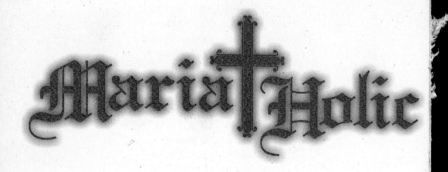

Volume 4

by Minari Endou

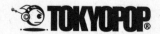

HAMBURG // LONDON // LOS ANGELES // TOKYO

Maria Holic Volume 4
Created by Minari Endou

Translation - Yuko Fukami
English Adaptation - Clint Bickham
Retouch and Lettering - Star Print Brokers
Copy Editor - Noora Kamel
Production Artist - Rui Kyo
Graphic Designer - Chelsea Windlinger

Editor - Cindy Suzuki
Print Production Manager - Lucas Rivera
Managing Editor - Vy Nguyen
Senior Designer - Louis Csontos
Art Director - Al-Insan Lashley
Director of Sales and Manufacturing - Allyson De Simone
Associate Publisher - Marco F. Pavia
President and C.O.O. - John Parker
C.E.O. and Chief Creative Officer - Stu Levy

A 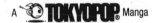 **TOKYOPOP** Manga

TOKYOPOP and 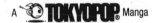 are trademarks or registered trademarks of TOKYOPOP Inc.

TOKYOPOP Inc.
5900 Wilshire Blvd. Suite 2000
Los Angeles, CA 90036

E-mail: info@TOKYOPOP.com
Come visit us online at www.TOKYOPOP.com

ISBN: 978-1-4278-1782-2

First TOKYOPOP printing: July 2010
10 9 8 7 6 5 4 3 2 1
Printed in the USA

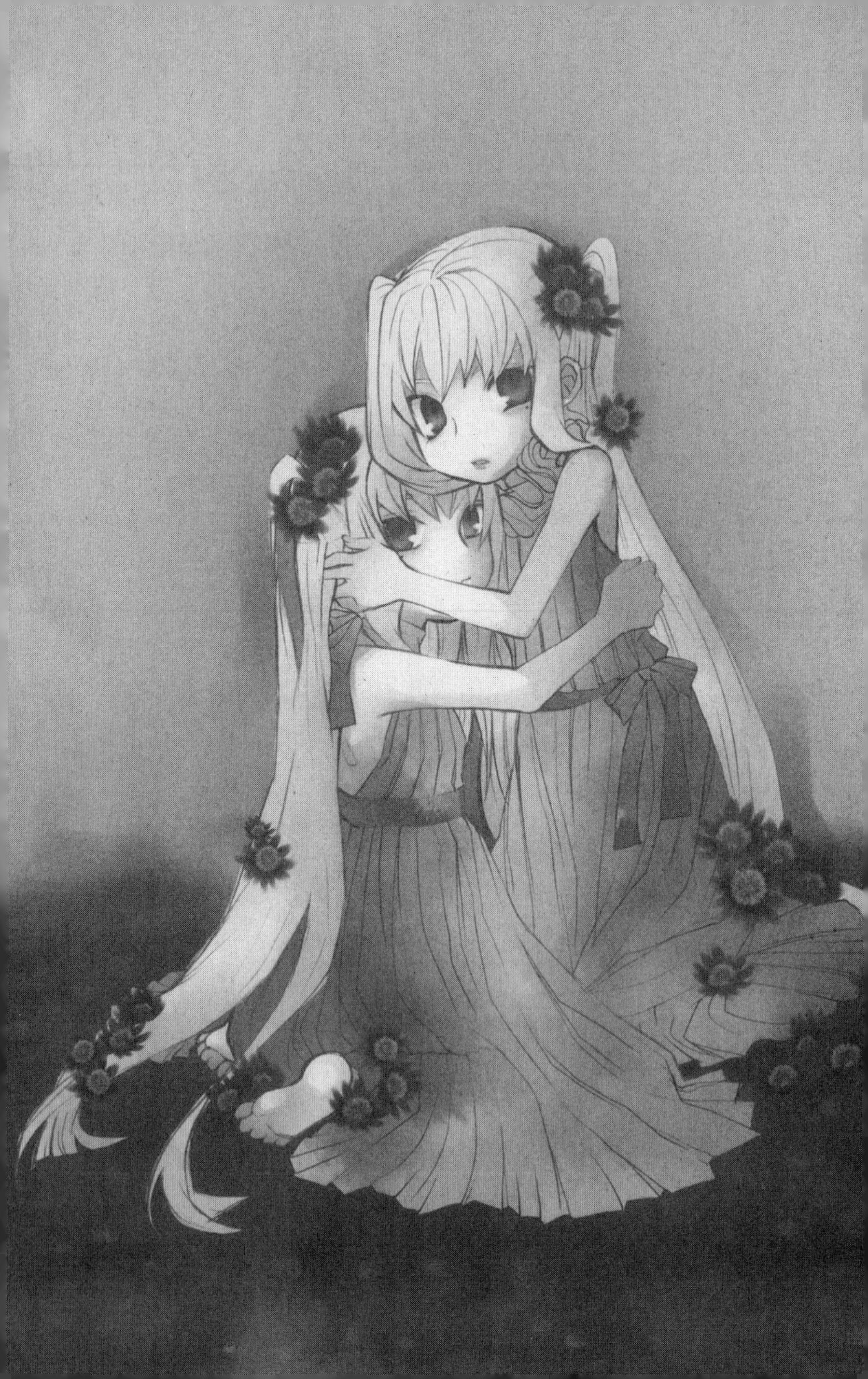

MARIA
HOLIC

4

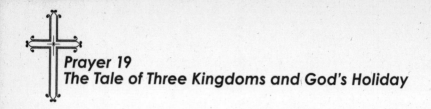

Prayer 19
The Tale of Three Kingdoms and God's Holiday

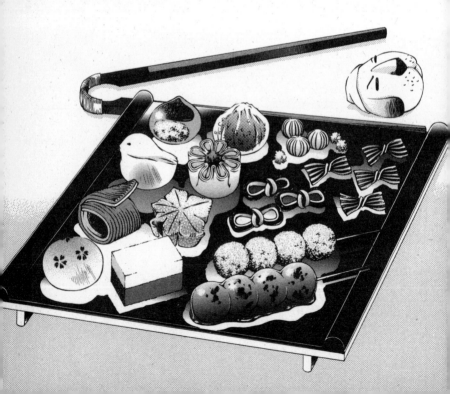

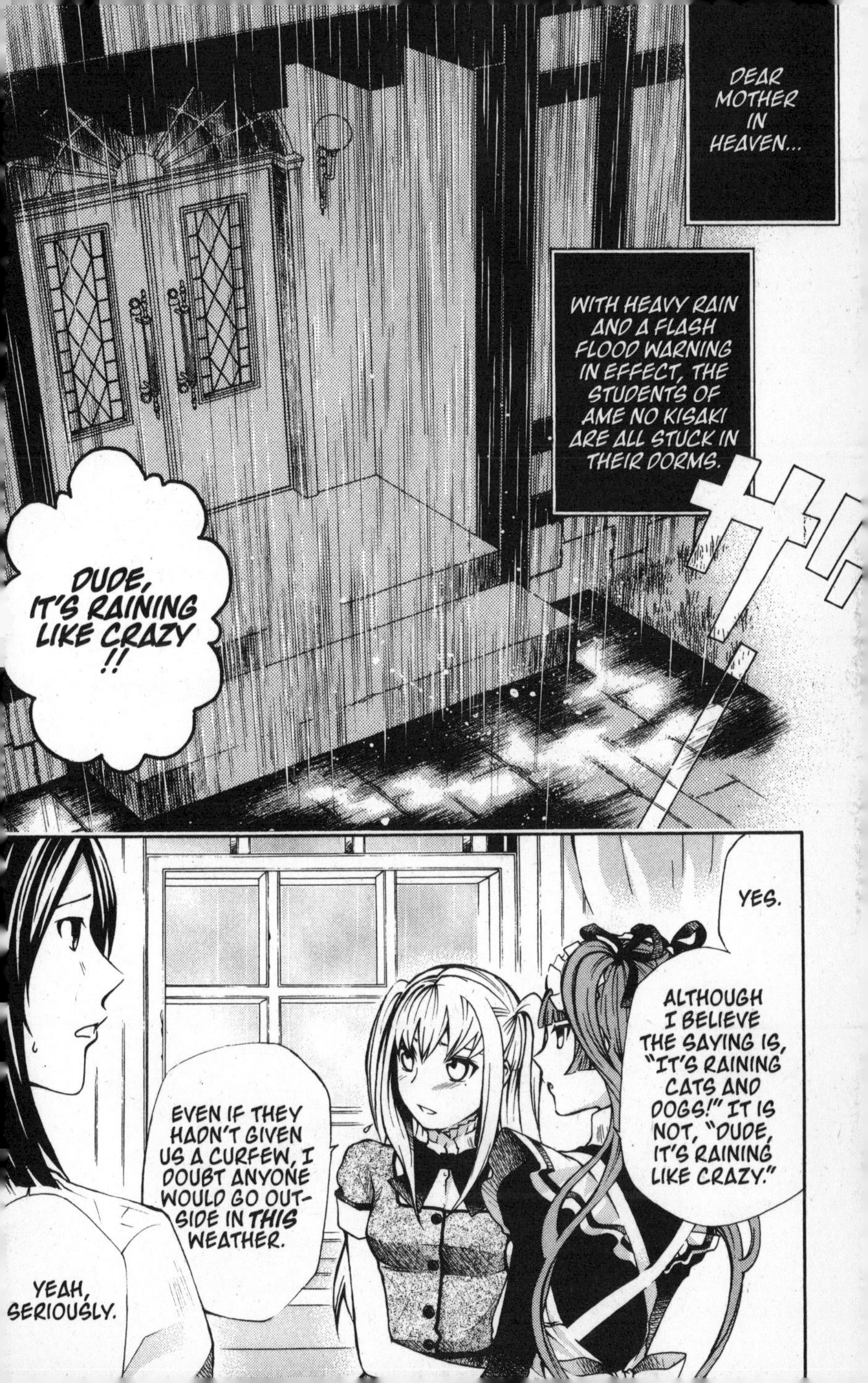
DEAR MOTHER IN HEAVEN...
WITH HEAVY RAIN AND A FLASH FLOOD WARNING IN EFFECT, THE STUDENTS OF AME NO KISAKI ARE ALL STUCK IN THEIR DORMS.
DUDE, IT'S RAINING LIKE CRAZY!!
YES.
ALTHOUGH I BELIEVE THE SAYING IS, "IT'S RAINING CATS AND DOGS!" IT IS NOT, "DUDE, IT'S RAINING LIKE CRAZY."
EVEN IF THEY HADN'T GIVEN US A CURFEW, I DOUBT ANYONE WOULD GO OUTSIDE IN THIS WEATHER.
YEAH, SERIOUSLY.

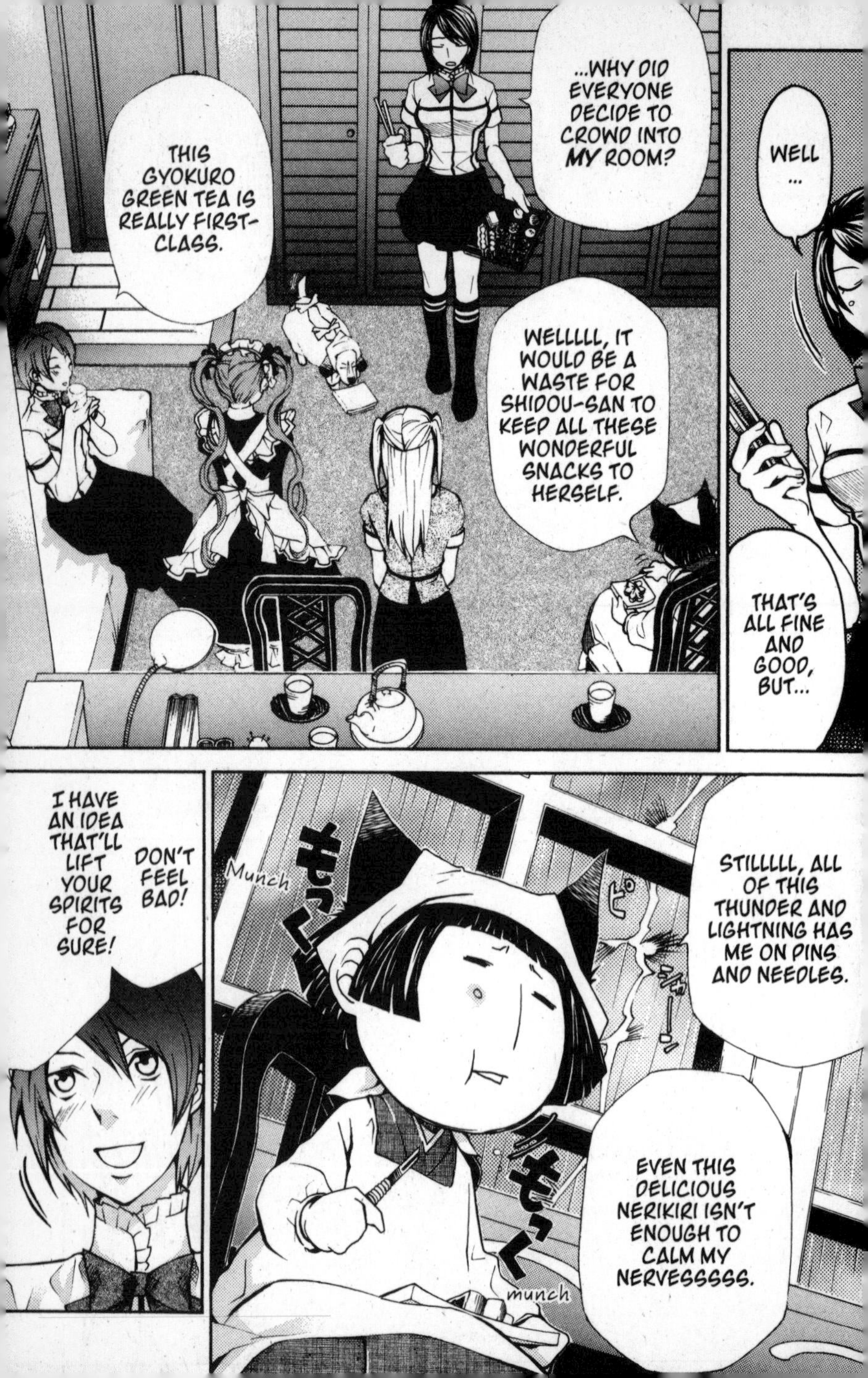
WELL ...
THAT'S ALL FINE AND GOOD, BUT...
...WHY DID EVERYONE DECIDE TO CROWD INTO *MY* ROOM?
WELLLLL, IT WOULD BE A WASTE FOR SHIDOU-SAN TO KEEP ALL THESE WONDERFUL SNACKS TO HERSELF.
THIS GYOKURO GREEN TEA IS REALLY FIRST-CLASS.
STILLLLL, ALL OF THIS THUNDER AND LIGHTNING HAS ME ON PINS AND NEEDLES.
Munch
munch
EVEN THIS DELICIOUS NERIKIRI ISN'T ENOUGH TO CALM MY NERVESSSSS.
DON'T FEEL BAD!
I HAVE AN IDEA THAT'LL LIFT YOUR SPIRITS FOR SURE!

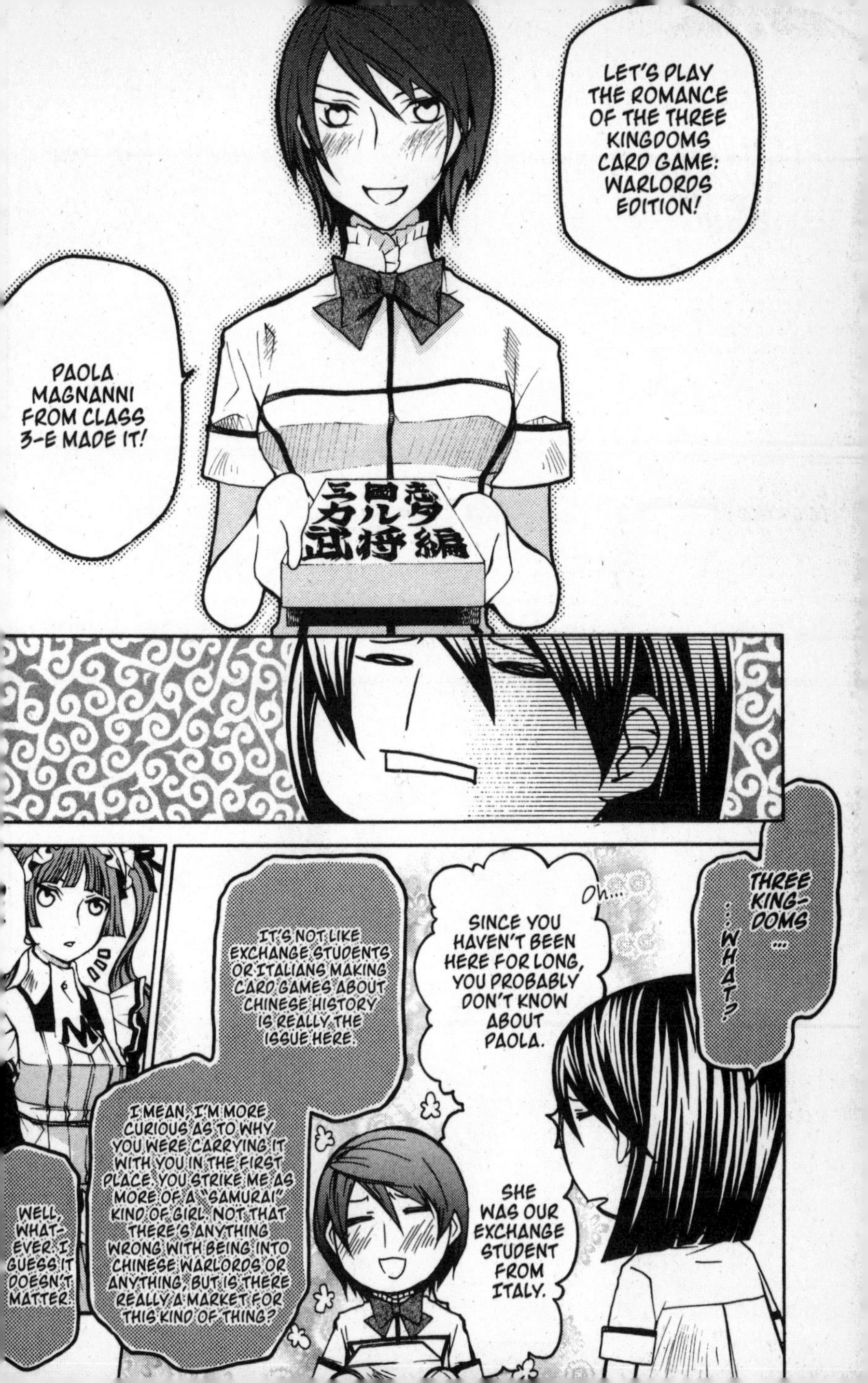
LET'S PLAY THE ROMANCE OF THE THREE KINGDOMS CARD GAME: WARLORDS EDITION!
PAOLA MAGNANNI FROM CLASS 3-E MADE IT!
三國志カルタ武将編
THREE KINGDOMS... ...WHAT?
Oh...
SINCE YOU HAVEN'T BEEN HERE FOR LONG, YOU PROBABLY DON'T KNOW ABOUT PAOLA.
SHE WAS OUR EXCHANGE STUDENT FROM ITALY.
IT'S NOT LIKE EXCHANGE STUDENTS OR ITALIANS MAKING CARD GAMES ABOUT CHINESE HISTORY IS REALLY THE ISSUE HERE.
I MEAN, I'M MORE CURIOUS AS TO WHY YOU WERE CARRYING IT WITH YOU IN THE FIRST PLACE. YOU STRIKE ME AS MORE OF A "SAMURAI" KIND OF GIRL. NOT THAT THERE'S ANYTHING WRONG WITH BEING INTO CHINESE WARLORDS OR ANYTHING, BUT IS THERE REALLY A MARKET FOR THIS KIND OF THING?
WELL, WHATEVER. I GUESS IT DOESN'T MATTER.

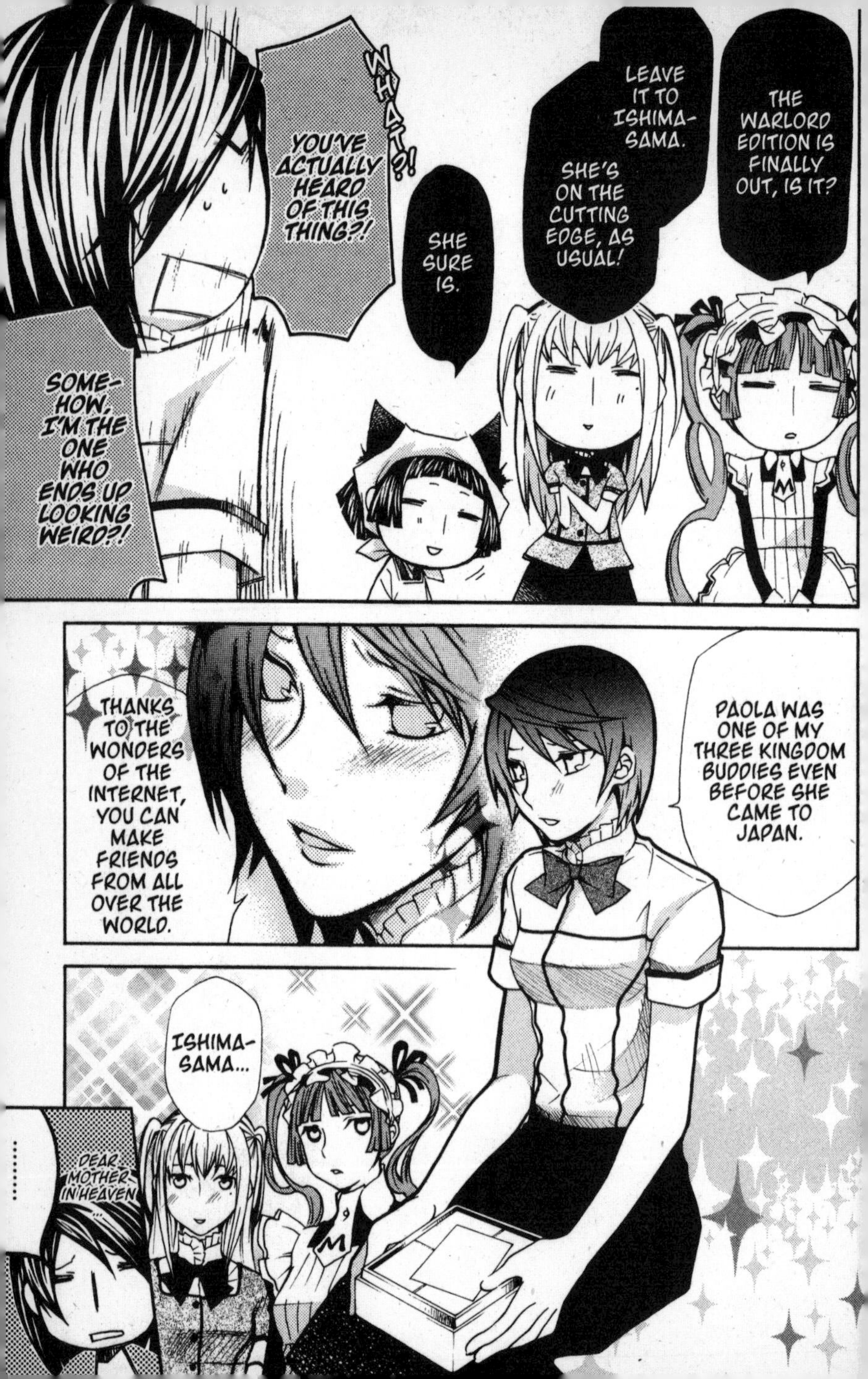
THE WARLORD EDITION IS FINALLY OUT, IS IT?
LEAVE IT TO ISHIMA-SAMA.
SHE'S ON THE CUTTING EDGE, AS USUAL!
SHE SURE IS.
WHAT?!
YOU'VE ACTUALLY HEARD OF THIS THING?!
SOME-HOW, I'M THE ONE WHO ENDS UP LOOKING WEIRD?!
PAOLA WAS ONE OF MY THREE KINGDOM BUDDIES EVEN BEFORE SHE CAME TO JAPAN.
THANKS TO THE WONDERS OF THE INTERNET, YOU CAN MAKE FRIENDS FROM ALL OVER THE WORLD.
ISHIMA-SAMA...
......
DEAR MOTHER IN HEAVEN...

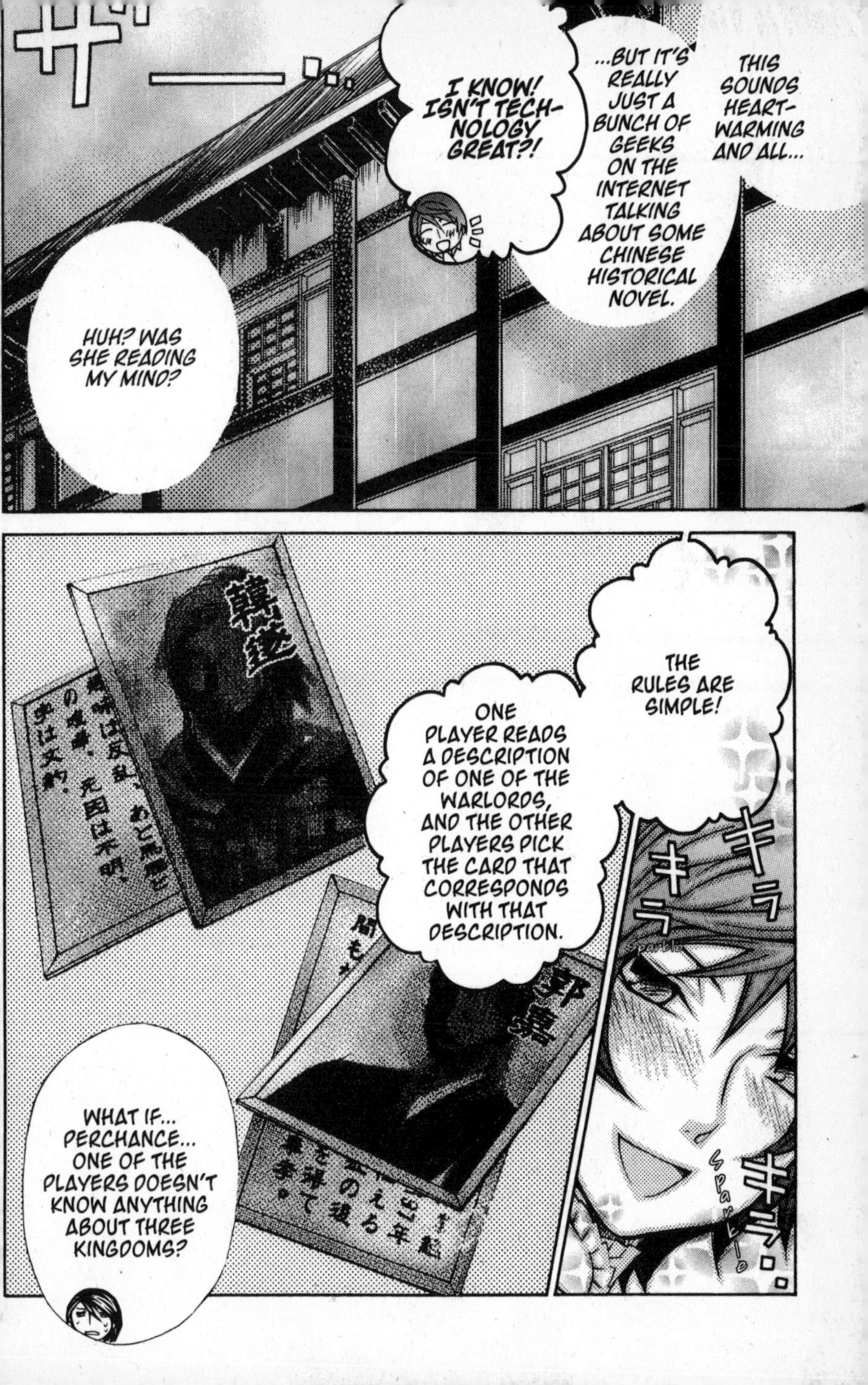
THIS SOUNDS HEART-WARMING AND ALL...
...BUT IT'S REALLY JUST A BUNCH OF GEEKS ON THE INTERNET TALKING ABOUT SOME CHINESE HISTORICAL NOVEL.
I KNOW! ISN'T TECH-NOLOGY GREAT?!
HUH? WAS SHE READING MY MIND?
THE RULES ARE SIMPLE!
ONE PLAYER READS A DESCRIPTION OF ONE OF THE WARLORDS, AND THE OTHER PLAYERS PICK THE CARD THAT CORRESPONDS WITH THAT DESCRIPTION.
韓遂
郭嘉
Sparkle
WHAT IF... PERCHANCE... ONE OF THE PLAYERS DOESN'T KNOW ANYTHING ABOUT THREE KINGDOMS?

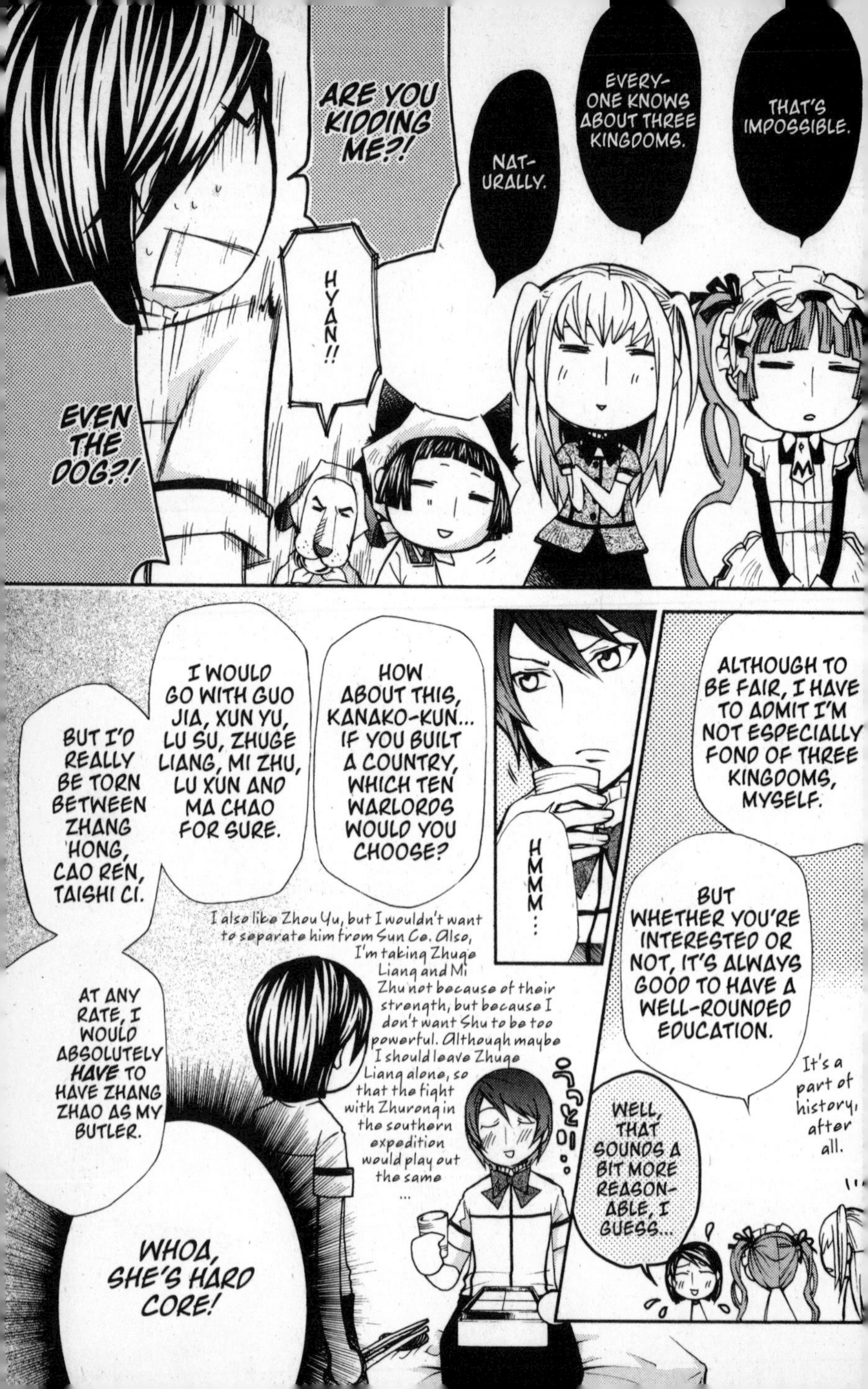

THAT'S IMPOSSIBLE.
EVERY-ONE KNOWS ABOUT THREE KINGDOMS.
NAT-URALLY.
ARE YOU KIDDING ME?!
HYAN!!
EVEN THE DOG?!
ALTHOUGH TO BE FAIR, I HAVE TO ADMIT I'M NOT ESPECIALLY FOND OF THREE KINGDOMS, MYSELF.
BUT WHETHER YOU'RE INTERESTED OR NOT, IT'S ALWAYS GOOD TO HAVE A WELL-ROUNDED EDUCATION.
It's a part of history, after all.
WELL, THAT SOUNDS A BIT MORE REASON-ABLE, I GUESS...
HMMM...
HOW ABOUT THIS, KANAKO-KUN... IF YOU BUILT A COUNTRY, WHICH TEN WARLORDS WOULD YOU CHOOSE?
I WOULD GO WITH GUO JIA, XUN YU, LU SU, ZHUGE LIANG, MI ZHU, LU XUN AND MA CHAO FOR SURE.
BUT I'D REALLY BE TORN BETWEEN ZHANG HONG, CAO REN, TAISHI CI.
AT ANY RATE, I WOULD ABSOLUTELY HAVE TO HAVE ZHANG ZHAO AS MY BUTLER.
I also like Zhou Yu, but I wouldn't want to separate him from Sun Ce. Also, I'm taking Zhuge Liang and Mi Zhu not because of their strength, but because I don't want Shu to be too powerful. Although maybe I should leave Zhuge Liang alone, so that the fight with Zhurong in the southern expedition would play out the same ...
WHOA, SHE'S HARD CORE!

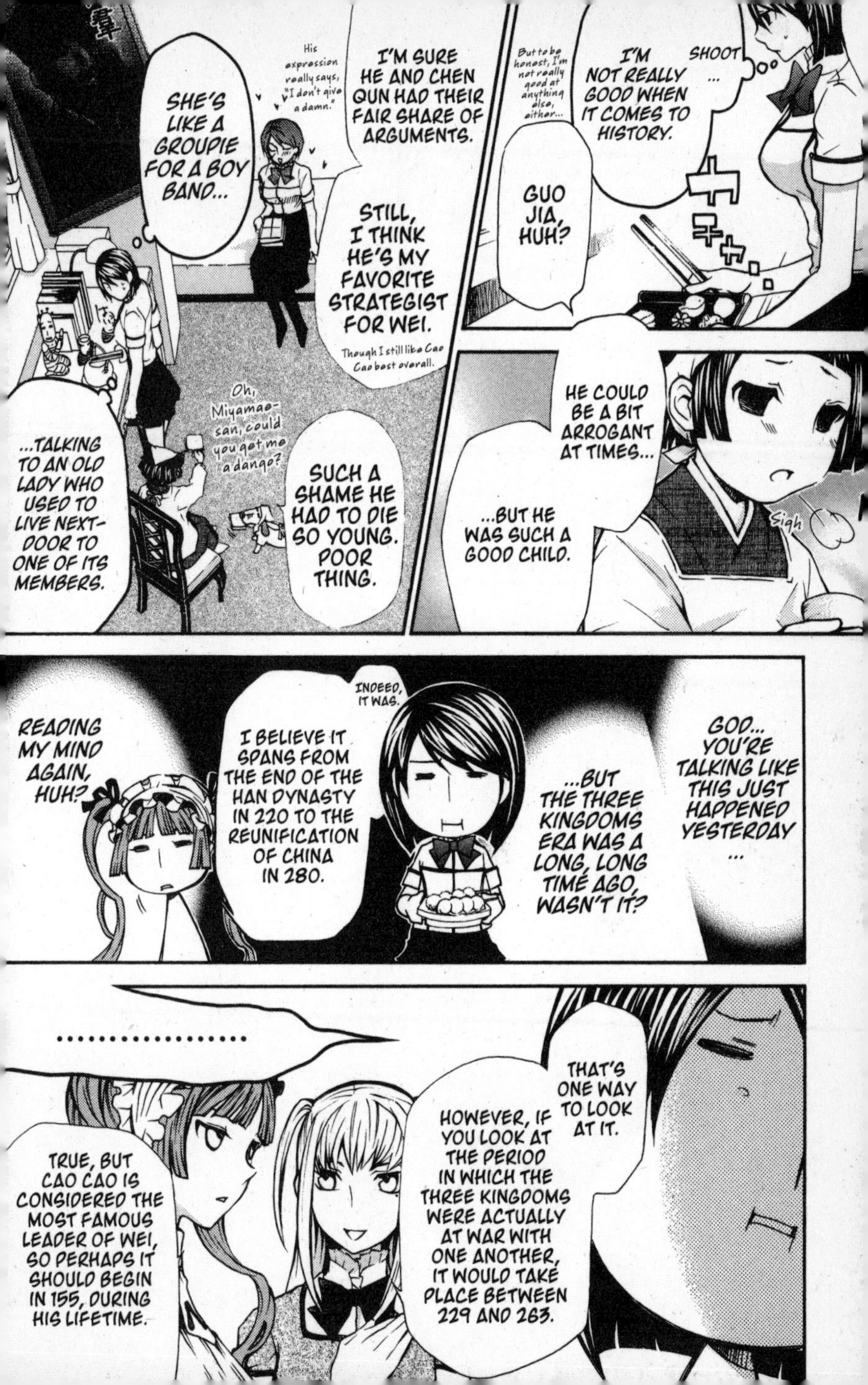
SHOOT...
I'M NOT REALLY GOOD WHEN IT COMES TO HISTORY.
But to be honest, I'm not really good at anything else, either...
GUO JIA, HUH?
HE COULD BE A BIT ARROGANT AT TIMES...
...BUT HE WAS SUCH A GOOD CHILD.
Sigh
I'M SURE HE AND CHEN QUN HAD THEIR FAIR SHARE OF ARGUMENTS.
His expression really says, "I don't give a damn."
SHE'S LIKE A GROUPIE FOR A BOY BAND...
STILL, I THINK HE'S MY FAVORITE STRATEGIST FOR WEI.
Though I still like Cao Cao best overall.
SUCH A SHAME HE HAD TO DIE SO YOUNG. POOR THING.
Oh, Miyamae-san, could you get me a dango?
...TALKING TO AN OLD LADY WHO USED TO LIVE NEXT-DOOR TO ONE OF ITS MEMBERS.
GOD... YOU'RE TALKING LIKE THIS JUST HAPPENED YESTERDAY...
...BUT THE THREE KINGDOMS ERA WAS A LONG, LONG TIME AGO, WASN'T IT?
INDEED, IT WAS.
I BELIEVE IT SPANS FROM THE END OF THE HAN DYNASTY IN 220 TO THE REUNIFICATION OF CHINA IN 280.
READING MY MIND AGAIN, HUH?
THAT'S ONE WAY TO LOOK AT IT.
HOWEVER, IF YOU LOOK AT THE PERIOD IN WHICH THE THREE KINGDOMS WERE ACTUALLY AT WAR WITH ONE ANOTHER, IT WOULD TAKE PLACE BETWEEN 229 AND 263.
....
TRUE, BUT CAO CAO IS CONSIDERED THE MOST FAMOUS LEADER OF WEI, SO PERHAPS IT SHOULD BEGIN IN 155, DURING HIS LIFETIME.

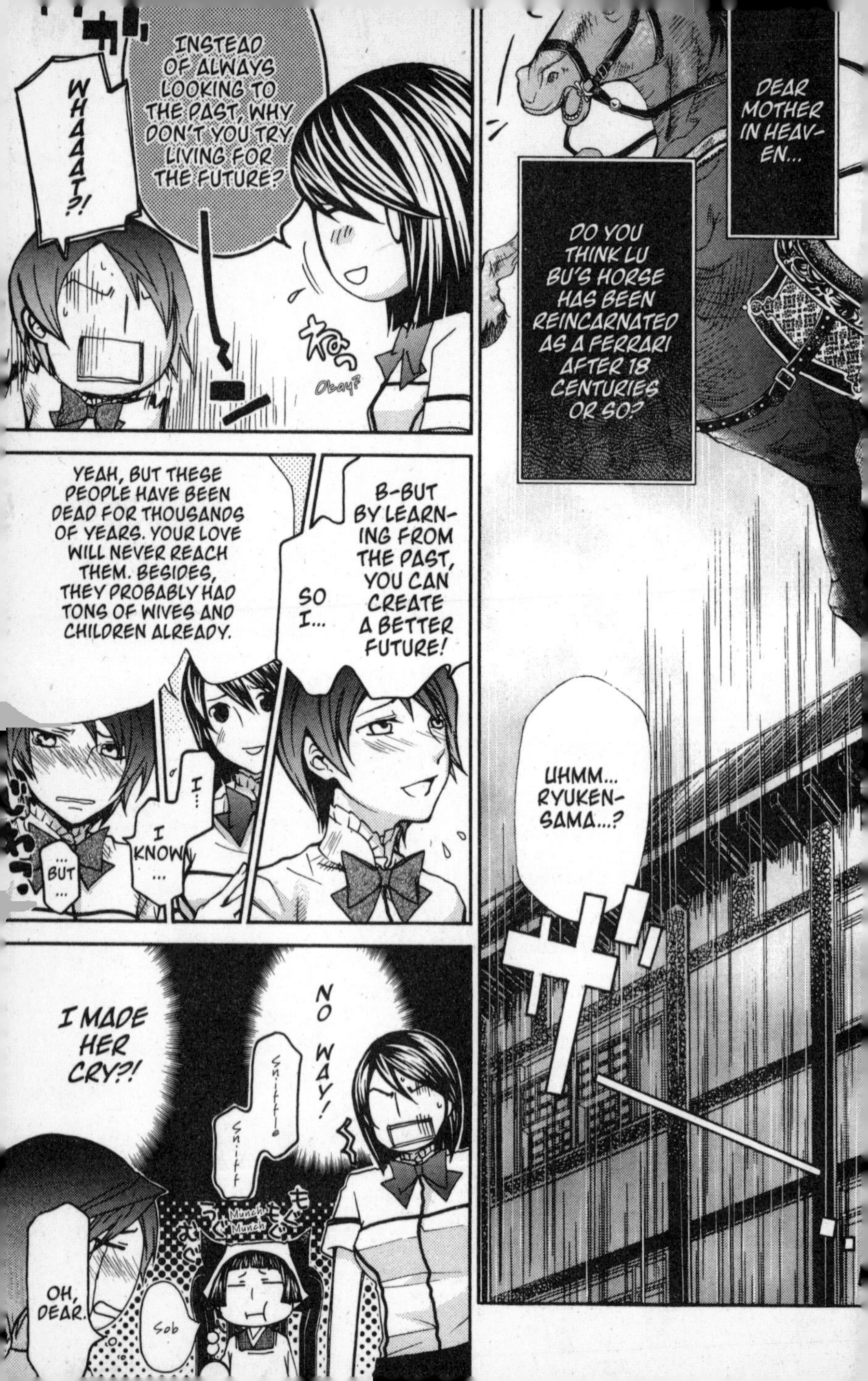
DEAR MOTHER IN HEAVEN...
DO YOU THINK LU BU'S HORSE HAS BEEN REINCARNATED AS A FERRARI AFTER 18 CENTURIES OR SO?
UHMM... RYUKEN-SAMA...?
INSTEAD OF ALWAYS LOOKING TO THE PAST, WHY DON'T YOU TRY LIVING FOR THE FUTURE?
ねっ
Okay?
WHAAAAT?!
B-BUT BY LEARNING FROM THE PAST, YOU CAN CREATE A BETTER FUTURE!
SO I...
YEAH, BUT THESE PEOPLE HAVE BEEN DEAD FOR THOUSANDS OF YEARS. YOUR LOVE WILL NEVER REACH THEM. BESIDES, THEY PROBABLY HAD TONS OF WIVES AND CHILDREN ALREADY.
I... I KNOW...
...BUT...
NO WAY!
Sniffle
Sniff
I MADE HER CRY?!
Munch Munch
OH, DEAR.
Sob

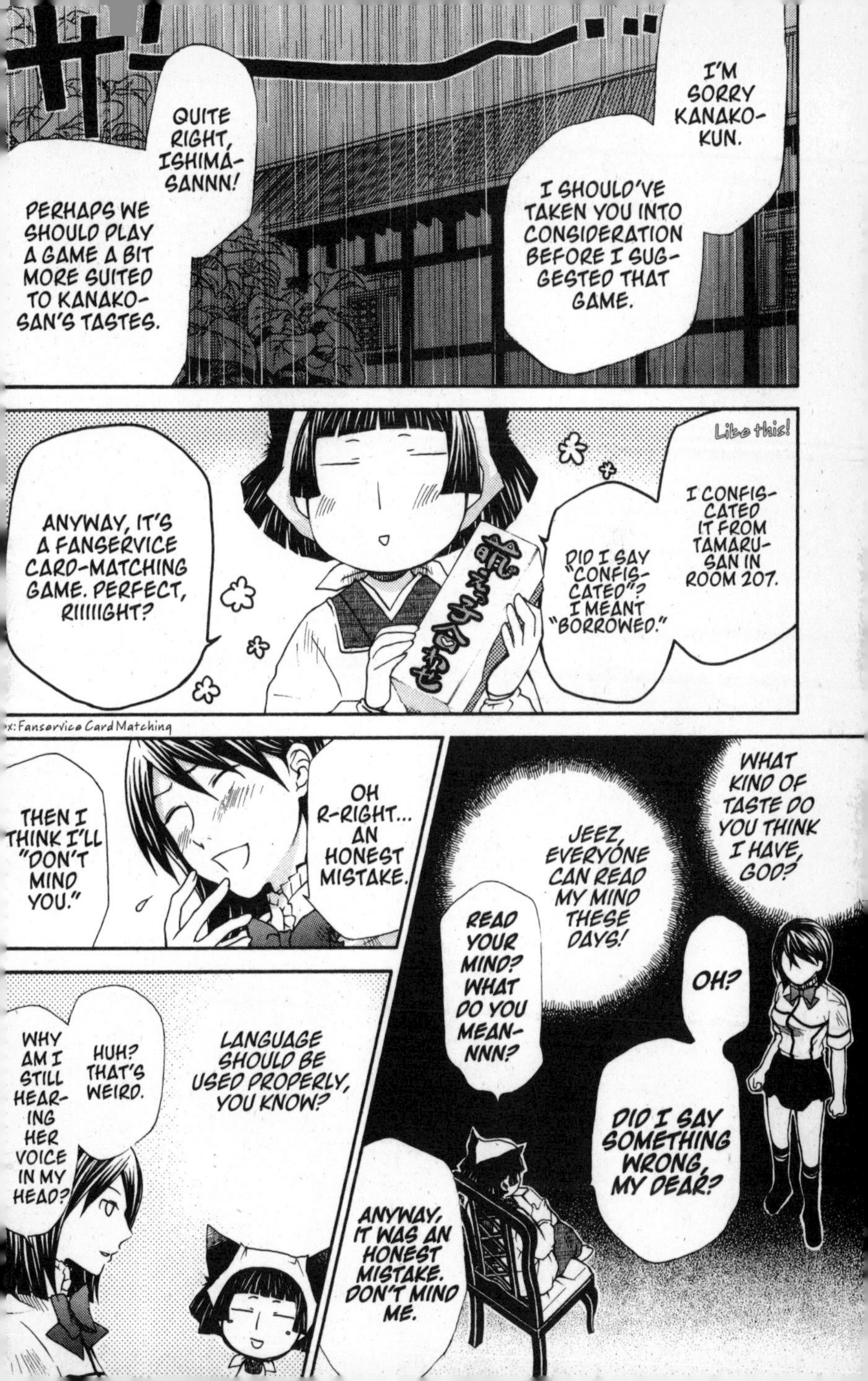
I'M SORRY KANAKO-KUN.
I SHOULD'VE TAKEN YOU INTO CONSIDERATION BEFORE I SUG-GESTED THAT GAME.
QUITE RIGHT, ISHIMA-SANNN!
PERHAPS WE SHOULD PLAY A GAME A BIT MORE SUITED TO KANAKO-SAN'S TASTES.
Like this!
I CONFIS-CATED IT FROM TAMARU-SAN IN ROOM 207.
DID I SAY "CONFIS-CATED"? I MEANT "BORROWED."
ANYWAY, IT'S A FANSERVICE CARD-MATCHING GAME. PERFECT, RIIIIIGHT?
x: Fanservice Card Matching
WHAT KIND OF TASTE DO YOU THINK I HAVE, GOD?
JEEZ, EVERYONE CAN READ MY MIND THESE DAYS!
READ YOUR MIND? WHAT DO YOU MEAN-NNN?
OH?
DID I SAY SOMETHING WRONG, MY DEAR?
ANYWAY, IT WAS AN HONEST MISTAKE. DON'T MIND ME.
OH R-RIGHT... AN HONEST MISTAKE.
THEN I THINK I'LL "DON'T MIND YOU."
LANGUAGE SHOULD BE USED PROPERLY, YOU KNOW?
HUH? THAT'S WEIRD.
WHY AM I STILL HEAR-ING HER VOICE IN MY HEAD?

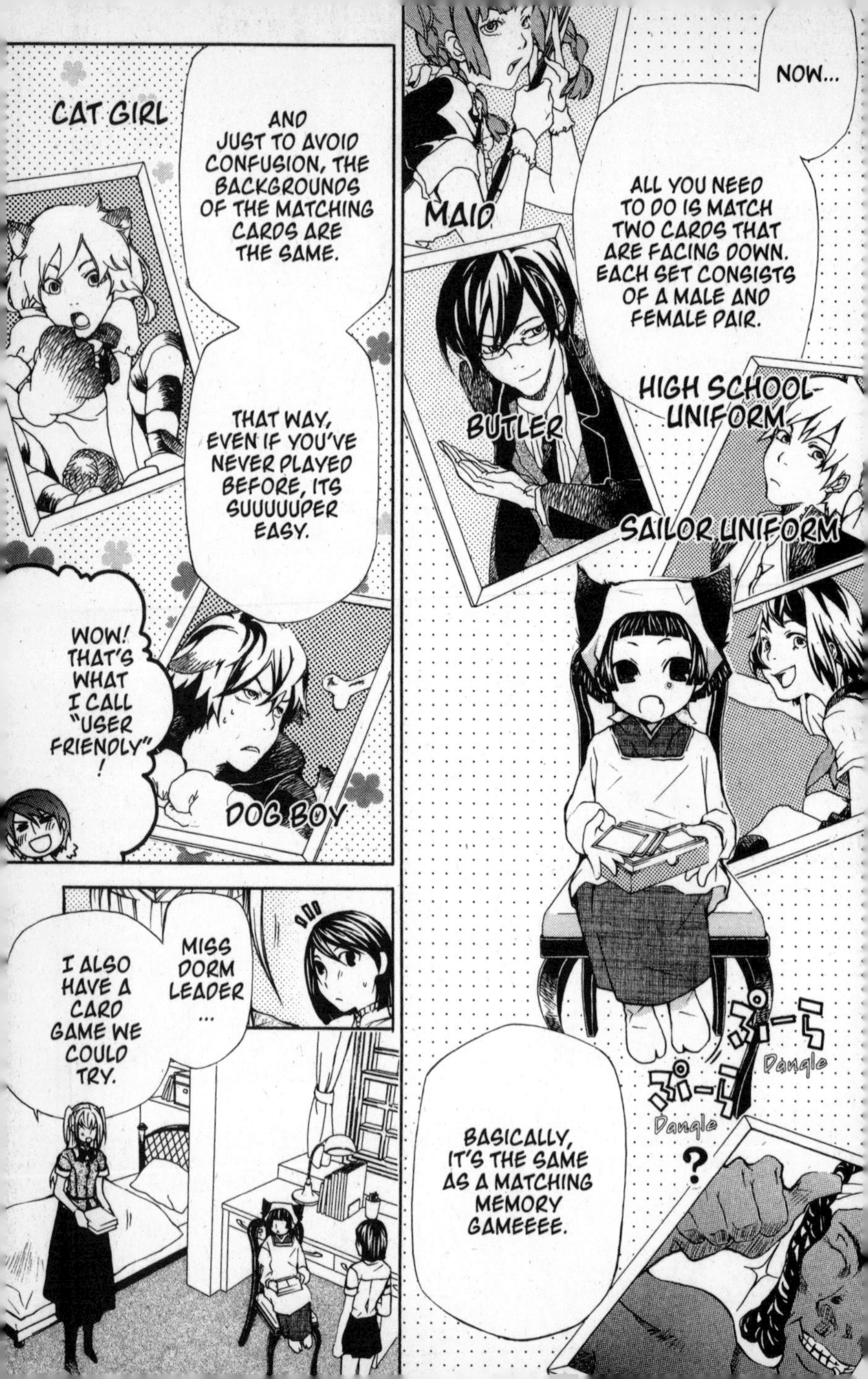
NOW...
ALL YOU NEED TO DO IS MATCH TWO CARDS THAT ARE FACING DOWN. EACH SET CONSISTS OF A MALE AND FEMALE PAIR.
MAID
HIGH SCHOOL UNIFORM
BUTLER
SAILOR UNIFORM
Dangle
Dangle
?
BASICALLY, IT'S THE SAME AS A MATCHING MEMORY GAMEEEE.
AND JUST TO AVOID CONFUSION, THE BACKGROUNDS OF THE MATCHING CARDS ARE THE SAME.
CAT GIRL
THAT WAY, EVEN IF YOU'VE NEVER PLAYED BEFORE, ITS SUUUUUPER EASY.
WOW! THAT'S WHAT I CALL "USER FRIENDLY"!
DOG BOY
MISS DORM LEADER ...
I ALSO HAVE A CARD GAME WE COULD TRY.

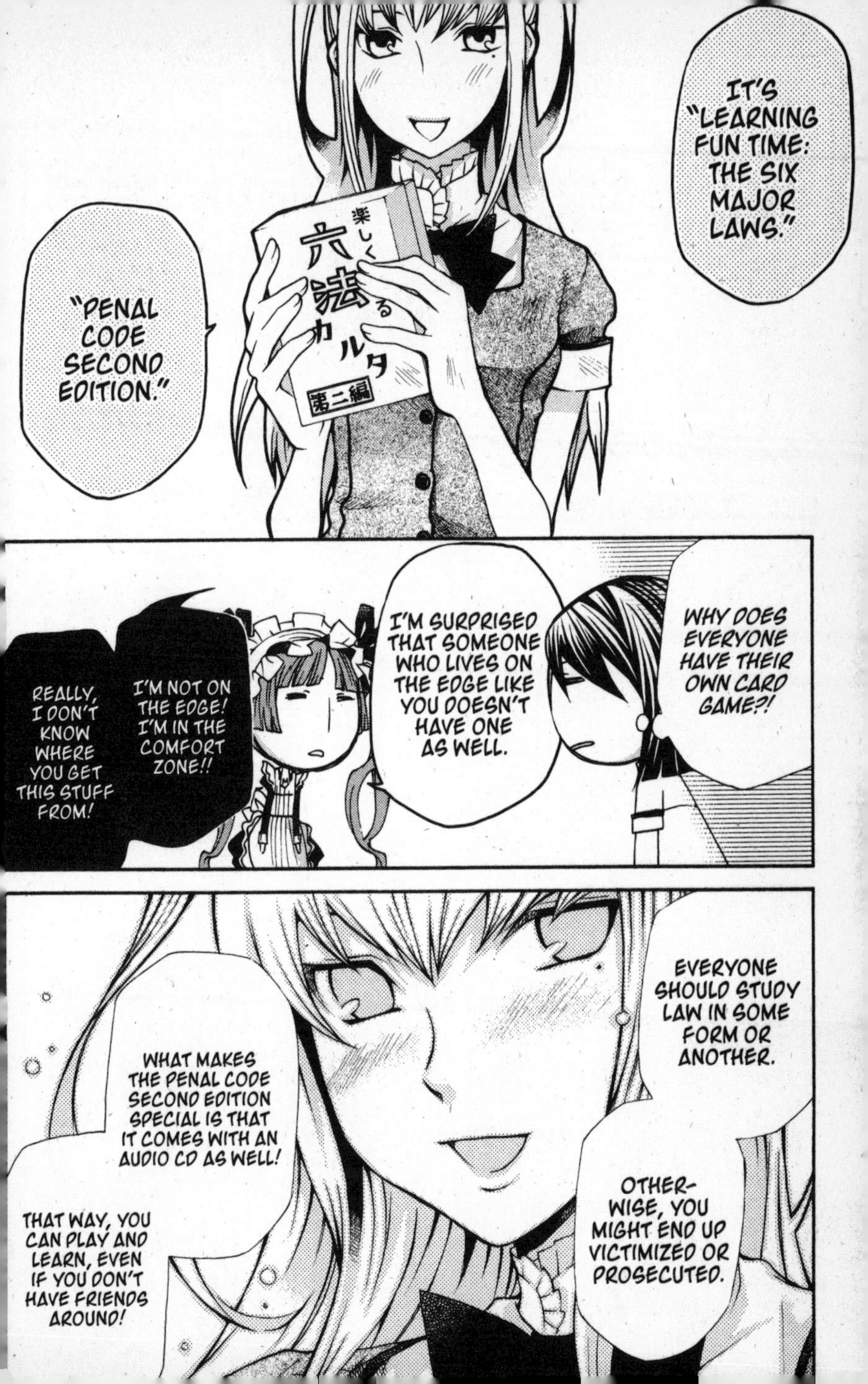
IT'S "LEARNING FUN TIME: THE SIX MAJOR LAWS."
楽しく六法るカルタ
第二編
"PENAL CODE SECOND EDITION."
WHY DOES EVERYONE HAVE THEIR OWN CARD GAME?!
I'M SURPRISED THAT SOMEONE WHO LIVES ON THE EDGE LIKE YOU DOESN'T HAVE ONE AS WELL.
I'M NOT ON THE EDGE! I'M IN THE COMFORT ZONE!!
REALLY, I DON'T KNOW WHERE YOU GET THIS STUFF FROM!
EVERYONE SHOULD STUDY LAW IN SOME FORM OR ANOTHER.
WHAT MAKES THE PENAL CODE SECOND EDITION SPECIAL IS THAT IT COMES WITH AN AUDIO CD AS WELL!
OTHER-WISE, YOU MIGHT END UP VICTIMIZED OR PROSECUTED.
THAT WAY, YOU CAN PLAY AND LEARN, EVEN IF YOU DON'T HAVE FRIENDS AROUND!

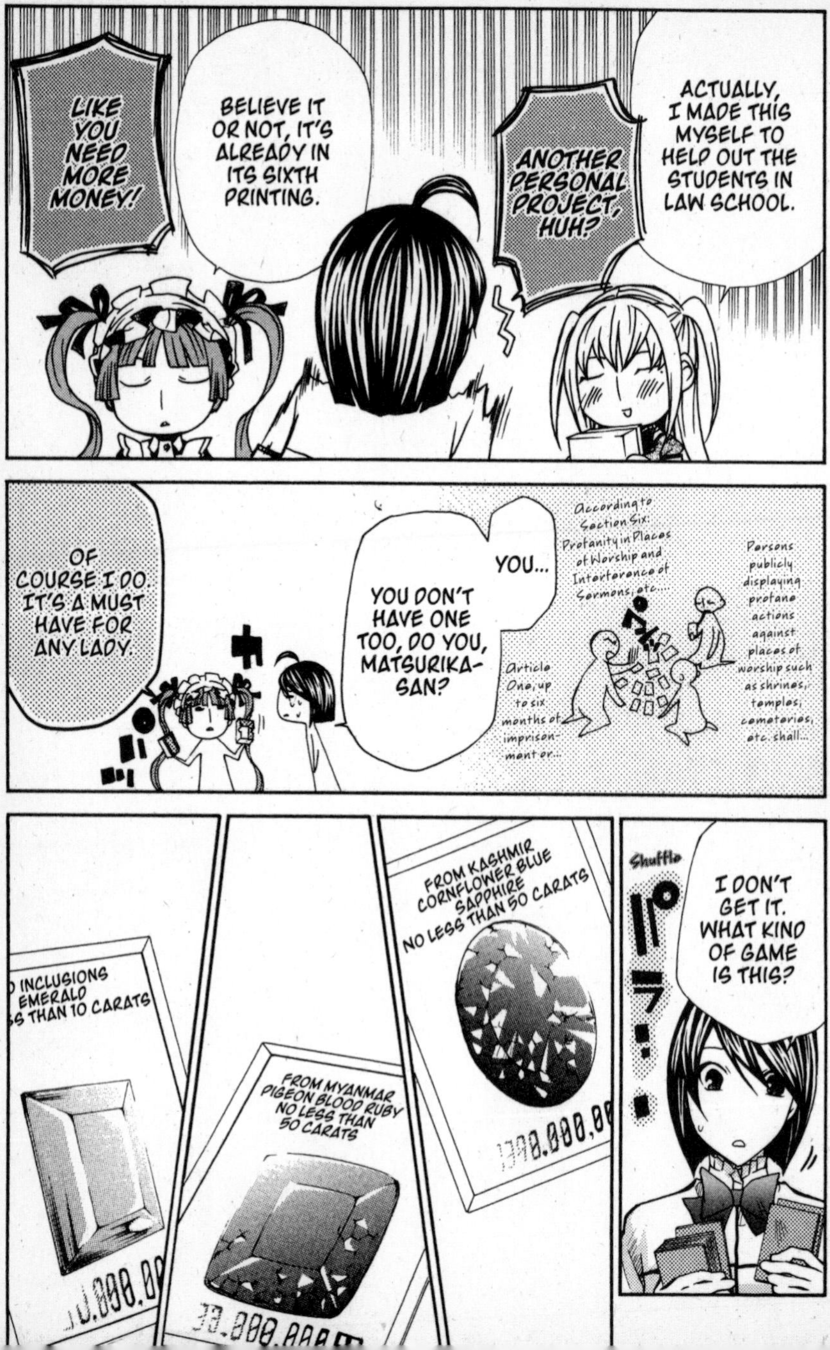
ACTUALLY, I MADE THIS MYSELF TO HELP OUT THE STUDENTS IN LAW SCHOOL.
ANOTHER PERSONAL PROJECT, HUH?
BELIEVE IT OR NOT, IT'S ALREADY IN ITS SIXTH PRINTING.
LIKE YOU NEED MORE MONEY!
Persons publicly displaying profane actions against places of worship such as shrines, temples, cemeteries, etc. shall...
According to Section Six: Profanity in Places of Worship and Interference of Sermons, etc....
Article One, up to six months of imprisonment or...
YOU...
YOU DON'T HAVE ONE TOO, DO YOU, MATSURIKA-SAN?
OF COURSE I DO. IT'S A MUST HAVE FOR ANY LADY.
Shuffle
I DON'T GET IT. WHAT KIND OF GAME IS THIS?
FROM KASHMIR CORNFLOWER BLUE SAPPHIRE NO LESS THAN 50 CARATS
FROM MYANMAR PIGEON BLOOD RUBY NO LESS THAN 50 CARATS
INCLUSIONS EMERALD
THAN 10 CARATS

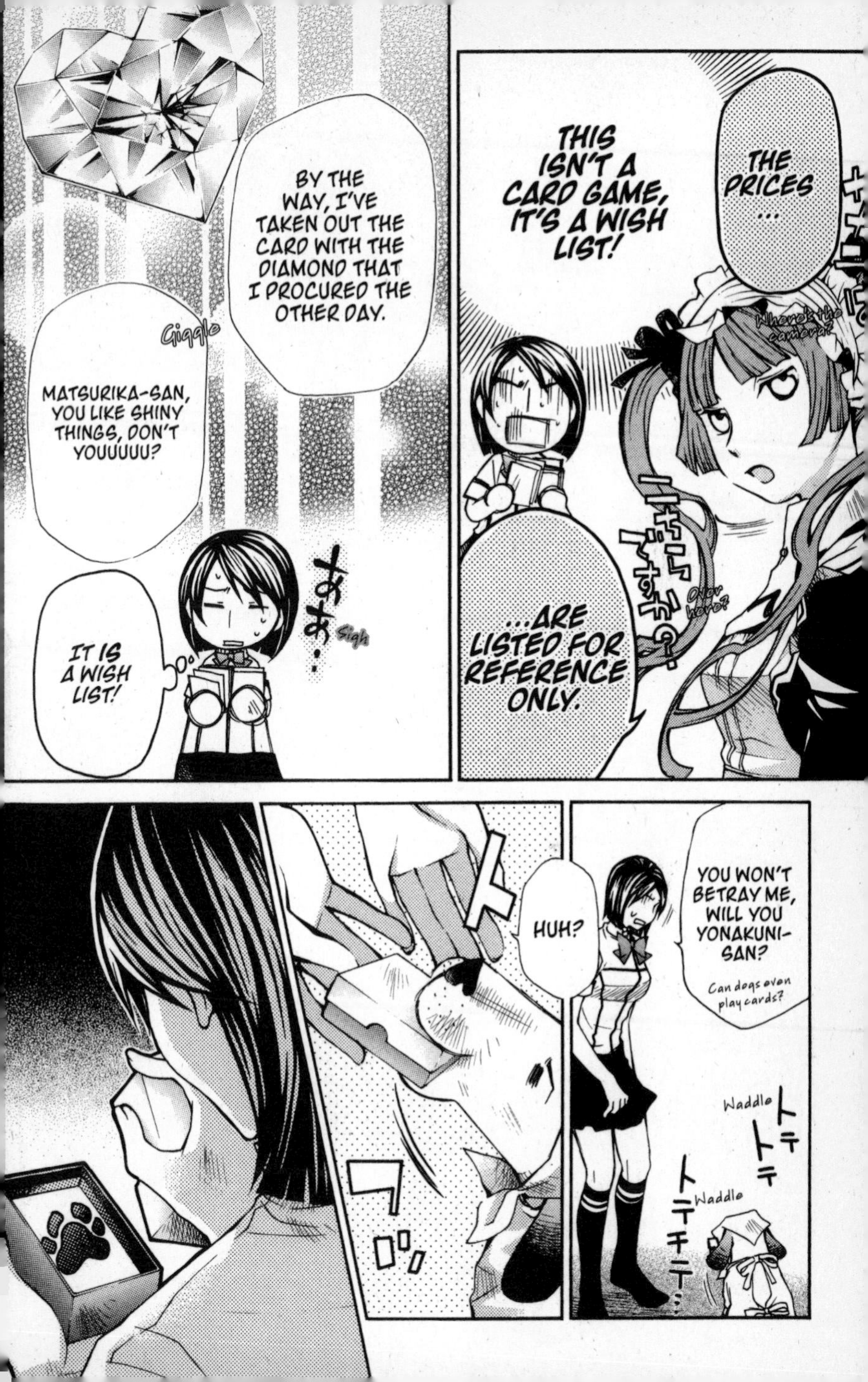
THE PRICES ...
Where's the camera?
...ARE LISTED FOR REFERENCE ONLY.
Over here?
THIS ISN'T A CARD GAME, IT'S A WISH LIST!
BY THE WAY, I'VE TAKEN OUT THE CARD WITH THE DIAMOND THAT I PROCURED THE OTHER DAY.
Giggle
MATSURIKA-SAN, YOU LIKE SHINY THINGS, DON'T YOUUUUU?
Sigh
IT IS A WISH LIST!
YOU WON'T BETRAY ME, WILL YOU YONAKUNI-SAN?
Can dogs even play cards?
HUH?
Waddle
Waddle

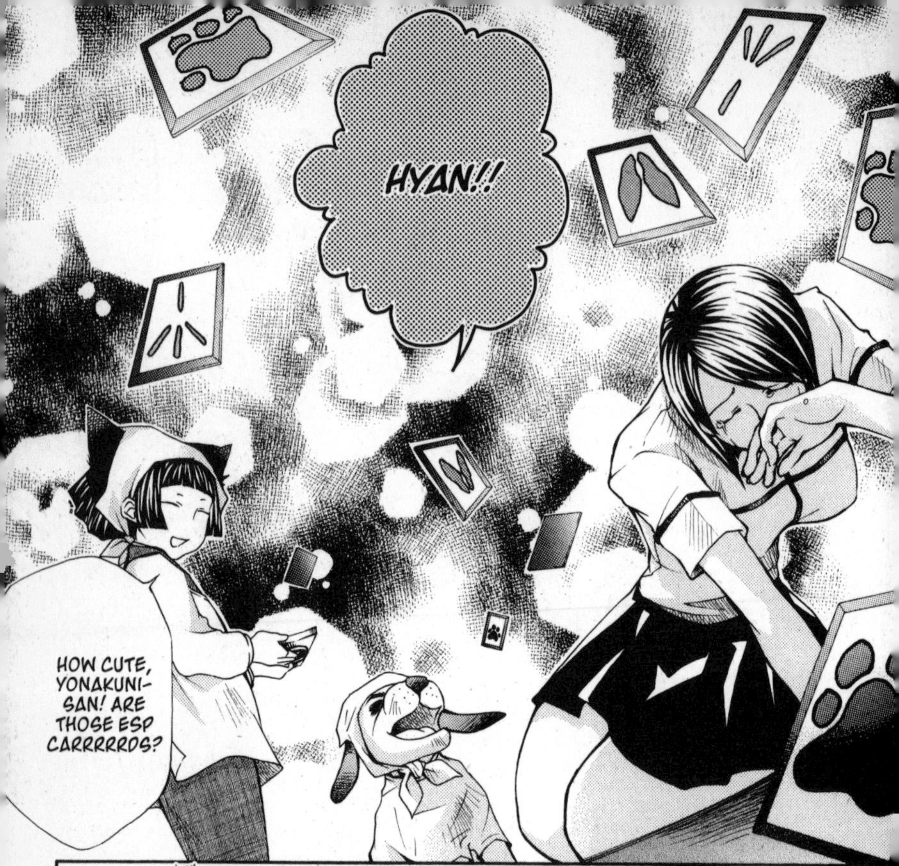
HYAN!!
HOW CUTE, YONAKUNI-SAN! ARE THOSE ESP CARRRRRDS?
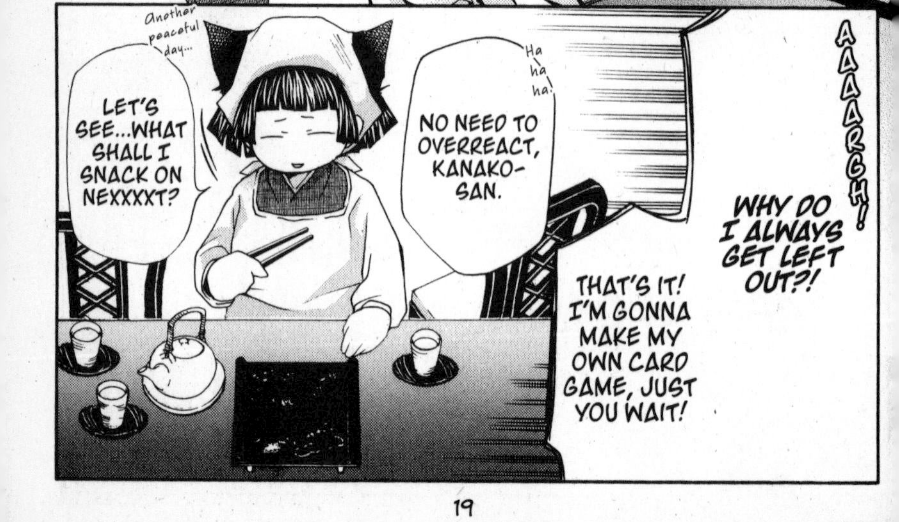
AAAARGH!
WHY DO I ALWAYS GET LEFT OUT?!
THAT'S IT! I'M GONNA MAKE MY OWN CARD GAME, JUST YOU WAIT!
Ha ha ha!
NO NEED TO OVERREACT, KANAKO-SAN.
Another peaceful day...
LET'S SEE...WHAT SHALL I SNACK ON NEXXXXT?

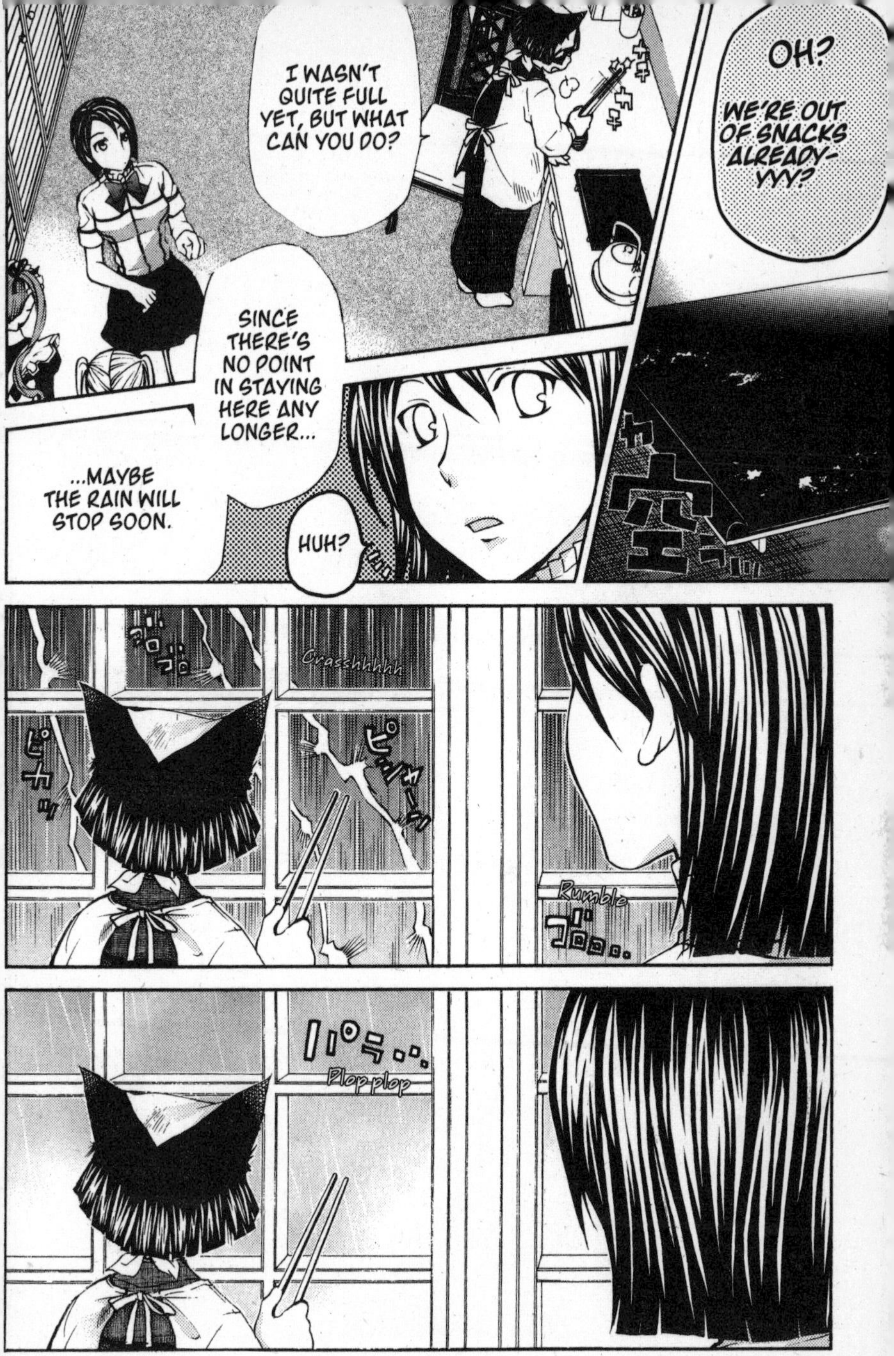
OH?
WE'RE OUT OF SNACKS ALREADY-YYY?
I WASN'T QUITE FULL YET, BUT WHAT CAN YOU DO?
SINCE THERE'S NO POINT IN STAYING HERE ANY LONGER...
...MAYBE THE RAIN WILL STOP SOON.
HUH?
Rumble
Crasshhhhh
Plop plop

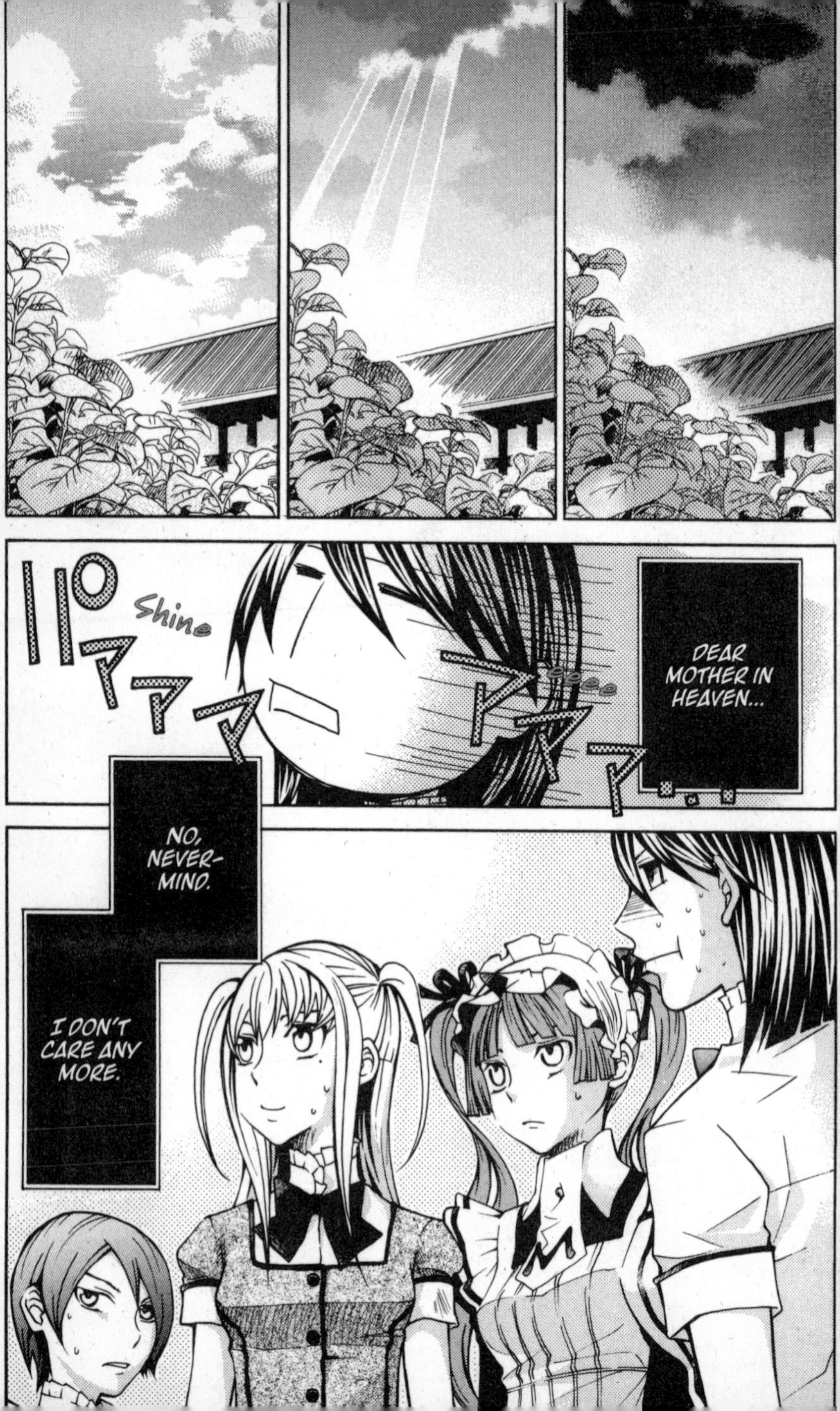
DEAR MOTHER IN HEAVEN...
パアアアアアア..
Shine
NO, NEVER-MIND.
I DON'T CARE ANY MORE.

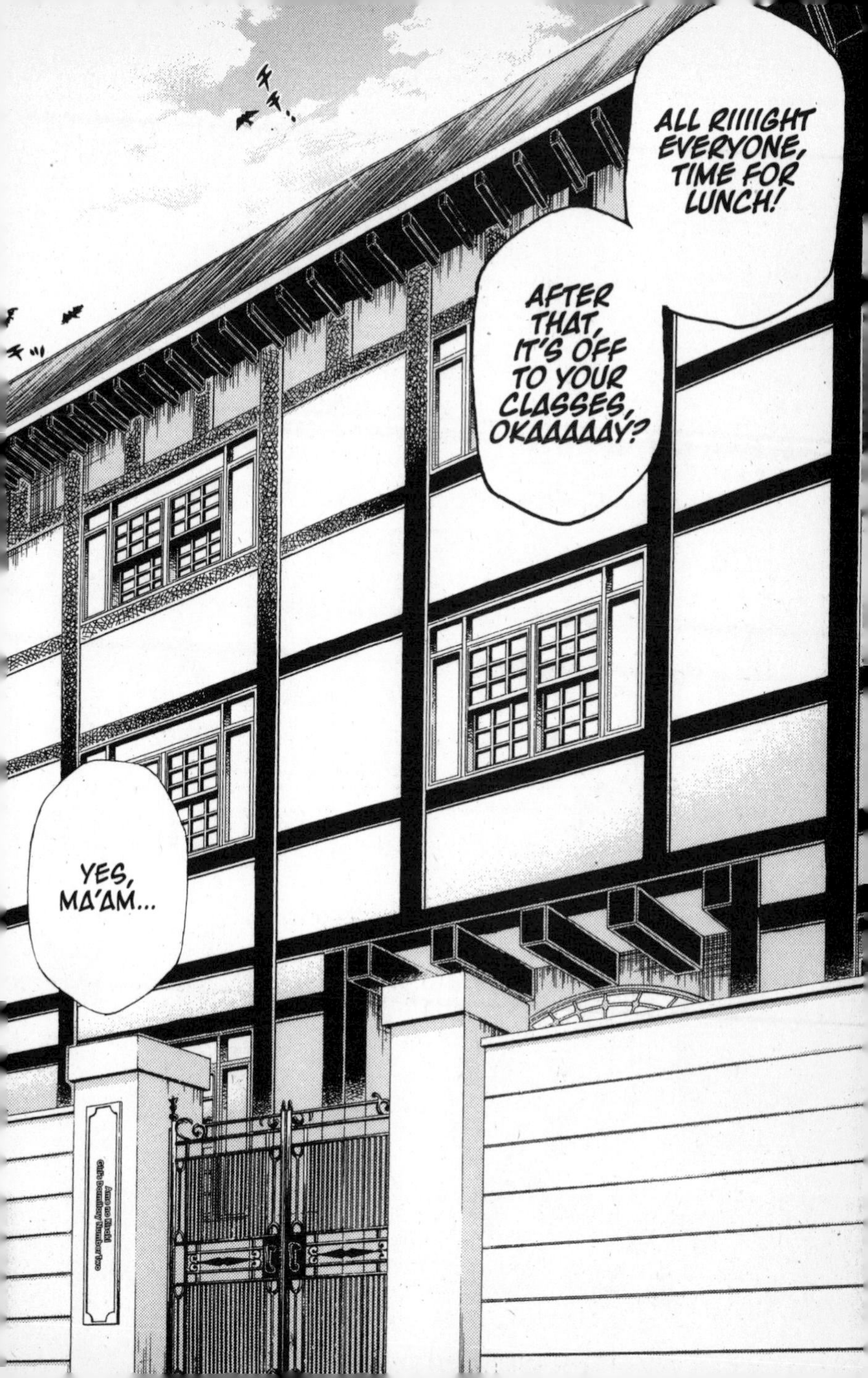
ALL RIIIIGHT EVERYONE, TIME FOR LUNCH!
AFTER THAT, IT'S OFF TO YOUR CLASSES, OKAAAAAY?
チチ..
チッ
YES, MA'AM...

Maria✝Holic

M A R I A H O L I C

Maria Holic

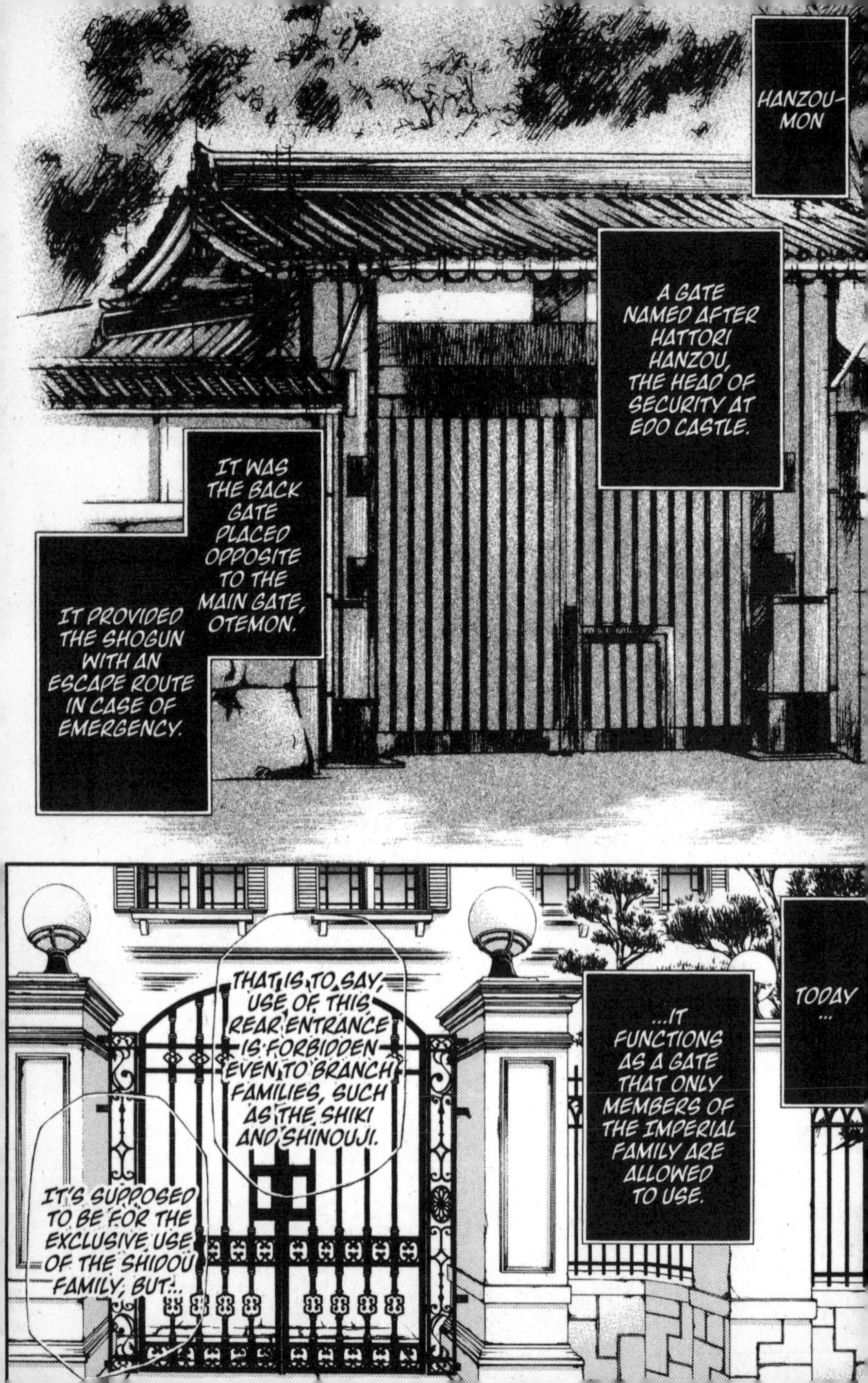
HANZOU-MON
A GATE NAMED AFTER HATTORI HANZOU, THE HEAD OF SECURITY AT EDO CASTLE.
IT WAS THE BACK GATE PLACED OPPOSITE TO THE MAIN GATE, OTEMON.
IT PROVIDED THE SHOGUN WITH AN ESCAPE ROUTE IN CASE OF EMERGENCY.
TODAY...
...IT FUNCTIONS AS A GATE THAT ONLY MEMBERS OF THE IMPERIAL FAMILY ARE ALLOWED TO USE.
THAT IS TO SAY, USE OF THIS REAR ENTRANCE IS FORBIDDEN EVEN TO BRANCH FAMILIES, SUCH AS THE SHIKI AND SHINOUJI.
IT'S SUPPOSED TO BE FOR THE EXCLUSIVE USE OF THE SHIDOU FAMILY, BUT...

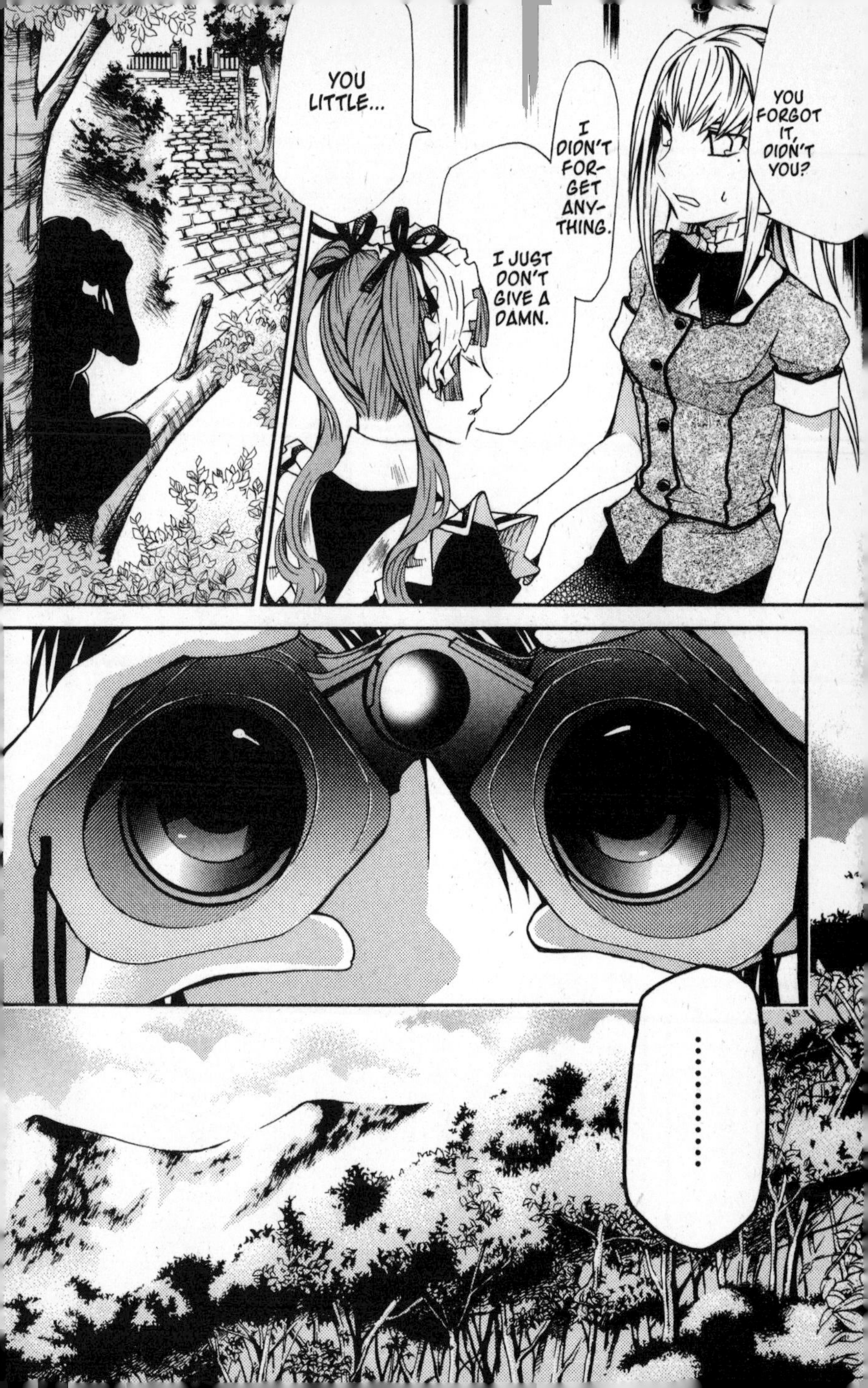
YOU FORGOT IT, DIDN'T YOU?
I DIDN'T FOR-GET ANY-THING.
I JUST DON'T GIVE A DAMN.
YOU LITTLE...
....

Prayer 20
The Tale of Shizu is Mariya and Mariya is Shizu and...

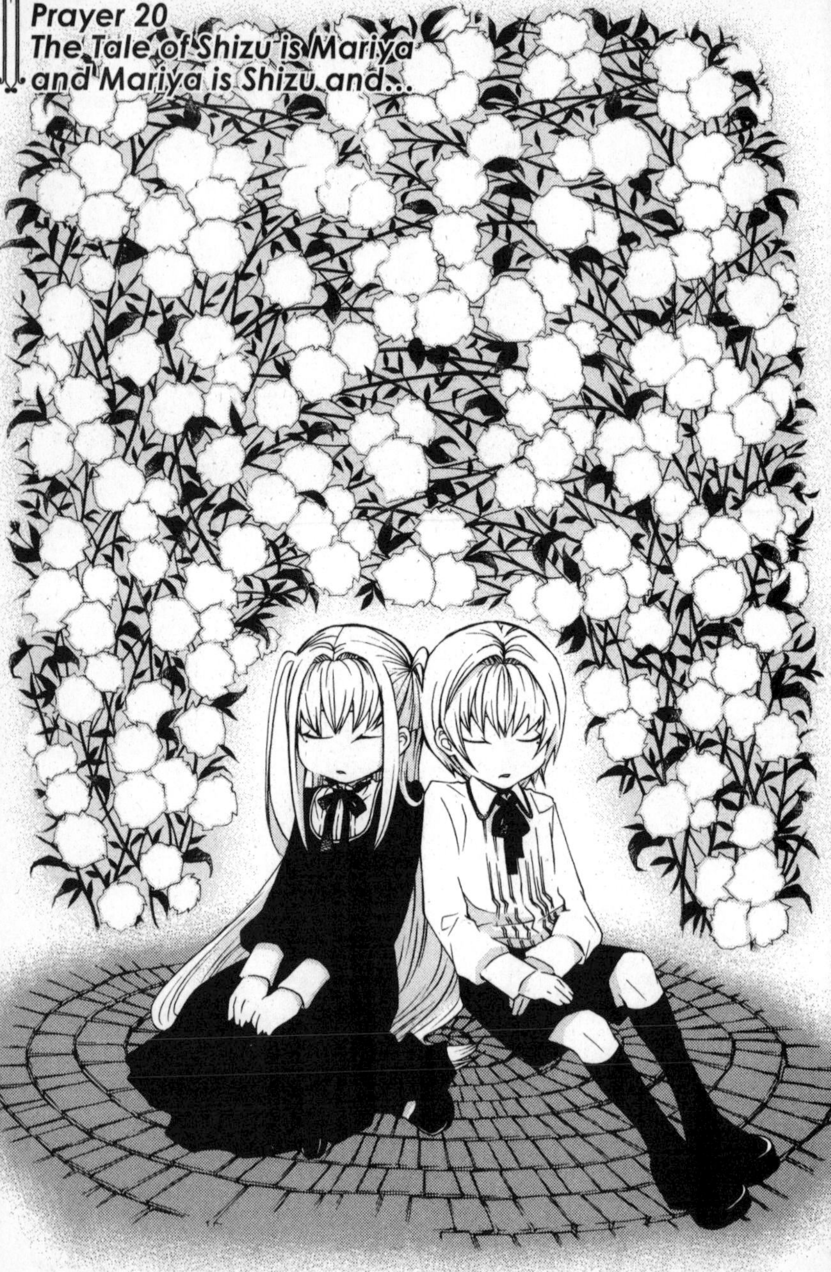

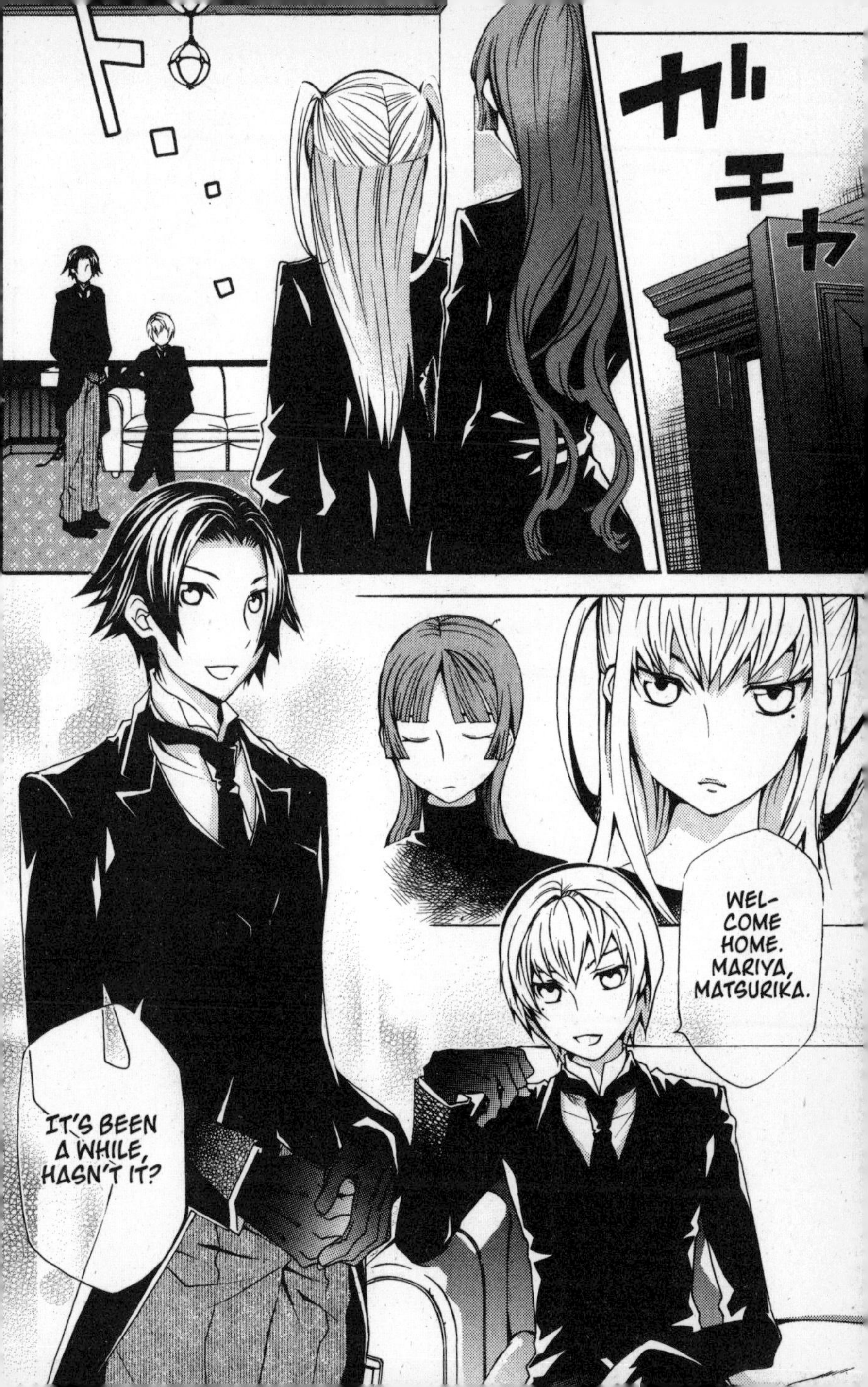
ガチャ
WEL-COME HOME. MARIYA, MATSURIKA.
IT'S BEEN A WHILE, HASN'T IT?

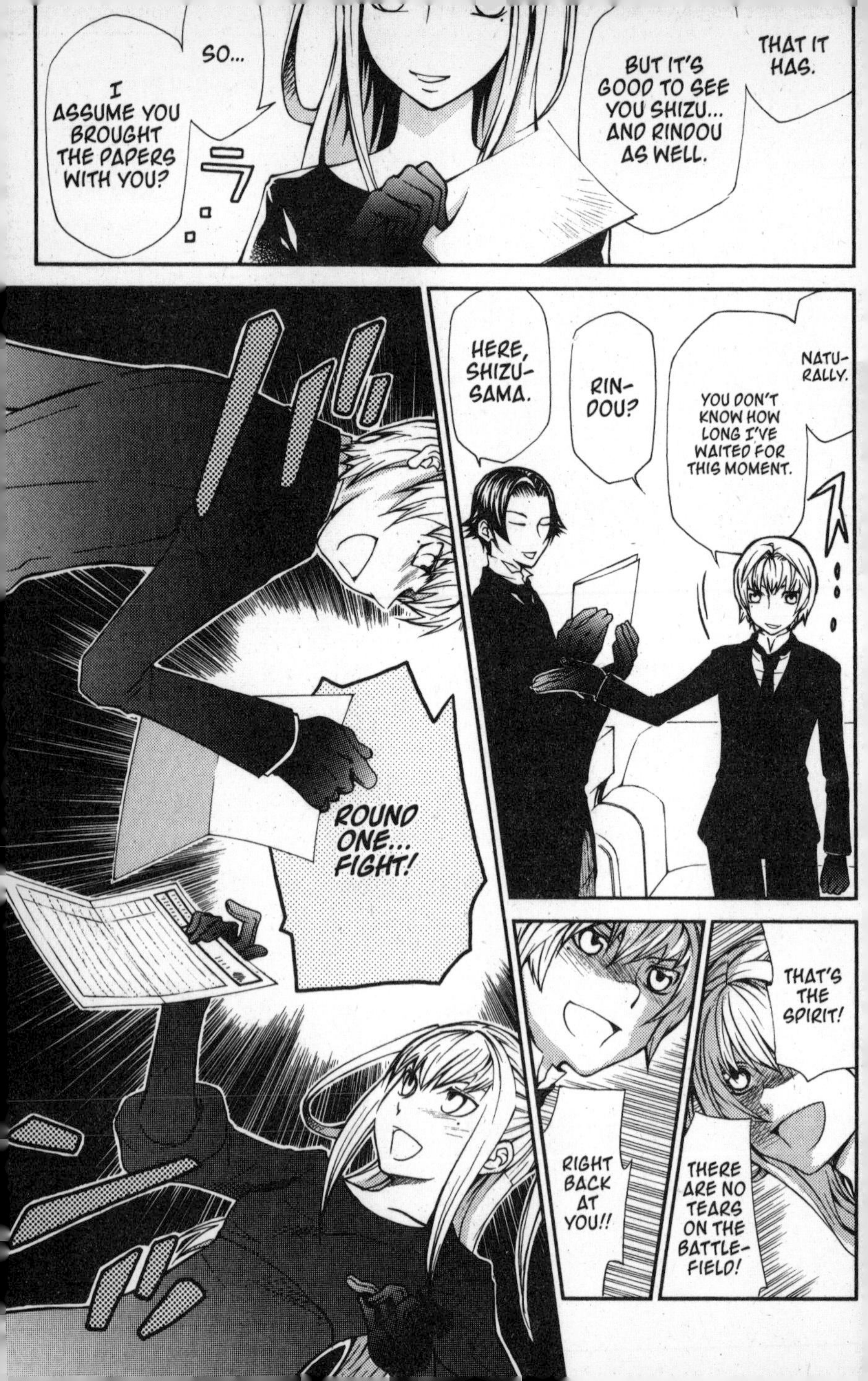
THAT IT HAS.
BUT IT'S GOOD TO SEE YOU SHIZU... AND RINDOU AS WELL.
SO...
I ASSUME YOU BROUGHT THE PAPERS WITH YOU?
NATU-RALLY.
YOU DON'T KNOW HOW LONG I'VE WAITED FOR THIS MOMENT.
RIN-DOU?
HERE, SHIZU-SAMA.
THAT'S THE SPIRIT!
THERE ARE NO TEARS ON THE BATTLE-FIELD!
RIGHT BACK AT YOU!!
ROUND ONE... FIGHT!

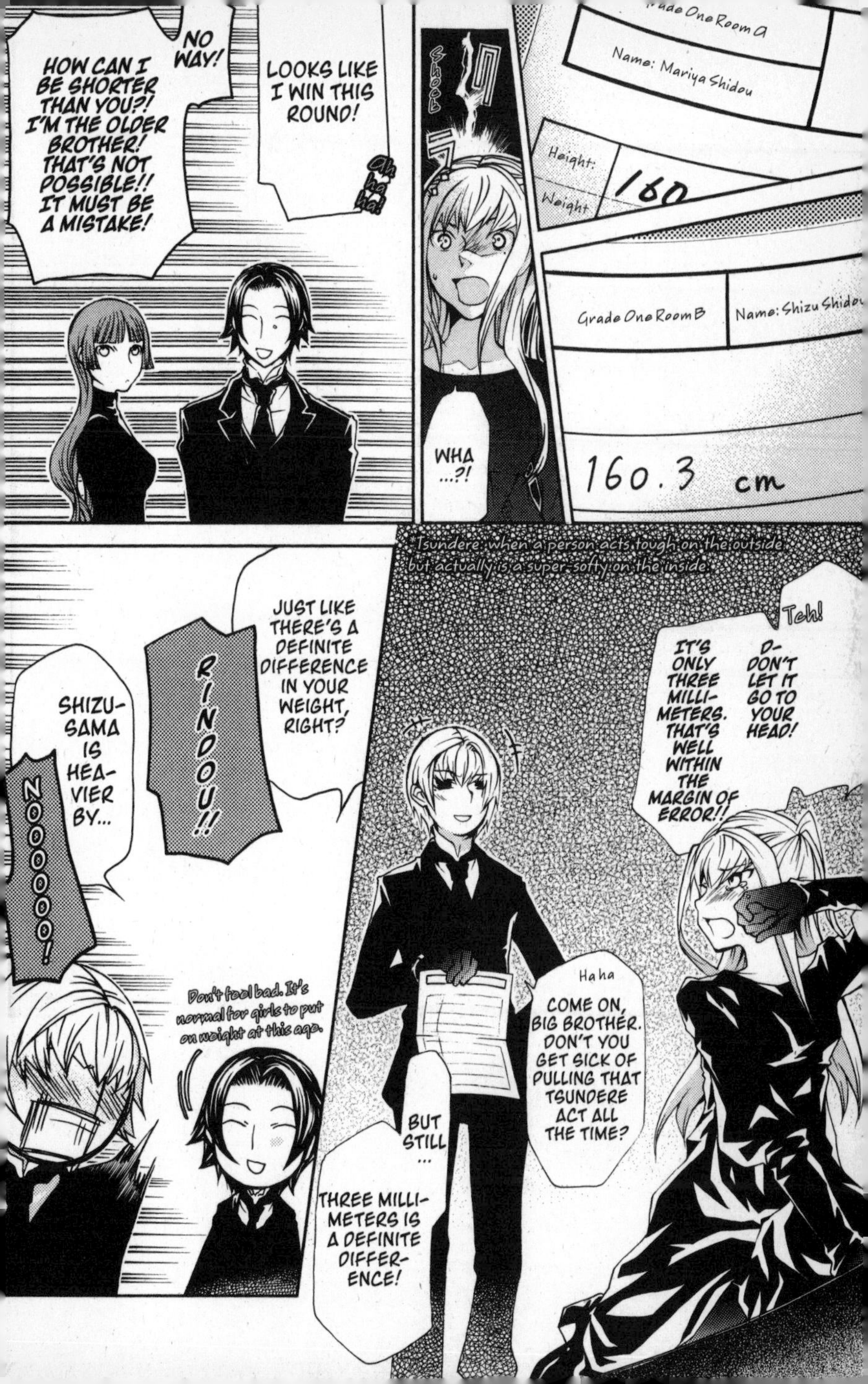
rade One Room A
Name: Mariya Shidou
Height: 160
Weight
Grade One Room B
Name: Shizu Shidou
160.3 cm
Shock
WHA ...?!
LOOKS LIKE I WIN THIS ROUND!
Oh ha ha!
NO WAY!
HOW CAN I BE SHORTER THAN YOU?! I'M THE OLDER BROTHER! THAT'S NOT POSSIBLE!! IT MUST BE A MISTAKE!
*Tsundere: when a person acts tough on the outside but actually is a super-softy on the inside.
Tch!
D-DON'T LET IT GO TO YOUR HEAD!
IT'S ONLY THREE MILLIMETERS. THAT'S WELL WITHIN THE MARGIN OF ERROR!!
Haha
COME ON, BIG BROTHER. DON'T YOU GET SICK OF PULLING THAT TSUNDERE ACT ALL THE TIME?
BUT STILL ...
THREE MILLIMETERS IS A DEFINITE DIFFERENCE!
JUST LIKE THERE'S A DEFINITE DIFFERENCE IN YOUR WEIGHT, RIGHT?
RINDOU!!
SHIZU-SAMA IS HEAVIER BY...
NOOOOOOO!
Don't feel bad. It's normal for girls to put on weight at this age.

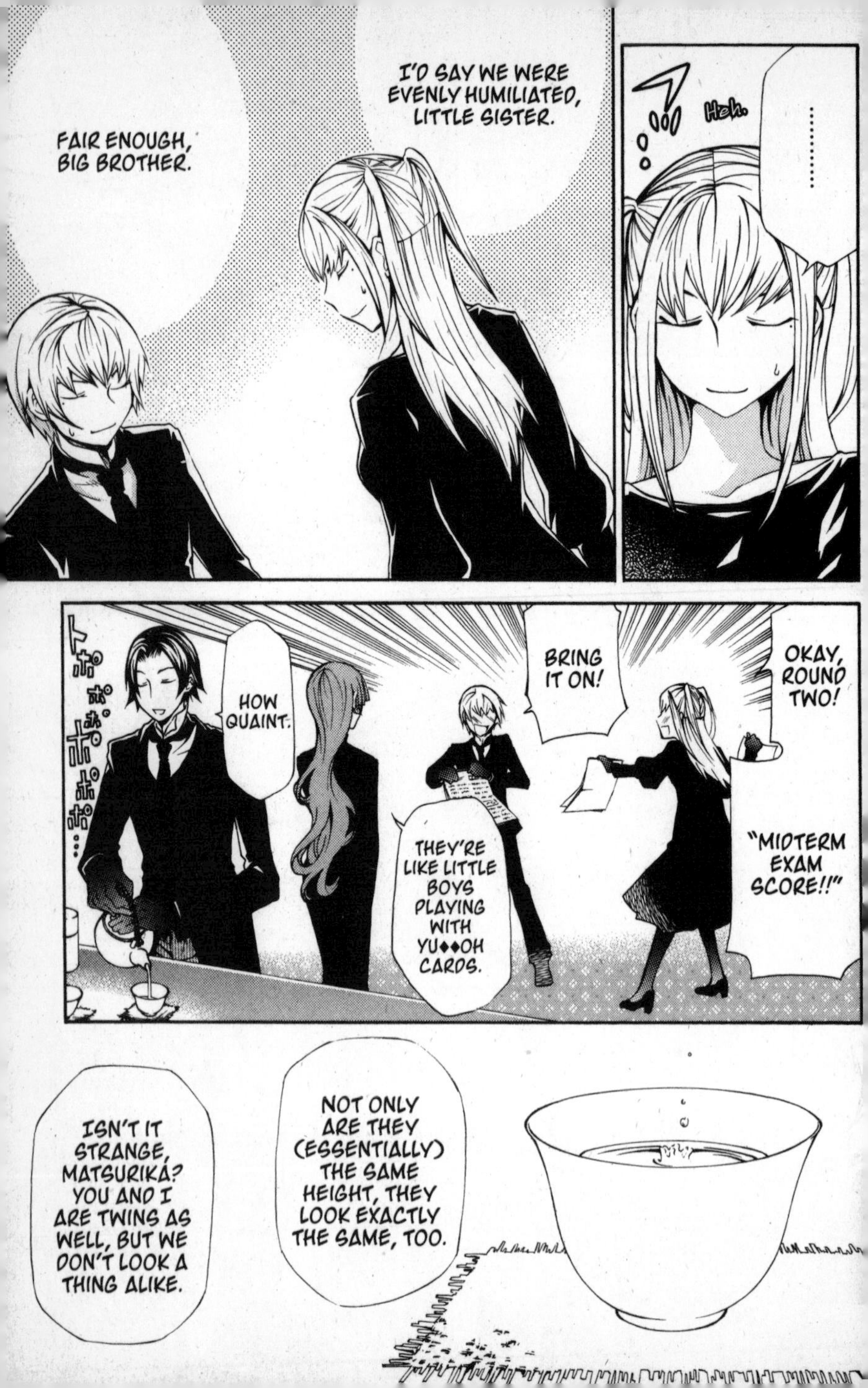
......
Heh.
I'D SAY WE WERE EVENLY HUMILIATED, LITTLE SISTER.
FAIR ENOUGH, BIG BROTHER.
OKAY, ROUND TWO!
"MIDTERM EXAM SCORE!!"
BRING IT ON!
THEY'RE LIKE LITTLE BOYS PLAYING WITH YU◆◆OH CARDS.
HOW QUAINT.
NOT ONLY ARE THEY (ESSENTIALLY) THE SAME HEIGHT, THEY LOOK EXACTLY THE SAME, TOO.
ISN'T IT STRANGE, MATSURIKA? YOU AND I ARE TWINS AS WELL, BUT WE DON'T LOOK A THING ALIKE.

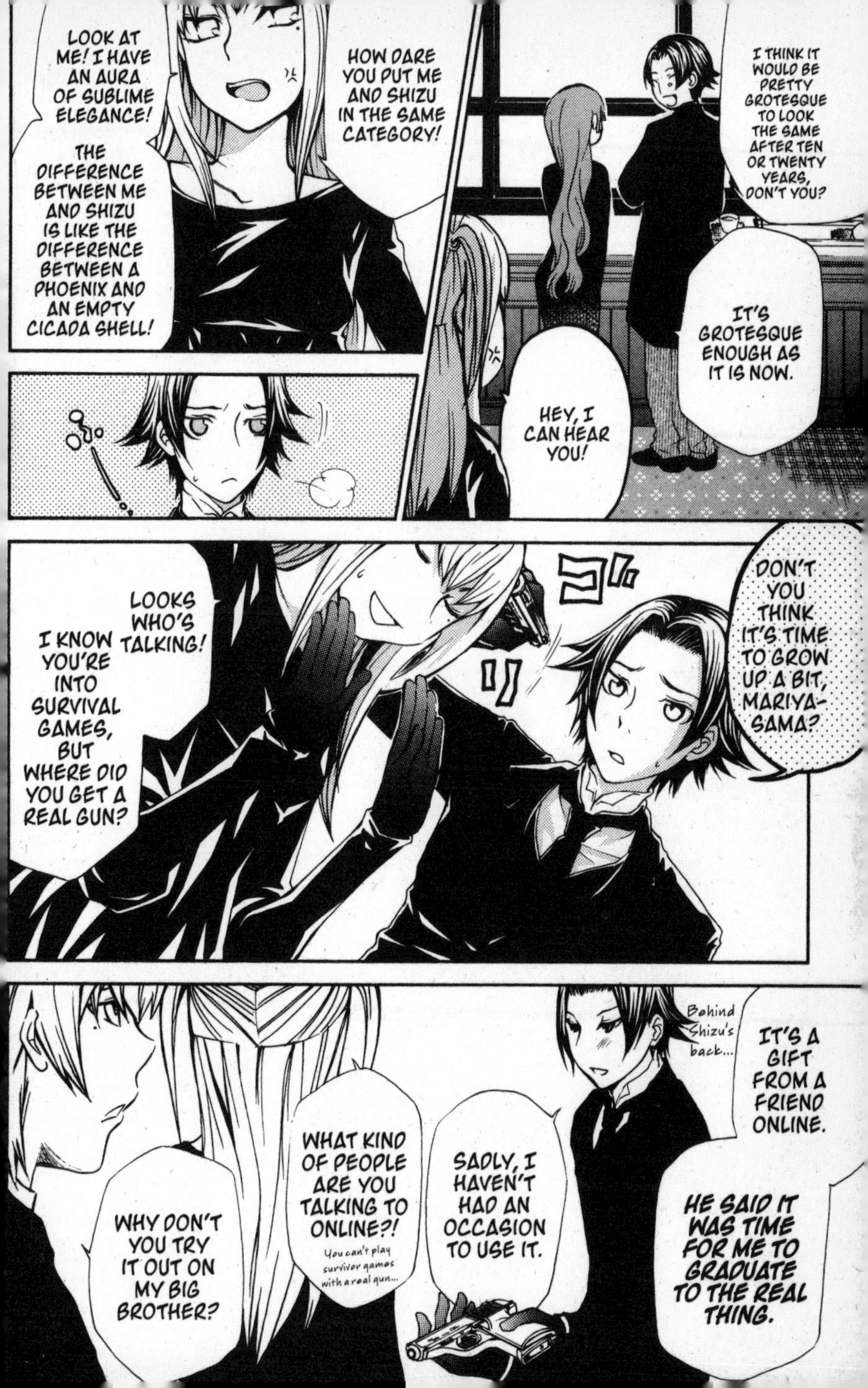
I THINK IT WOULD BE PRETTY GROTESQUE TO LOOK THE SAME AFTER TEN OR TWENTY YEARS, DON'T YOU?
IT'S GROTESQUE ENOUGH AS IT IS NOW.
HEY, I CAN HEAR YOU!
HOW DARE YOU PUT ME AND SHIZU IN THE SAME CATEGORY!
LOOK AT ME! I HAVE AN AURA OF SUBLIME ELEGANCE!
THE DIFFERENCE BETWEEN ME AND SHIZU IS LIKE THE DIFFERENCE BETWEEN A PHOENIX AND AN EMPTY CICADA SHELL!
DON'T YOU THINK IT'S TIME TO GROW UP A BIT, MARIYA-SAMA?
LOOKS WHO'S TALKING!
I KNOW YOU'RE INTO SURVIVAL GAMES, BUT WHERE DID YOU GET A REAL GUN?
Behind Shizu's back...
IT'S A GIFT FROM A FRIEND ONLINE.
HE SAID IT WAS TIME FOR ME TO GRADUATE TO THE REAL THING.
SADLY, I HAVEN'T HAD AN OCCASION TO USE IT.
WHAT KIND OF PEOPLE ARE YOU TALKING TO ONLINE?!
You can't play survivor games with a real gun...
WHY DON'T YOU TRY IT OUT ON MY BIG BROTHER?

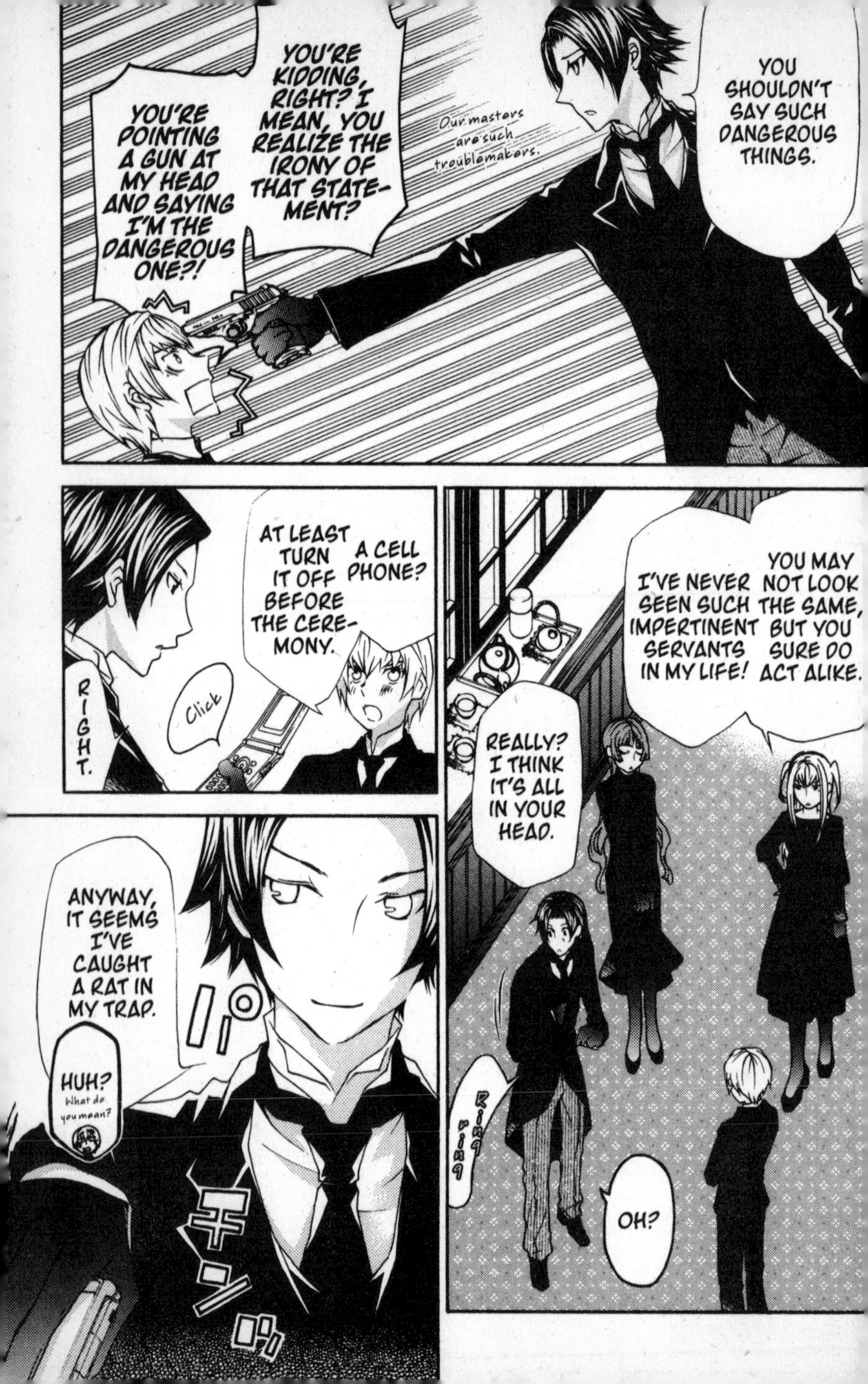
YOU SHOULDN'T SAY SUCH DANGEROUS THINGS.
Our masters are such troublemakers.
YOU'RE KIDDING, RIGHT? I MEAN, YOU REALIZE THE IRONY OF THAT STATEMENT?
YOU'RE POINTING A GUN AT MY HEAD AND SAYING I'M THE DANGEROUS ONE?!
YOU MAY NOT LOOK THE SAME, BUT YOU SURE DO ACT ALIKE.
I'VE NEVER SEEN SUCH IMPERTINENT SERVANTS IN MY LIFE!
REALLY? I THINK IT'S ALL IN YOUR HEAD.
Ring ring
OH?
A CELL PHONE?
AT LEAST TURN IT OFF BEFORE THE CEREMONY.
Click
RIGHT.
ANYWAY, IT SEEMS I'VE CAUGHT A RAT IN MY TRAP.
HUH?
What do you mean?

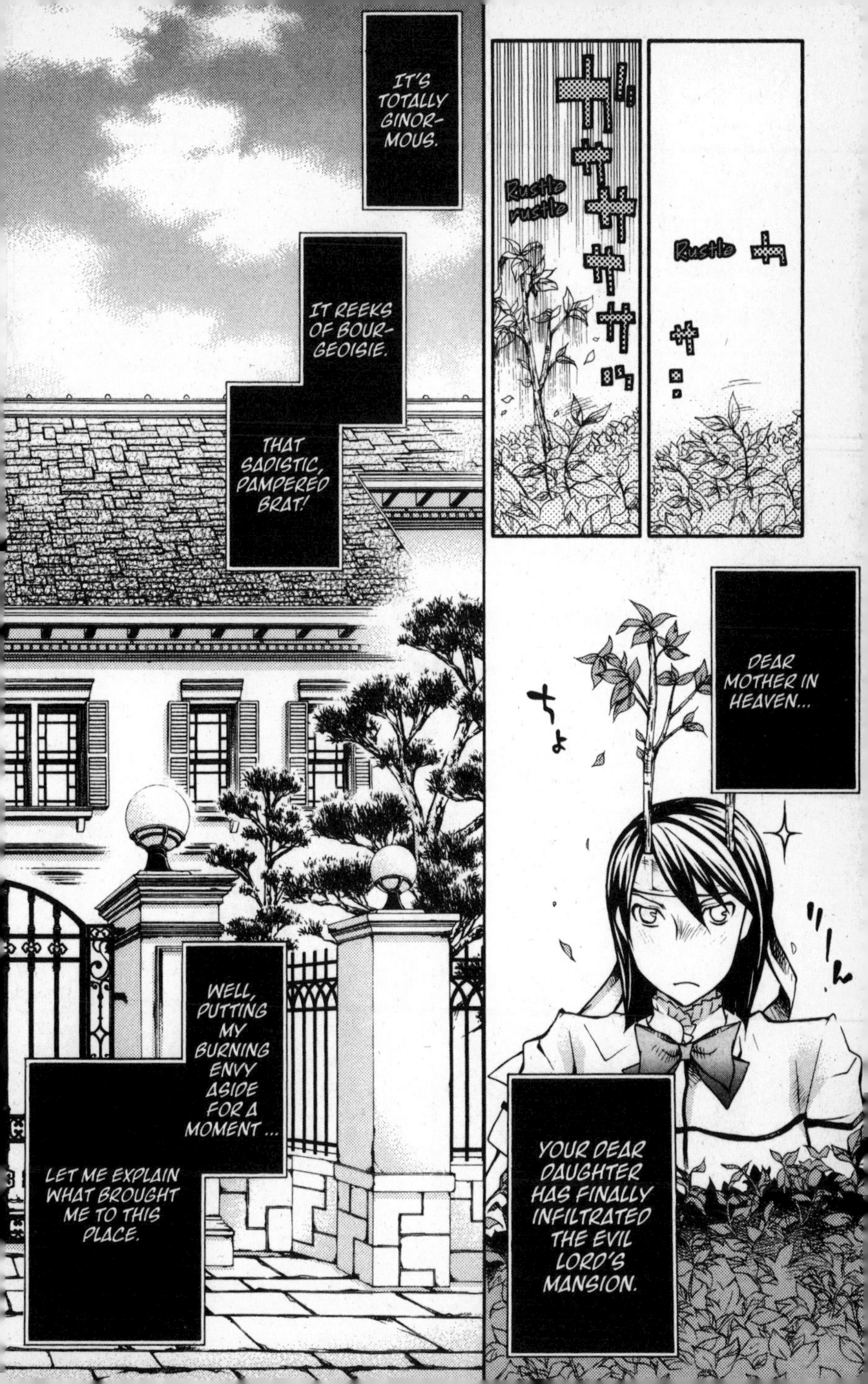
Rustle
Rustle rustle
ちょ
DEAR MOTHER IN HEAVEN...
YOUR DEAR DAUGHTER HAS FINALLY INFILTRATED THE EVIL LORD'S MANSION.
IT'S TOTALLY GINOR-MOUS.
IT REEKS OF BOUR-GEOISIE.
THAT SADISTIC, PAMPERED BRAT!
WELL, PUTTING MY BURNING ENVY ASIDE FOR A MOMENT ...
LET ME EXPLAIN WHAT BROUGHT ME TO THIS PLACE.

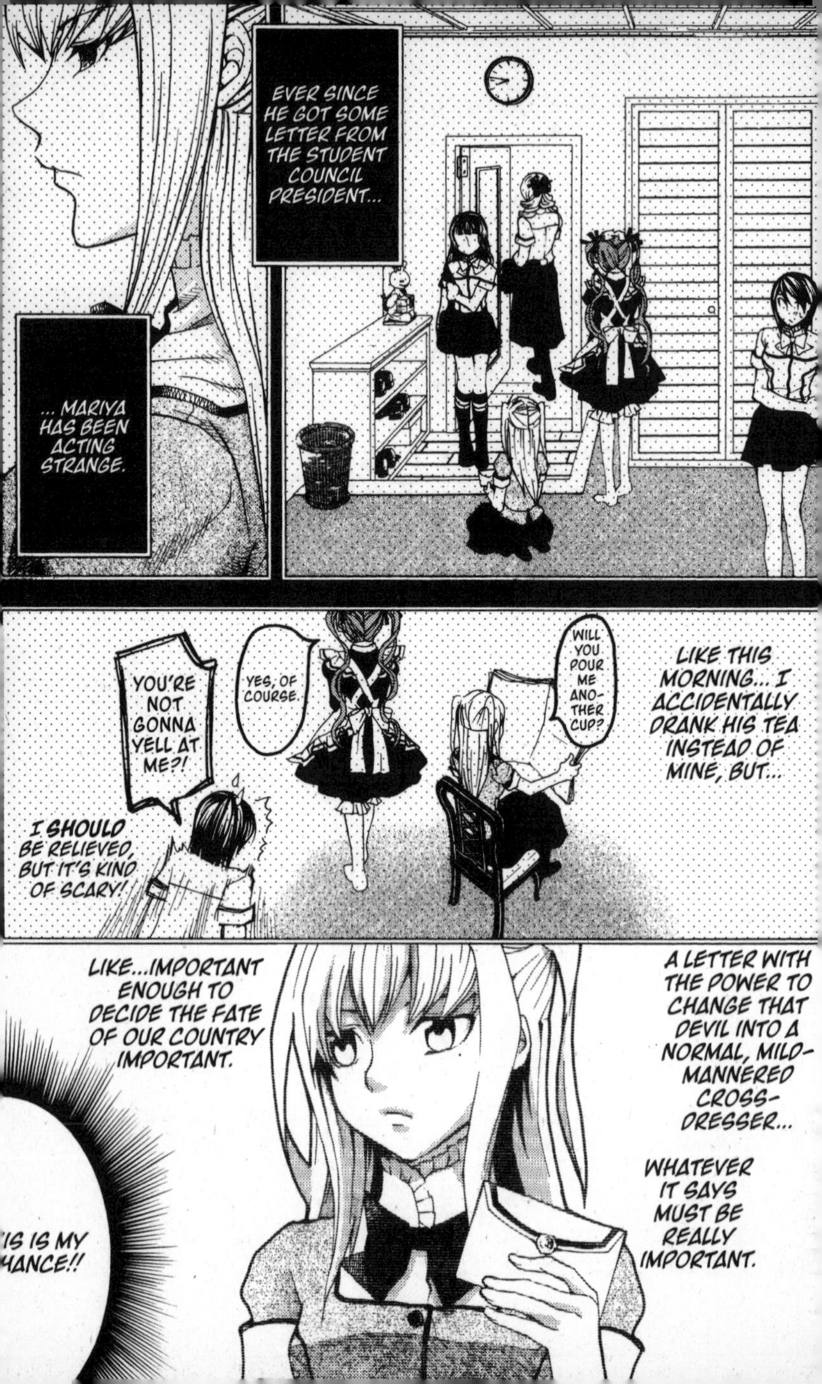
EVER SINCE HE GOT SOME LETTER FROM THE STUDENT COUNCIL PRESIDENT...
...MARIYA HAS BEEN ACTING STRANGE.
LIKE THIS MORNING... I ACCIDENTALLY DRANK HIS TEA INSTEAD OF MINE, BUT...
WILL YOU POUR ME ANOTHER CUP?
YES, OF COURSE.
YOU'RE NOT GONNA YELL AT ME?!
I SHOULD BE RELIEVED, BUT IT'S KIND OF SCARY!
A LETTER WITH THE POWER TO CHANGE THAT DEVIL INTO A NORMAL, MILD-MANNERED CROSS-DRESSER...
WHATEVER IT SAYS MUST BE REALLY IMPORTANT.
LIKE...IMPORTANT ENOUGH TO DECIDE THE FATE OF OUR COUNTRY IMPORTANT.
IS IS MY
HANCE!!

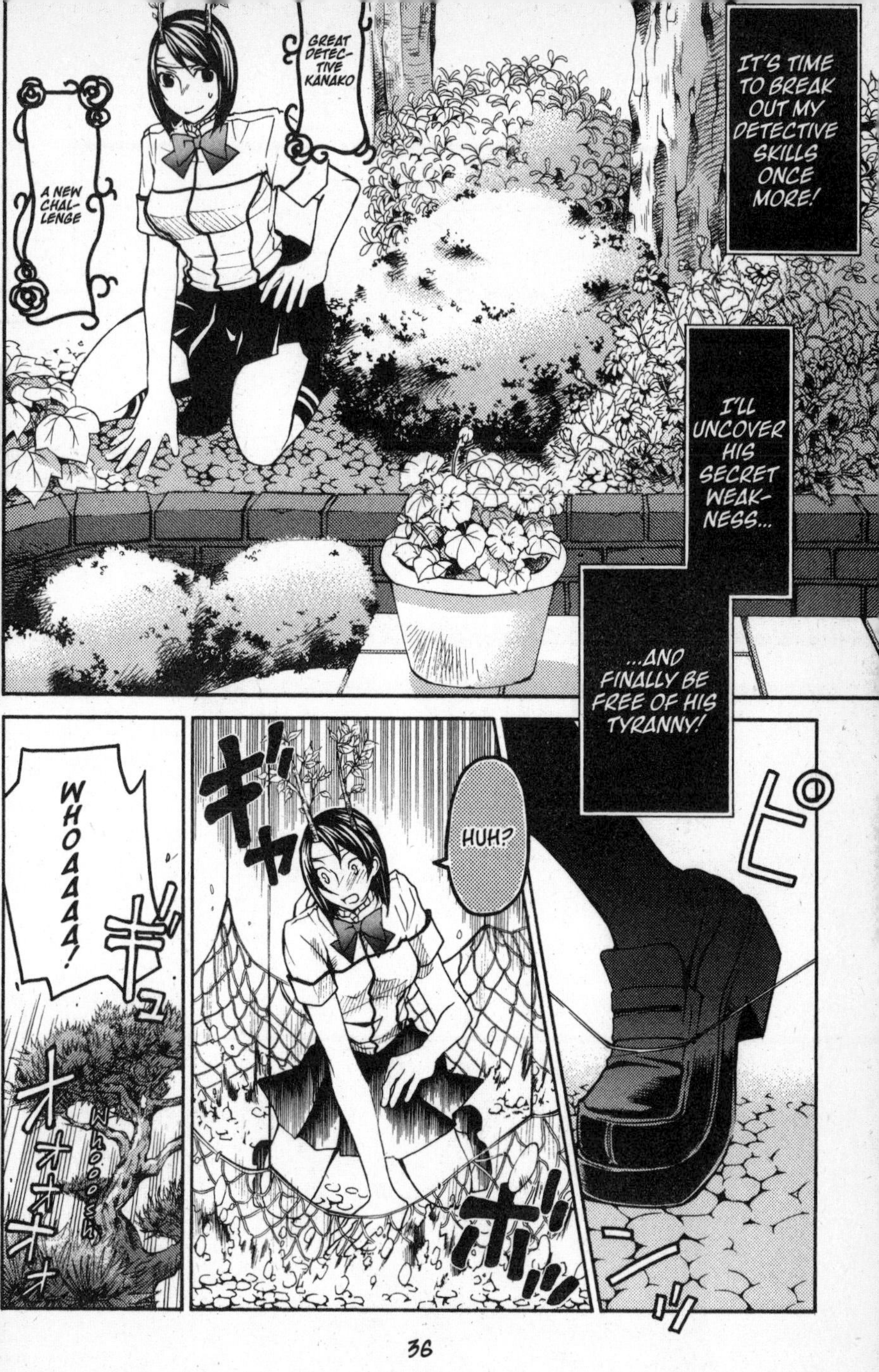
IT'S TIME TO BREAK OUT MY DETECTIVE SKILLS ONCE MORE!
GREAT DETECTIVE KANAKO
A NEW CHALLENGE
I'LL UNCOVER HIS SECRET WEAKNESS...
...AND FINALLY BE FREE OF HIS TYRANNY!
ピ
HUH?
ギャ
ボッ
WHOAAAAA!
ギュ
オオオオ
Whoooosh

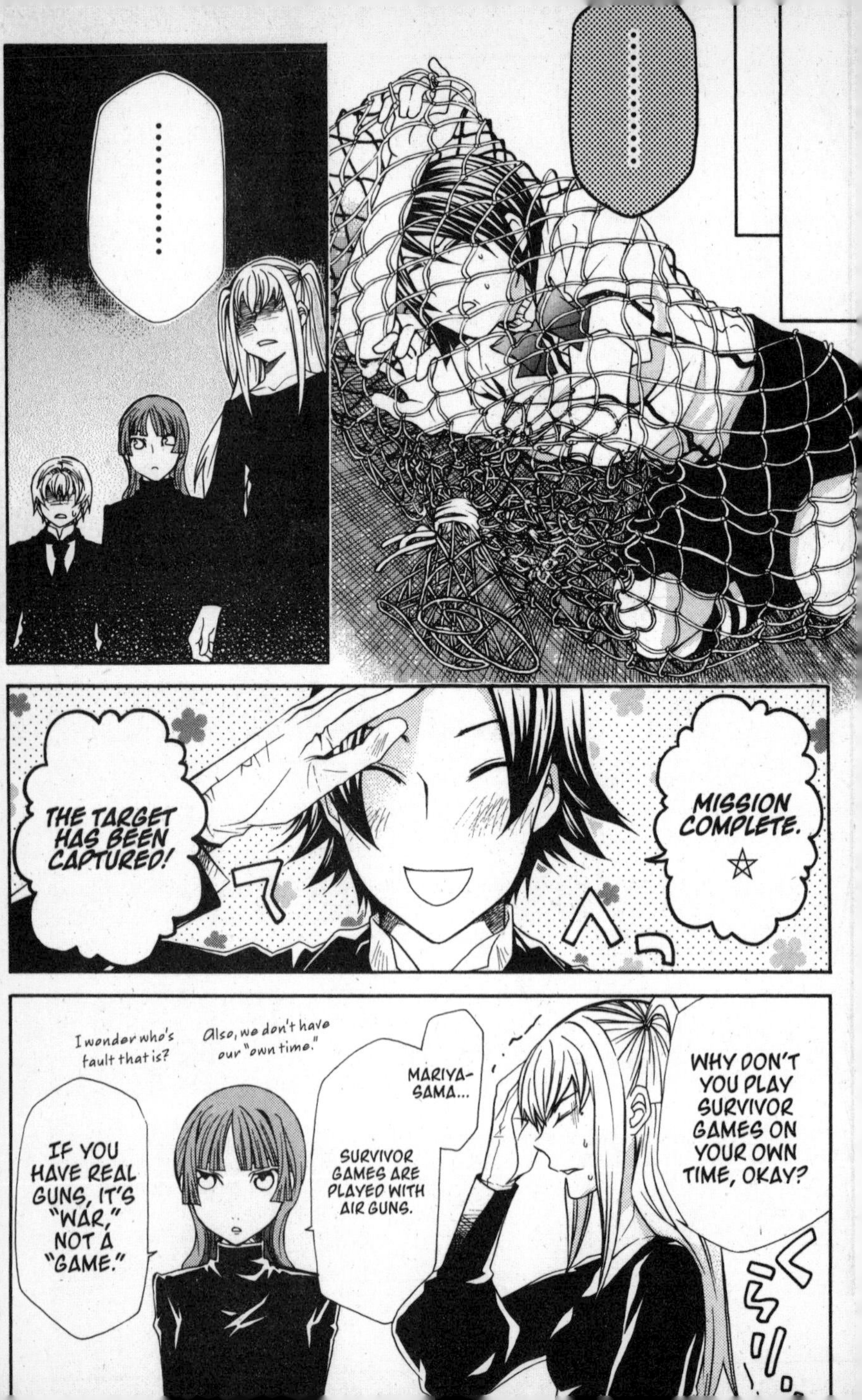
......
......
MISSION COMPLETE. ☆
THE TARGET HAS BEEN CAPTURED!
WHY DON'T YOU PLAY SURVIVOR GAMES ON YOUR OWN TIME, OKAY?
MARIYA-SAMA...
SURVIVOR GAMES ARE PLAYED WITH AIR GUNS.
Also, we don't have our "own time."
IF YOU HAVE REAL GUNS, IT'S "WAR," NOT A "GAME."
I wonder who's fault that is?

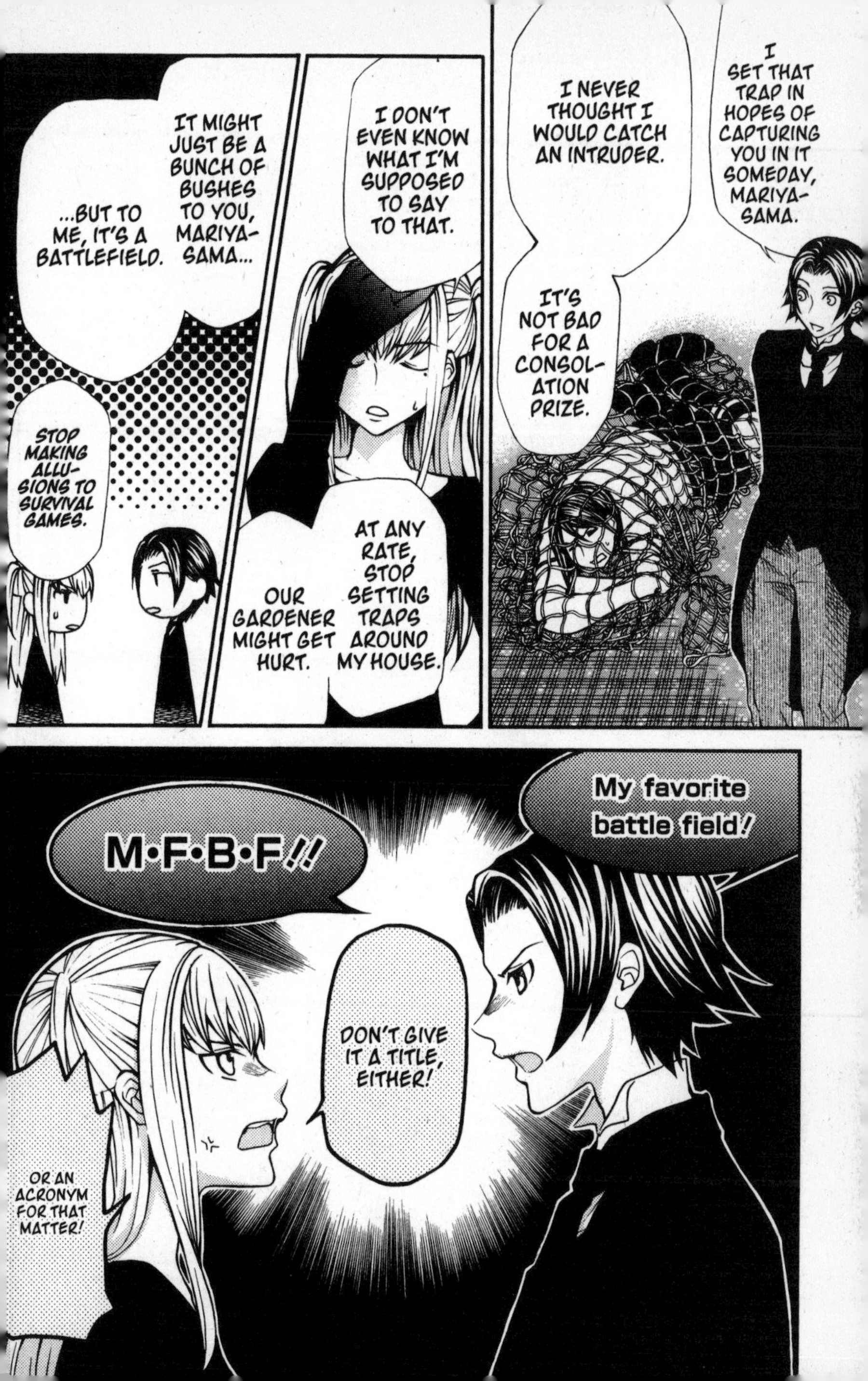
I SET THAT TRAP IN HOPES OF CAPTURING YOU IN IT SOMEDAY, MARIYA-SAMA.
I NEVER THOUGHT I WOULD CATCH AN INTRUDER.
IT'S NOT BAD FOR A CONSOL-ATION PRIZE.
I DON'T EVEN KNOW WHAT I'M SUPPOSED TO SAY TO THAT.
AT ANY RATE, STOP SETTING TRAPS AROUND MY HOUSE.
OUR GARDENER MIGHT GET HURT.
IT MIGHT JUST BE A BUNCH OF BUSHES TO YOU, MARIYA-SAMA...
...BUT TO ME, IT'S A BATTLEFIELD.
STOP MAKING ALLU-SIONS TO SURVIVAL GAMES.
My favorite battle field!
M·F·B·F!!
DON'T GIVE IT A TITLE, EITHER!
OR AN ACRONYM FOR THAT MATTER!

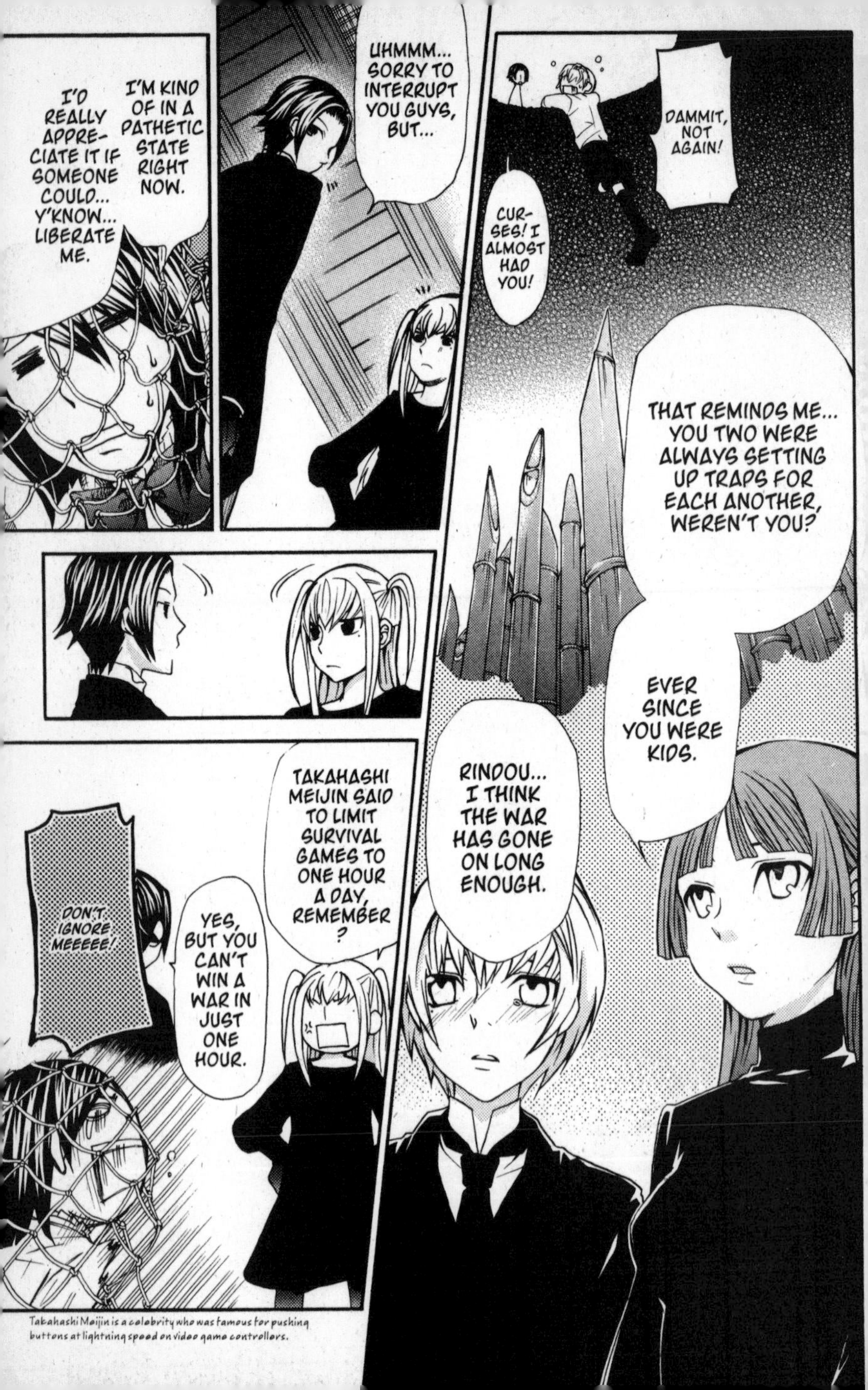
DAMMIT, NOT AGAIN!
CURSES! I ALMOST HAD YOU!
THAT REMINDS ME... YOU TWO WERE ALWAYS SETTING UP TRAPS FOR EACH ANOTHER, WEREN'T YOU?
EVER SINCE YOU WERE KIDS.
RINDOU... I THINK THE WAR HAS GONE ON LONG ENOUGH.
UHMMM... SORRY TO INTERRUPT YOU GUYS, BUT...
I'M KIND OF IN A PATHETIC STATE RIGHT NOW.
I'D REALLY APPRECIATE IT IF SOMEONE COULD... Y'KNOW... LIBERATE ME.
TAKAHASHI MEIJIN SAID TO LIMIT SURVIVAL GAMES TO ONE HOUR A DAY, REMEMBER?
YES, BUT YOU CAN'T WIN A WAR IN JUST ONE HOUR.
DON'T IGNORE MEEEEE!

Takahashi Meijin is a celebrity who was famous for pushing buttons at lightning speed on video game controllers.

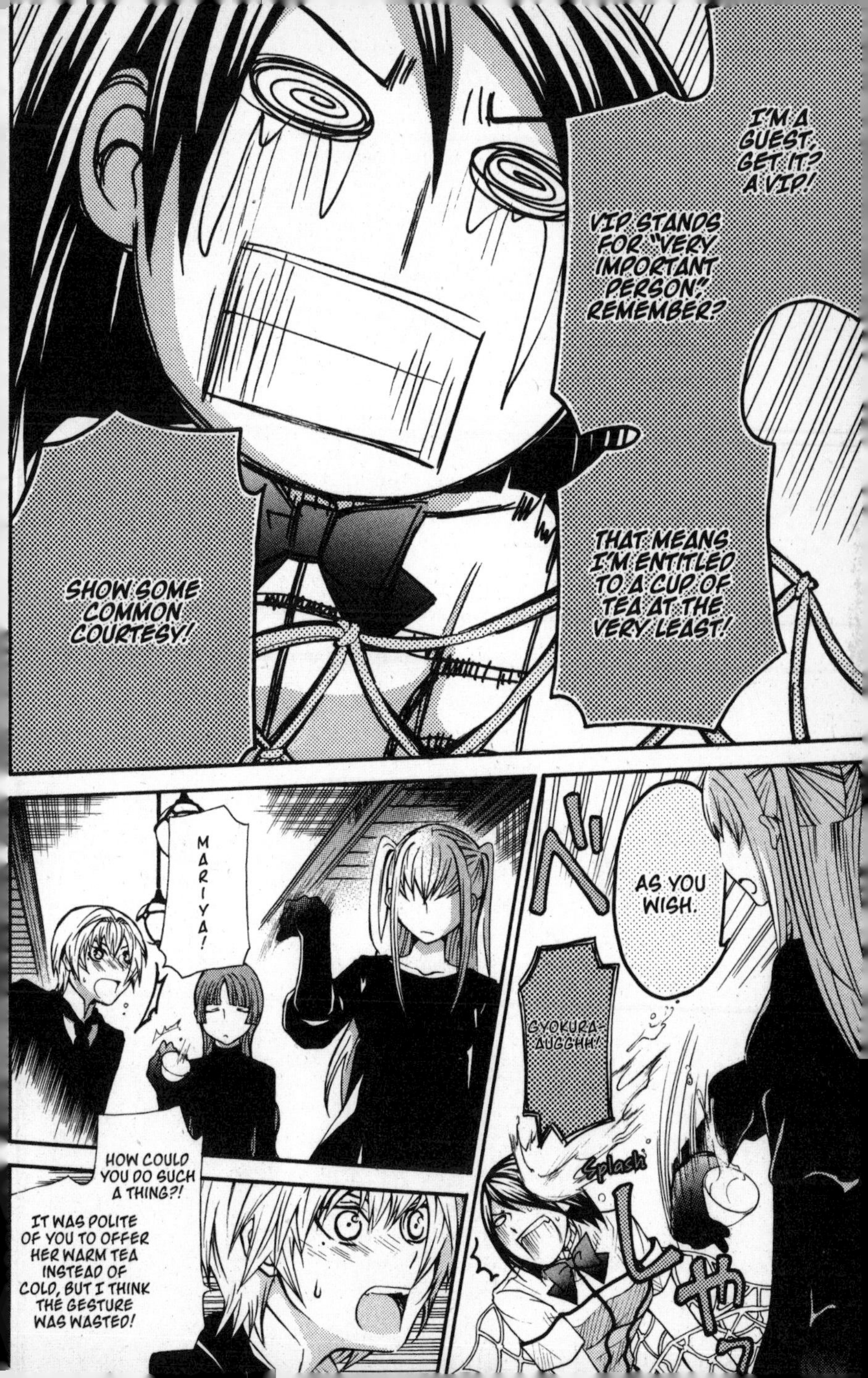

I'M A GUEST, GET IT? A VIP!
VIP STANDS FOR "VERY IMPORTANT PERSON," REMEMBER?
THAT MEANS I'M ENTITLED TO A CUP OF TEA AT THE VERY LEAST!
SHOW SOME COMMON COURTESY!
AS YOU WISH.
GYOKURA-AUGGHH!
Splash
MARIYA!
HOW COULD YOU DO SUCH A THING?!
IT WAS POLITE OF YOU TO OFFER HER WARM TEA INSTEAD OF COLD, BUT I THINK THE GESTURE WAS WASTED!

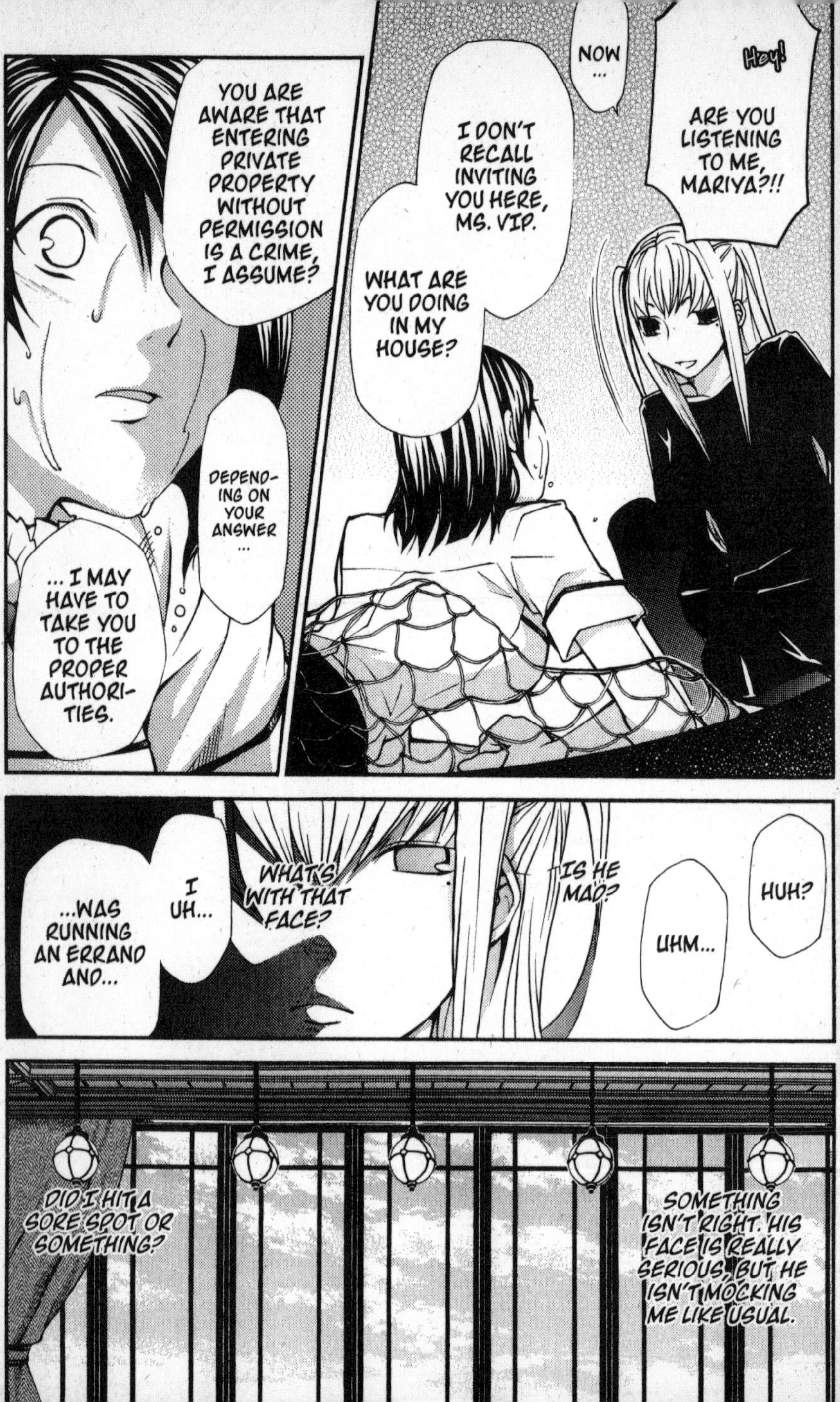
Hey!
ARE YOU LISTENING TO ME, MARIYA?!!
NOW ...
I DON'T RECALL INVITING YOU HERE, MS. VIP.
WHAT ARE YOU DOING IN MY HOUSE?
YOU ARE AWARE THAT ENTERING PRIVATE PROPERTY WITHOUT PERMISSION IS A CRIME, I ASSUME?
DEPEND-ING ON YOUR ANSWER ...
... I MAY HAVE TO TAKE YOU TO THE PROPER AUTHORI-TIES.
HUH?
UHM...
IS HE MAD?
WHAT'S WITH THAT FACE?
I UH...
...WAS RUNNING AN ERRAND AND...
SOMETHING ISN'T RIGHT. HIS FACE IS REALLY SERIOUS, BUT HE ISN'T MOCKING ME LIKE USUAL.
DID I HIT A SORE SPOT OR SOMETHING?

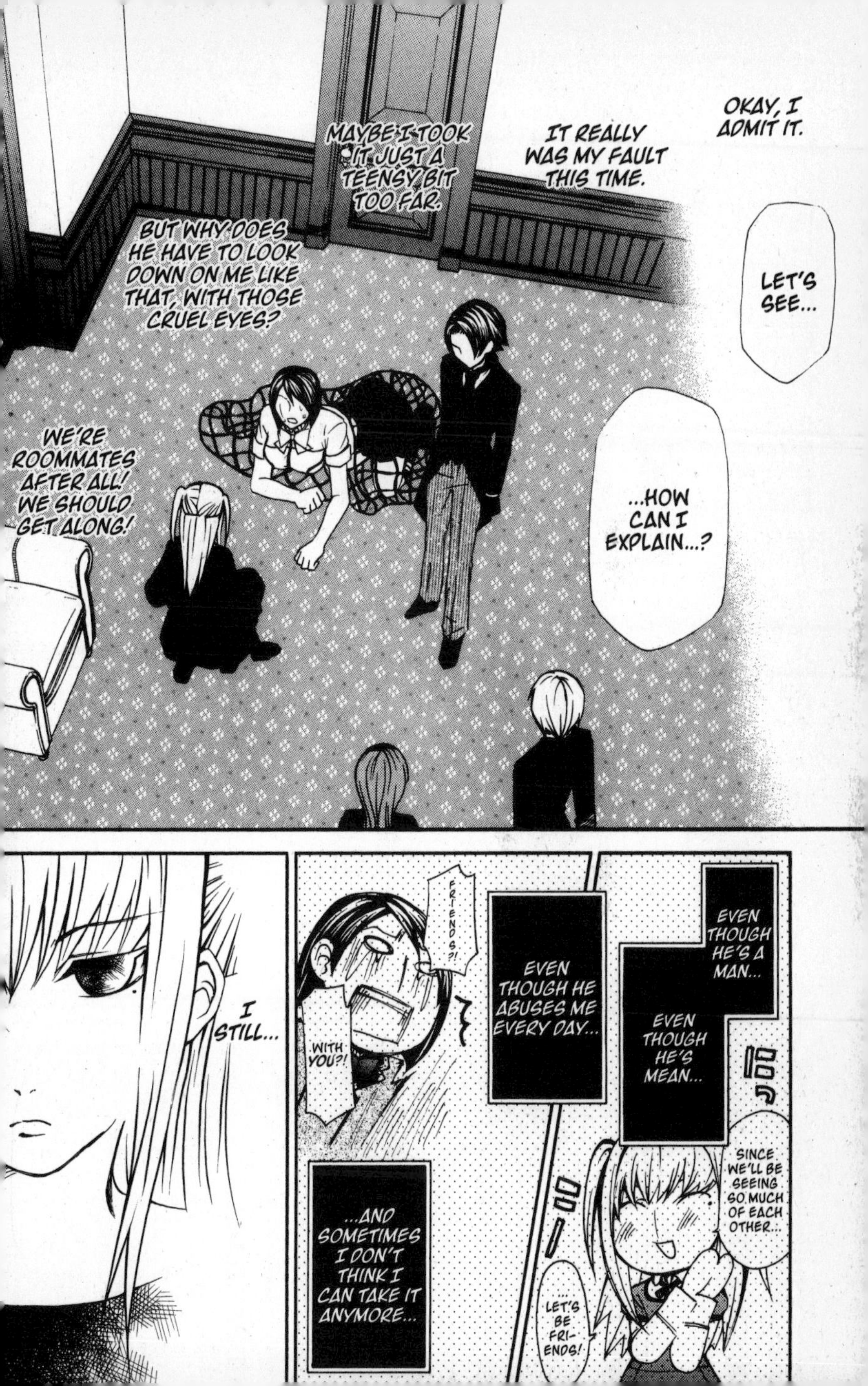

OKAY, I ADMIT IT.
IT REALLY WAS MY FAULT THIS TIME.
MAYBE I TOOK IT JUST A TEENSY BIT TOO FAR.
BUT WHY DOES HE HAVE TO LOOK DOWN ON ME LIKE THAT, WITH THOSE CRUEL EYES?
LET'S SEE...
...HOW CAN I EXPLAIN...?
WE'RE ROOMMATES AFTER ALL! WE SHOULD GET ALONG!
EVEN THOUGH HE'S A MAN...
EVEN THOUGH HE'S MEAN...
SINCE WE'LL BE SEEING SO MUCH OF EACH OTHER...
...LET'S BE FRI-ENDS!
FRIENDS?!
WITH YOU?!
EVEN THOUGH HE ABUSES ME EVERY DAY...
...AND SOMETIMES I DON'T THINK I CAN TAKE IT ANYMORE...
I STILL...

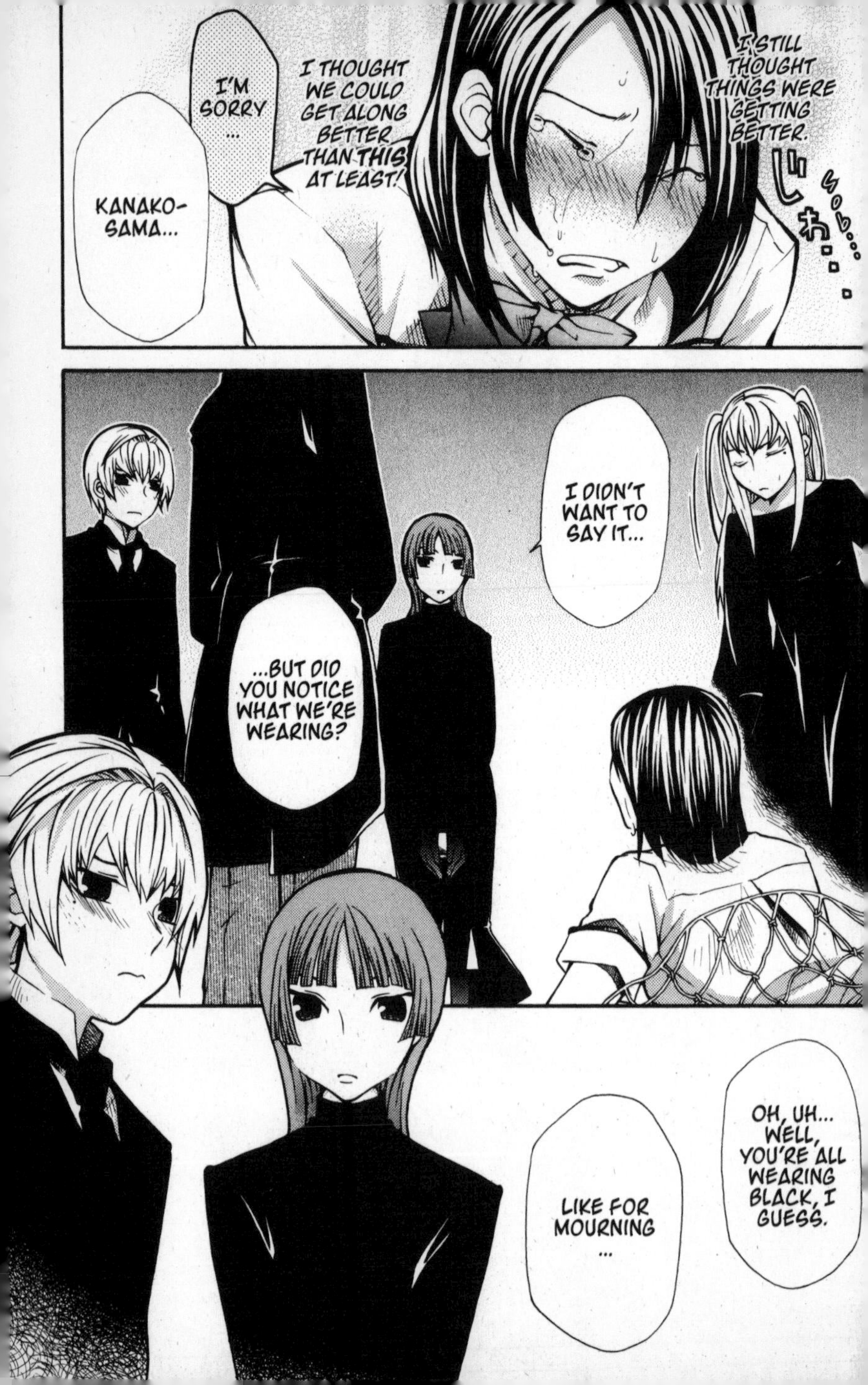
I STILL THOUGHT THINGS WERE GETTING BETTER.
sob...
じわ...
I THOUGHT WE COULD GET ALONG BETTER THAN THIS AT LEAST!
I'M SORRY...
KANAKO-SAMA...
I DIDN'T WANT TO SAY IT...
...BUT DID YOU NOTICE WHAT WE'RE WEARING?
OH, UH... WELL, YOU'RE ALL WEARING BLACK, I GUESS.
LIKE FOR MOURNING...

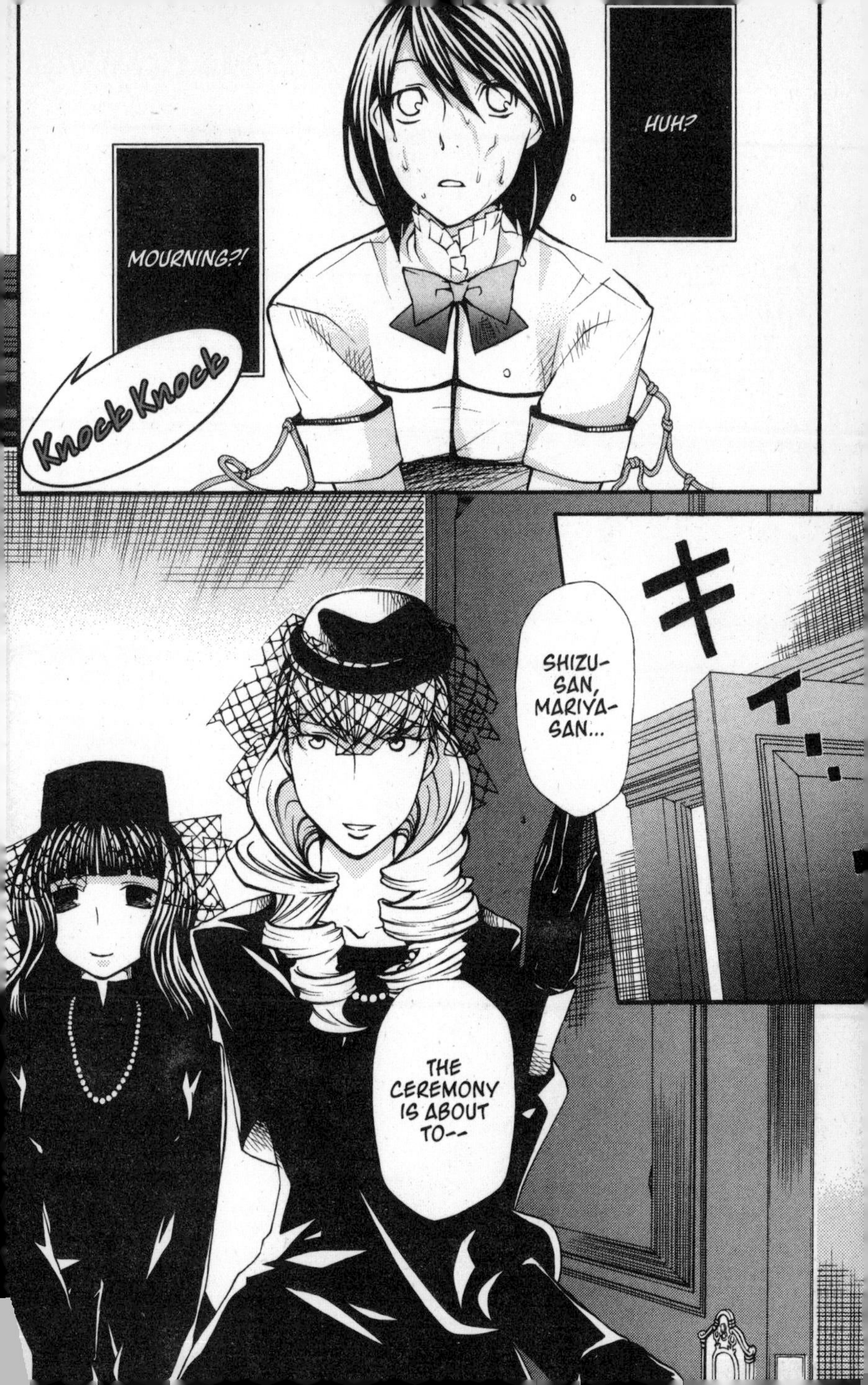
HUH?
MOURNING?!
Knock Knock
キイ・・
SHIZU-SAN, MARIYA-SAN...
THE CEREMONY IS ABOUT TO--

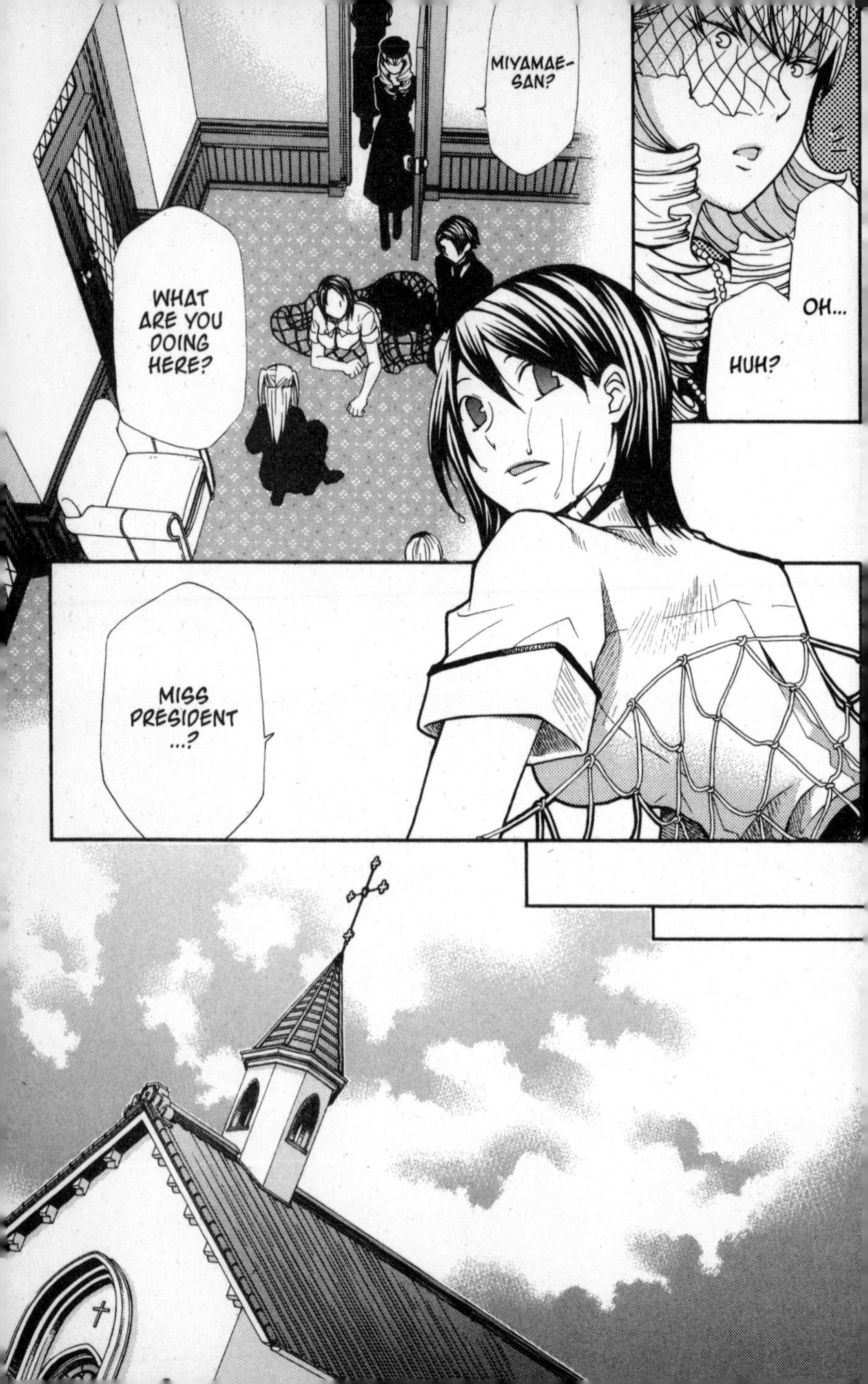
OH...
HUH?
MIYAMAE-SAN?
WHAT ARE YOU DOING HERE?
MISS PRESIDENT ...?

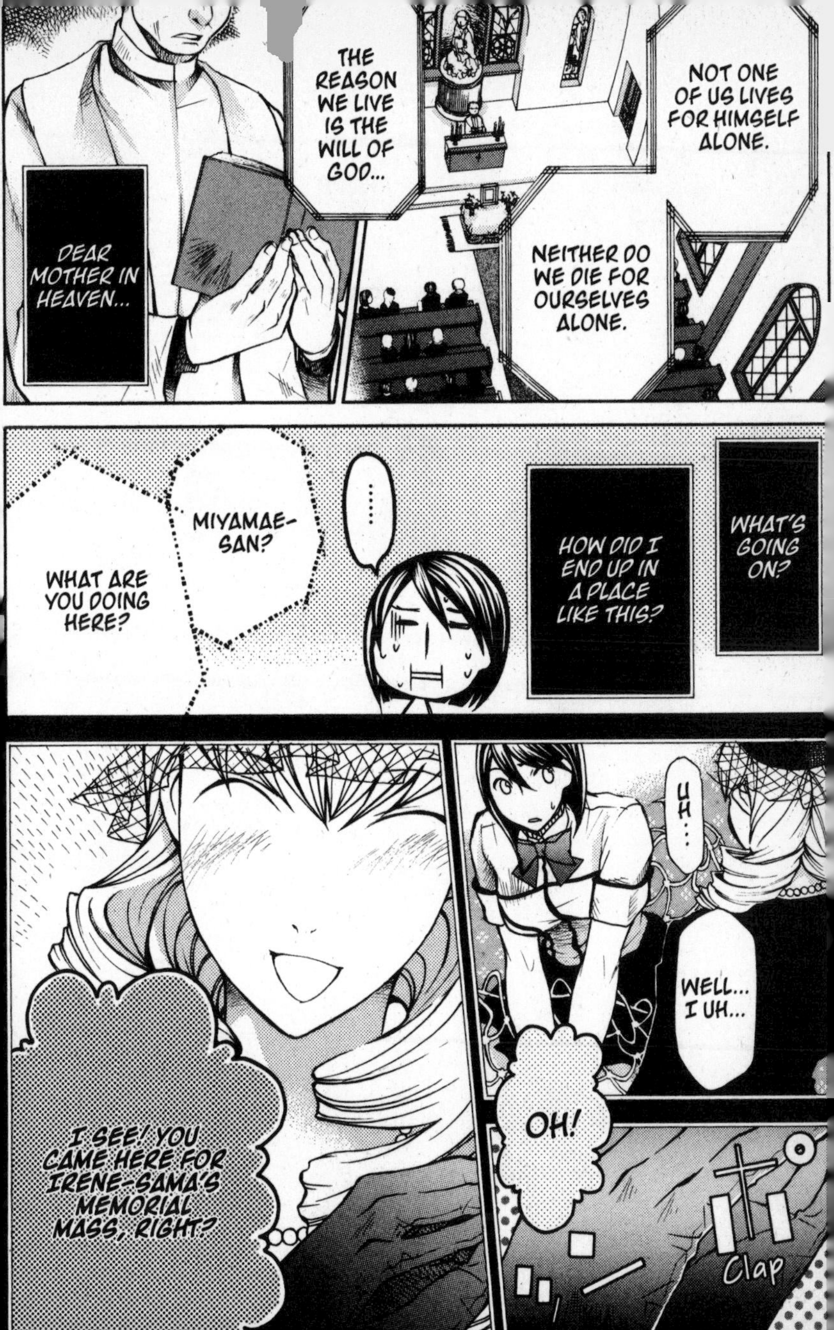
NOT ONE OF US LIVES FOR HIMSELF ALONE.
NEITHER DO WE DIE FOR OURSELVES ALONE.
THE REASON WE LIVE IS THE WILL OF GOD...
DEAR MOTHER IN HEAVEN...
WHAT'S GOING ON?
HOW DID I END UP IN A PLACE LIKE THIS?
......
MIYAMAE-SAN?
WHAT ARE YOU DOING HERE?
UH...
WELL... I UH...
OH!
Clap
I SEE! YOU CAME HERE FOR IRENE-SAMA'S MEMORIAL MASS, RIGHT?

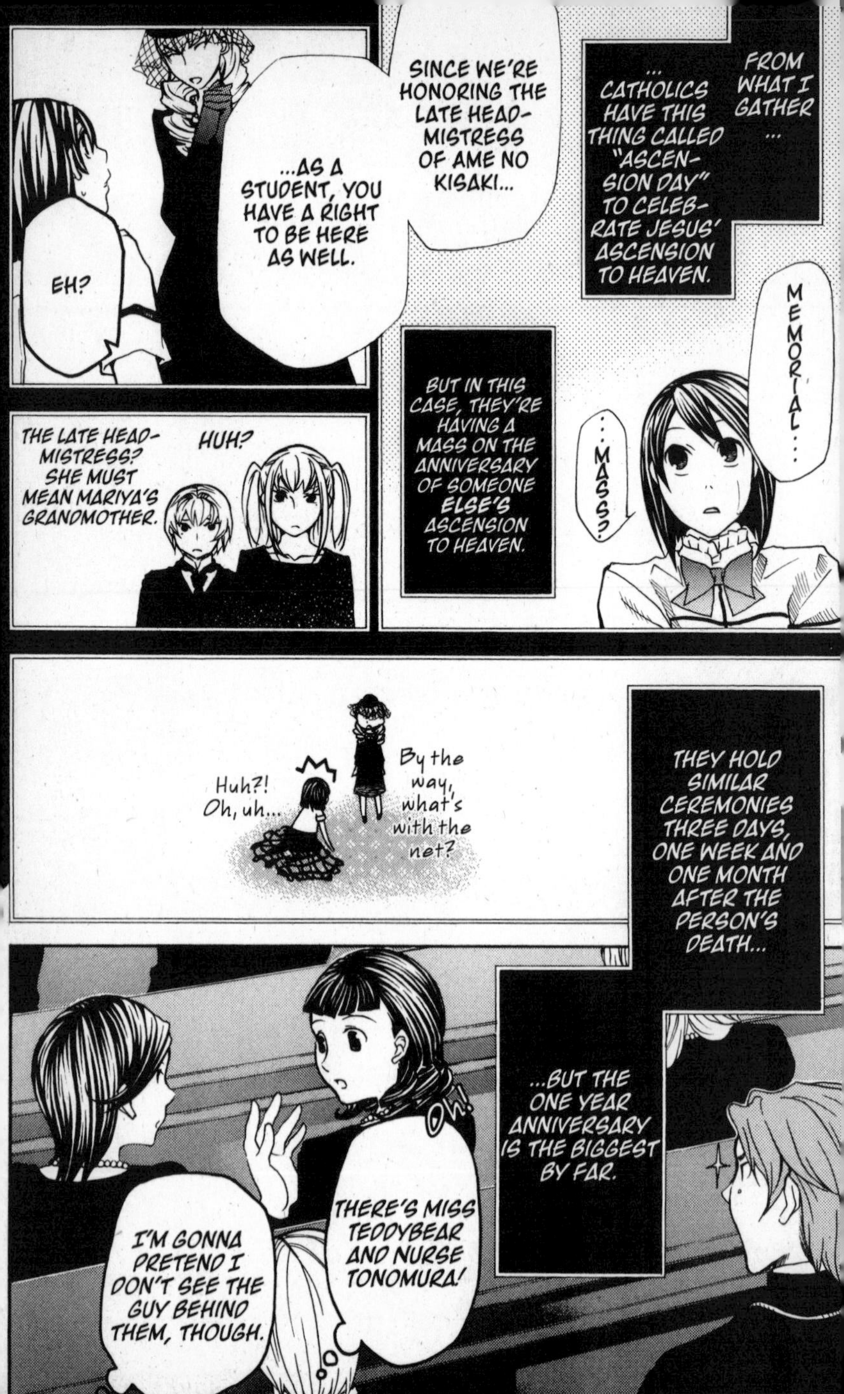
FROM WHAT I GATHER...
...CATHOLICS HAVE THIS THING CALLED "ASCENSION DAY" TO CELEBRATE JESUS' ASCENSION TO HEAVEN.
MEMORIAL...
...MASS?
BUT IN THIS CASE, THEY'RE HAVING A MASS ON THE ANNIVERSARY OF SOMEONE **ELSE'S** ASCENSION TO HEAVEN.
SINCE WE'RE HONORING THE LATE HEADMISTRESS OF AME NO KISAKI...
...AS A STUDENT, YOU HAVE A RIGHT TO BE HERE AS WELL.
EH?
HUH?
THE LATE HEADMISTRESS? SHE MUST MEAN MARIYA'S GRANDMOTHER.
THEY HOLD SIMILAR CEREMONIES THREE DAYS, ONE WEEK AND ONE MONTH AFTER THE PERSON'S DEATH...
By the way, what's with the net?
Huh?! Oh, uh...
...BUT THE ONE YEAR ANNIVERSARY IS THE BIGGEST BY FAR.
THERE'S MISS TEDDYBEAR AND NURSE TONOMURA!
Oh!
I'M GONNA PRETEND I DON'T SEE THE GUY BEHIND THEM, THOUGH.

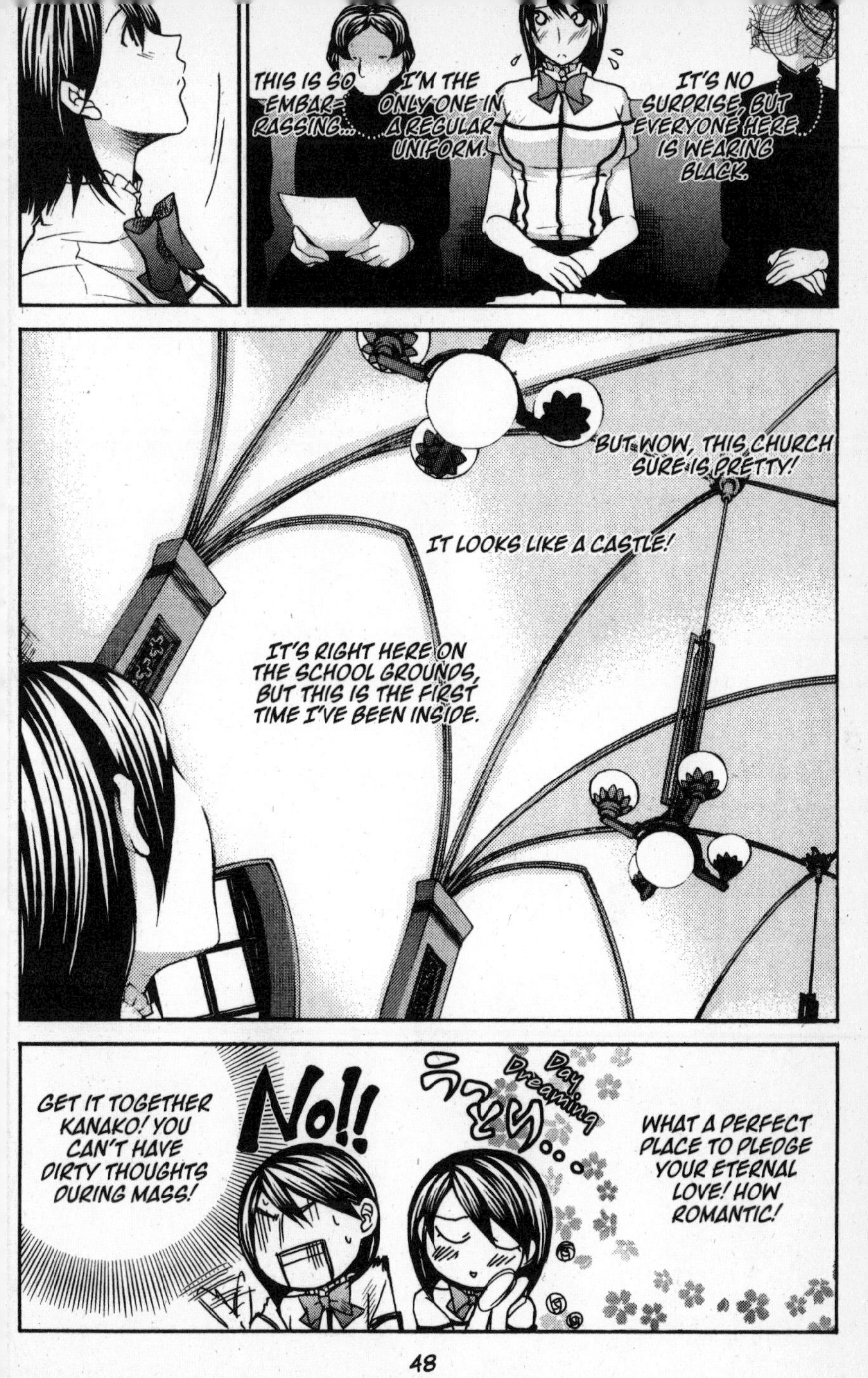
IT'S NO SURPRISE, BUT EVERYONE HERE IS WEARING BLACK.
I'M THE ONLY ONE IN A REGULAR UNIFORM.
THIS IS SO EMBARRASSING...
BUT WOW, THIS CHURCH SURE IS PRETTY!
IT LOOKS LIKE A CASTLE!
IT'S RIGHT HERE ON THE SCHOOL GROUNDS, BUT THIS IS THE FIRST TIME I'VE BEEN INSIDE.
WHAT A PERFECT PLACE TO PLEDGE YOUR ETERNAL LOVE! HOW ROMANTIC!
Day Dreaming
うっとり。。。
No!!
GET IT TOGETHER KANAKO! YOU CAN'T HAVE DIRTY THOUGHTS DURING MASS!

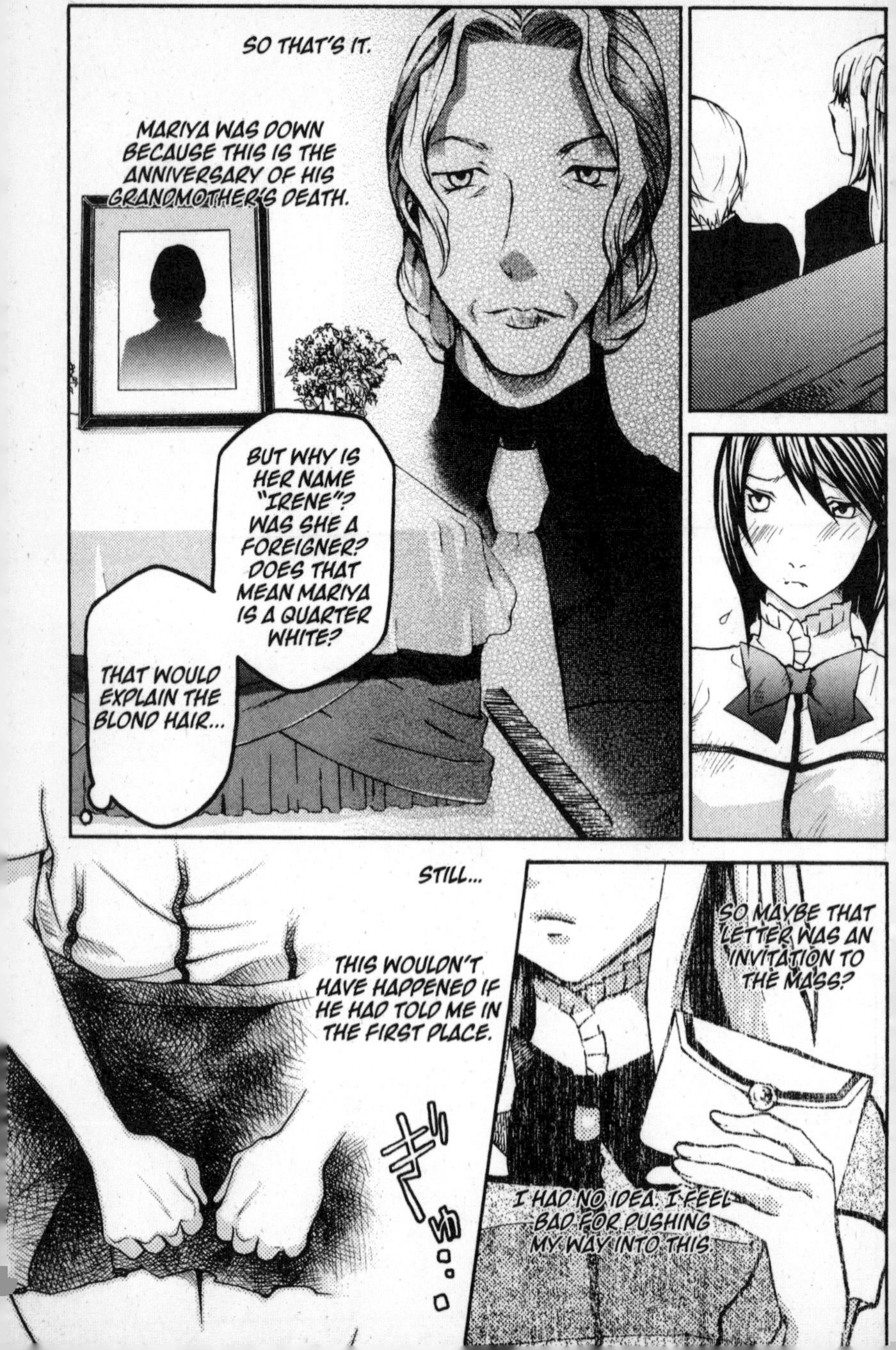
SO THAT'S IT.
MARIYA WAS DOWN BECAUSE THIS IS THE ANNIVERSARY OF HIS GRANDMOTHER'S DEATH.
BUT WHY IS HER NAME "IRENE"? WAS SHE A FOREIGNER? DOES THAT MEAN MARIYA IS A QUARTER WHITE?
THAT WOULD EXPLAIN THE BLOND HAIR...
SO MAYBE THAT LETTER WAS AN INVITATION TO THE MASS?
I HAD NO IDEA. I FEEL BAD FOR PUSHING MY WAY INTO THIS.
STILL...
THIS WOULDN'T HAVE HAPPENED IF HE HAD TOLD ME IN THE FIRST PLACE.

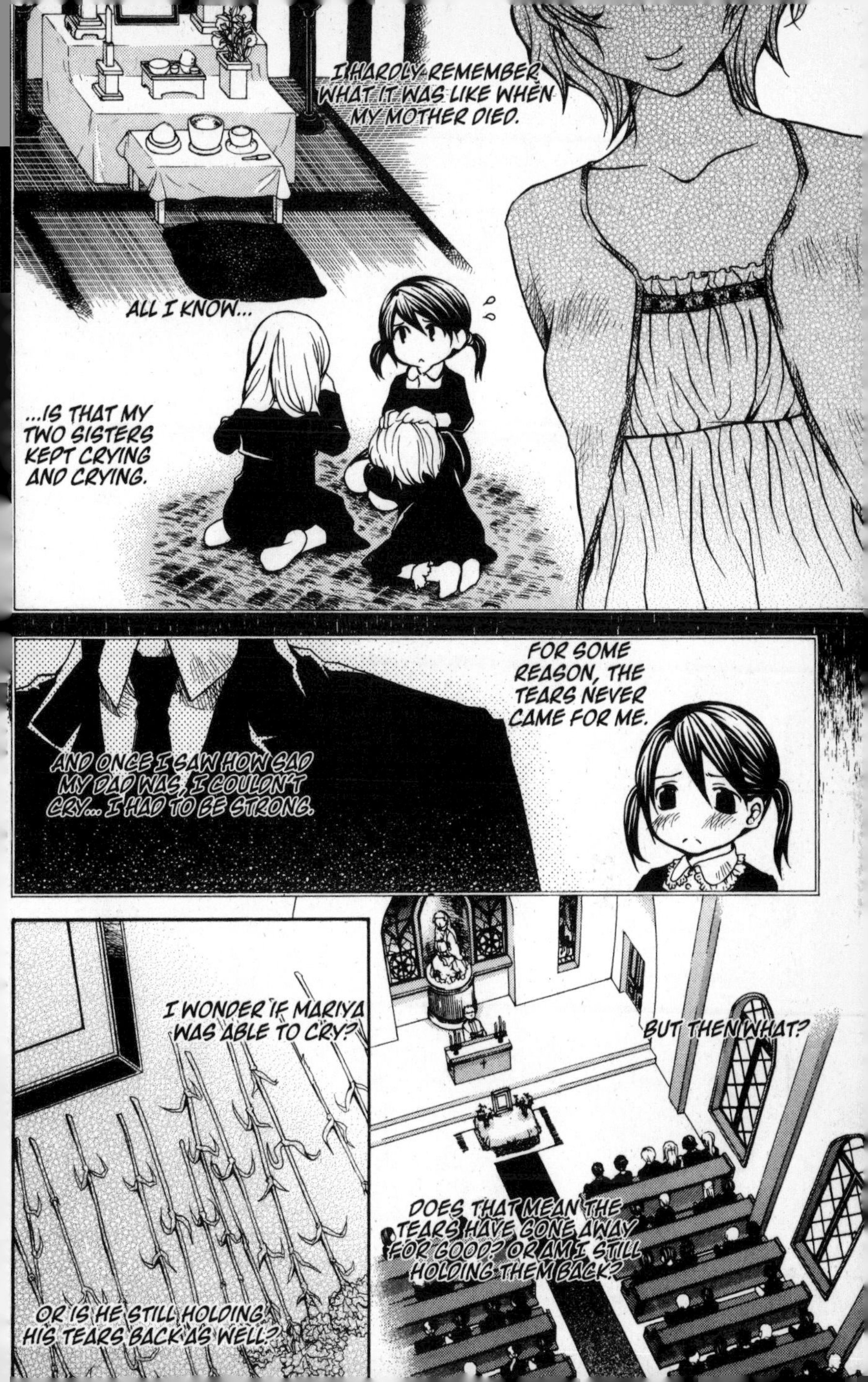
I HARDLY REMEMBER WHAT IT WAS LIKE WHEN MY MOTHER DIED.
ALL I KNOW...
...IS THAT MY TWO SISTERS KEPT CRYING AND CRYING.
FOR SOME REASON, THE TEARS NEVER CAME FOR ME.
AND ONCE I SAW HOW SAD MY DAD WAS, I COULDN'T CRY... I HAD TO BE STRONG.
BUT THEN WHAT?
DOES THAT MEAN THE TEARS HAVE GONE AWAY FOR GOOD? OR AM I STILL HOLDING THEM BACK?
I WONDER IF MARIYA WAS ABLE TO CRY?
OR IS HE STILL HOLDING HIS TEARS BACK AS WELL?

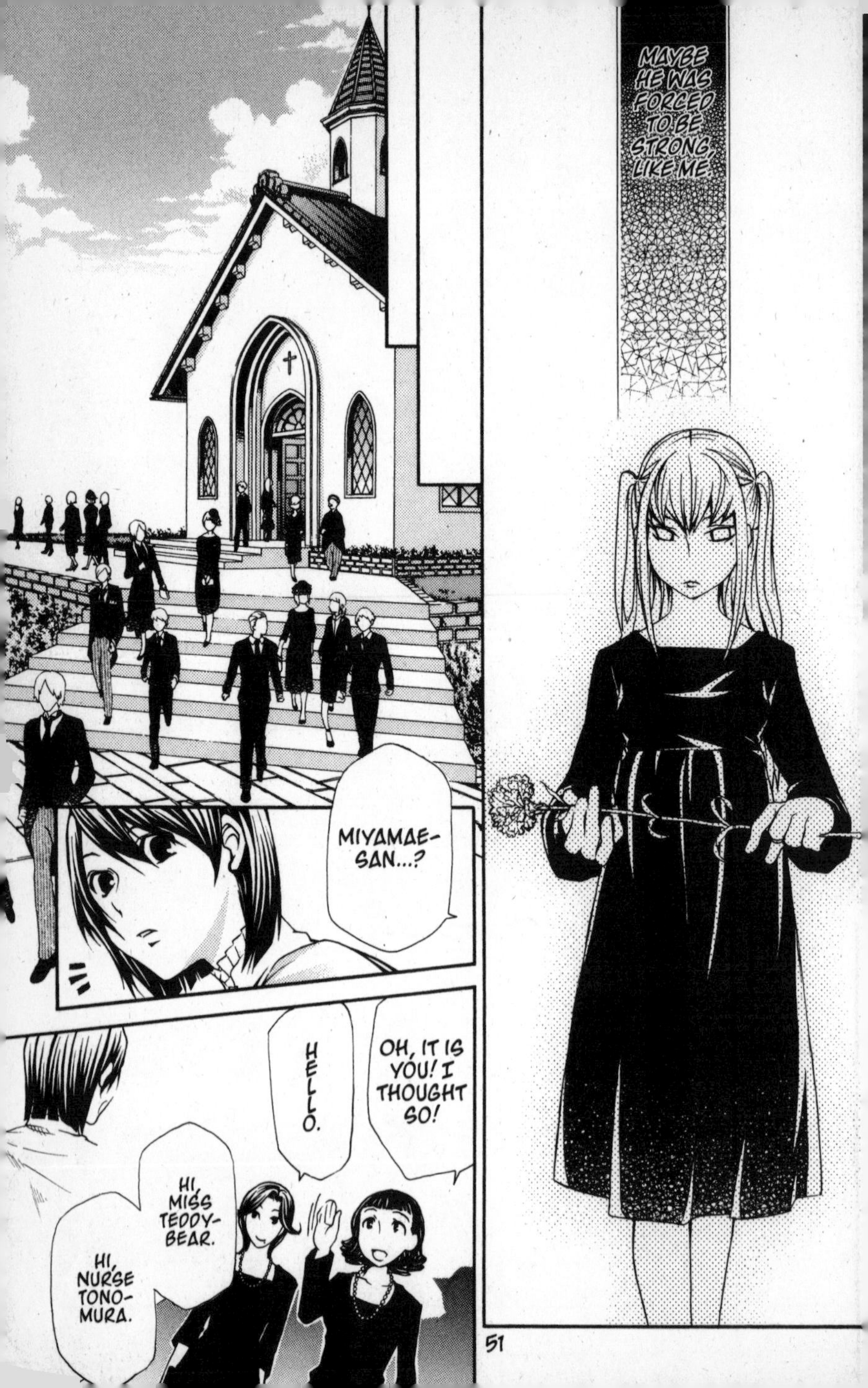

MAYBE HE WAS FORCED TO BE STRONG, LIKE ME.
MIYAMAE-SAN...?
OH, IT IS YOU! I THOUGHT SO!
HELLO.
HI, MISS TEDDY-BEAR.
HI, NURSE TONOMURA.

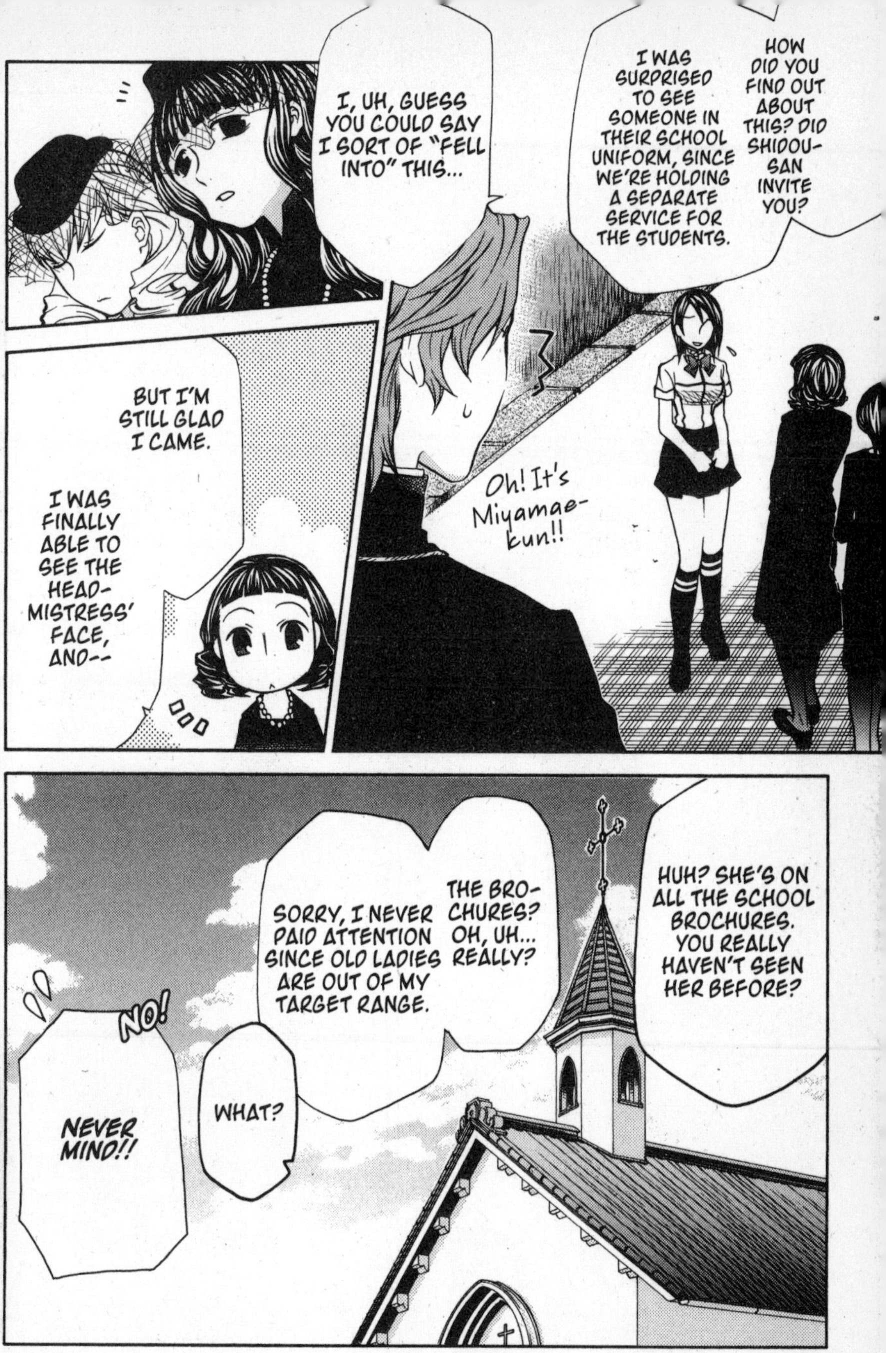
HOW DID YOU FIND OUT ABOUT THIS? DID SHIDOU-SAN INVITE YOU?
I WAS SURPRISED TO SEE SOMEONE IN THEIR SCHOOL UNIFORM, SINCE WE'RE HOLDING A SEPARATE SERVICE FOR THE STUDENTS.
I, UH, GUESS YOU COULD SAY I SORT OF "FELL INTO" THIS...
Oh! It's Miyamae-kun!!
BUT I'M STILL GLAD I CAME.
I WAS FINALLY ABLE TO SEE THE HEADMISTRESS' FACE, AND--
HUH? SHE'S ON ALL THE SCHOOL BROCHURES. YOU REALLY HAVEN'T SEEN HER BEFORE?
THE BROCHURES? OH, UH... REALLY?
SORRY, I NEVER PAID ATTENTION SINCE OLD LADIES ARE OUT OF MY TARGET RANGE.
WHAT?
NO!
NEVER MIND!!

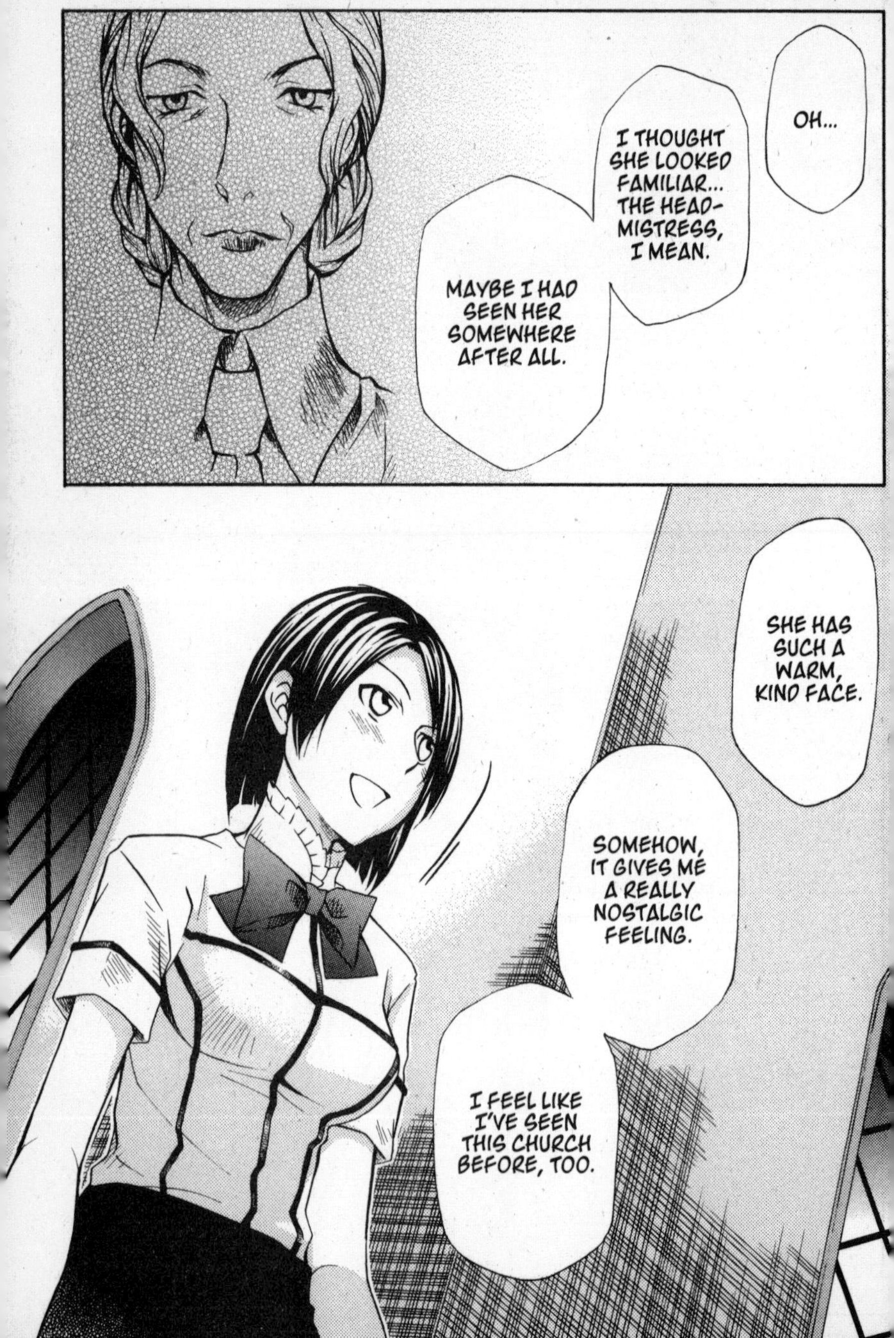
OH...
I THOUGHT SHE LOOKED FAMILIAR... THE HEAD-MISTRESS, I MEAN.
MAYBE I HAD SEEN HER SOMEWHERE AFTER ALL.
SHE HAS SUCH A WARM, KIND FACE.
SOMEHOW, IT GIVES ME A REALLY NOSTALGIC FEELING.
I FEEL LIKE I'VE SEEN THIS CHURCH BEFORE, TOO.

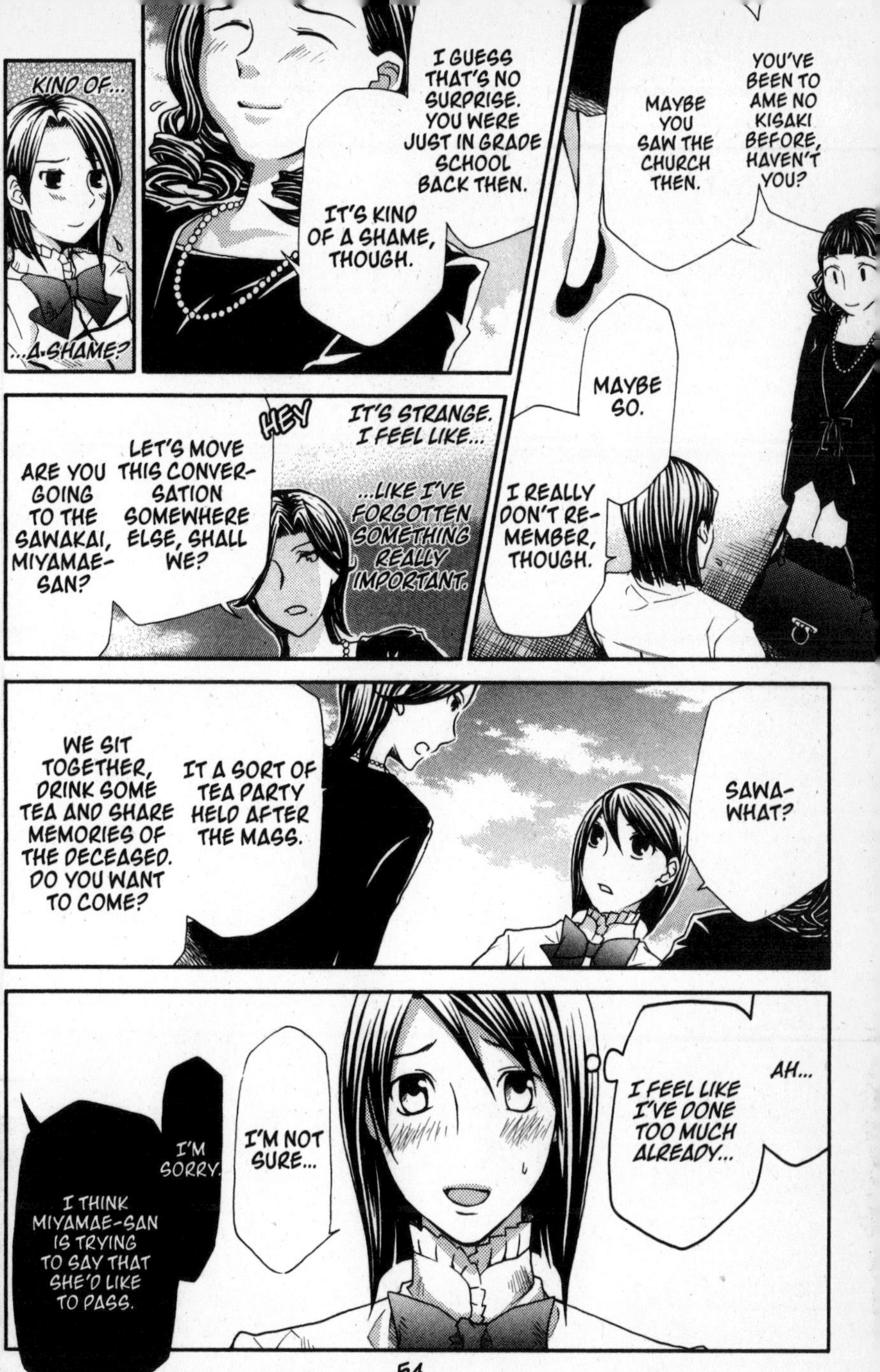
YOU'VE BEEN TO AME NO KISAKI BEFORE, HAVEN'T YOU?
MAYBE YOU SAW THE CHURCH THEN.
MAYBE SO.
I REALLY DON'T RE-MEMBER, THOUGH.
I GUESS THAT'S NO SURPRISE. YOU WERE JUST IN GRADE SCHOOL BACK THEN.
IT'S KIND OF A SHAME, THOUGH.
KIND OF...
...A SHAME?
IT'S STRANGE. I FEEL LIKE...
...LIKE I'VE FORGOTTEN SOMETHING REALLY IMPORTANT.
HEY
LET'S MOVE THIS CONVER-SATION SOMEWHERE ELSE, SHALL WE?
ARE YOU GOING TO THE SAWAKAI, MIYAMAE-SAN?
SAWA-WHAT?
IT A SORT OF TEA PARTY HELD AFTER THE MASS.
WE SIT TOGETHER, DRINK SOME TEA AND SHARE MEMORIES OF THE DECEASED. DO YOU WANT TO COME?
AH...
I FEEL LIKE I'VE DONE TOO MUCH ALREADY...
I'M NOT SURE...
I'M SORRY.
I THINK MIYAMAE-SAN IS TRYING TO SAY THAT SHE'D LIKE TO PASS.

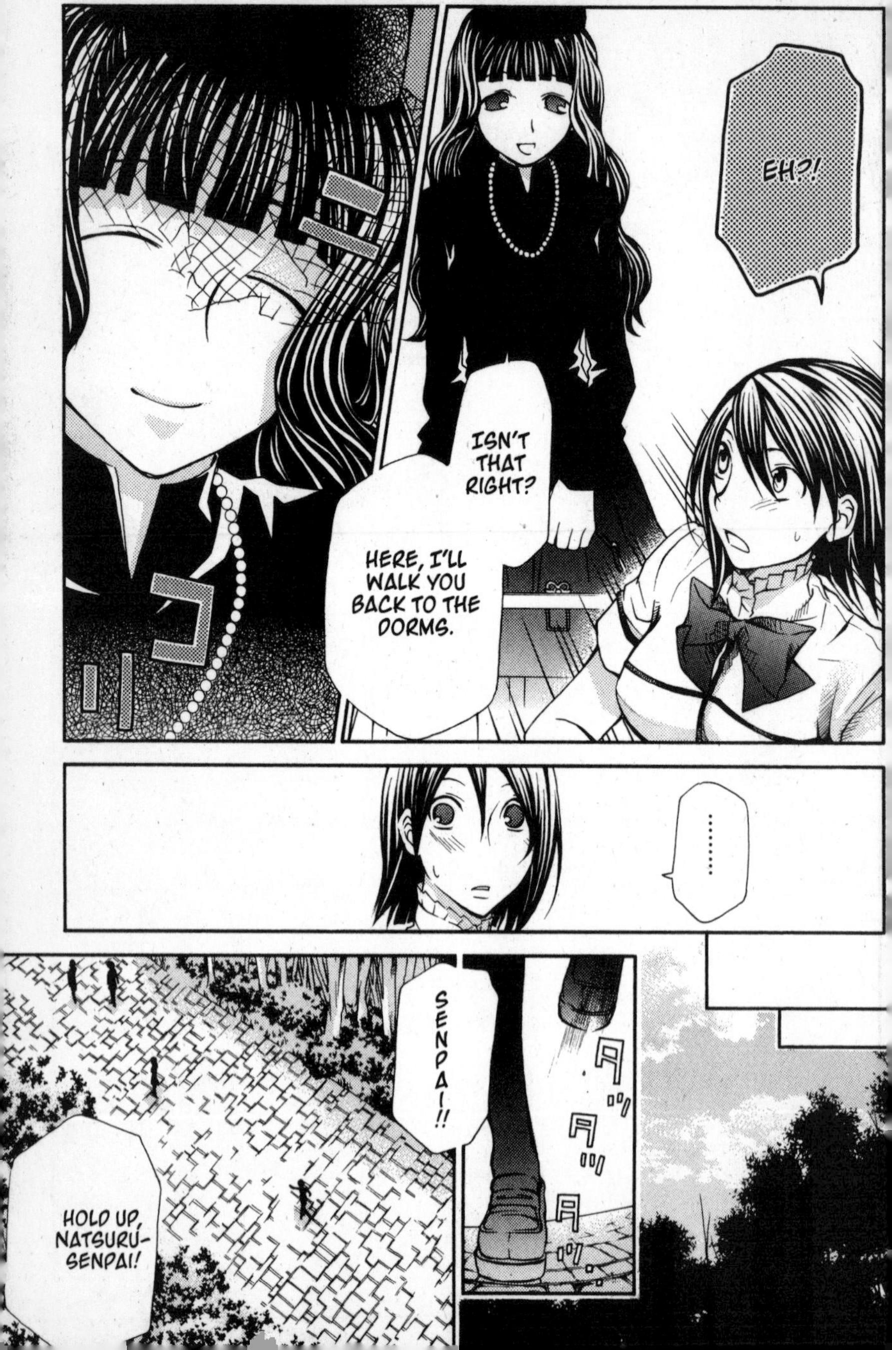
EH?!
ISN'T THAT RIGHT?
HERE, I'LL WALK YOU BACK TO THE DORMS.
....
SENPAI!!
HOLD UP, NATSURU-SENPAI!

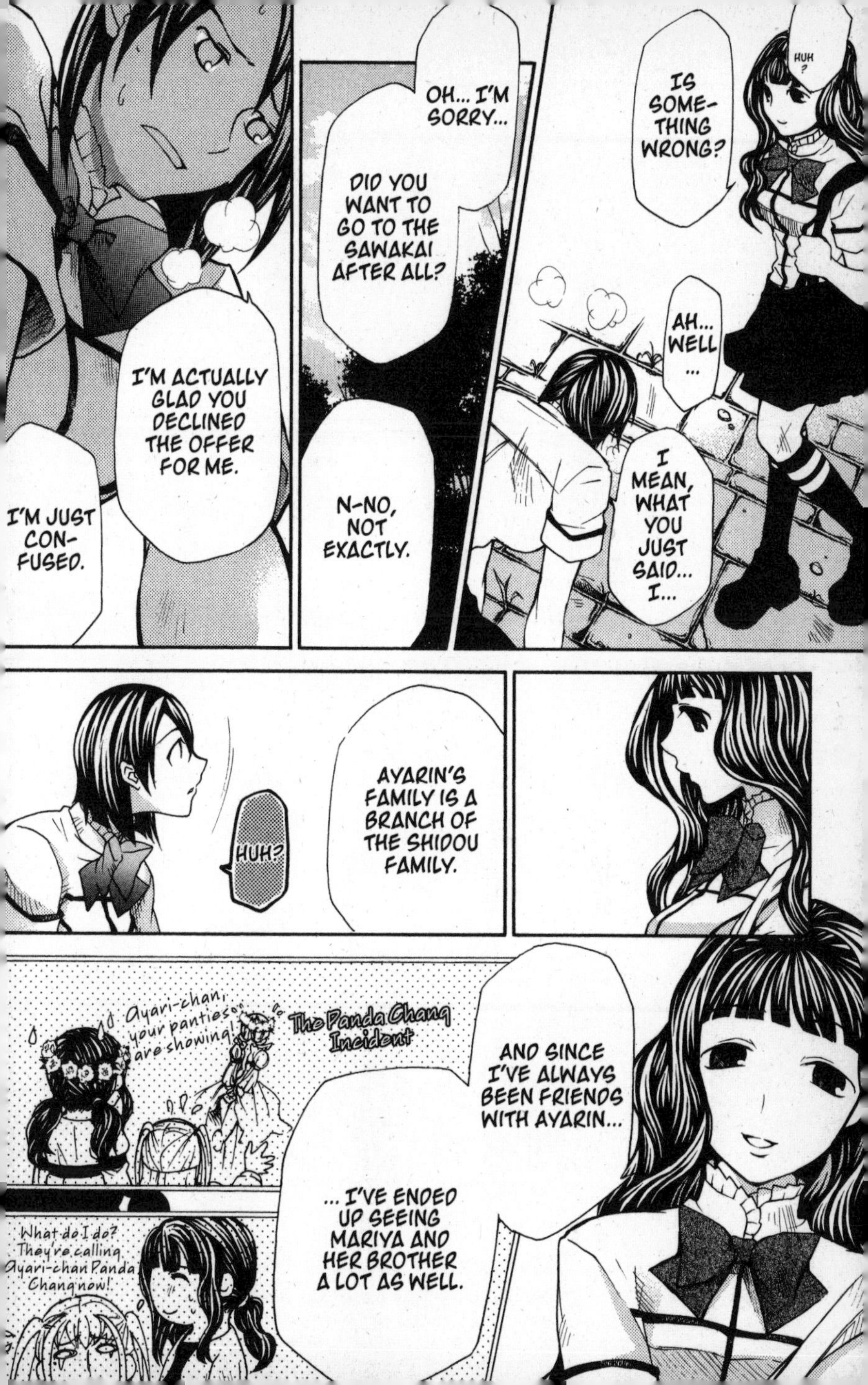
HUH?
IS SOME-THING WRONG?
AH... WELL...
I MEAN, WHAT YOU JUST SAID... I...
OH... I'M SORRY...
DID YOU WANT TO GO TO THE SAWAKAI AFTER ALL?
N-NO, NOT EXACTLY.
I'M ACTUALLY GLAD YOU DECLINED THE OFFER FOR ME.
I'M JUST CON-FUSED.
AYARIN'S FAMILY IS A BRANCH OF THE SHIDOU FAMILY.
HUH?
AND SINCE I'VE ALWAYS BEEN FRIENDS WITH AYARIN...
... I'VE ENDED UP SEEING MARIYA AND HER BROTHER A LOT AS WELL.
The Panda Chang Incident
Ayari-chan, your panties are showing!
What do I do? They're calling Ayari-chan Panda Chang now!

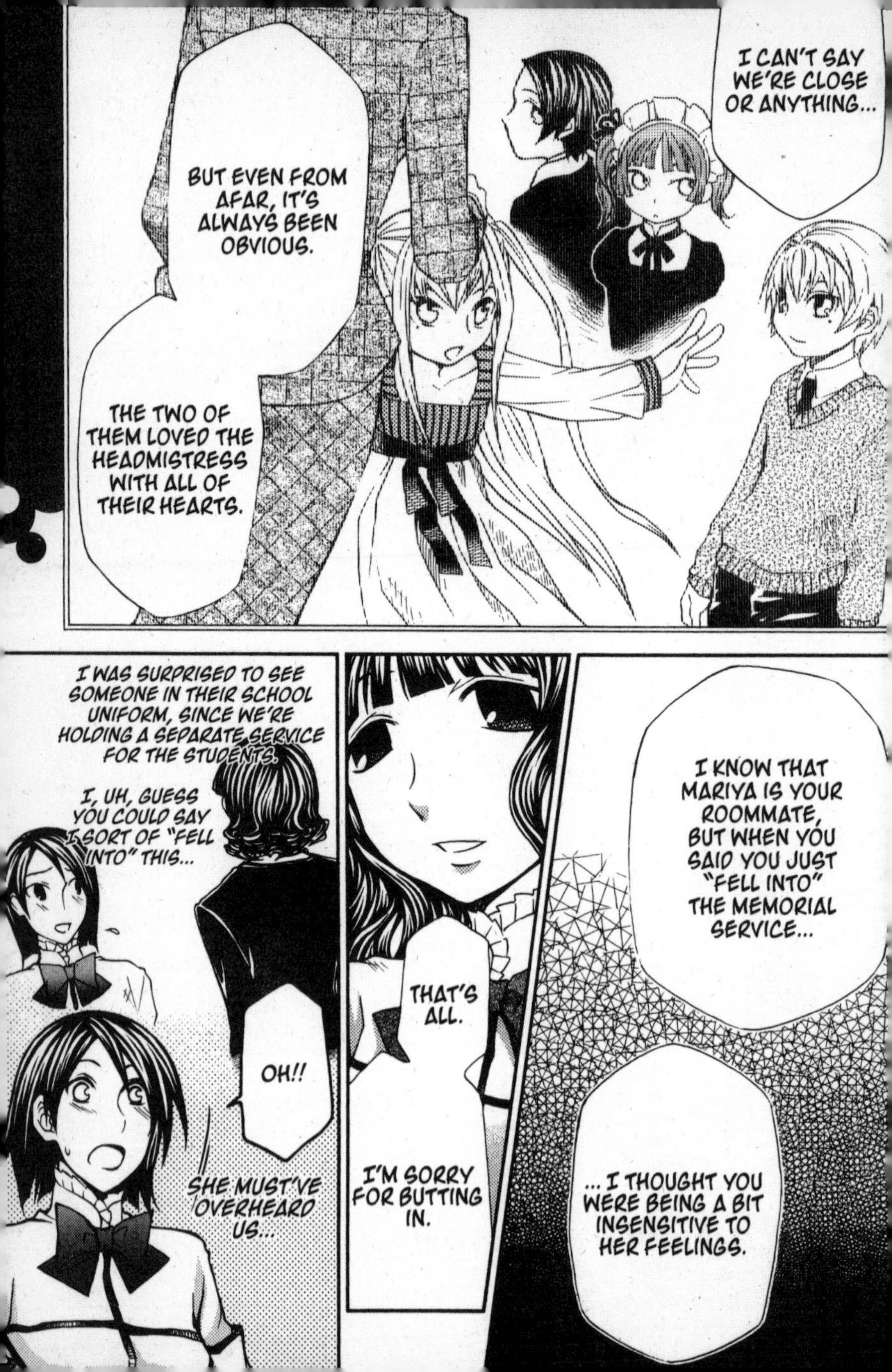
I CAN'T SAY WE'RE CLOSE OR ANYTHING...
BUT EVEN FROM AFAR, IT'S ALWAYS BEEN OBVIOUS.
THE TWO OF THEM LOVED THE HEADMISTRESS WITH ALL OF THEIR HEARTS.
I KNOW THAT MARIYA IS YOUR ROOMMATE, BUT WHEN YOU SAID YOU JUST "FELL INTO" THE MEMORIAL SERVICE...
...I THOUGHT YOU WERE BEING A BIT INSENSITIVE TO HER FEELINGS.
THAT'S ALL.
I'M SORRY FOR BUTTING IN.
I WAS SURPRISED TO SEE SOMEONE IN THEIR SCHOOL UNIFORM, SINCE WE'RE HOLDING A SEPARATE SERVICE FOR THE STUDENTS.
I, UH, GUESS YOU COULD SAY I SORT OF "FELL INTO" THIS...
OH!!
SHE MUST'VE OVERHEARD US...

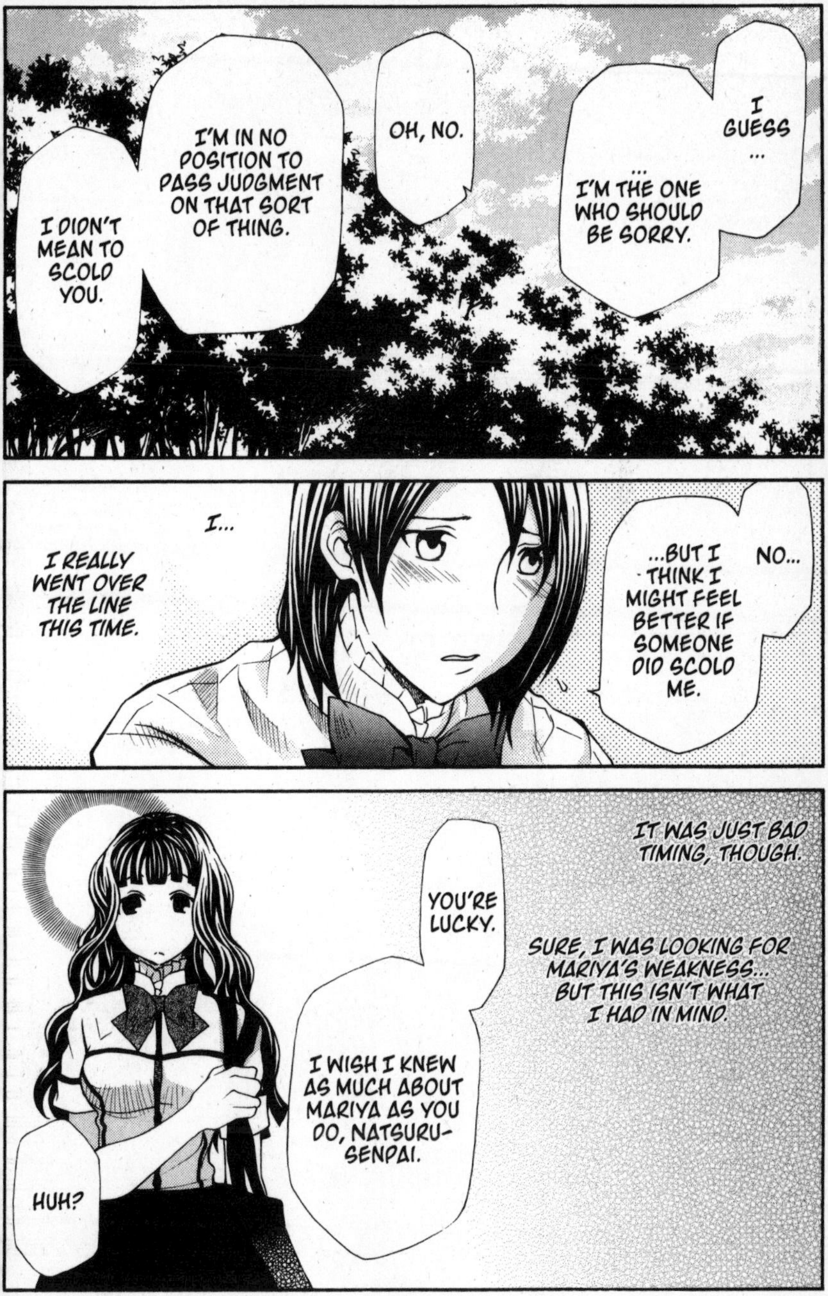
I GUESS...
...I'M THE ONE WHO SHOULD BE SORRY.
OH, NO.
I'M IN NO POSITION TO PASS JUDGMENT ON THAT SORT OF THING.
I DIDN'T MEAN TO SCOLD YOU.
NO...
...BUT I THINK I MIGHT FEEL BETTER IF SOMEONE DID SCOLD ME.
I...
I REALLY WENT OVER THE LINE THIS TIME.
IT WAS JUST BAD TIMING, THOUGH.
SURE, I WAS LOOKING FOR MARIYA'S WEAKNESS... BUT THIS ISN'T WHAT I HAD IN MIND.
YOU'RE LUCKY.
I WISH I KNEW AS MUCH ABOUT MARIYA AS YOU DO, NATSURU-SENPAI.
HUH?

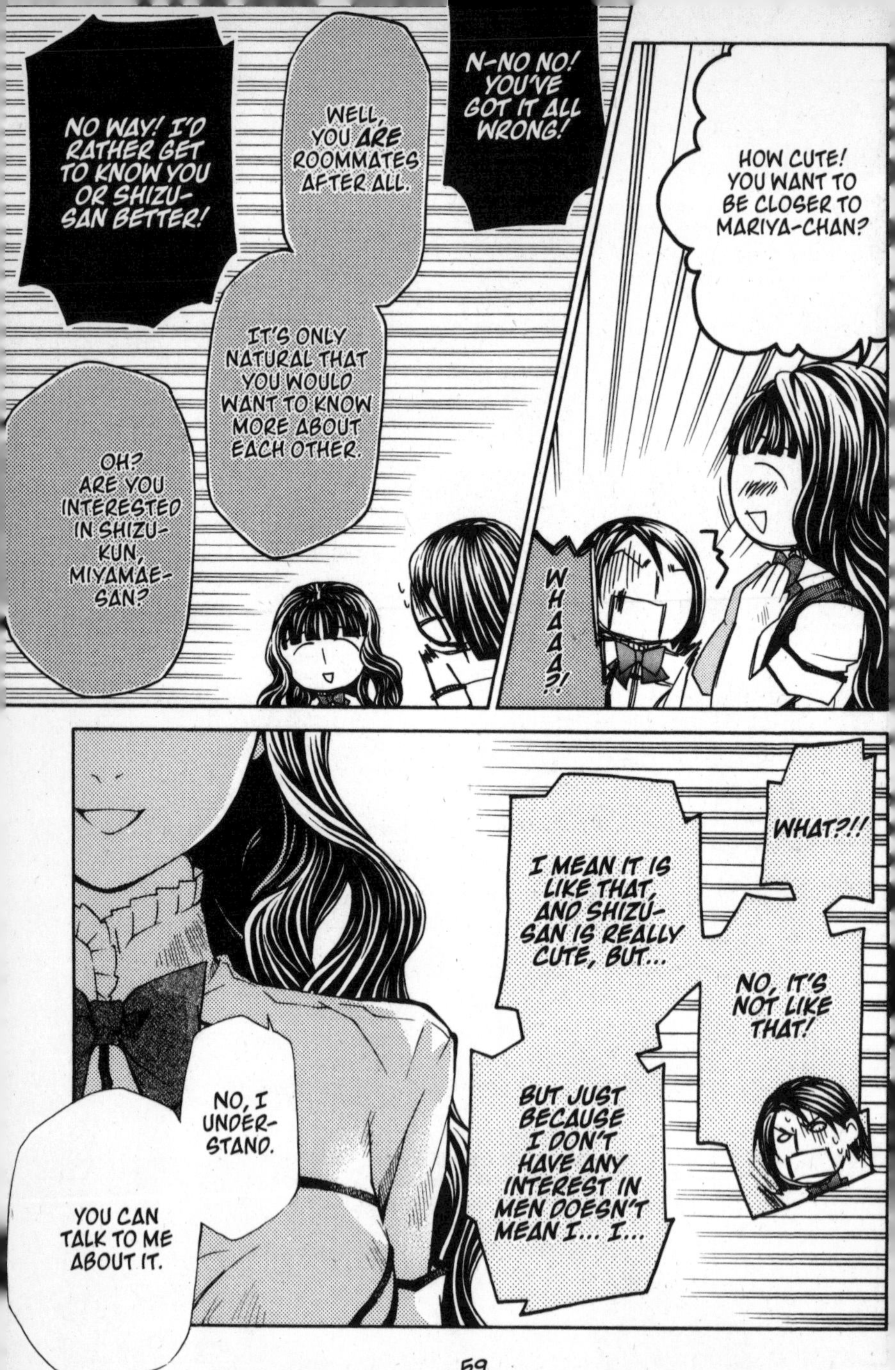
HOW CUTE! YOU WANT TO BE CLOSER TO MARIYA-CHAN?
N-NO NO! YOU'VE GOT IT ALL WRONG!
WELL, YOU ARE ROOMMATES AFTER ALL.
IT'S ONLY NATURAL THAT YOU WOULD WANT TO KNOW MORE ABOUT EACH OTHER.
NO WAY! I'D RATHER GET TO KNOW YOU OR SHIZU-SAN BETTER!
OH? ARE YOU INTERESTED IN SHIZU-KUN, MIYAMAE-SAN?
WHAAAA?!
WHAT?!!
NO, IT'S NOT LIKE THAT!
I MEAN IT IS LIKE THAT, AND SHIZU-SAN IS REALLY CUTE, BUT...
BUT JUST BECAUSE I DON'T HAVE ANY INTEREST IN MEN DOESN'T MEAN I... I...
NO, I UNDER-STAND.
YOU CAN TALK TO ME ABOUT IT.

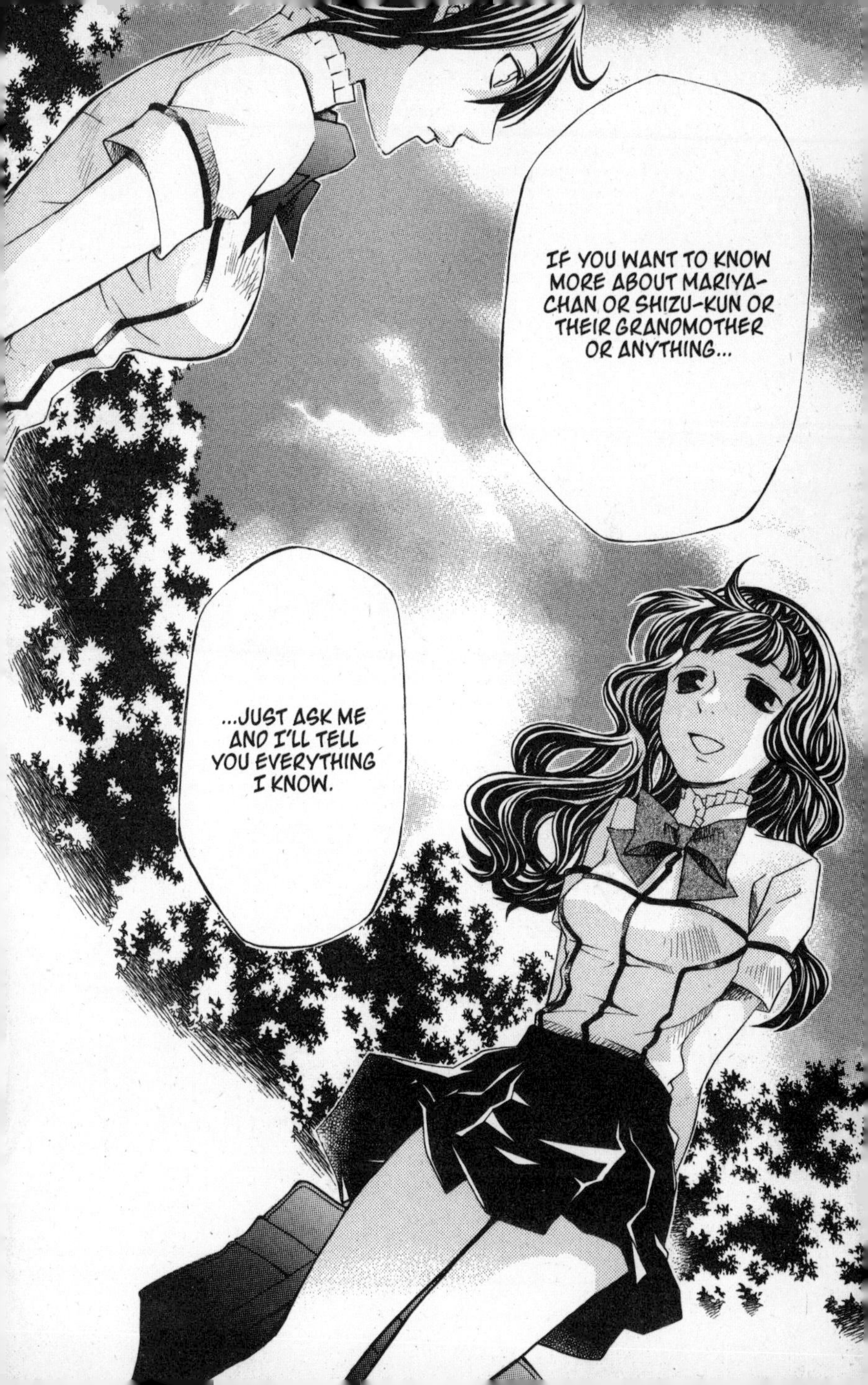
IF YOU WANT TO KNOW MORE ABOUT MARIYA-CHAN OR SHIZU-KUN OR THEIR GRANDMOTHER OR ANYTHING...
...JUST ASK ME AND I'LL TELL YOU EVERYTHING I KNOW.

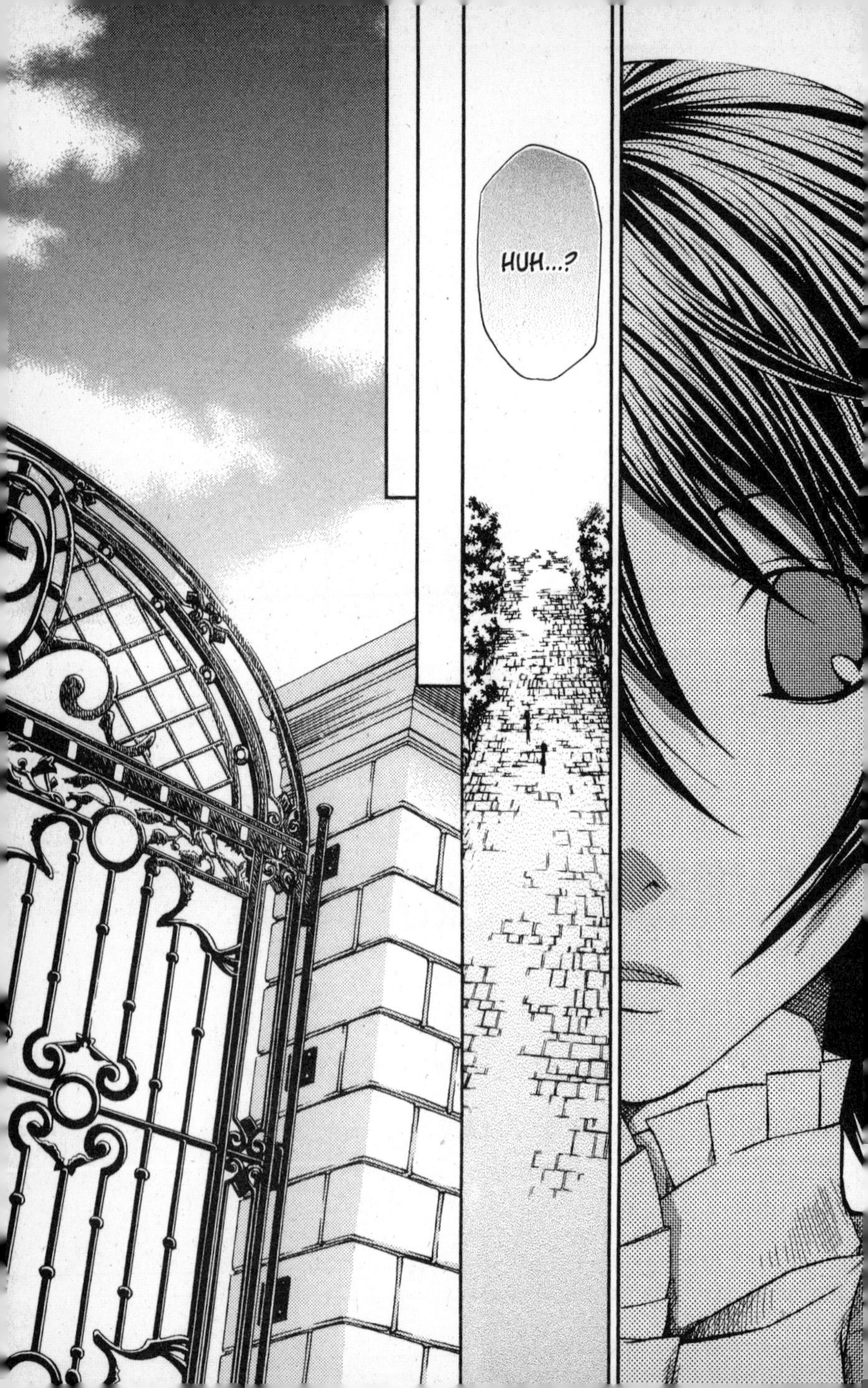
HUH...?

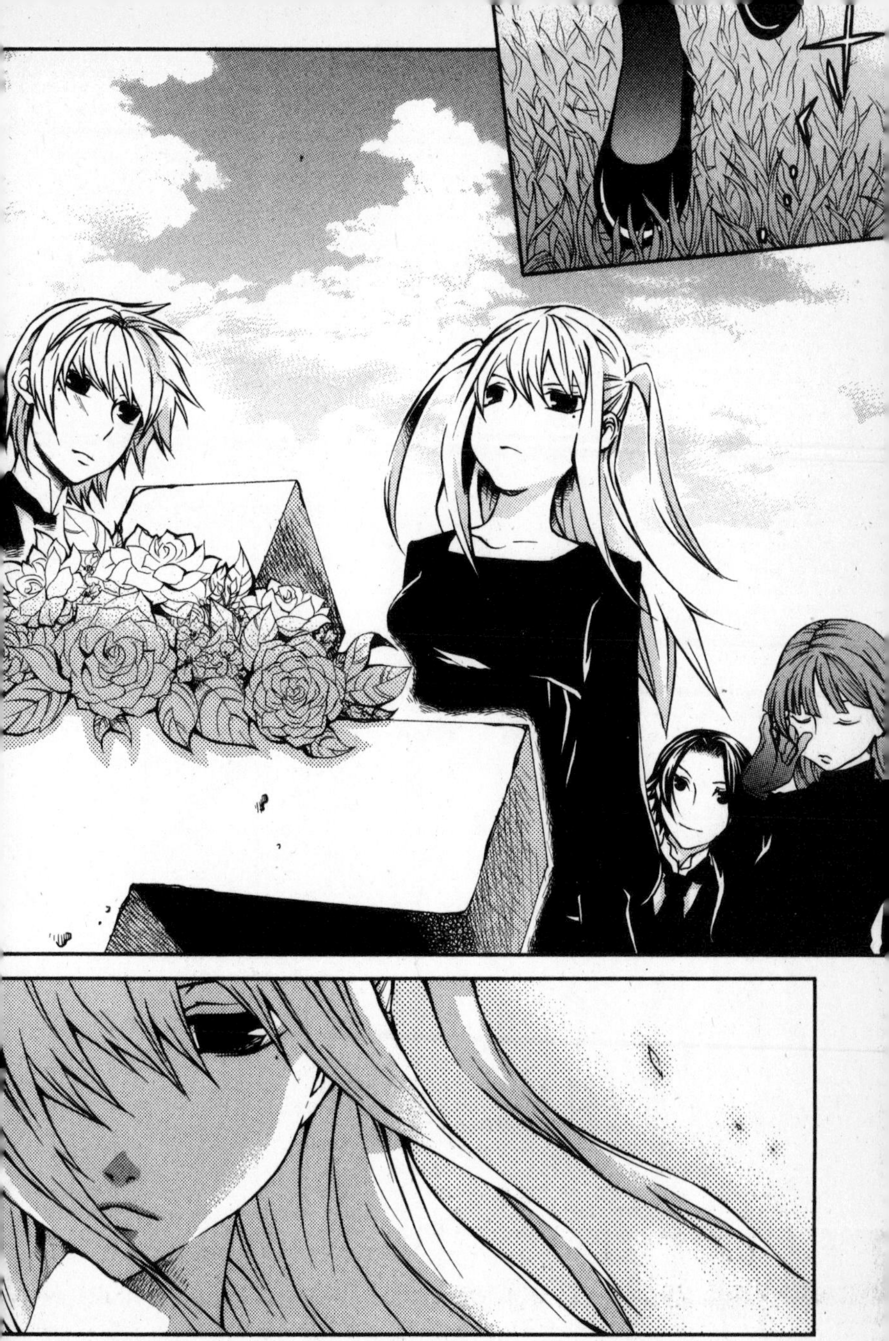

Maria✝Holic

Maria✝Holic

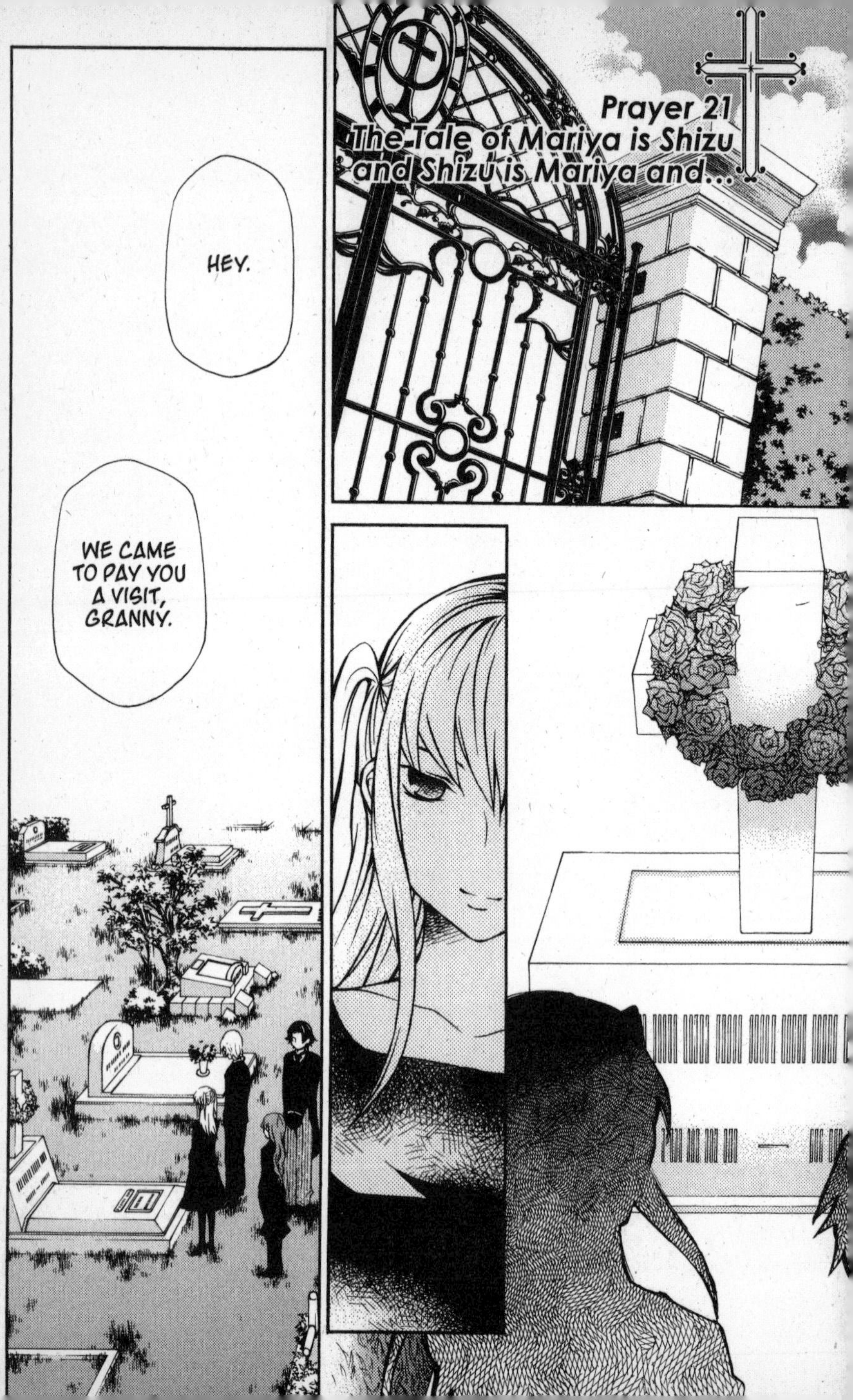
Prayer 21
The Tale of Mariya is Shizu and Shizu is Mariya and...
HEY.
WE CAME TO PAY YOU A VISIT, GRANNY.

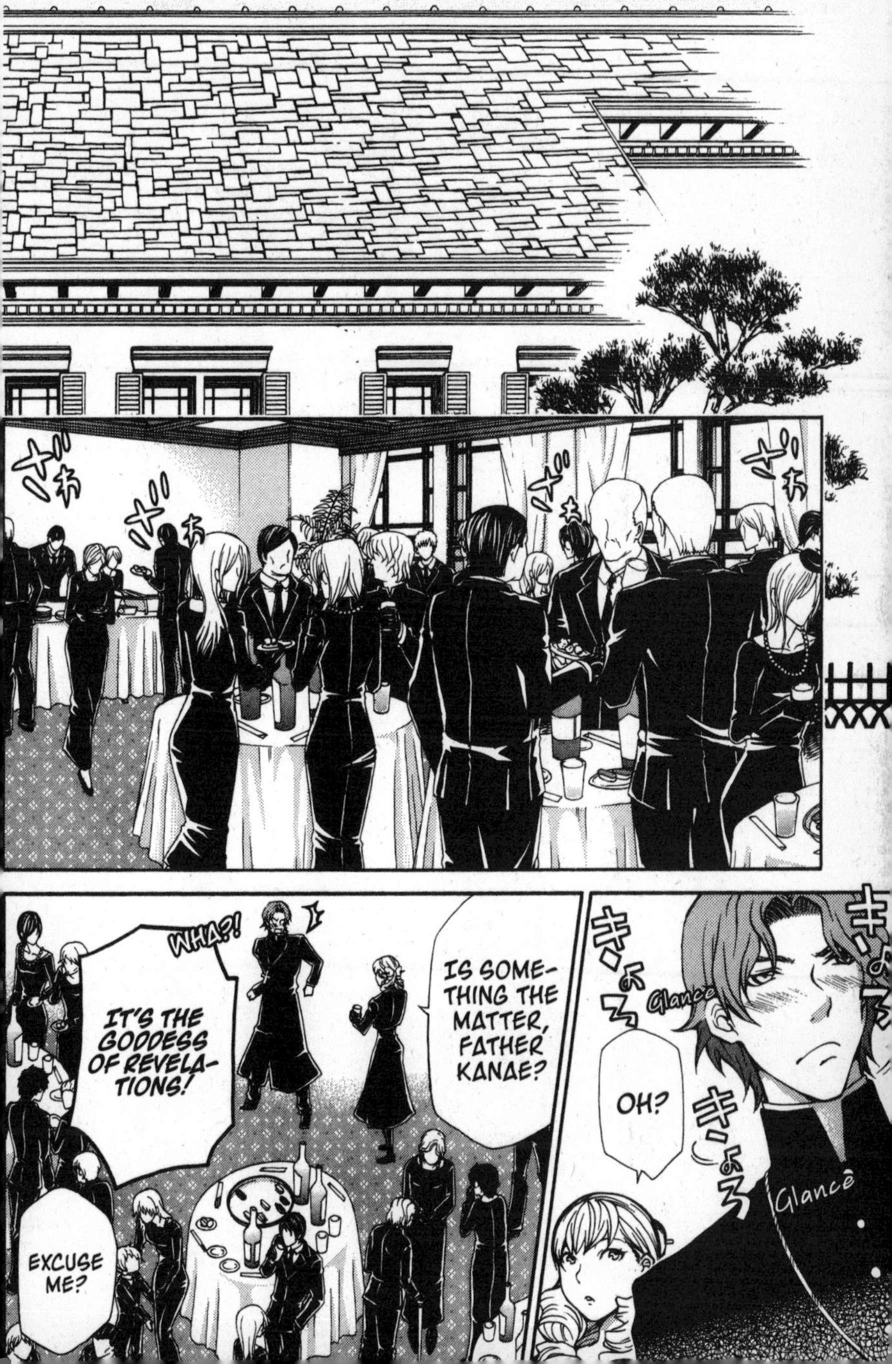
ざわ
ざわ
ざわ
ざわ
きょろ
Glance
OH?
きょろ
Glance
IS SOMETHING THE MATTER, FATHER KANAE?
WHA?!
IT'S THE GODDESS OF REVELATIONS!
EXCUSE ME?

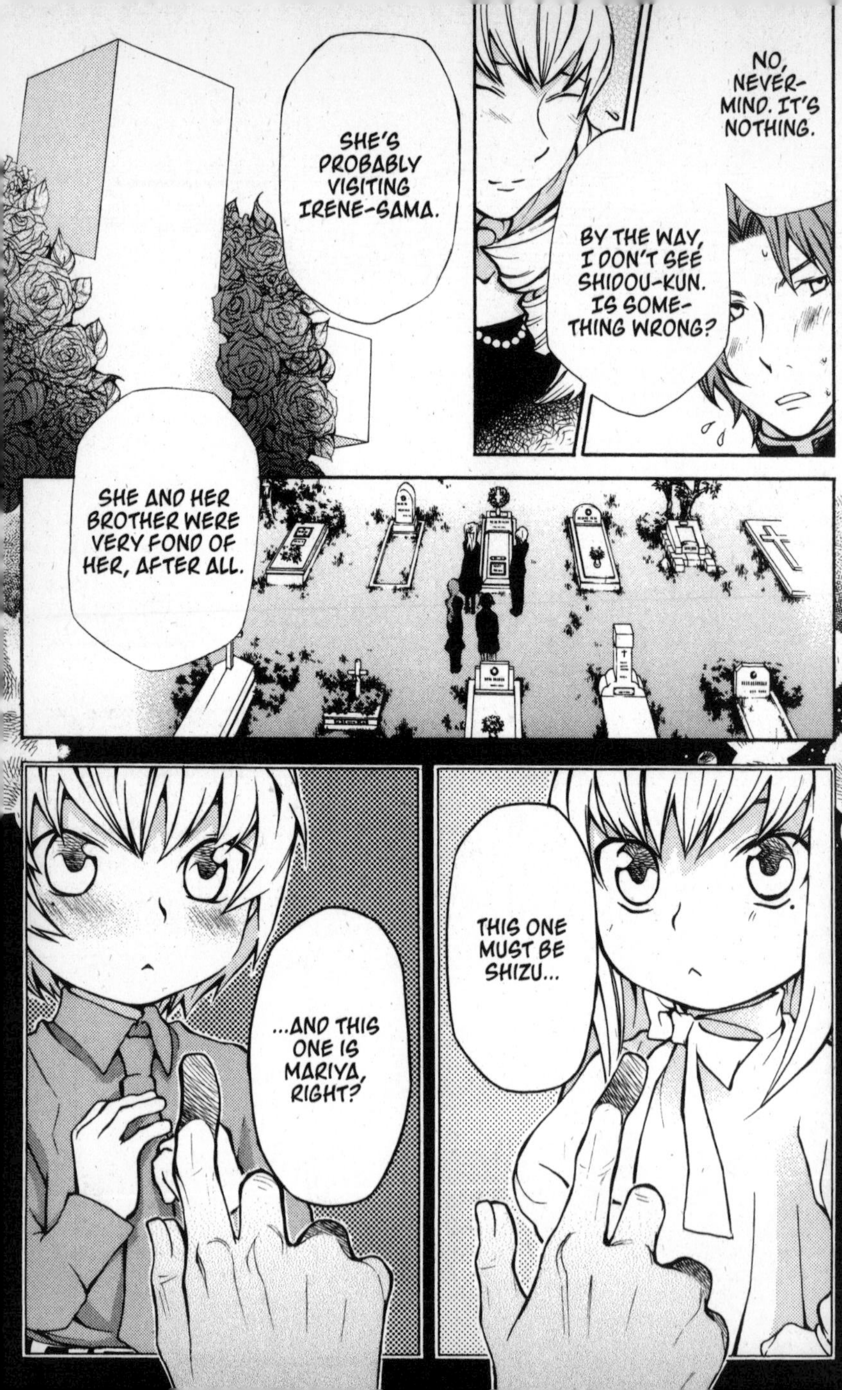
NO, NEVER-MIND. IT'S NOTHING.
BY THE WAY, I DON'T SEE SHIDOU-KUN. IS SOME-THING WRONG?
SHE'S PROBABLY VISITING IRENE-SAMA.
SHE AND HER BROTHER WERE VERY FOND OF HER, AFTER ALL.
THIS ONE MUST BE SHIZU...
...AND THIS ONE IS MARIYA, RIGHT?

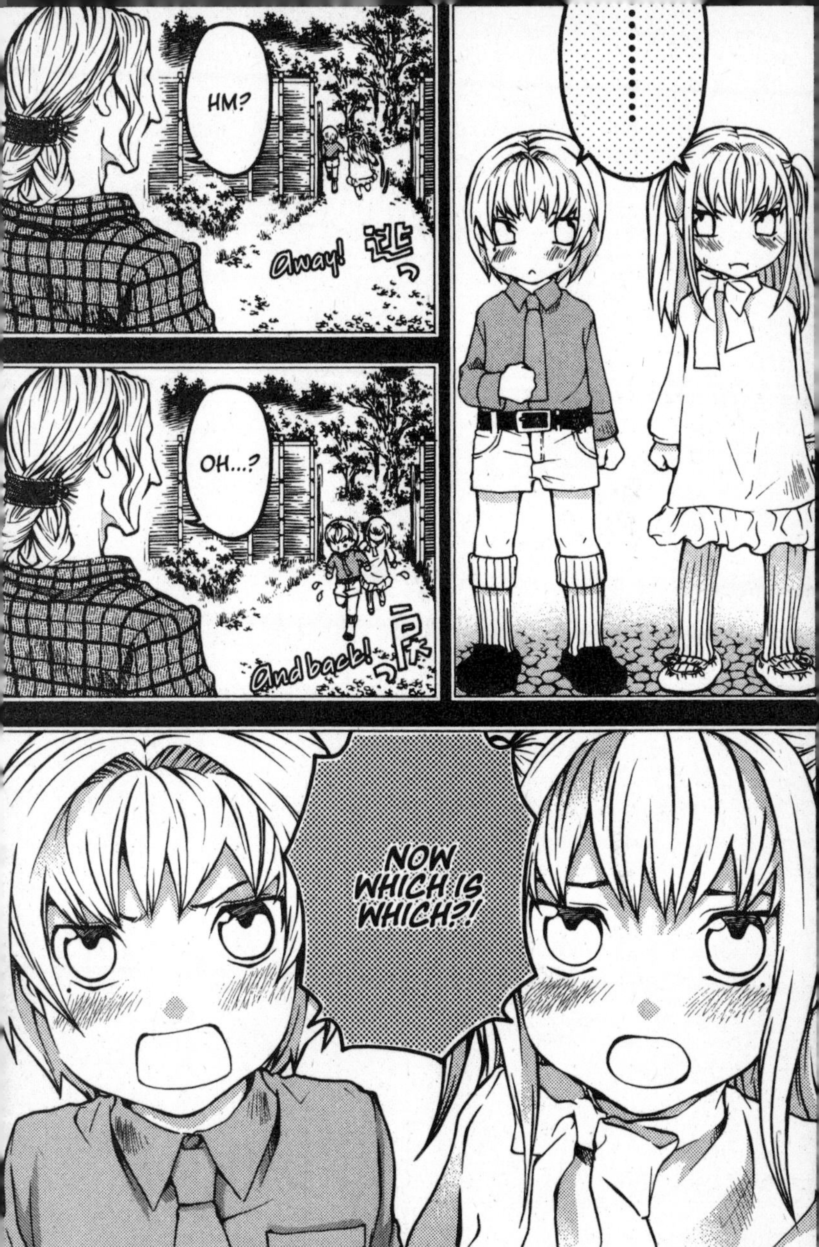
......
HM?
Away!
逃っ
OH...?
And back!
戻っ
NOW WHICH IS WHICH?!

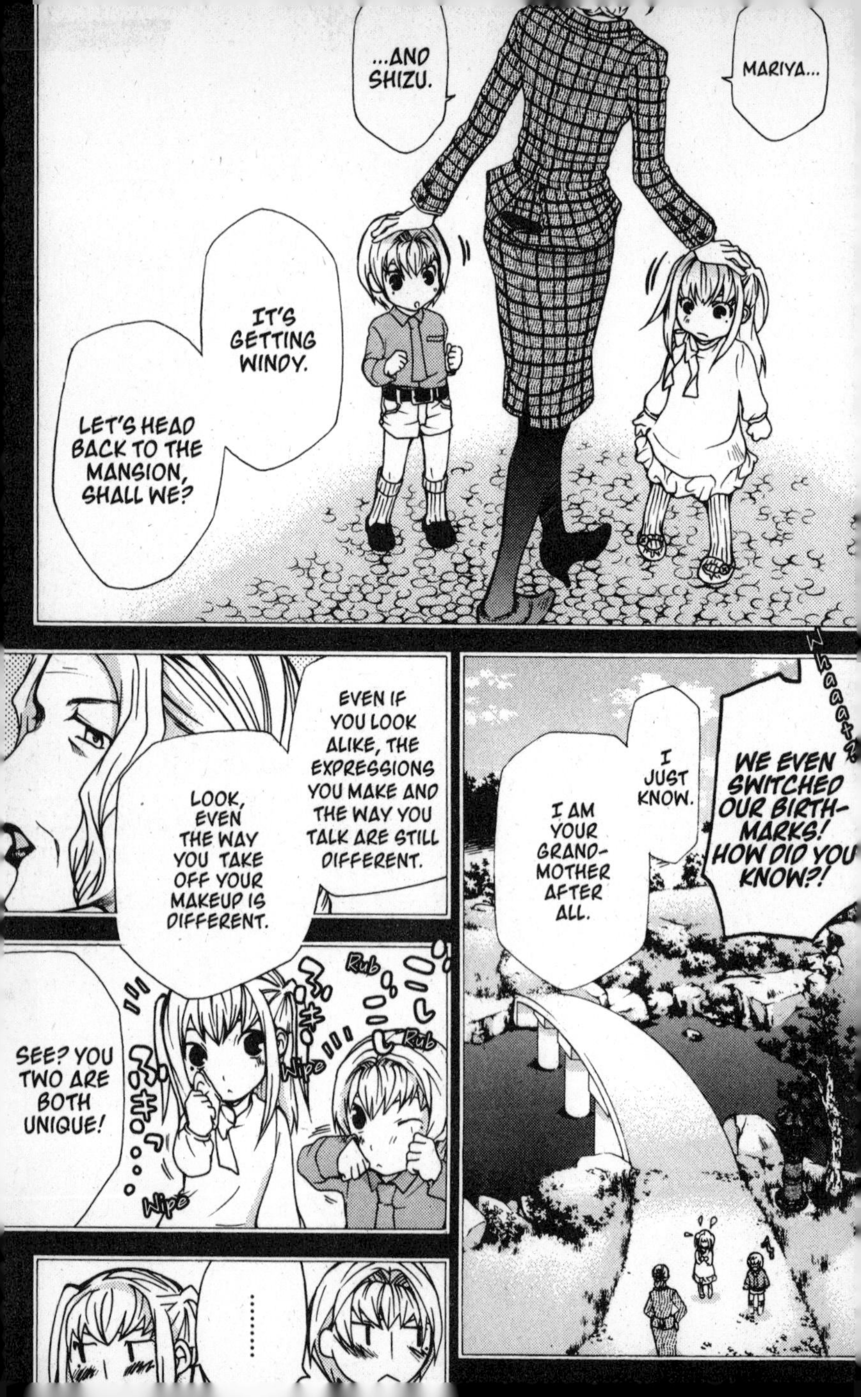
MARIYA...
...AND SHIZU.
IT'S GETTING WINDY.
LET'S HEAD BACK TO THE MANSION, SHALL WE?
Whaaaat?!
WE EVEN SWITCHED OUR BIRTH-MARKS! HOW DID YOU KNOW?!
I JUST KNOW.
I AM YOUR GRANDMOTHER AFTER ALL.
EVEN IF YOU LOOK ALIKE, THE EXPRESSIONS YOU MAKE AND THE WAY YOU TALK ARE STILL DIFFERENT.
LOOK, EVEN THE WAY YOU TAKE OFF YOUR MAKEUP IS DIFFERENT.
Rub
Rub
Wipe
Wipe
SEE? YOU TWO ARE BOTH UNIQUE!
......

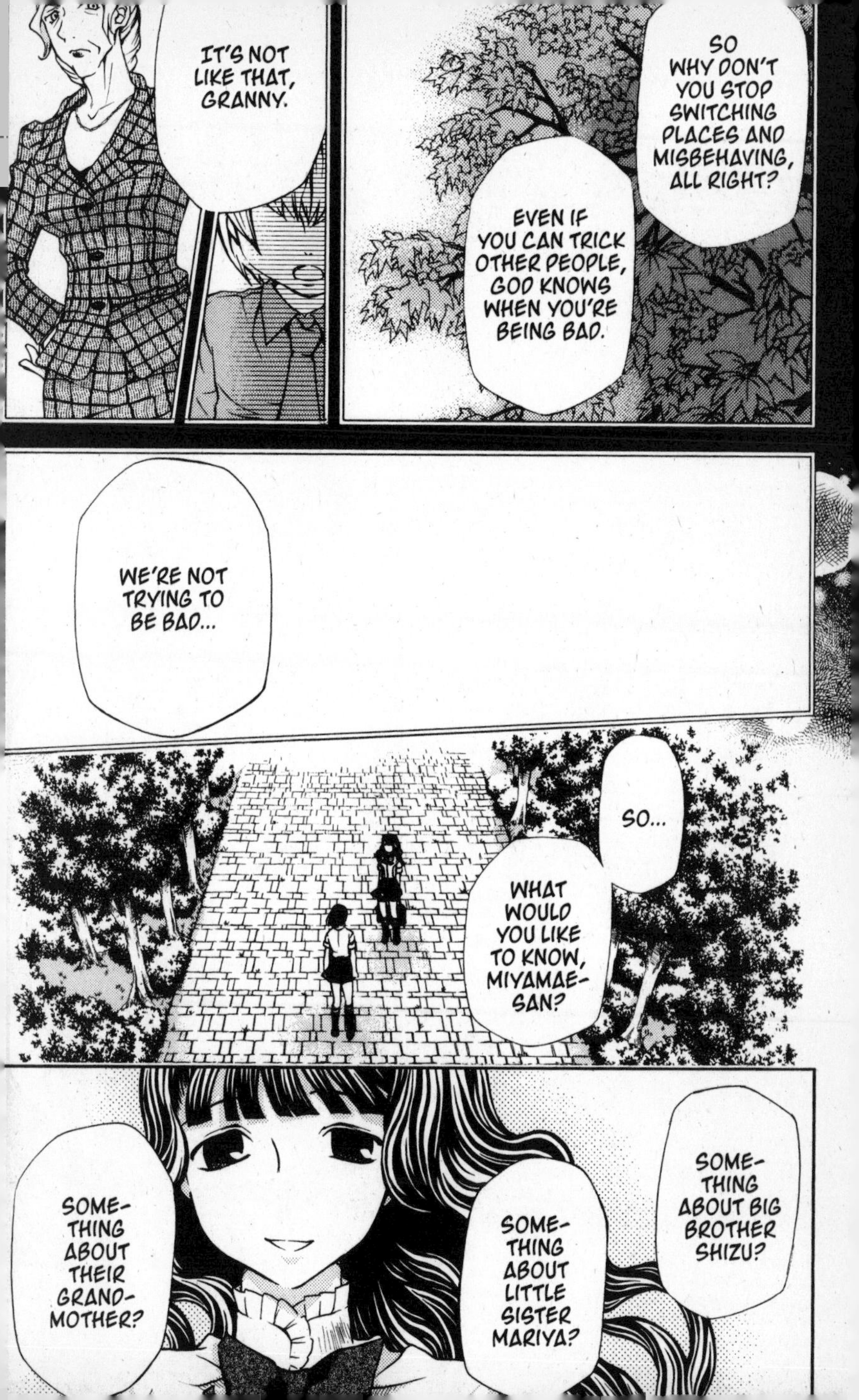
SO WHY DON'T YOU STOP SWITCHING PLACES AND MISBEHAVING, ALL RIGHT?
EVEN IF YOU CAN TRICK OTHER PEOPLE, GOD KNOWS WHEN YOU'RE BEING BAD.
IT'S NOT LIKE THAT, GRANNY.
WE'RE NOT TRYING TO BE BAD...
SO...
WHAT WOULD YOU LIKE TO KNOW, MIYAMAE-SAN?
SOMETHING ABOUT BIG BROTHER SHIZU?
SOMETHING ABOUT LITTLE SISTER MARIYA?
SOMETHING ABOUT THEIR GRANDMOTHER?

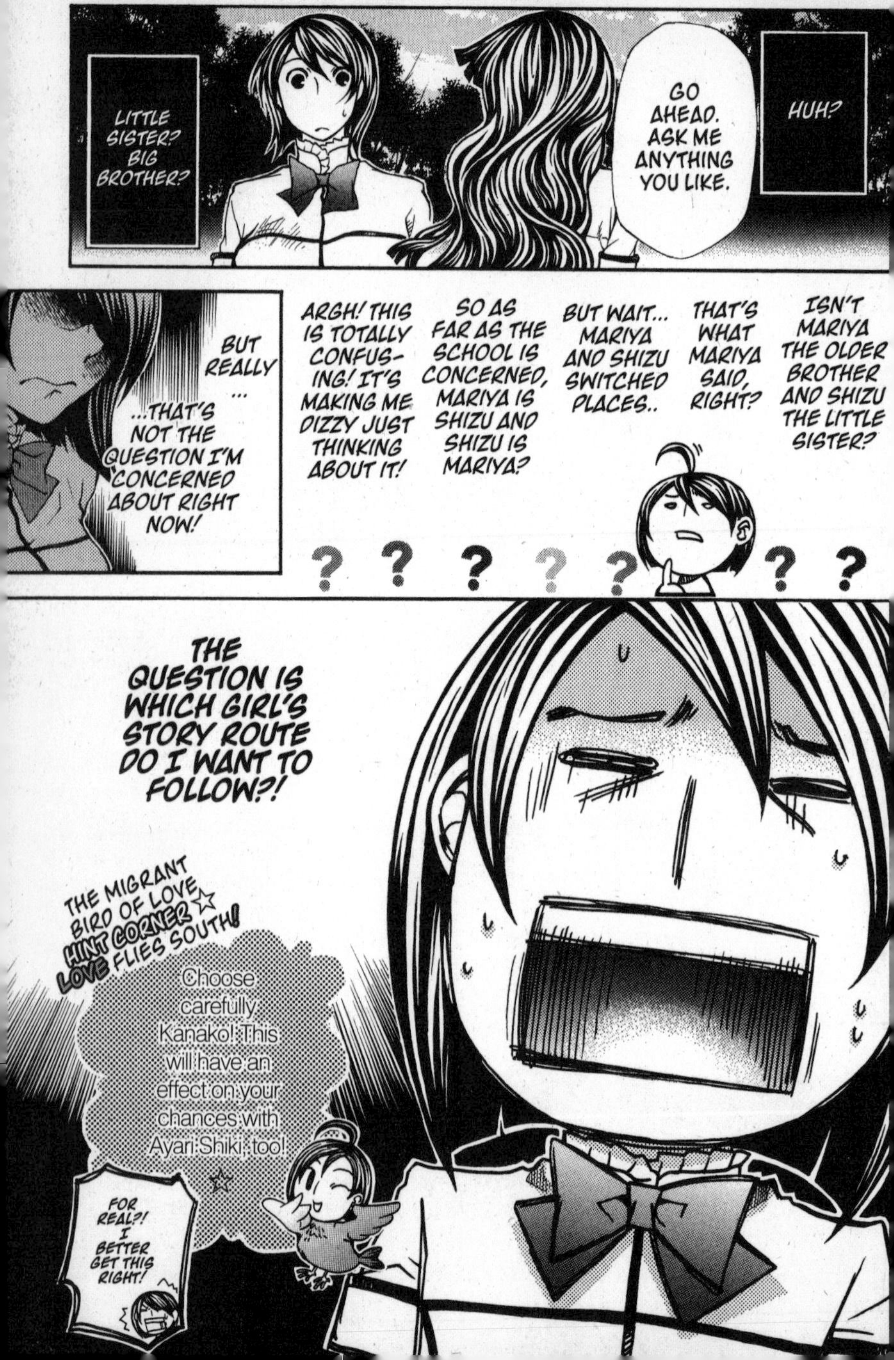

HUH?
GO AHEAD. ASK ME ANYTHING YOU LIKE.
LITTLE SISTER? BIG BROTHER?
ISN'T MARIYA THE OLDER BROTHER AND SHIZU THE LITTLE SISTER?
THAT'S WHAT MARIYA SAID, RIGHT?
BUT WAIT... MARIYA AND SHIZU SWITCHED PLACES..
SO AS FAR AS THE SCHOOL IS CONCERNED, MARIYA IS SHIZU AND SHIZU IS MARIYA?
ARGH! THIS IS TOTALLY CONFUS-ING! IT'S MAKING ME DIZZY JUST THINKING ABOUT IT!
? ? ? ? ? ? ?
BUT REALLY ...
...THAT'S NOT THE QUESTION I'M CONCERNED ABOUT RIGHT NOW!
THE QUESTION IS WHICH GIRL'S STORY ROUTE DO I WANT TO FOLLOW?!
THE MIGRANT BIRD OF LOVE☆
HINT CORNER
LOVE FLIES SOUTH!
Choose carefully, Kanako! This will have an effect on your chances with Ayari Shiki, too! ☆
FOR REAL?! I BETTER GET THIS RIGHT!

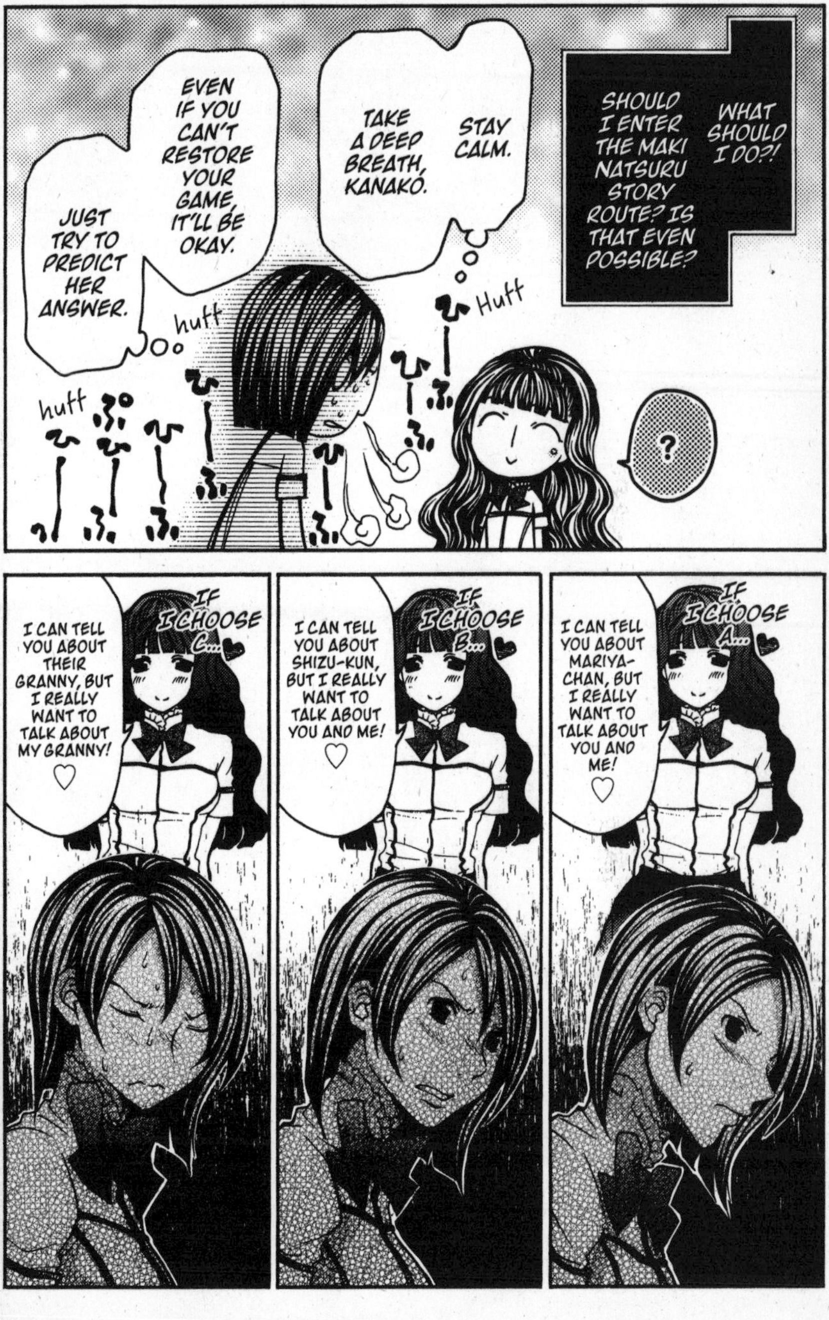
WHAT SHOULD I DO?!
SHOULD I ENTER THE MAKI NATSURU STORY ROUTE? IS THAT EVEN POSSIBLE?
STAY CALM.
TAKE A DEEP BREATH, KANAKO.
EVEN IF YOU CAN'T RESTORE YOUR GAME, IT'LL BE OKAY.
JUST TRY TO PREDICT HER ANSWER.
?
Huff
huff
huff
ひーふー
IF I CHOOSE A...
I CAN TELL YOU ABOUT MARIYA-CHAN, BUT I REALLY WANT TO TALK ABOUT YOU AND ME! ♡
IF I CHOOSE B...
I CAN TELL YOU ABOUT SHIZU-KUN, BUT I REALLY WANT TO TALK ABOUT YOU AND ME! ♡
IF I CHOOSE C...
I CAN TELL YOU ABOUT THEIR GRANNY, BUT I REALLY WANT TO TALK ABOUT MY GRANNY! ♡

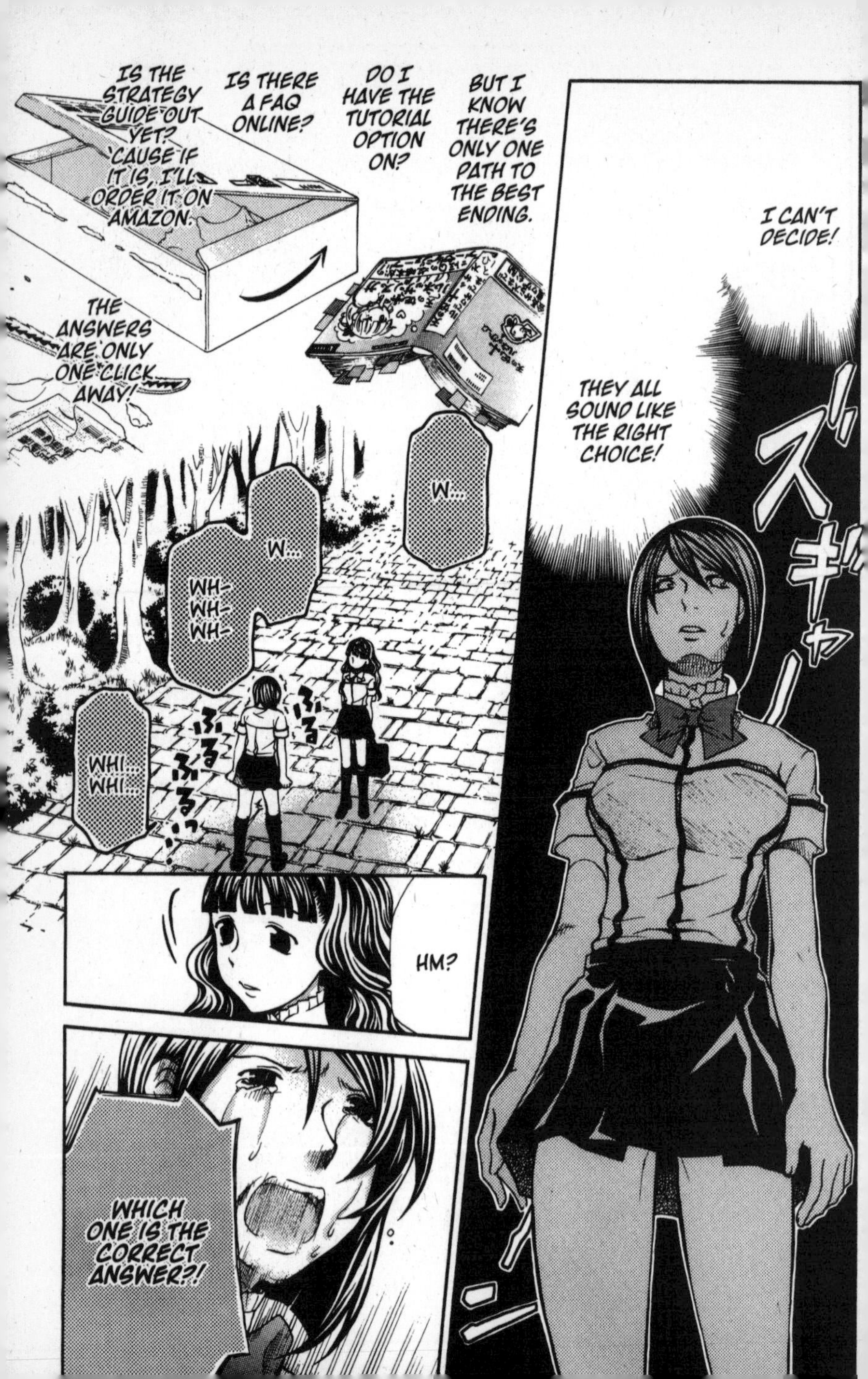

I CAN'T DECIDE!
THEY ALL SOUND LIKE THE RIGHT CHOICE!
ズギャーン
BUT I KNOW THERE'S ONLY ONE PATH TO THE BEST ENDING.
DO I HAVE THE TUTORIAL OPTION ON?
IS THERE A FAQ ONLINE?
IS THE STRATEGY GUIDE OUT YET? 'CAUSE IF IT IS, I'LL ORDER IT ON AMAZON.
THE ANSWERS ARE ONLY ONE CLICK AWAY!
W...
W... WH- WH- WH-
WHI... WHI...
HM?
WHICH ONE IS THE CORRECT ANSWER?!

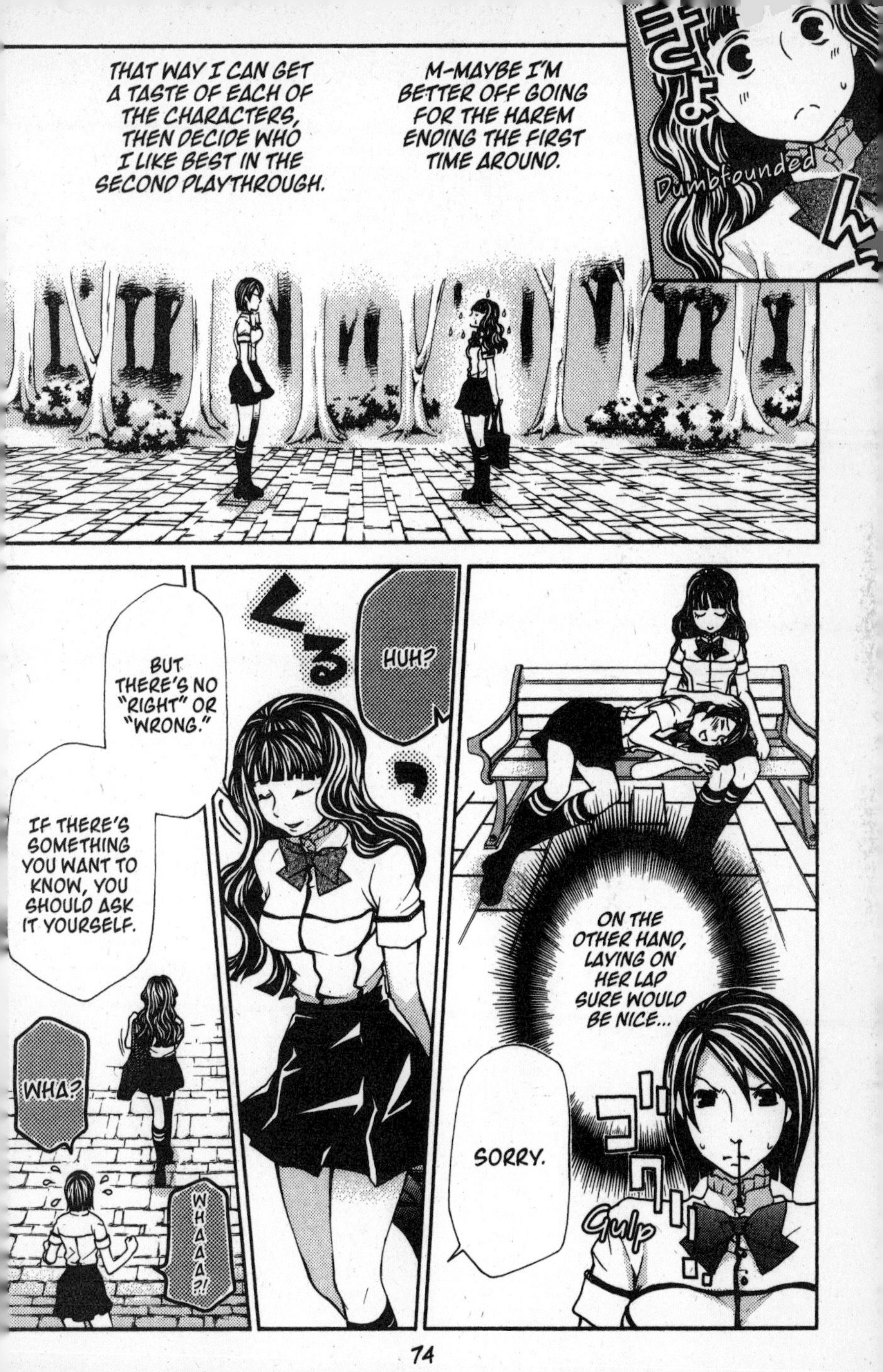

きょ
ん
Dumbfounded
M-MAYBE I'M BETTER OFF GOING FOR THE HAREM ENDING THE FIRST TIME AROUND.
THAT WAY I CAN GET A TASTE OF EACH OF THE CHARACTERS, THEN DECIDE WHO I LIKE BEST IN THE SECOND PLAYTHROUGH.
ON THE OTHER HAND, LAYING ON HER LAP SURE WOULD BE NICE...
SORRY.
Gulp
HUH?
くる
BUT THERE'S NO "RIGHT" OR "WRONG."
IF THERE'S SOMETHING YOU WANT TO KNOW, YOU SHOULD ASK IT YOURSELF.
WHA?
WHAAAA?!

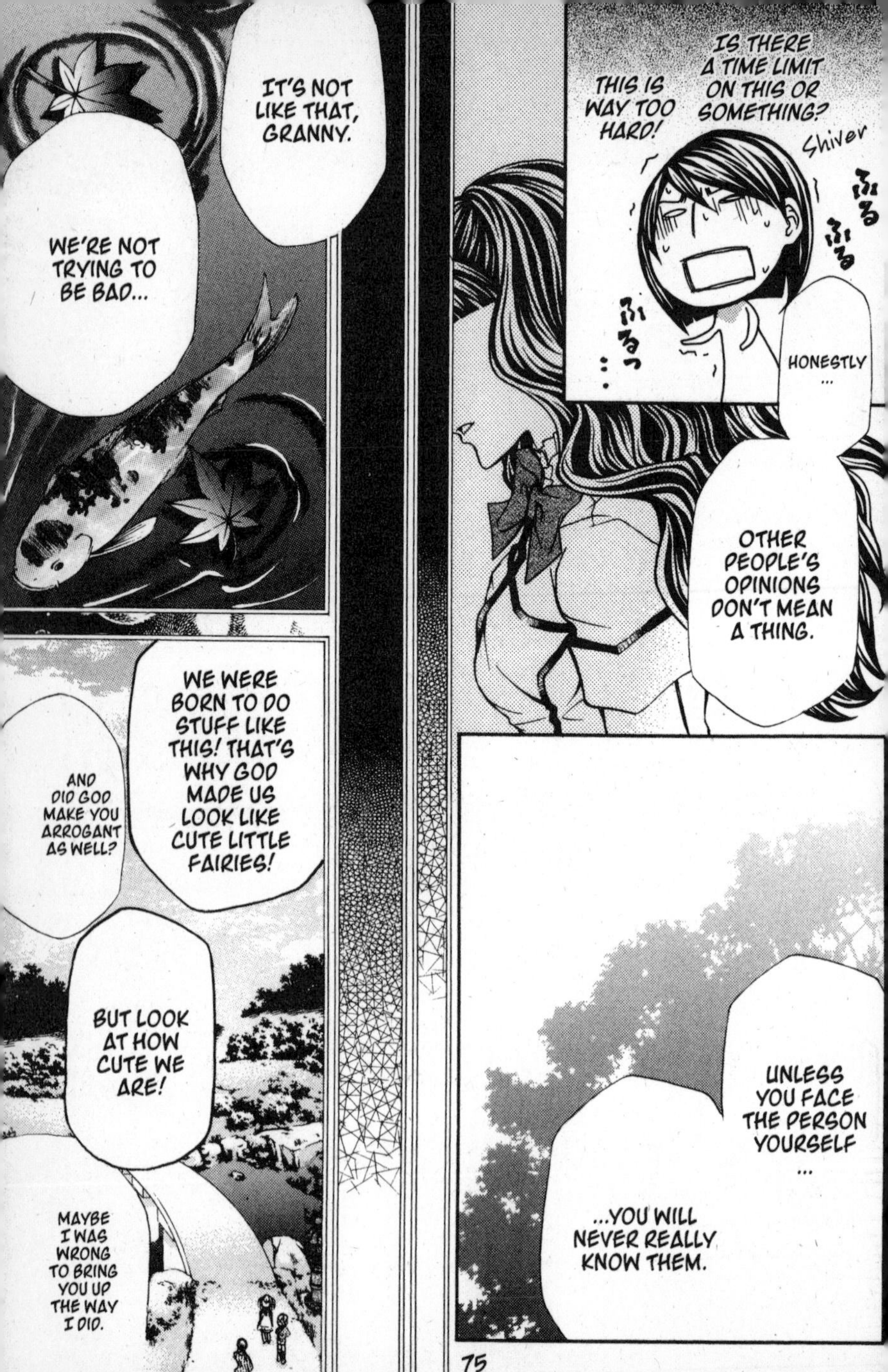
IS THERE A TIME LIMIT ON THIS OR SOMETHING?
THIS IS WAY TOO HARD!
Shiver
ふる
ふる
ふるっ…
HONESTLY...
OTHER PEOPLE'S OPINIONS DON'T MEAN A THING.
UNLESS YOU FACE THE PERSON YOURSELF...
...YOU WILL NEVER REALLY KNOW THEM.
IT'S NOT LIKE THAT, GRANNY.
WE'RE NOT TRYING TO BE BAD...
WE WERE BORN TO DO STUFF LIKE THIS! THAT'S WHY GOD MADE US LOOK LIKE CUTE LITTLE FAIRIES!
AND DID GOD MAKE YOU ARROGANT AS WELL?
BUT LOOK AT HOW CUTE WE ARE!
MAYBE I WAS WRONG TO BRING YOU UP THE WAY I DID.

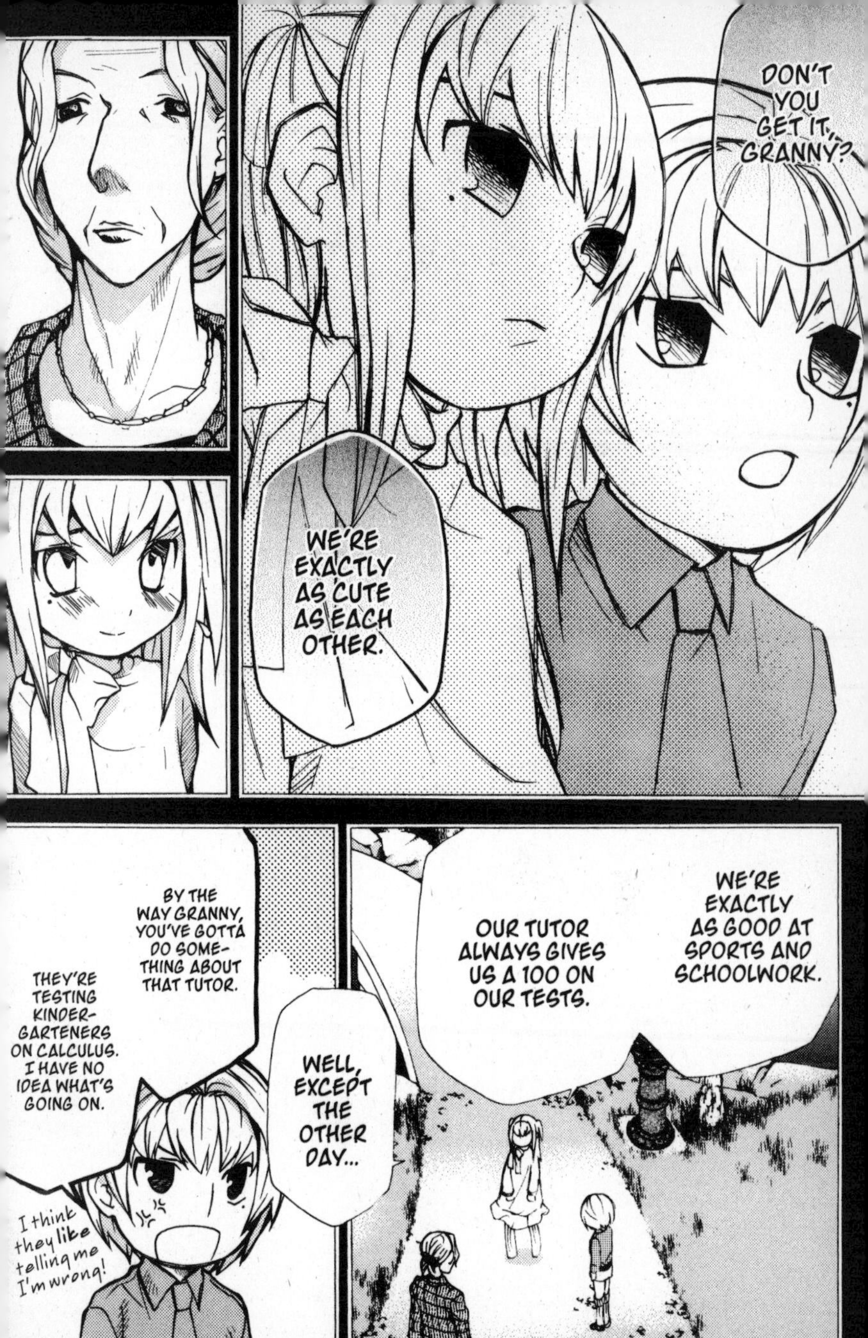
DON'T YOU GET IT, GRANNY?
WE'RE EXACTLY AS CUTE AS EACH OTHER.
WE'RE EXACTLY AS GOOD AT SPORTS AND SCHOOLWORK.
OUR TUTOR ALWAYS GIVES US A 100 ON OUR TESTS.
WELL, EXCEPT THE OTHER DAY...
BY THE WAY GRANNY, YOU'VE GOTTA DO SOME-THING ABOUT THAT TUTOR.
THEY'RE TESTING KINDER-GARTENERS ON CALCULUS. I HAVE NO IDEA WHAT'S GOING ON.
I think they like telling me I'm wrong!

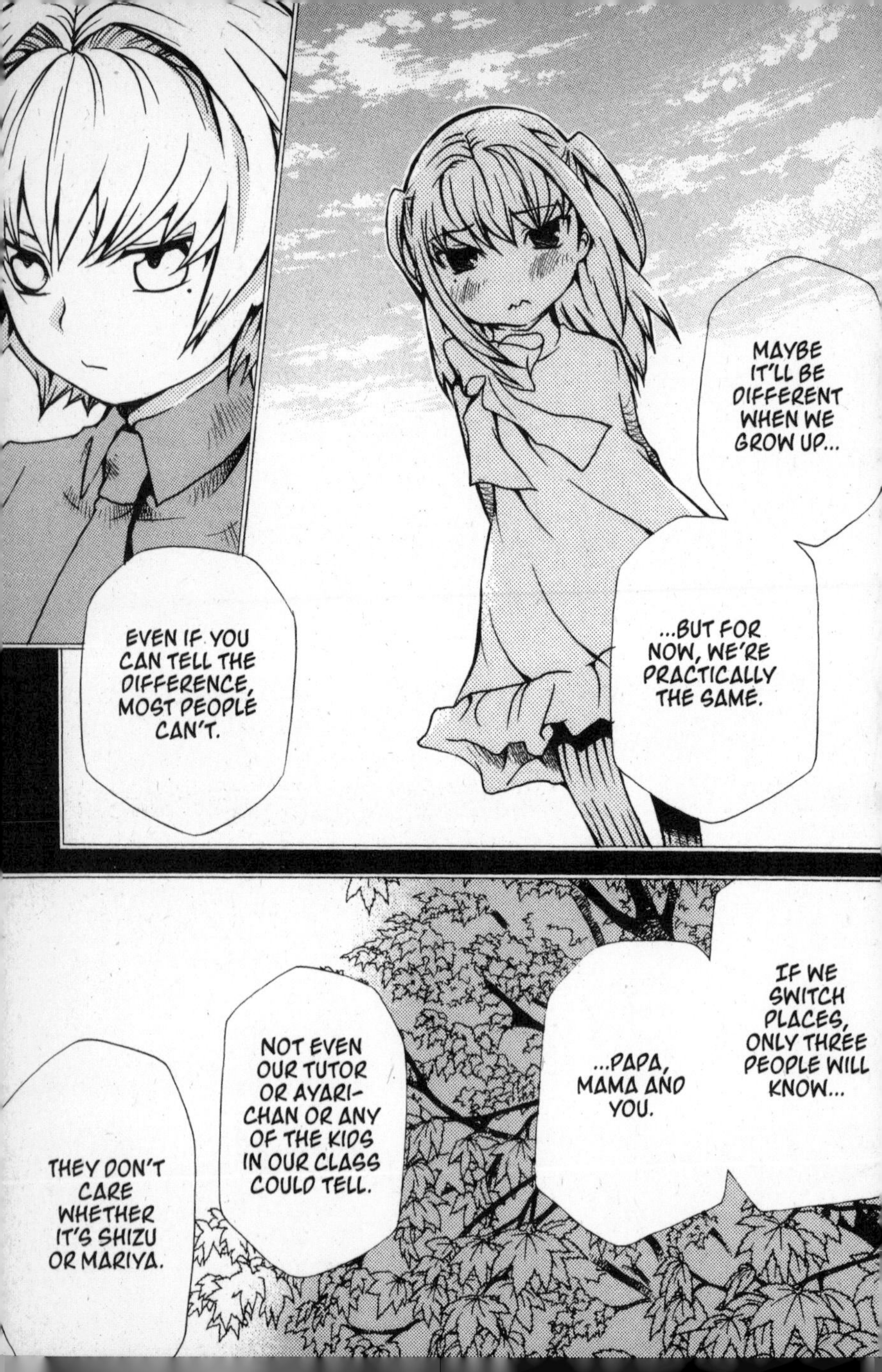
MAYBE IT'LL BE DIFFERENT WHEN WE GROW UP...
...BUT FOR NOW, WE'RE PRACTICALLY THE SAME.
EVEN IF YOU CAN TELL THE DIFFERENCE, MOST PEOPLE CAN'T.
IF WE SWITCH PLACES, ONLY THREE PEOPLE WILL KNOW...
...PAPA, MAMA AND YOU.
NOT EVEN OUR TUTOR OR AYARI-CHAN OR ANY OF THE KIDS IN OUR CLASS COULD TELL.
THEY DON'T CARE WHETHER IT'S SHIZU OR MARIYA.

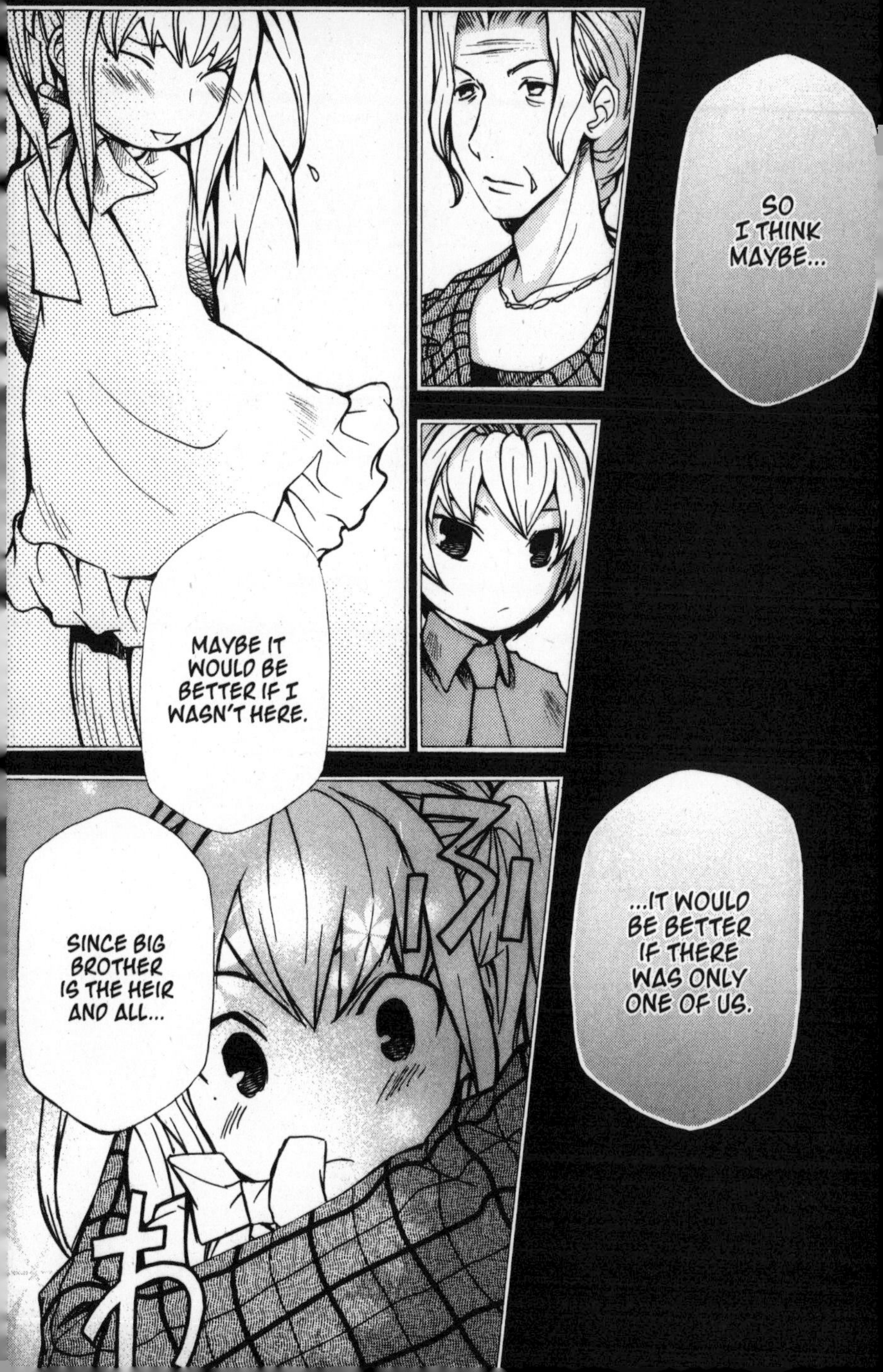
SO I THINK MAYBE...
MAYBE IT WOULD BE BETTER IF I WASN'T HERE.
...IT WOULD BE BETTER IF THERE WAS ONLY ONE OF US.
SINCE BIG BROTHER IS THE HEIR AND ALL...

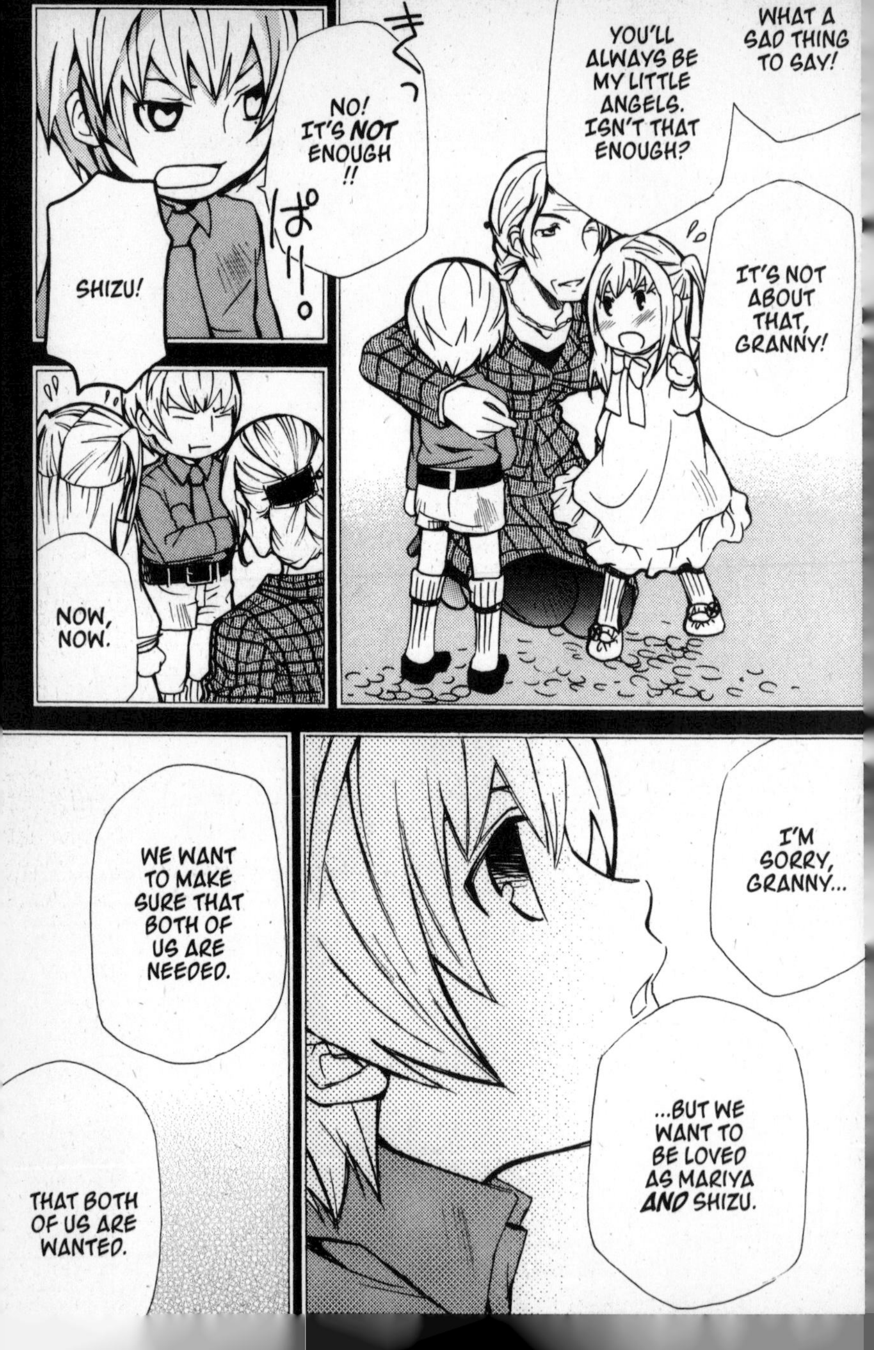
WHAT A SAD THING TO SAY!
YOU'LL ALWAYS BE MY LITTLE ANGELS. ISN'T THAT ENOUGH?
IT'S NOT ABOUT THAT, GRANNY!
きっ
NO! IT'S **NOT** ENOUGH!!
SHIZU!
NOW, NOW.
I'M SORRY, GRANNY...
...BUT WE WANT TO BE LOVED AS MARIYA ***AND*** SHIZU.
WE WANT TO MAKE SURE THAT BOTH OF US ARE NEEDED.
THAT BOTH OF US ARE WANTED.

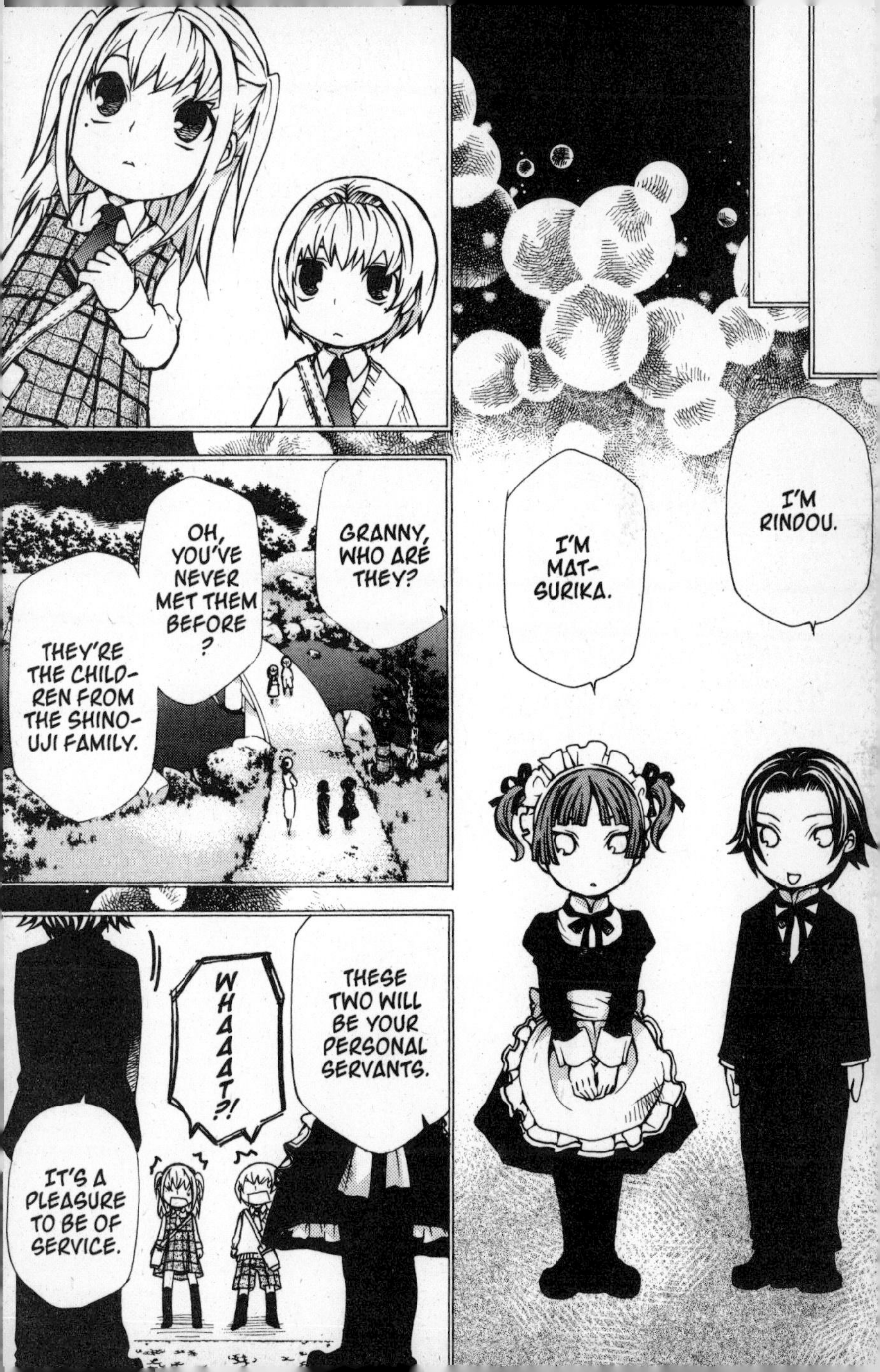
I'M RINDOU.
I'M MAT-SURIKA.
GRANNY, WHO ARE THEY?
OH, YOU'VE NEVER MET THEM BEFORE?
THEY'RE THE CHILD-REN FROM THE SHINO-UJI FAMILY.
THESE TWO WILL BE YOUR PERSONAL SERVANTS.
WHAAAAT?!
IT'S A PLEASURE TO BE OF SERVICE.

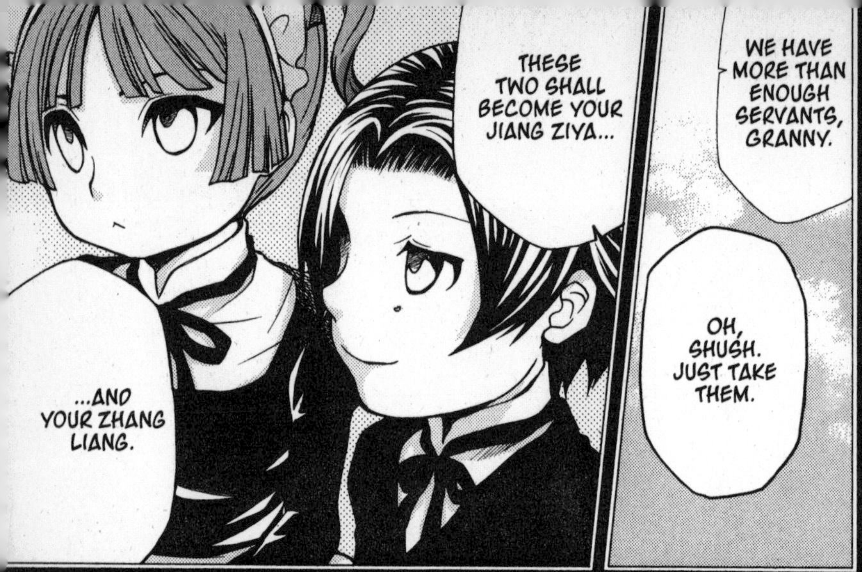
WE HAVE MORE THAN ENOUGH SERVANTS, GRANNY.
OH, SHUSH. JUST TAKE THEM.
THESE TWO SHALL BECOME YOUR JIANG ZIYA...
...AND YOUR ZHANG LIANG.

Note: AKA Taikoubou: an ancient Chinese sage that helped King Wu of Zhou defeat last king of the Shang Dynasty in 11BC

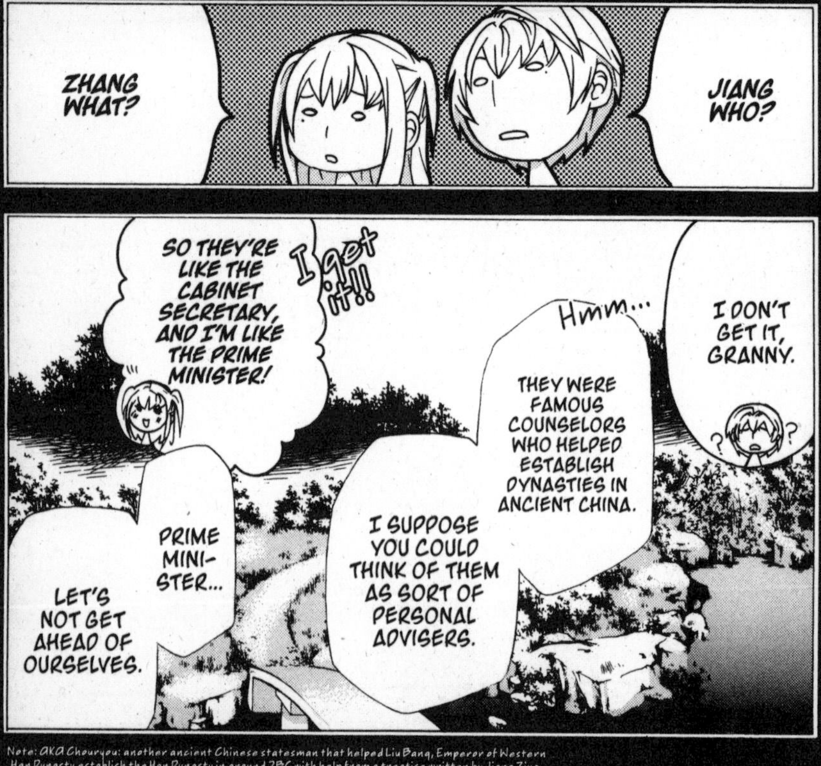
JIANG WHO?
ZHANG WHAT?
I DON'T GET IT, GRANNY.
Hmm...
THEY WERE FAMOUS COUNSELORS WHO HELPED ESTABLISH DYNASTIES IN ANCIENT CHINA.
I SUPPOSE YOU COULD THINK OF THEM AS SORT OF PERSONAL ADVISERS.
SO THEY'RE LIKE THE CABINET SECRETARY, AND I'M LIKE THE PRIME MINISTER!
I get it!!
PRIME MINI-STER...
LET'S NOT GET AHEAD OF OURSELVES.

Note: AKA Chouryou: another ancient Chinese statesman that helped Liu Bang, Emperor of Western Han Dynasty establish the Han Dynasty in around 2BC with help from a treatise written by Jiang Ziya.

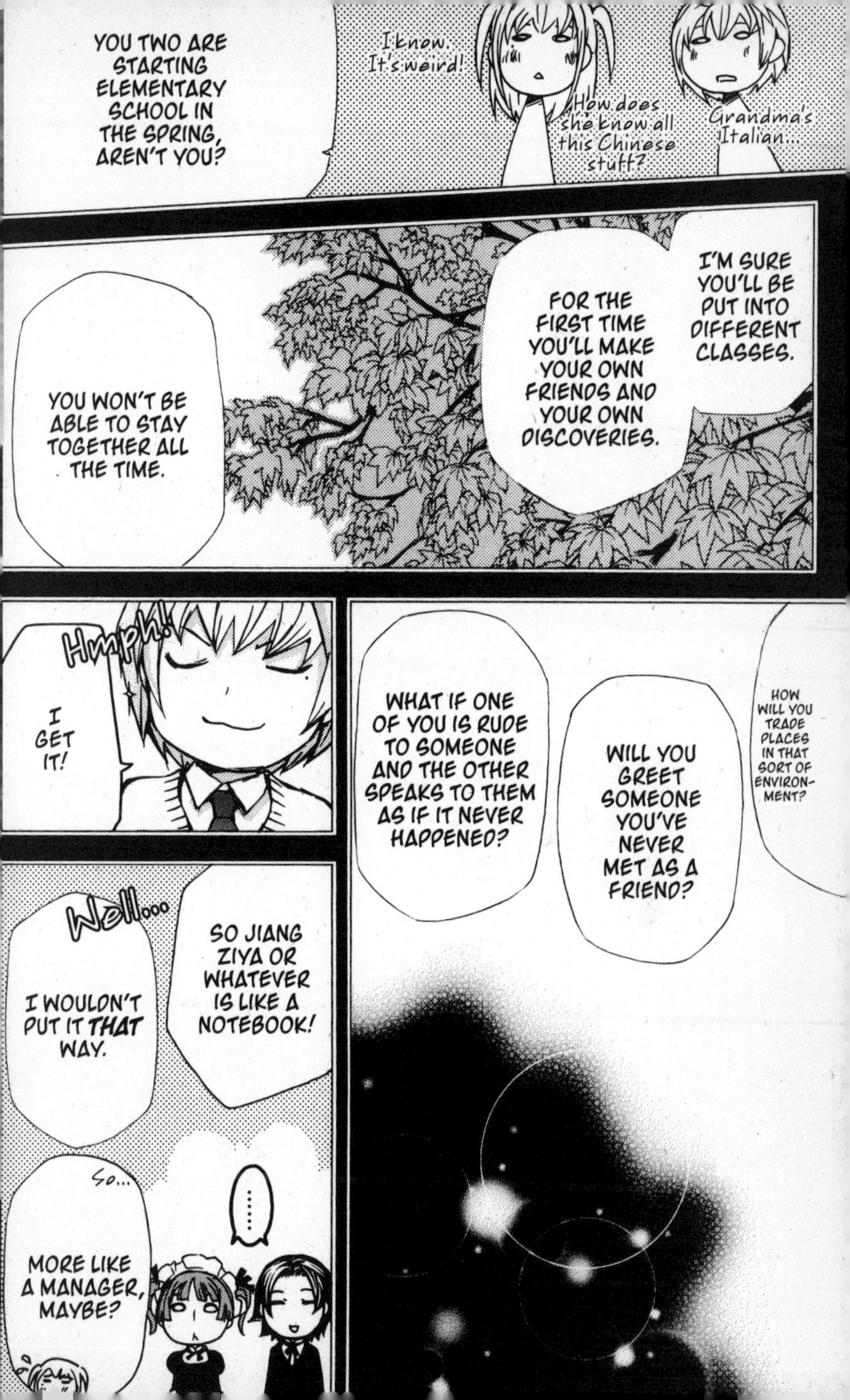
Grandma's Italian...
How does she know all this Chinese stuff?
I know. It's weird!
YOU TWO ARE STARTING ELEMENTARY SCHOOL IN THE SPRING, AREN'T YOU?
I'M SURE YOU'LL BE PUT INTO DIFFERENT CLASSES.
FOR THE FIRST TIME YOU'LL MAKE YOUR OWN FRIENDS AND YOUR OWN DISCOVERIES.
YOU WON'T BE ABLE TO STAY TOGETHER ALL THE TIME.
HOW WILL YOU TRADE PLACES IN THAT SORT OF ENVIRON-MENT?
WILL YOU GREET SOMEONE YOU'VE NEVER MET AS A FRIEND?
WHAT IF ONE OF YOU IS RUDE TO SOMEONE AND THE OTHER SPEAKS TO THEM AS IF IT NEVER HAPPENED?
Hmph!
I GET IT!
SO JIANG ZIYA OR WHATEVER IS LIKE A NOTEBOOK!
Well...
I WOULDN'T PUT IT *THAT* WAY.
......
So...
MORE LIKE A MANAGER, MAYBE?

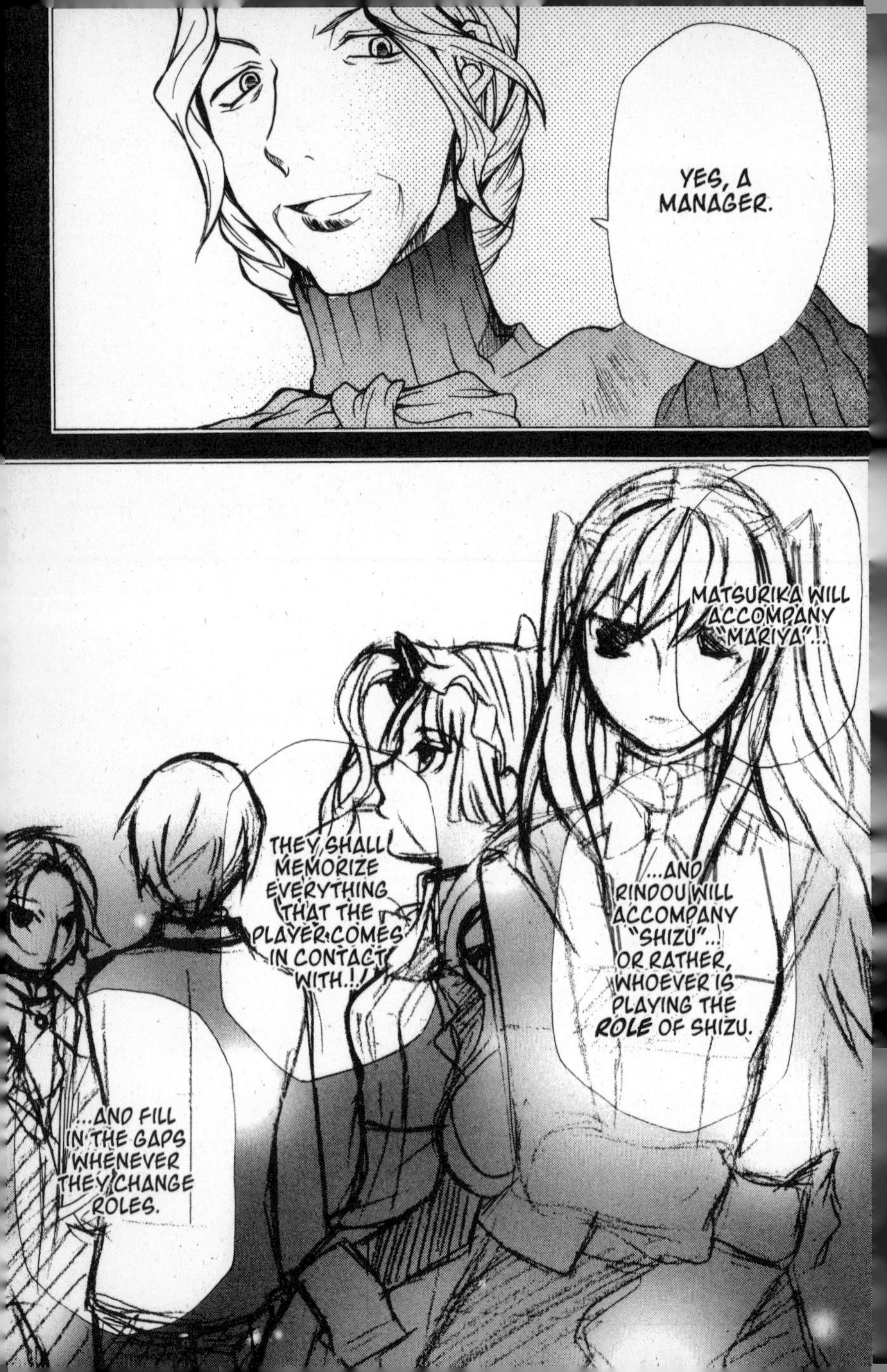
YES, A MANAGER.
MATSURIKA WILL ACCOMPANY "MARIYA"...
...AND RINDOU WILL ACCOMPANY "SHIZU"... OR RATHER, WHOEVER IS PLAYING THE ROLE OF SHIZU.
THEY SHALL MEMORIZE EVERYTHING THAT THE PLAYER COMES IN CONTACT WITH...
...AND FILL IN THE GAPS WHENEVER THEY CHANGE ROLES.

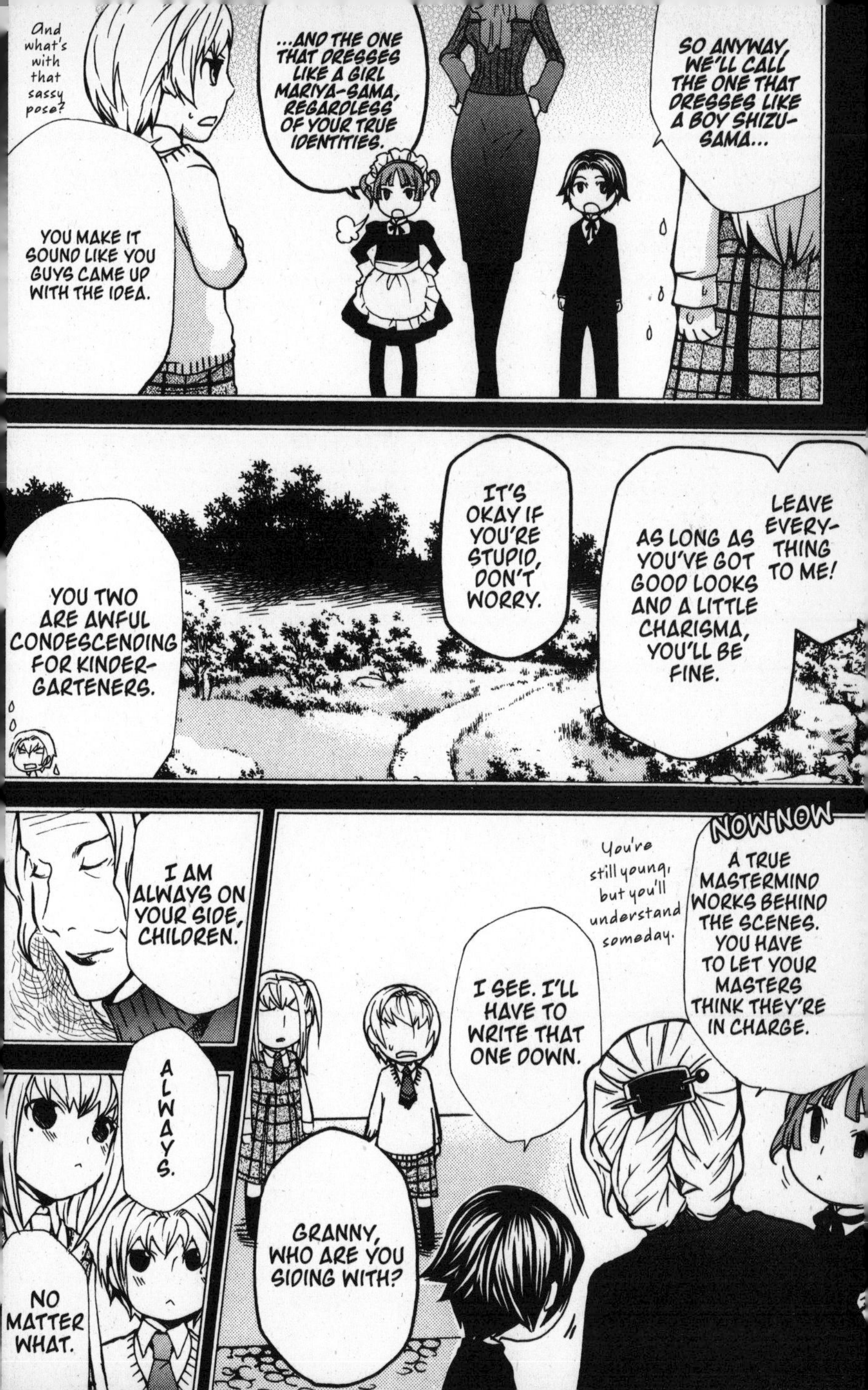
SO ANYWAY, WE'LL CALL THE ONE THAT DRESSES LIKE A BOY SHIZU-SAMA...
...AND THE ONE THAT DRESSES LIKE A GIRL MARIYA-SAMA, REGARDLESS OF YOUR TRUE IDENTITIES.
And what's with that sassy pose?
YOU MAKE IT SOUND LIKE YOU GUYS CAME UP WITH THE IDEA.
LEAVE EVERY-THING TO ME!
AS LONG AS YOU'VE GOT GOOD LOOKS AND A LITTLE CHARISMA, YOU'LL BE FINE.
IT'S OKAY IF YOU'RE STUPID, DON'T WORRY.
YOU TWO ARE AWFUL CONDESCENDING FOR KINDER-GARTENERS.
NOW NOW
A TRUE MASTERMIND WORKS BEHIND THE SCENES. YOU HAVE TO LET YOUR MASTERS THINK THEY'RE IN CHARGE.
You're still young, but you'll understand someday.
I SEE. I'LL HAVE TO WRITE THAT ONE DOWN.
GRANNY, WHO ARE YOU SIDING WITH?
I AM ALWAYS ON YOUR SIDE, CHILDREN.
ALWAYS.
NO MATTER WHAT.

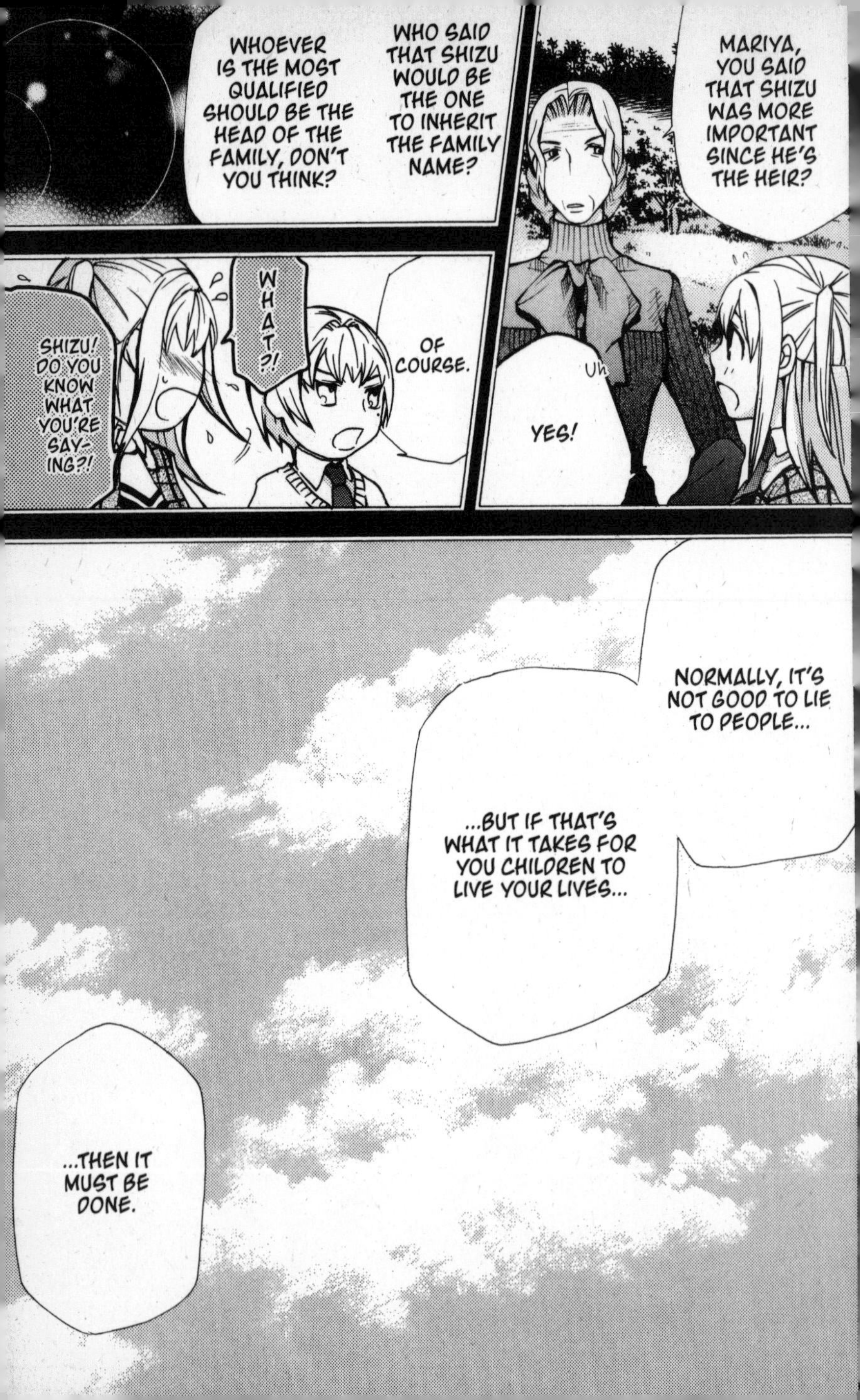
MARIYA, YOU SAID THAT SHIZU WAS MORE IMPORTANT SINCE HE'S THE HEIR?
Uh
YES!
WHO SAID THAT SHIZU WOULD BE THE ONE TO INHERIT THE FAMILY NAME?
WHOEVER IS THE MOST QUALIFIED SHOULD BE THE HEAD OF THE FAMILY, DON'T YOU THINK?
OF COURSE.
WHAT?!
SHIZU! DO YOU KNOW WHAT YOU'RE SAYING?!
NORMALLY, IT'S NOT GOOD TO LIE TO PEOPLE...
...BUT IF THAT'S WHAT IT TAKES FOR YOU CHILDREN TO LIVE YOUR LIVES...
...THEN IT MUST BE DONE.

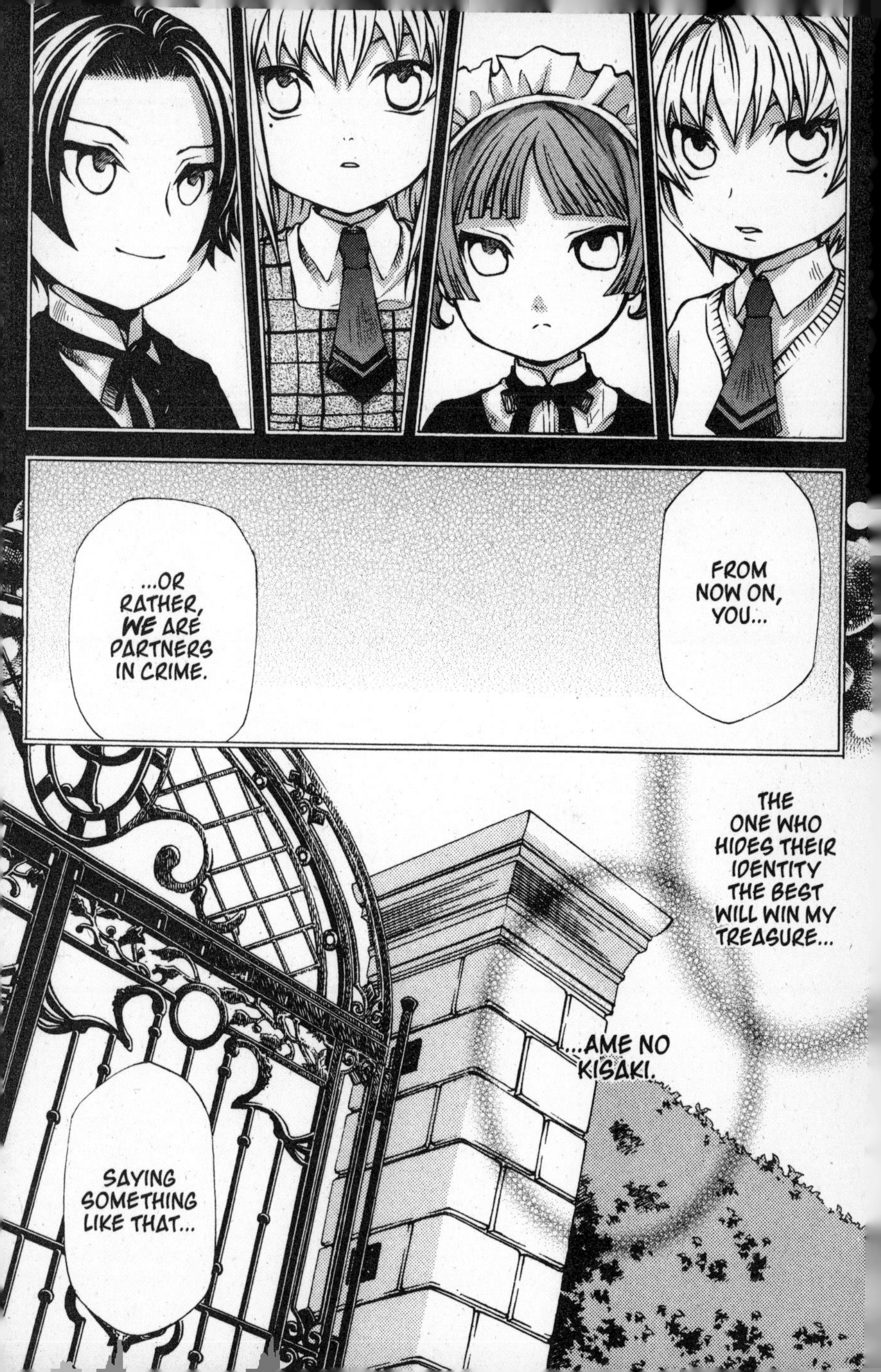
FROM NOW ON, YOU...
...OR RATHER, WE ARE PARTNERS IN CRIME.
THE ONE WHO HIDES THEIR IDENTITY THE BEST WILL WIN MY TREASURE...
...AME NO KISAKI.
SAYING SOMETHING LIKE THAT...

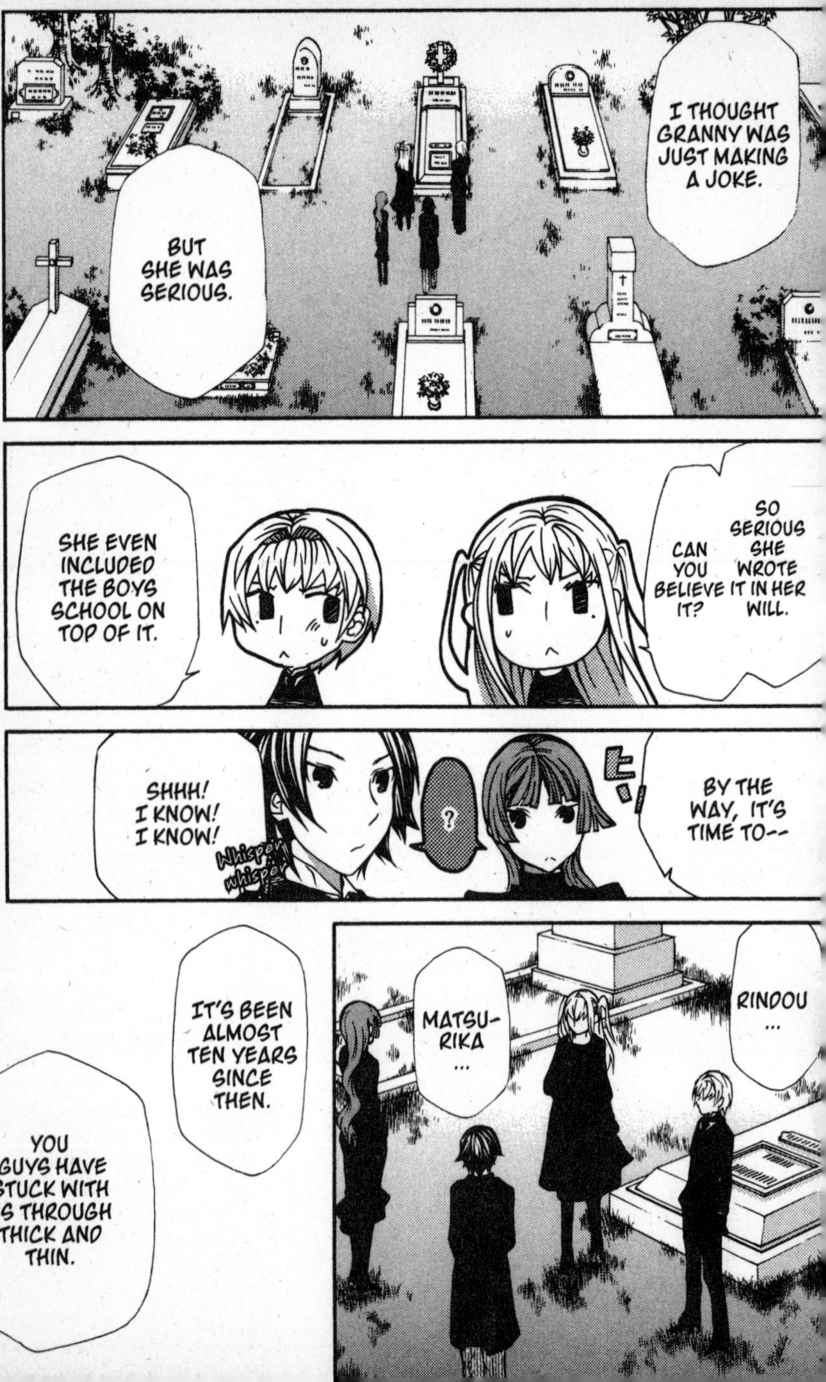

I THOUGHT GRANNY WAS JUST MAKING A JOKE.
BUT SHE WAS SERIOUS.
SO SERIOUS SHE WROTE IT IN HER WILL.
CAN YOU BELIEVE IT?
SHE EVEN INCLUDED THE BOYS SCHOOL ON TOP OF IT.
BY THE WAY, IT'S TIME TO--
?
SHHH! I KNOW! I KNOW!
Whisper whisper
RINDOU...
MATSU-RIKA...
IT'S BEEN ALMOST TEN YEARS SINCE THEN.
YOU GUYS HAVE STUCK WITH US THROUGH THICK AND THIN.

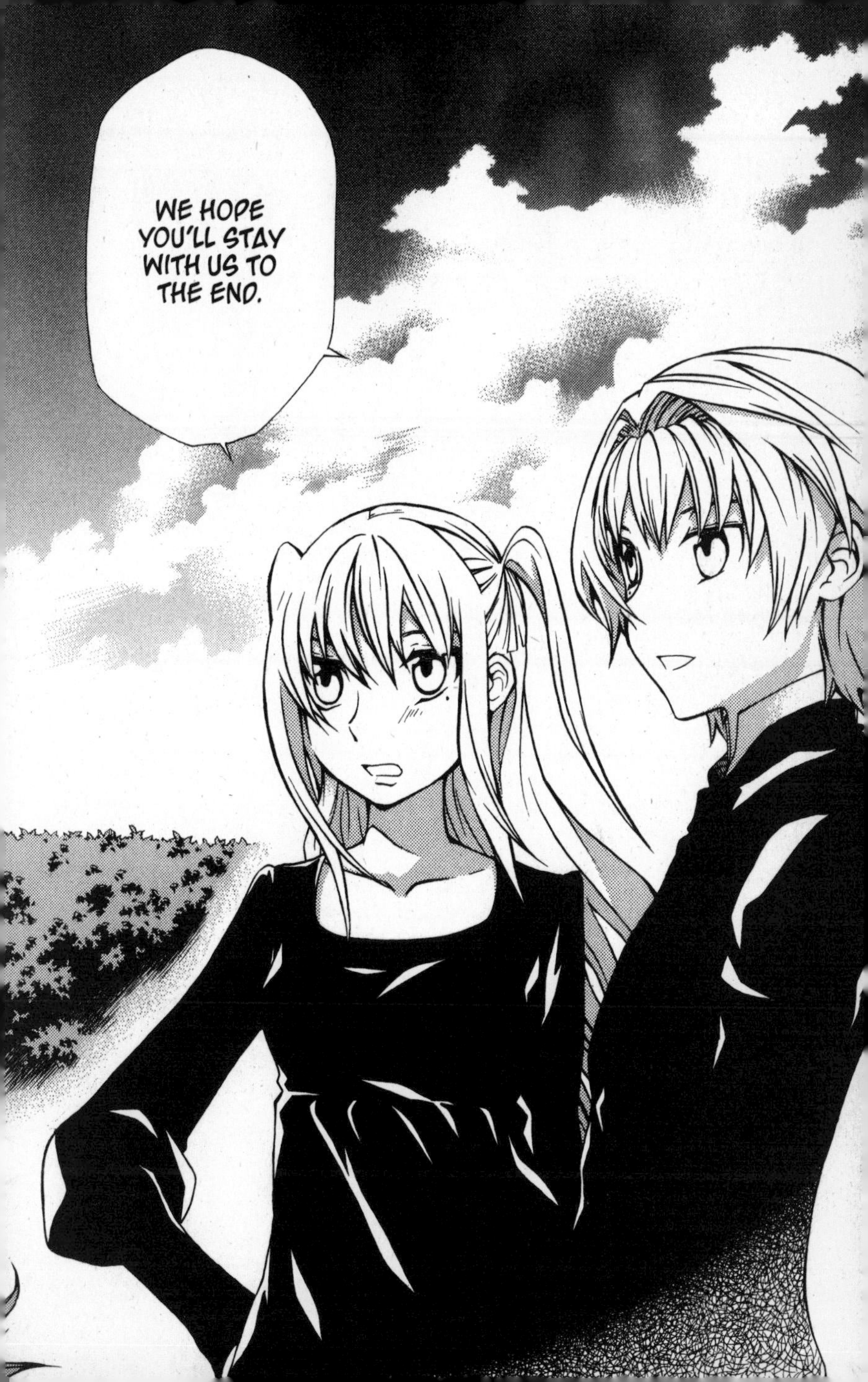
WE HOPE YOU'LL STAY WITH US TO THE END.

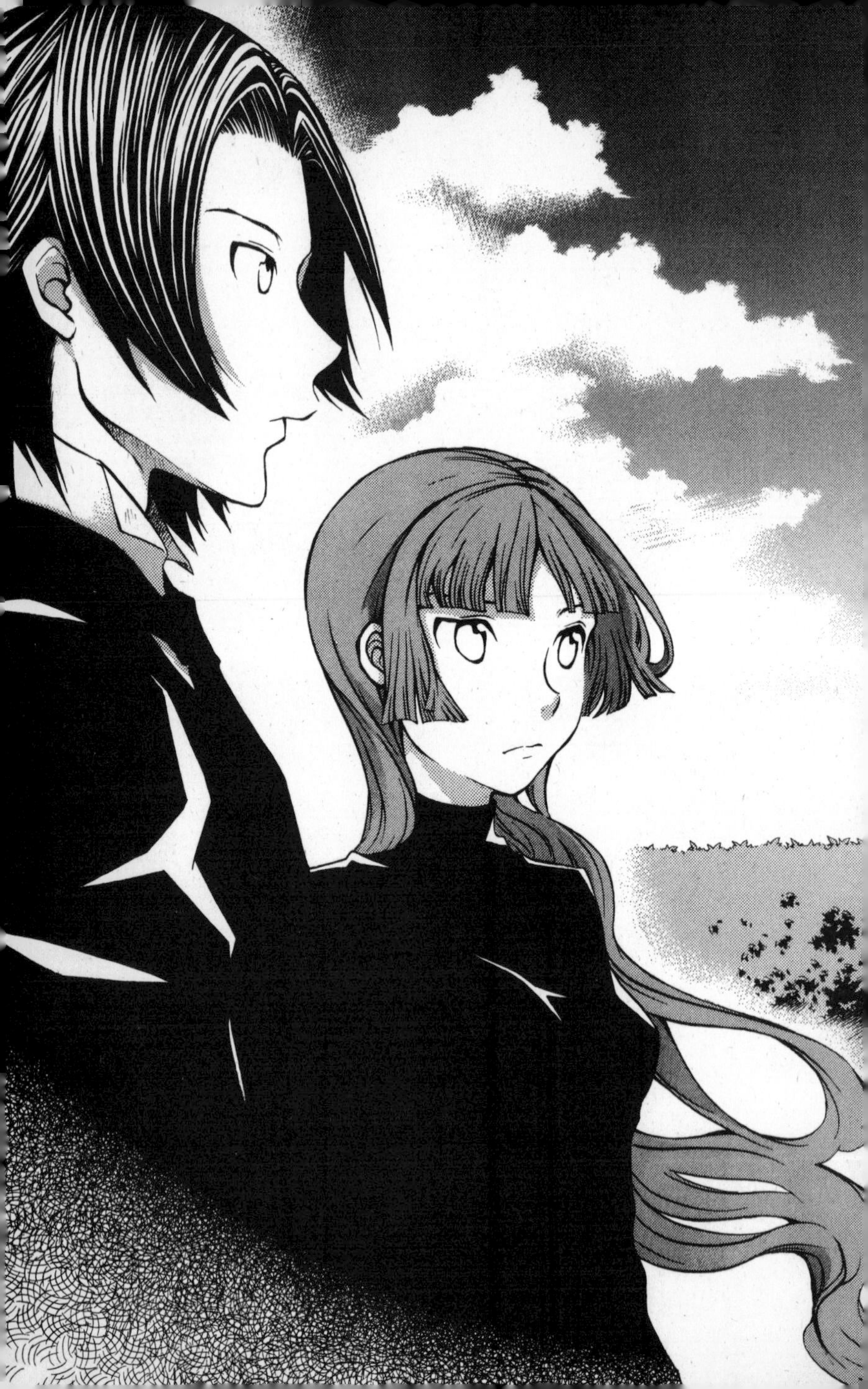

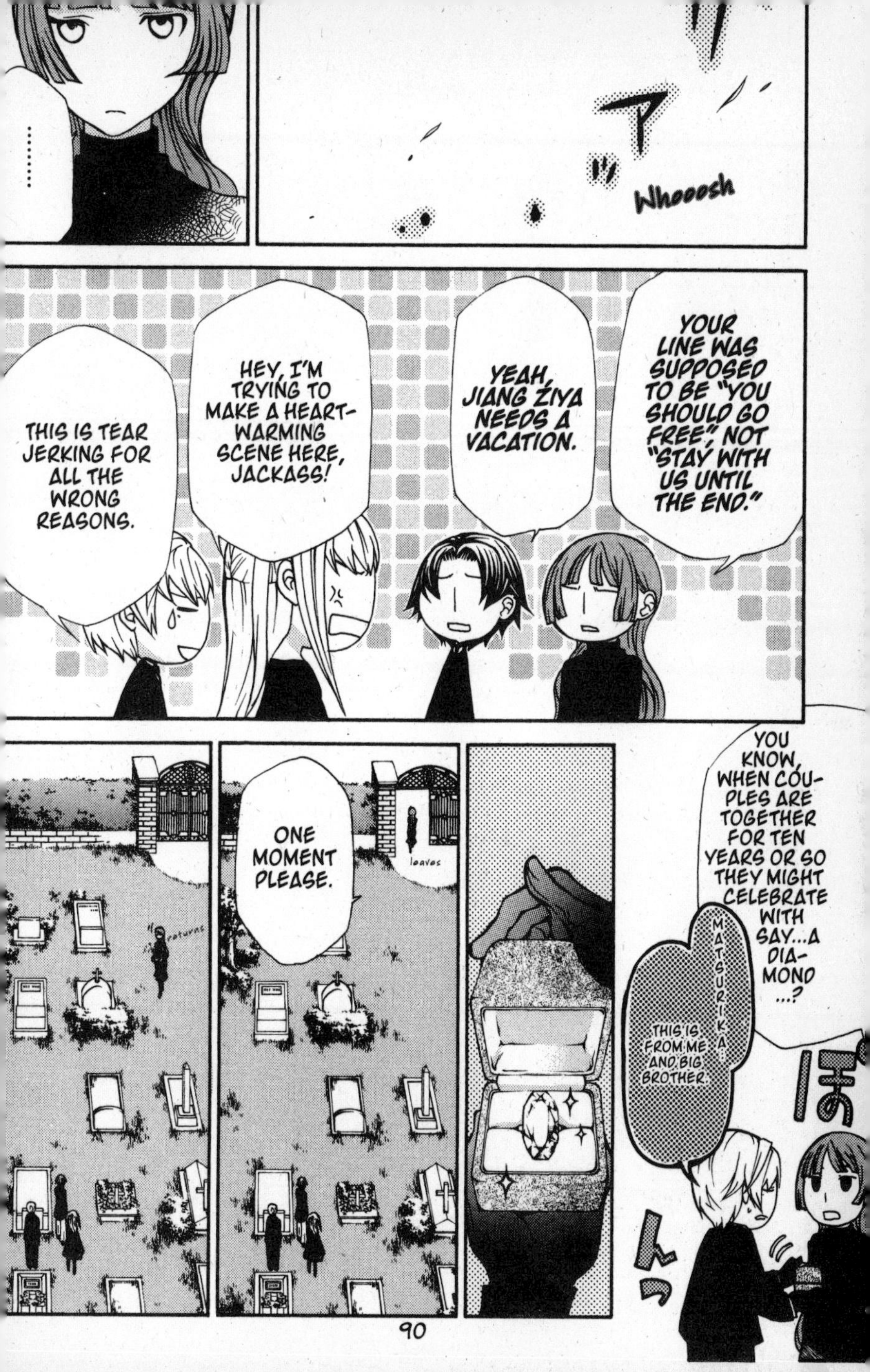
Whooosh
......
YOUR LINE WAS SUPPOSED TO BE "YOU SHOULD GO FREE," NOT "STAY WITH US UNTIL THE END."
YEAH, JIANG ZIYA NEEDS A VACATION.
HEY, I'M TRYING TO MAKE A HEART-WARMING SCENE HERE, JACKASS!
THIS IS TEAR JERKING FOR ALL THE WRONG REASONS.
YOU KNOW, WHEN COU-PLES ARE TOGETHER FOR TEN YEARS OR SO THEY MIGHT CELEBRATE WITH SAY...A DIA-MOND ...?
MATSURIKA...
THIS IS FROM ME AND BIG BROTHER.
ONE MOMENT PLEASE.
leaves
returns

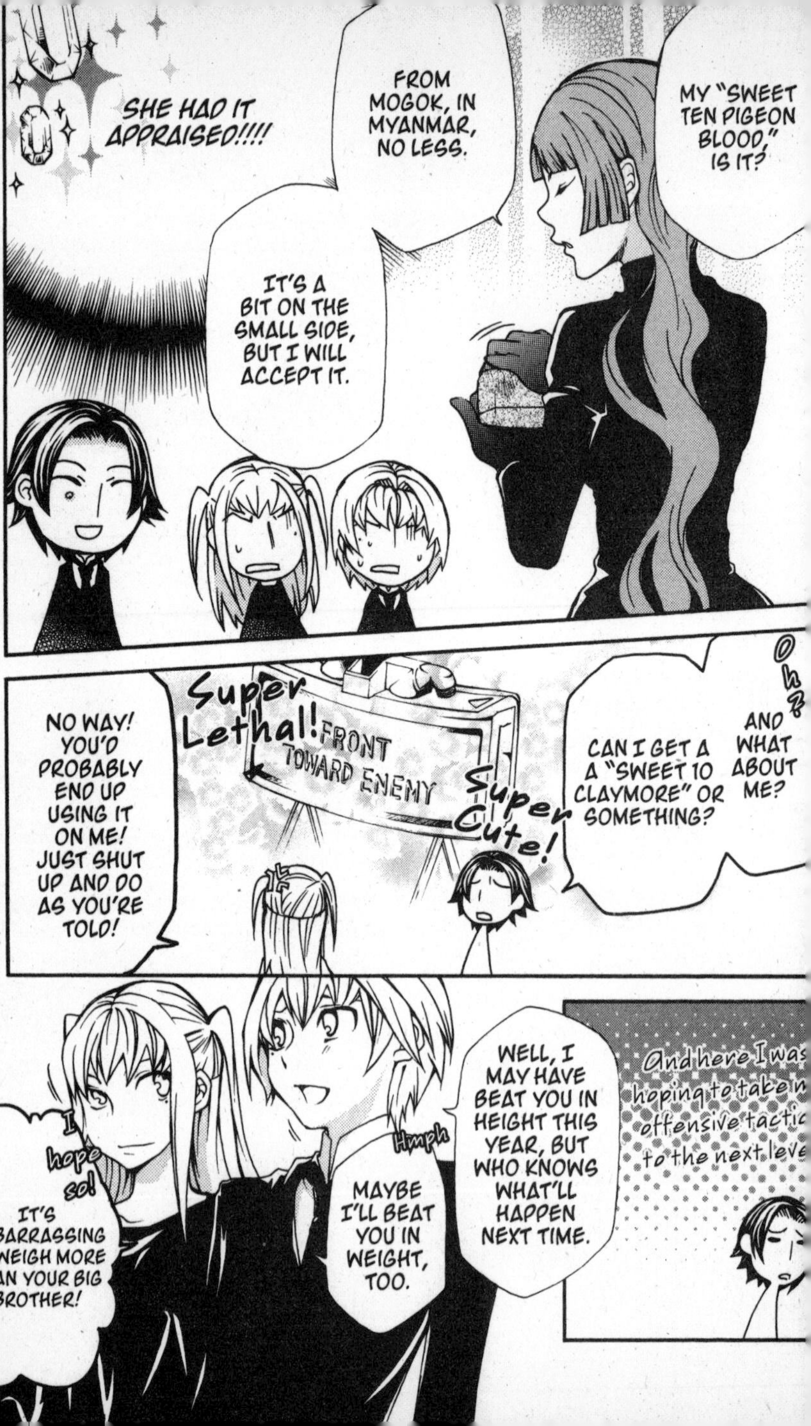

MY "SWEET TEN PIGEON BLOOD," IS IT?
FROM MOGOK, IN MYANMAR, NO LESS.
SHE HAD IT APPRAISED!!!!
IT'S A BIT ON THE SMALL SIDE, BUT I WILL ACCEPT IT.
Oh?
AND WHAT ABOUT ME?
CAN I GET A "SWEET 10 CLAYMORE" OR SOMETHING?
Super Cute!
FRONT TOWARD ENEMY
Super Lethal!
NO WAY! YOU'D PROBABLY END UP USING IT ON ME! JUST SHUT UP AND DO AS YOU'RE TOLD!
And here I was hoping to take m offensive tactic to the next leve
WELL, I MAY HAVE BEAT YOU IN HEIGHT THIS YEAR, BUT WHO KNOWS WHAT'LL HAPPEN NEXT TIME.
Hmph
MAYBE I'LL BEAT YOU IN WEIGHT, TOO.
I hope so!
IT'S EMBARRASSING TO WEIGH MORE THAN YOUR BIG BROTHER!

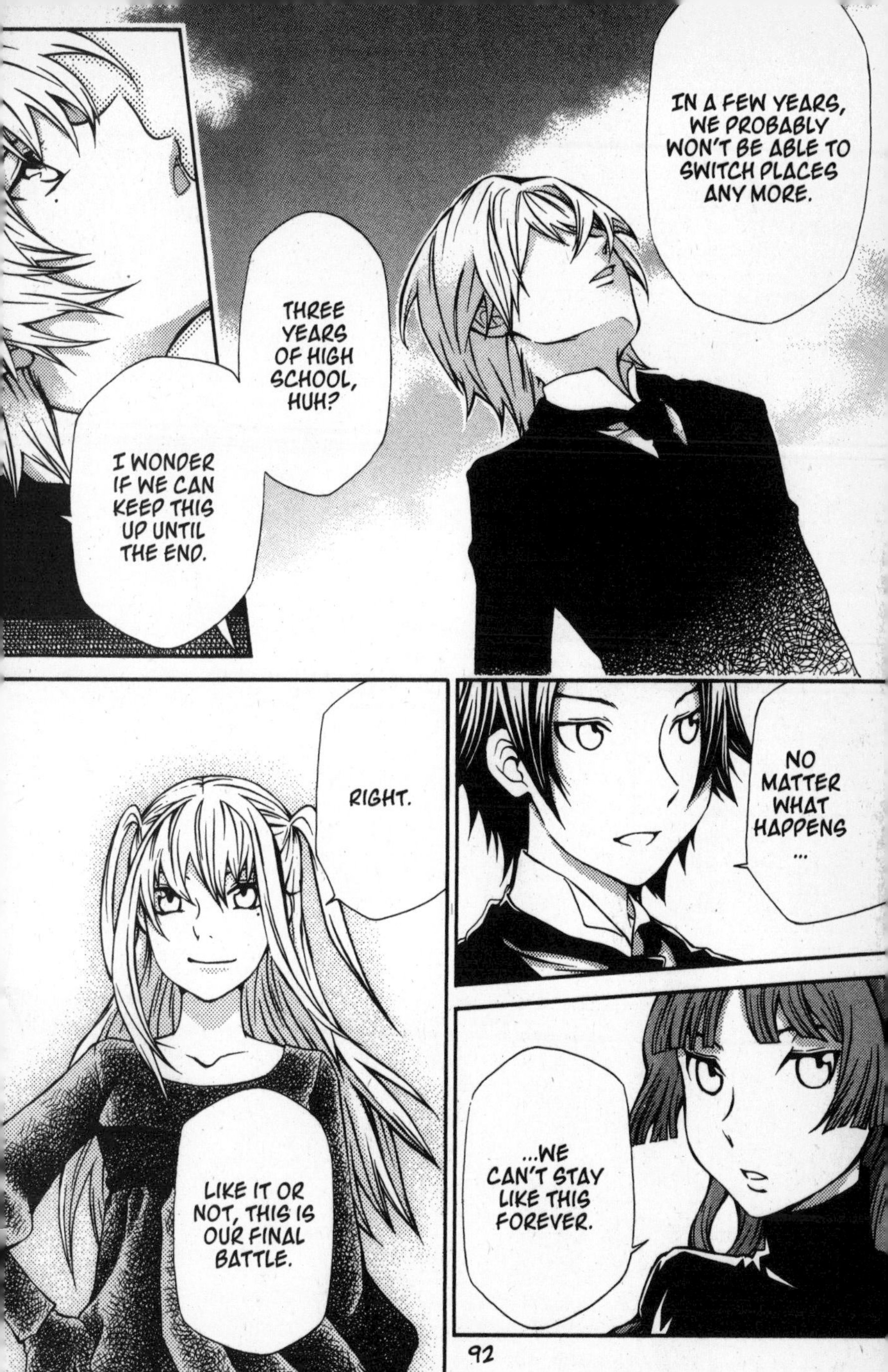
IN A FEW YEARS, WE PROBABLY WON'T BE ABLE TO SWITCH PLACES ANY MORE.
THREE YEARS OF HIGH SCHOOL, HUH?
I WONDER IF WE CAN KEEP THIS UP UNTIL THE END.
NO MATTER WHAT HAPPENS...
...WE CAN'T STAY LIKE THIS FOREVER.
RIGHT.
LIKE IT OR NOT, THIS IS OUR FINAL BATTLE.

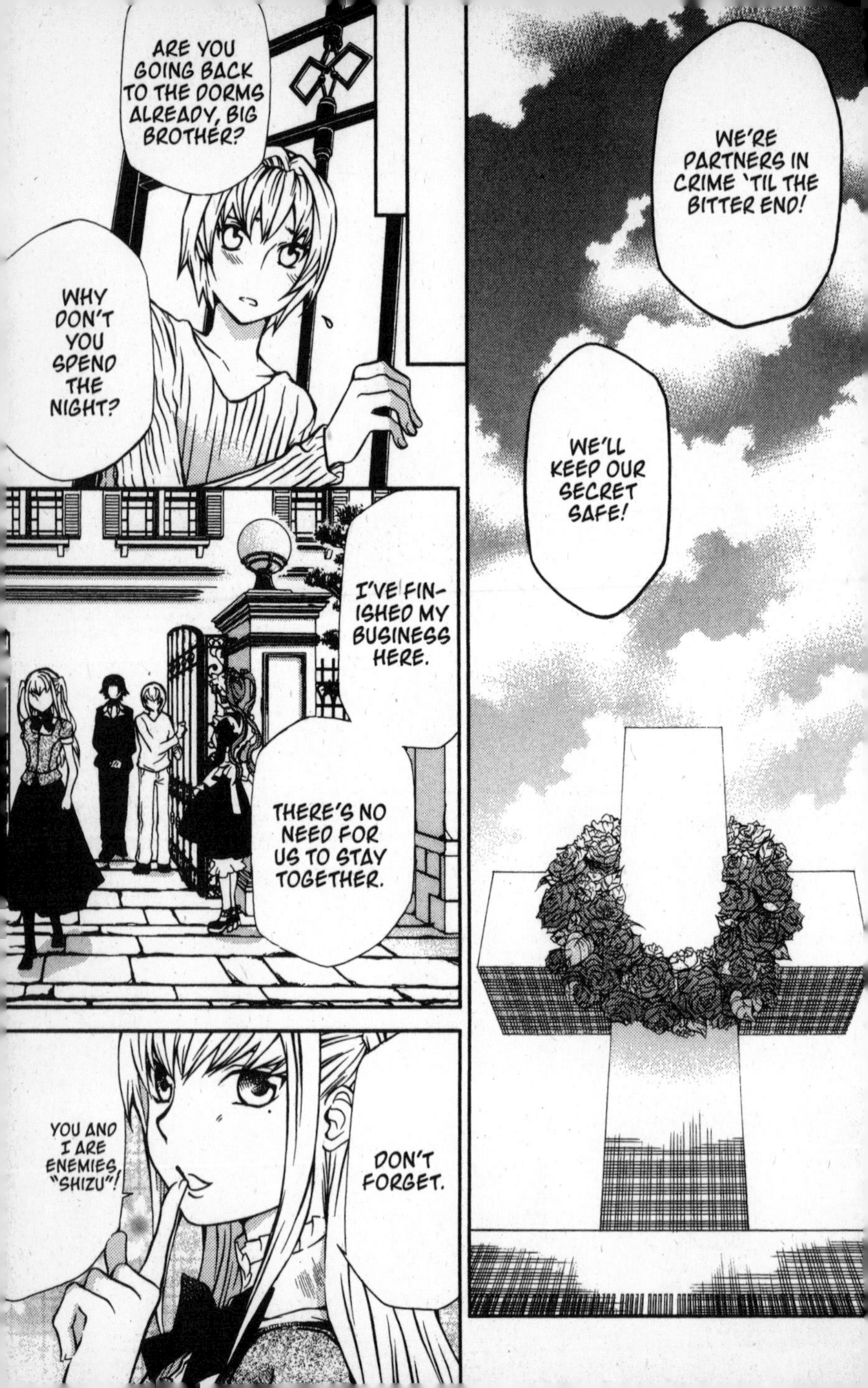
WE'RE PARTNERS IN CRIME 'TIL THE BITTER END!
WE'LL KEEP OUR SECRET SAFE!
ARE YOU GOING BACK TO THE DORMS ALREADY, BIG BROTHER?
WHY DON'T YOU SPEND THE NIGHT?
I'VE FIN-ISHED MY BUSINESS HERE.
THERE'S NO NEED FOR US TO STAY TOGETHER.
DON'T FORGET.
YOU AND I ARE ENEMIES, "SHIZU"!

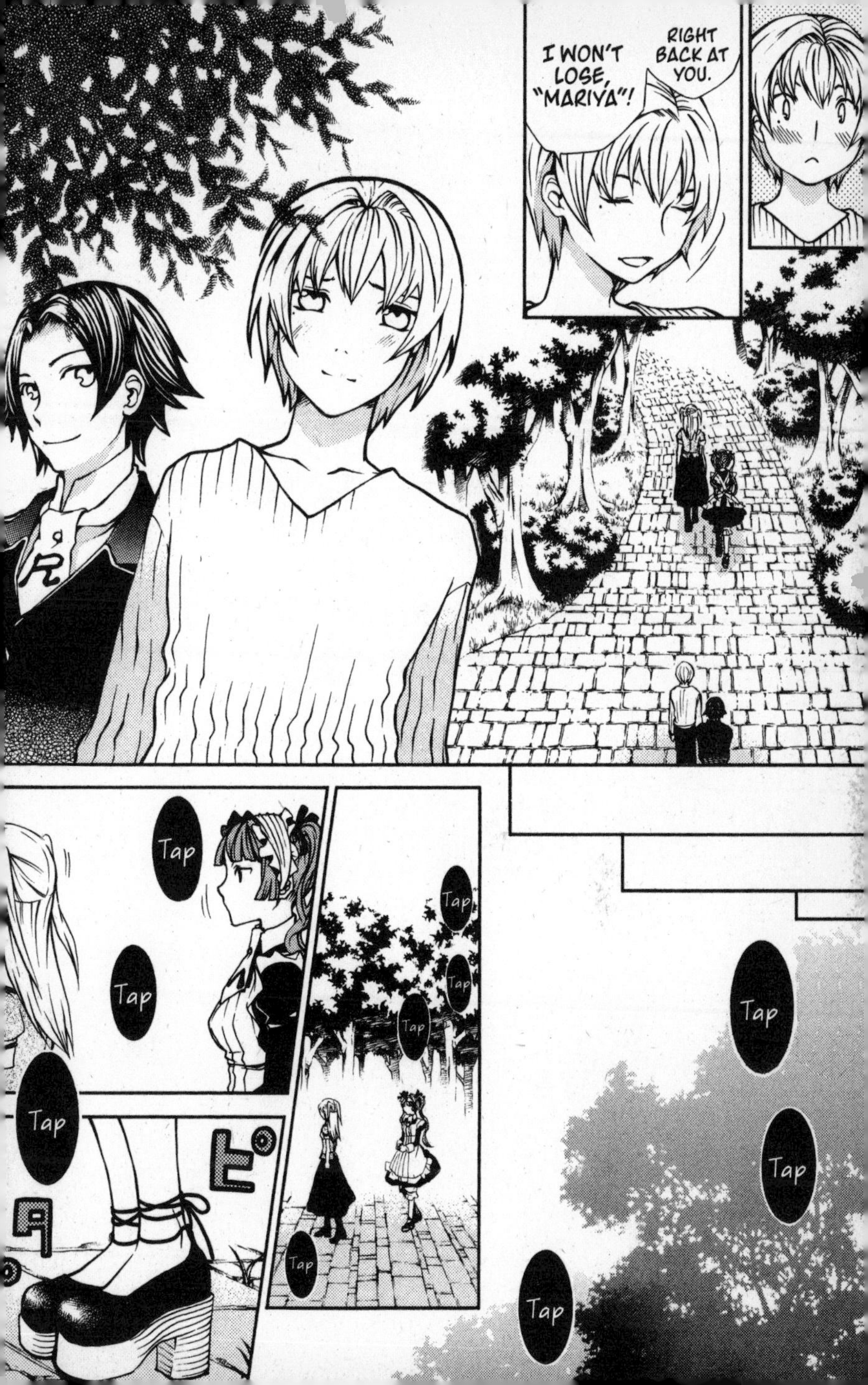
RIGHT BACK AT YOU.
I WON'T LOSE, "MARIYA"!
Tap
Tap
Tap
Tap
Tap
Tap
Tap
Tap
Tap
Tap
Tap

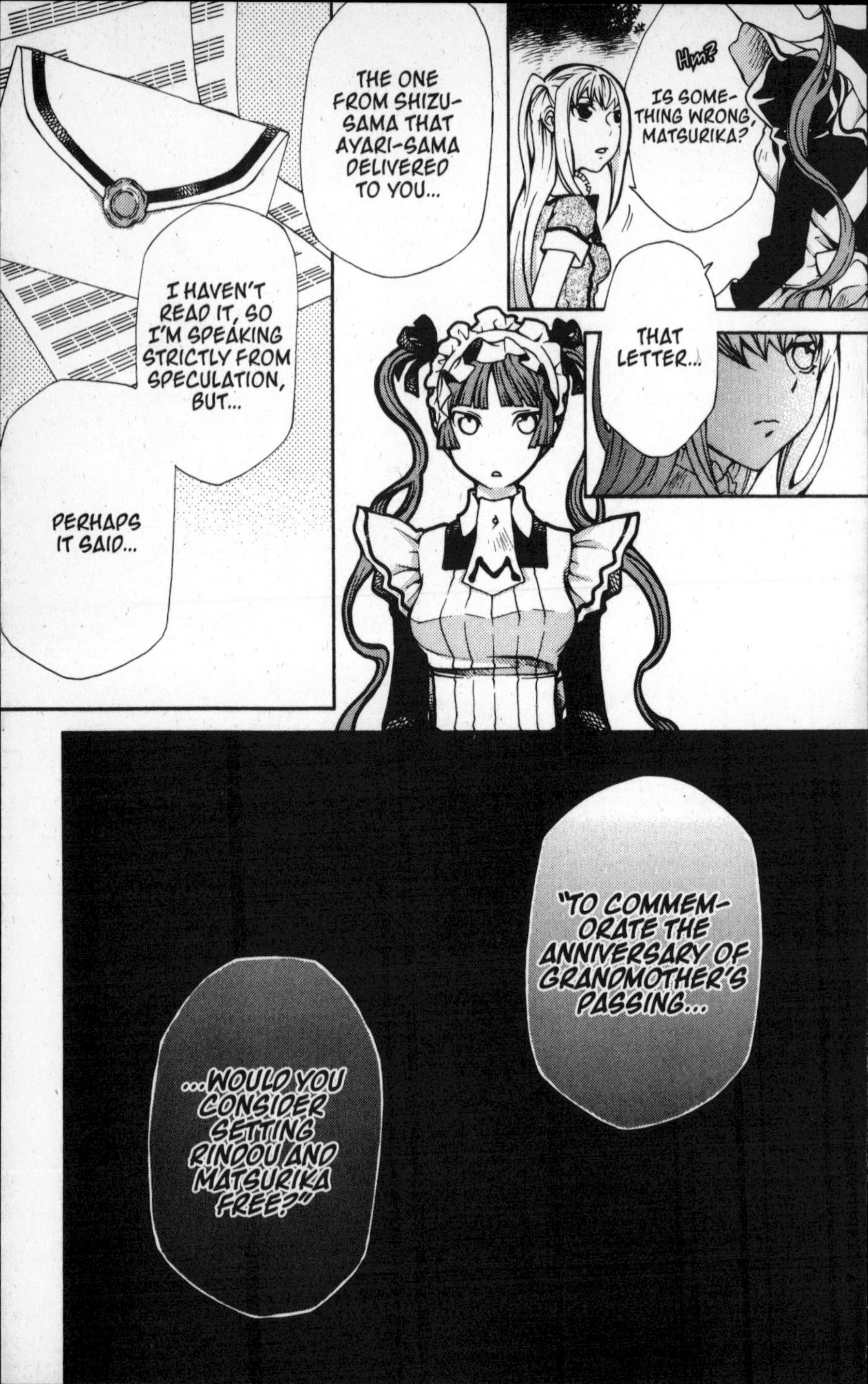

Hm?
IS SOME-THING WRONG, MATSURIKA?
THAT LETTER...
THE ONE FROM SHIZU-SAMA THAT AYARI-SAMA DELIVERED TO YOU...
I HAVEN'T READ IT, SO I'M SPEAKING STRICTLY FROM SPECULATION, BUT...
PERHAPS IT SAID...
"TO COMMEM-ORATE THE ANNIVERSARY OF GRANDMOTHER'S PASSING...
...WOULD YOU CONSIDER SETTING RINDOU AND MATSURIKA FREE?"

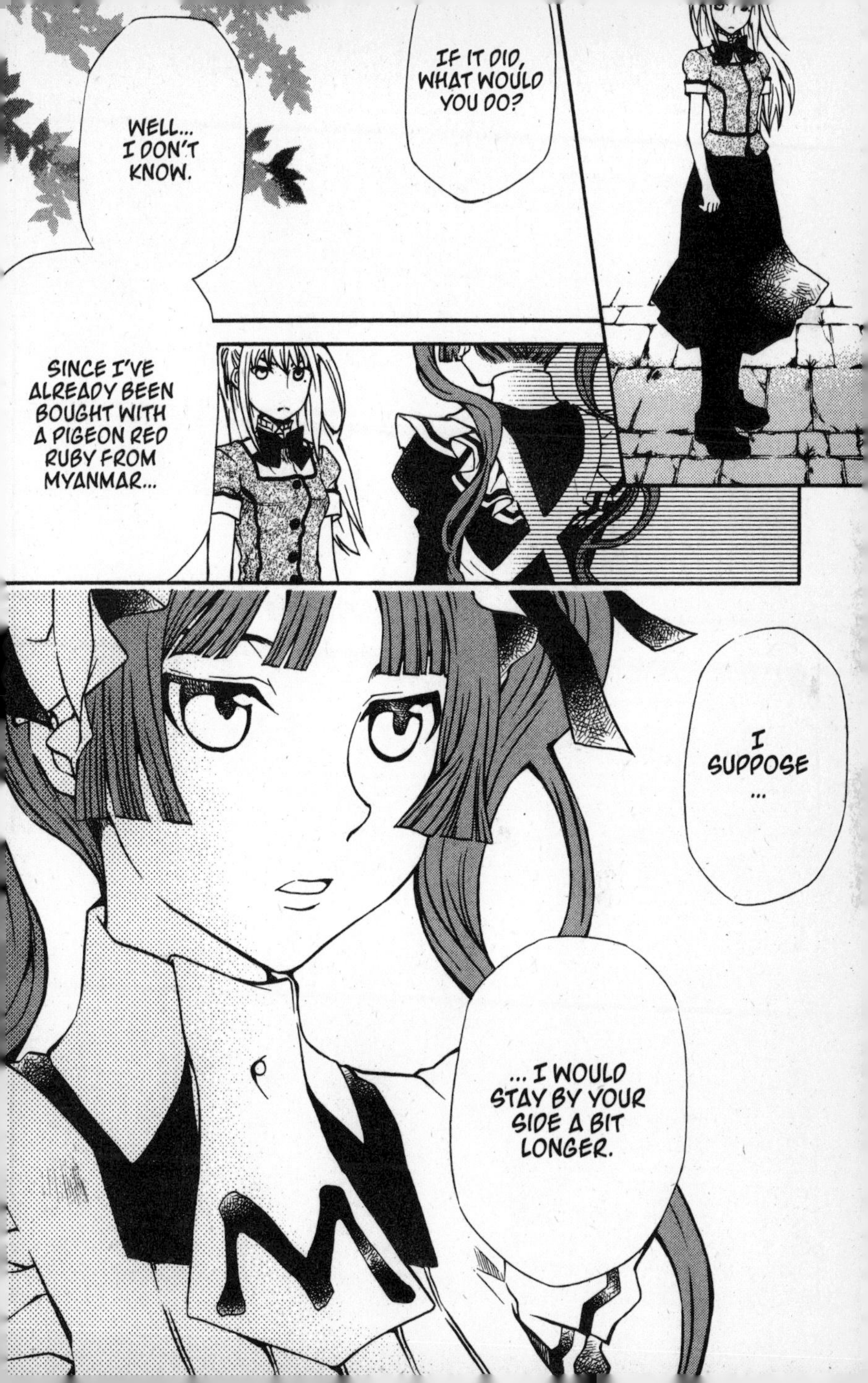
IF IT DID, WHAT WOULD YOU DO?
WELL... I DON'T KNOW.
SINCE I'VE ALREADY BEEN BOUGHT WITH A PIGEON RED RUBY FROM MYANMAR...
I SUPPOSE ...
... I WOULD STAY BY YOUR SIDE A BIT LONGER.

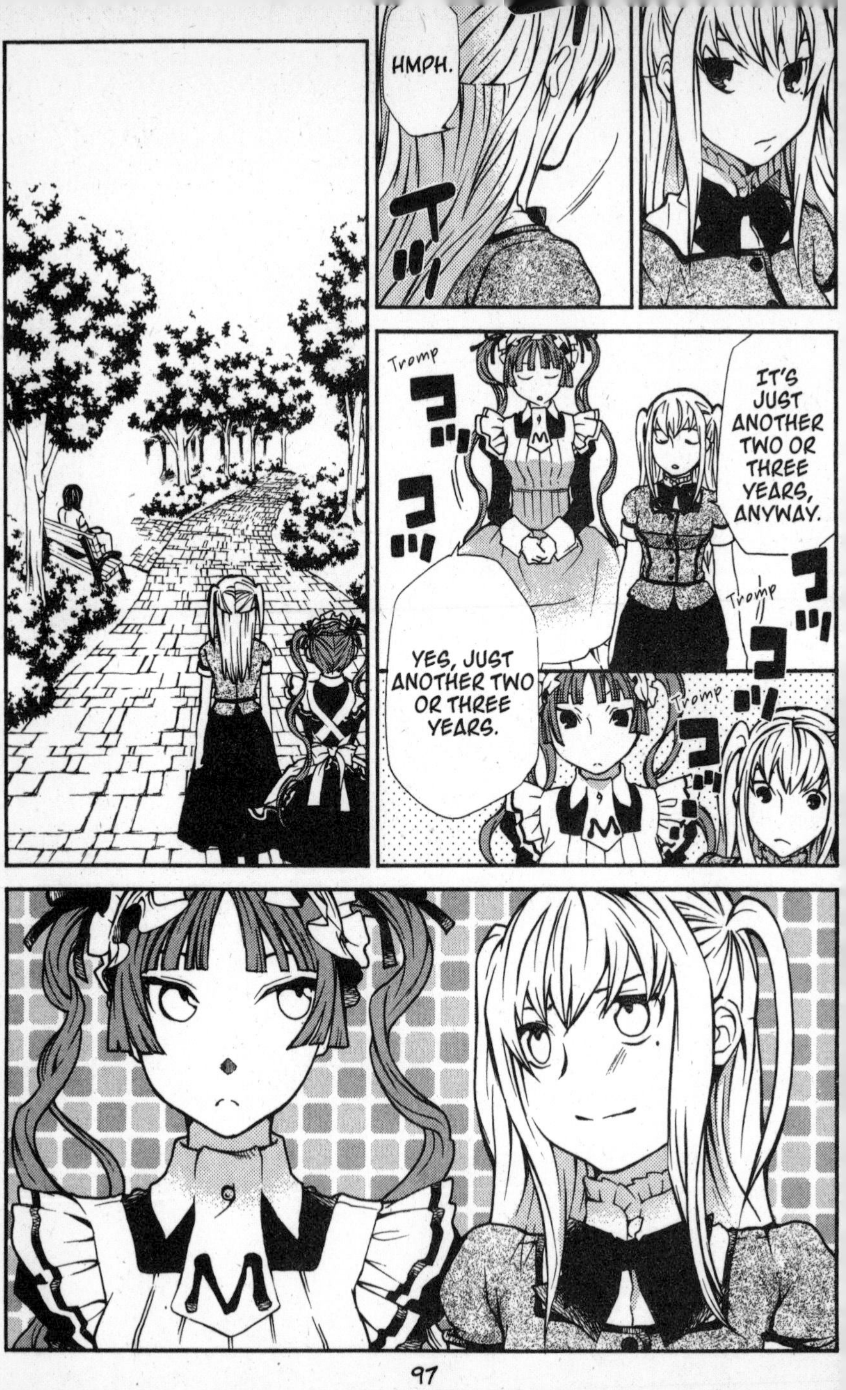
HMPH.
Tromp
IT'S JUST ANOTHER TWO OR THREE YEARS, ANYWAY.
Tromp
YES, JUST ANOTHER TWO OR THREE YEARS.
Tromp

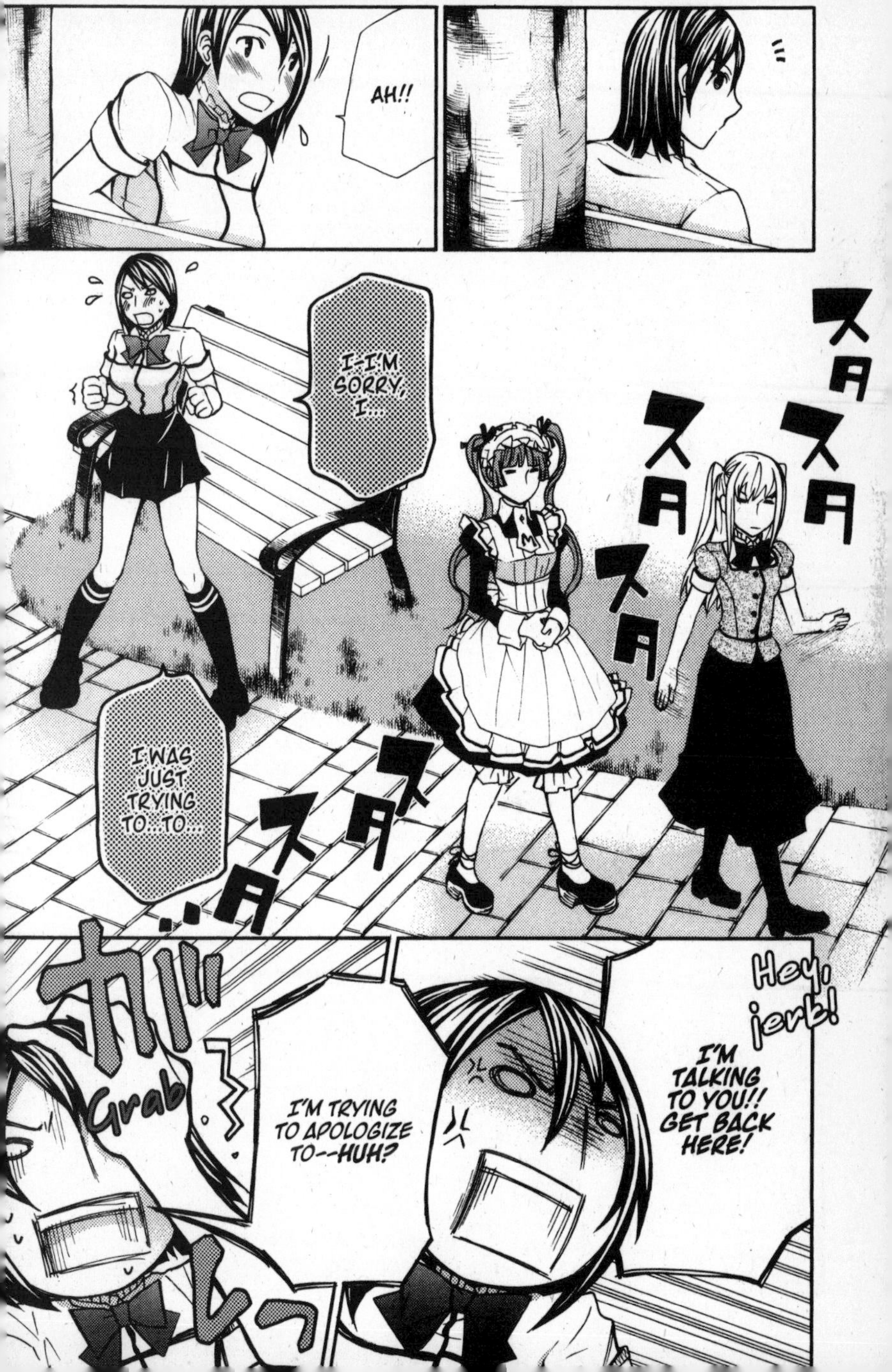
AH!!
I-I'M SORRY, I...
I WAS JUST TRYING TO...TO...
Hey, jerk!
I'M TALKING TO YOU!! GET BACK HERE!
I'M TRYING TO APOLOGIZE TO--HUH?
Grab

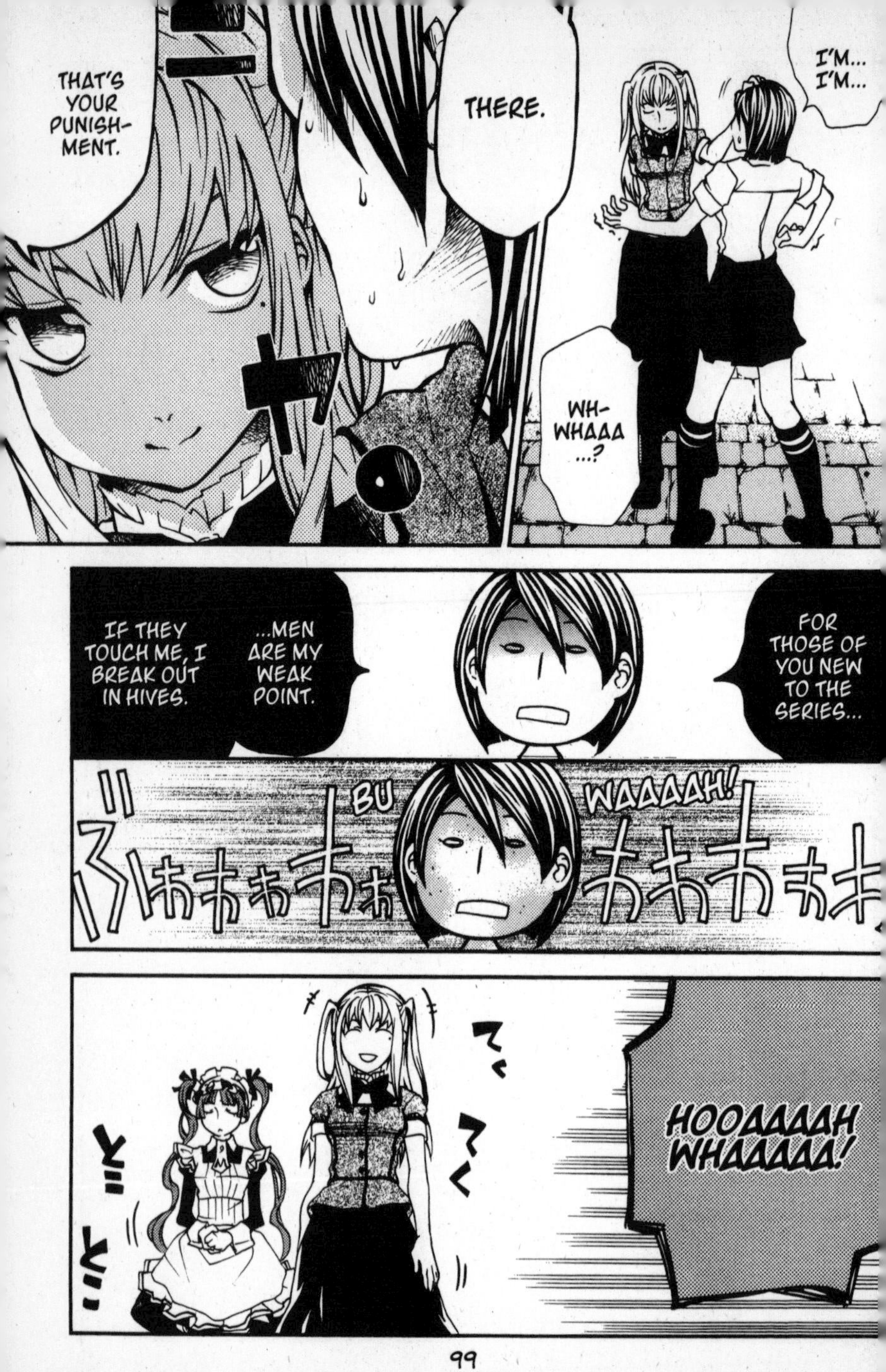
I'M... I'M...
WH- WHAAA ...?
THERE.
THAT'S YOUR PUNISH- MENT.
FOR THOSE OF YOU NEW TO THE SERIES...
...MEN ARE MY WEAK POINT.
IF THEY TOUCH ME, I BREAK OUT IN HIVES.
BU WAAAAH!
HOOAAAAH WHAAAAAA!

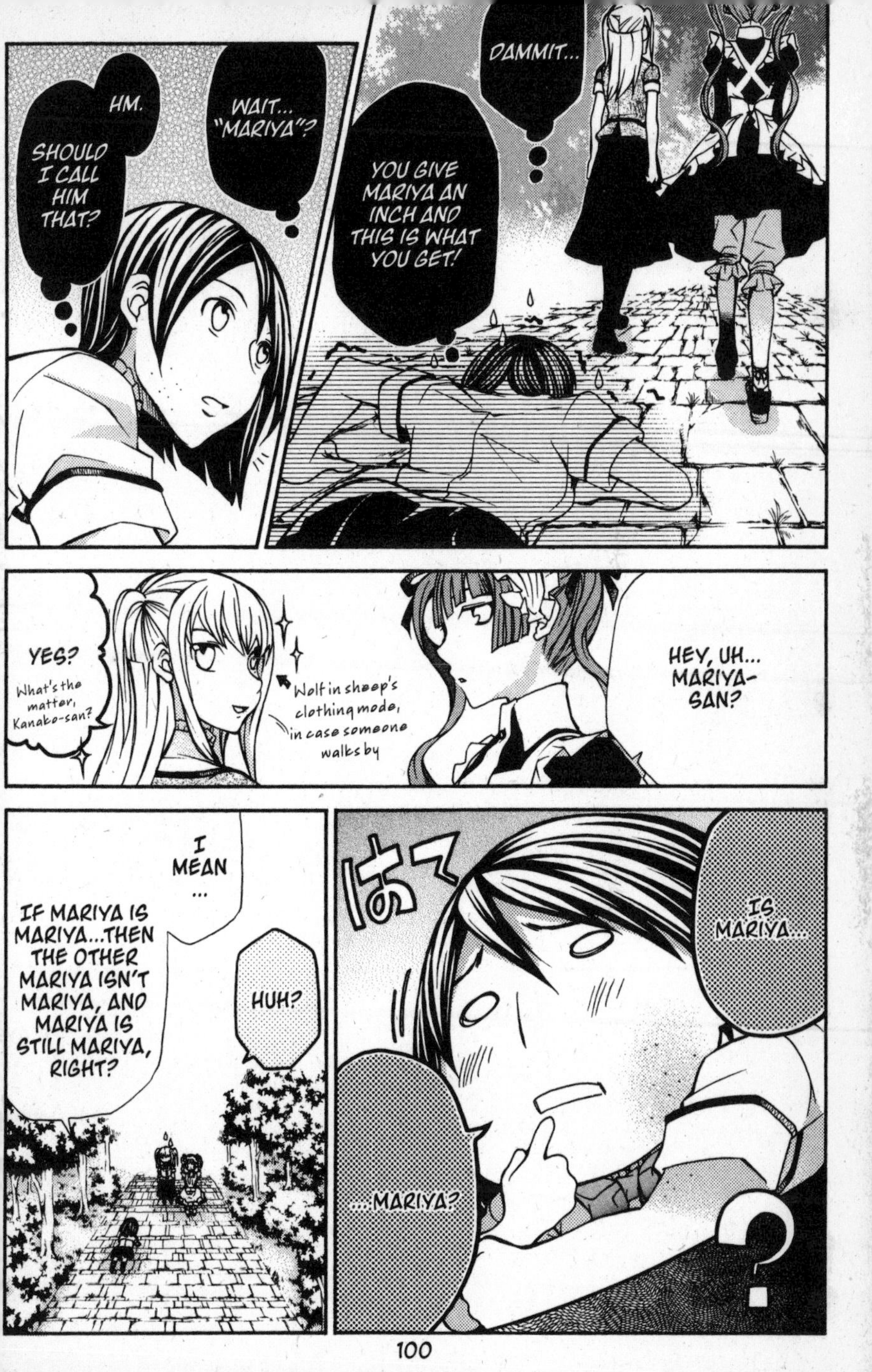
DAMMIT...
YOU GIVE MARIYA AN INCH AND THIS IS WHAT YOU GET!
WAIT... "MARIYA"?
HM.
SHOULD I CALL HIM THAT?
HEY, UH... MARIYA-SAN?
YES?
What's the matter, Kanako-san?
Wolf in sheep's clothing mode, in case someone walks by
IS MARIYA...
...MARIYA?
I MEAN...
IF MARIYA IS MARIYA...THEN THE OTHER MARIYA ISN'T MARIYA, AND MARIYA IS STILL MARIYA, RIGHT?
HUH?

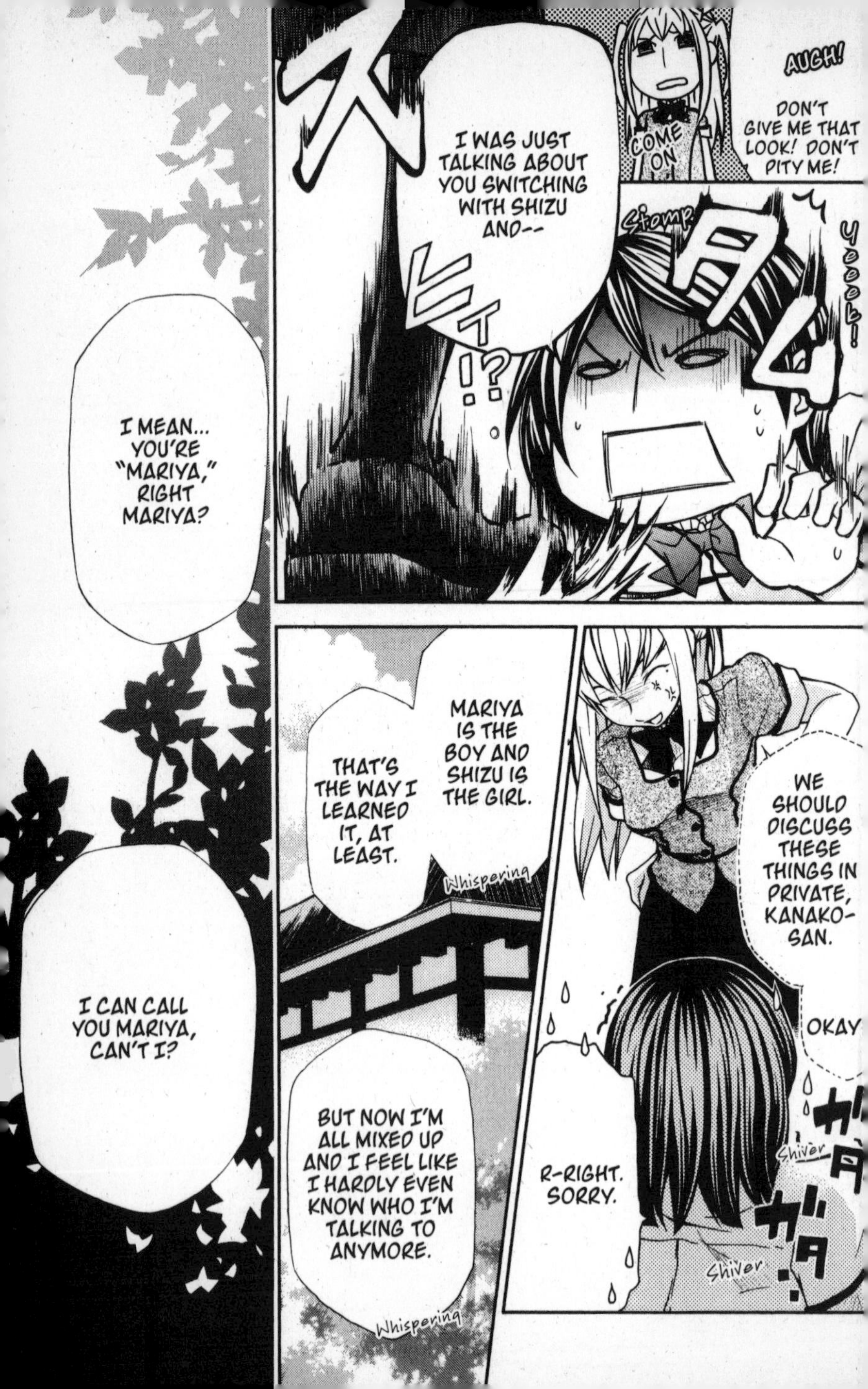
COME ON
AUGH!
DON'T GIVE ME THAT LOOK! DON'T PITY ME!
I WAS JUST TALKING ABOUT YOU SWITCHING WITH SHIZU AND--
Stomp
Yeeeek!
!?
WE SHOULD DISCUSS THESE THINGS IN PRIVATE, KANAKO-SAN.
OKAY
Shiver
R-RIGHT. SORRY.
Shiver
MARIYA IS THE BOY AND SHIZU IS THE GIRL.
THAT'S THE WAY I LEARNED IT, AT LEAST.
Whispering
BUT NOW I'M ALL MIXED UP AND I FEEL LIKE I HARDLY EVEN KNOW WHO I'M TALKING TO ANYMORE.
Whispering
I MEAN... YOU'RE "MARIYA," RIGHT MARIYA?
I CAN CALL YOU MARIYA, CAN'T I?

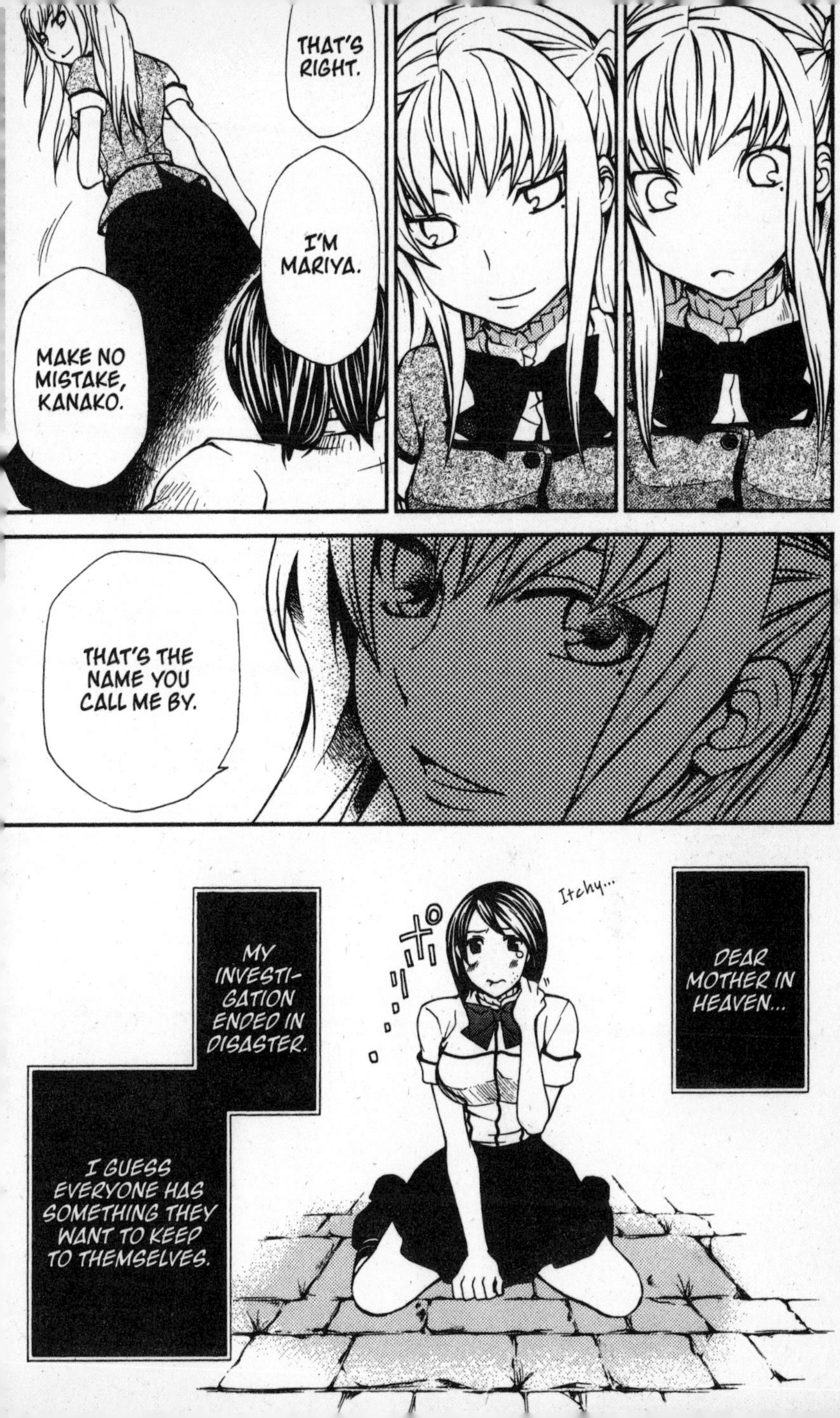
THAT'S RIGHT.
I'M MARIYA.
MAKE NO MISTAKE, KANAKO.
THAT'S THE NAME YOU CALL ME BY.
DEAR MOTHER IN HEAVEN...
Itchy...
MY INVESTIGATION ENDED IN DISASTER.
I GUESS EVERYONE HAS SOMETHING THEY WANT TO KEEP TO THEMSELVES.

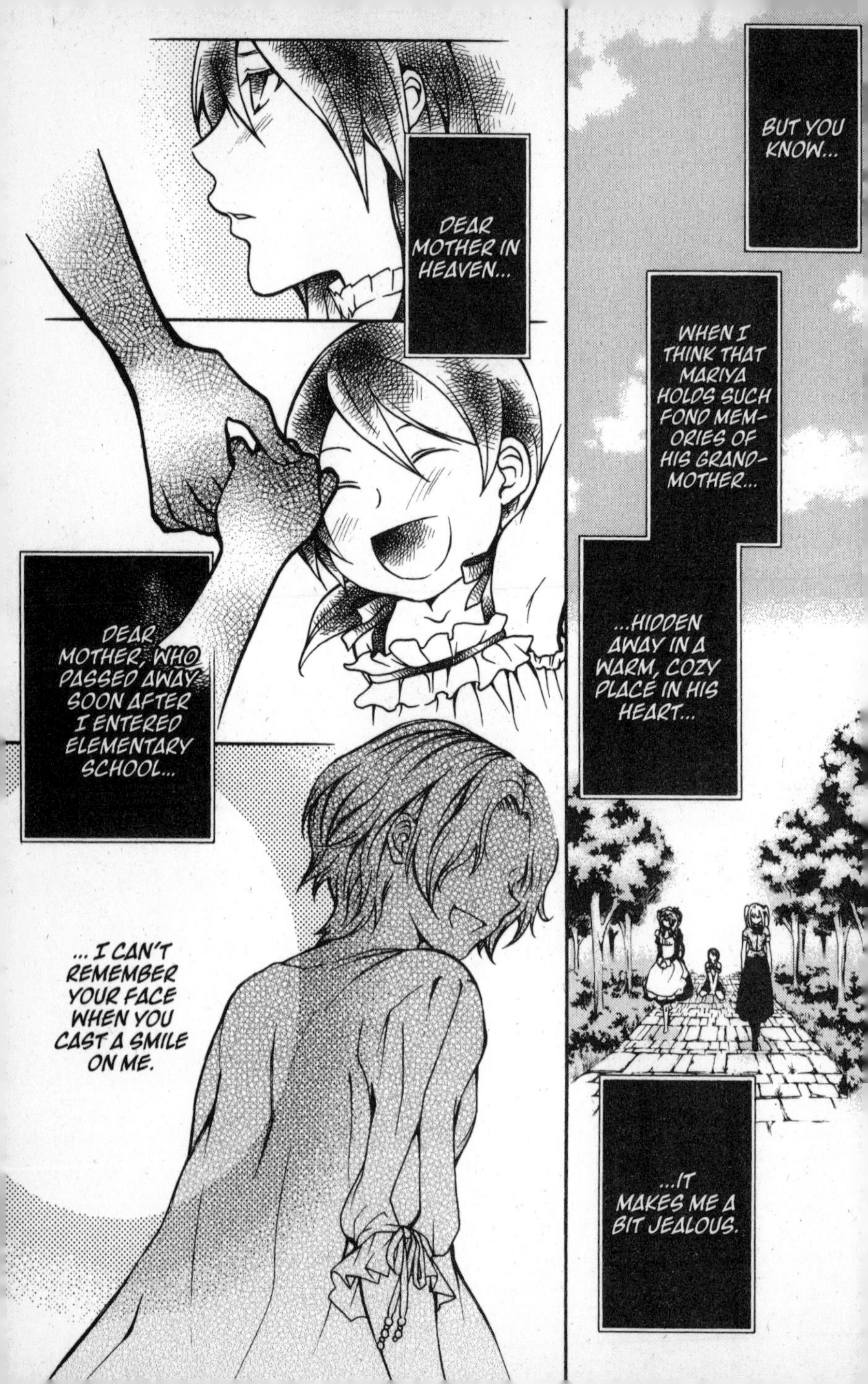
BUT YOU KNOW...
WHEN I THINK THAT MARIYA HOLDS SUCH FOND MEM-ORIES OF HIS GRAND-MOTHER...
...HIDDEN AWAY IN A WARM, COZY PLACE IN HIS HEART...
...IT MAKES ME A BIT JEALOUS.
DEAR MOTHER IN HEAVEN...
DEAR MOTHER, WHO PASSED AWAY SOON AFTER I ENTERED ELEMENTARY SCHOOL...
... I CAN'T REMEMBER YOUR FACE WHEN YOU CAST A SMILE ON ME.

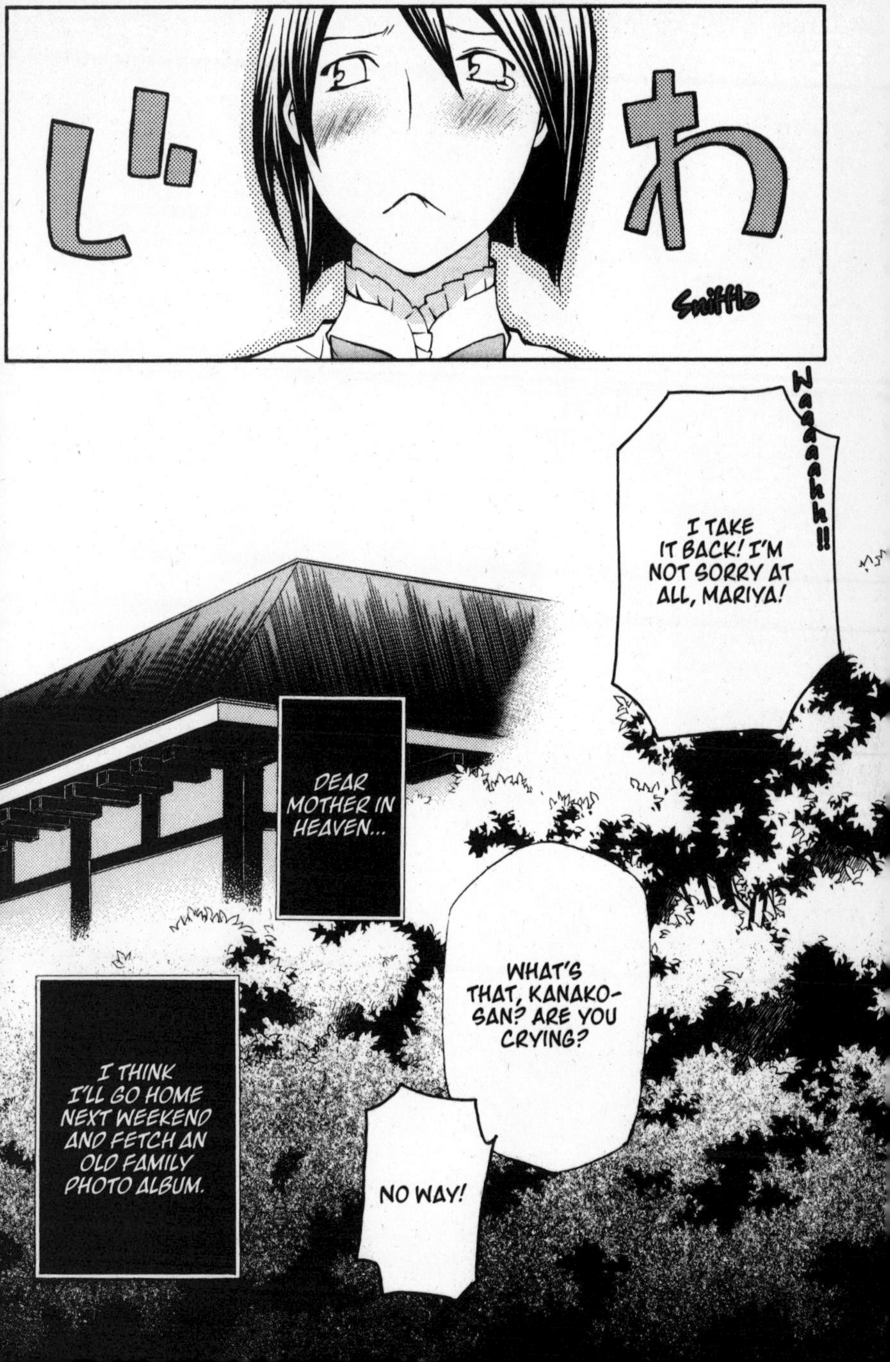
じわ
Sniffle
Waaaaahh!!
I TAKE IT BACK! I'M NOT SORRY AT ALL, MARIYA!
DEAR MOTHER IN HEAVEN...
WHAT'S THAT, KANAKO-SAN? ARE YOU CRYING?
NO WAY!
I THINK I'LL GO HOME NEXT WEEKEND AND FETCH AN OLD FAMILY PHOTO ALBUM.

M A R I A H O L I C

Maria Holic

M A R I A H O L I C

Maria Holic

Prayer 22
The Tale of the Sunday Hunt to Entertain Our Guest

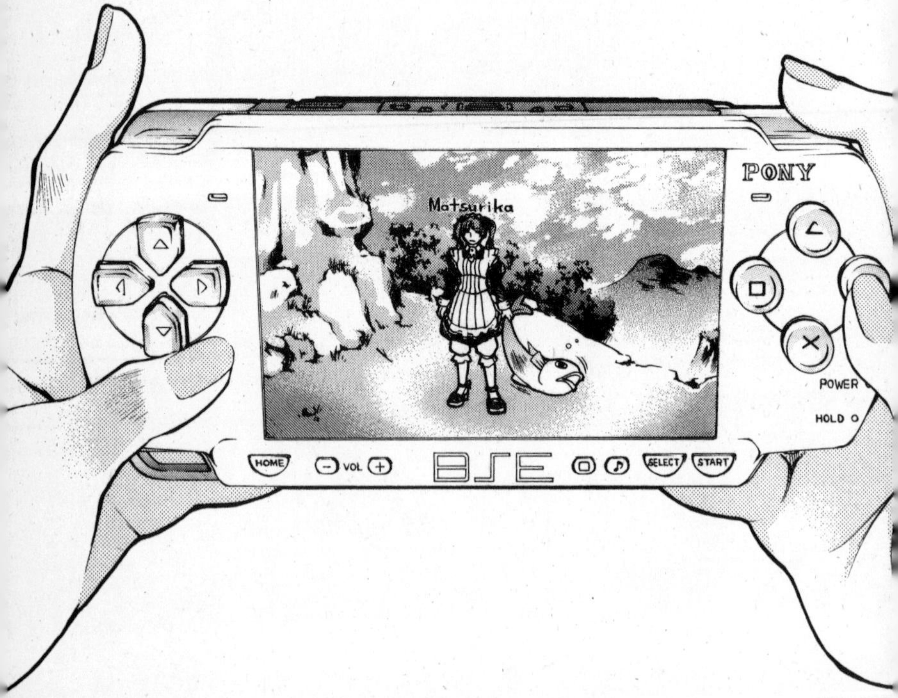

Matsurika
PONY
POWER
HOLD
HOME
VOL.
SELECT
START

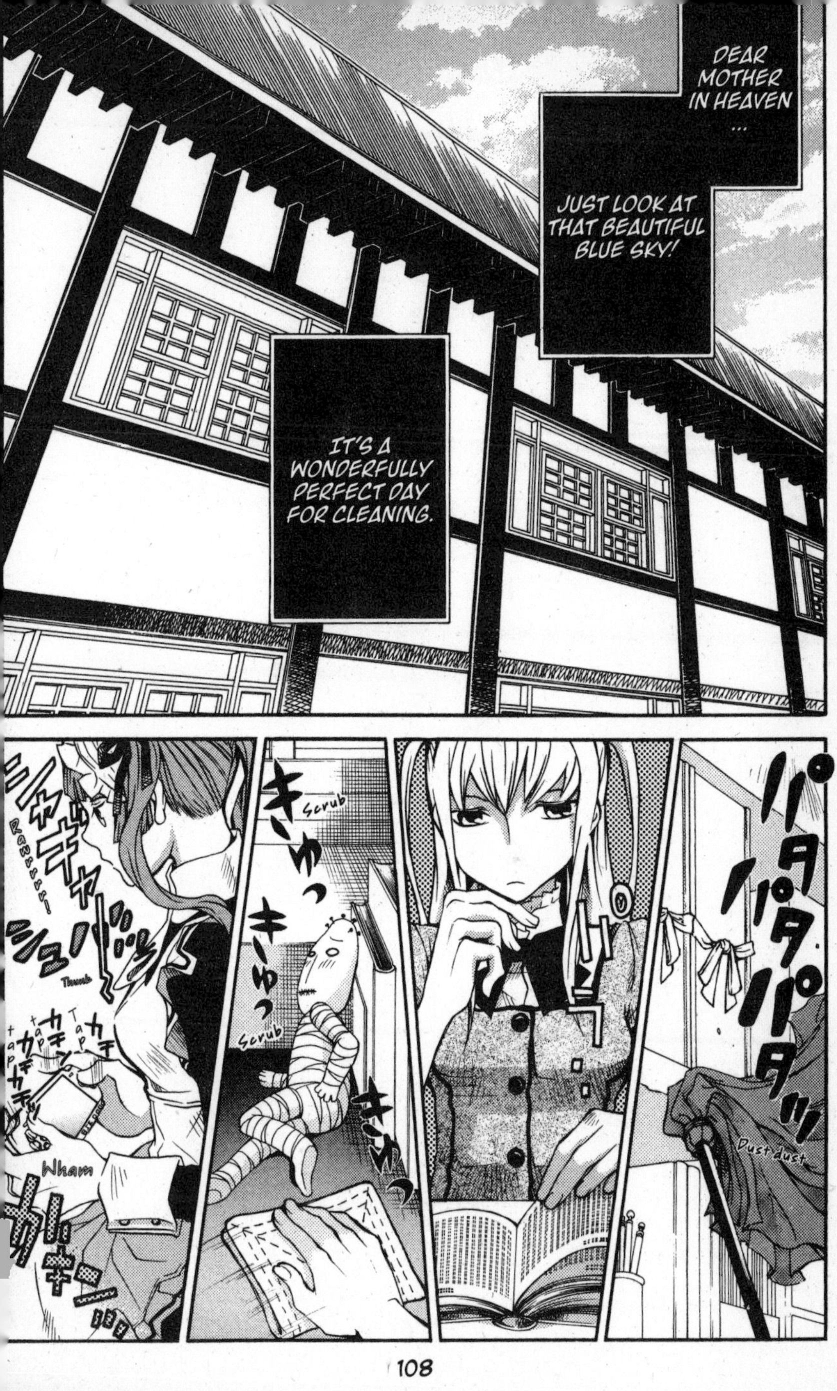
DEAR MOTHER IN HEAVEN ...
JUST LOOK AT THAT BEAUTIFUL BLUE SKY!
IT'S A WONDERFULLY PERFECT DAY FOR CLEANING.
Dust dust
Scrub
Scrub
Rawrrrrr!
Thunk
tap tap
Tap
tap
Wham

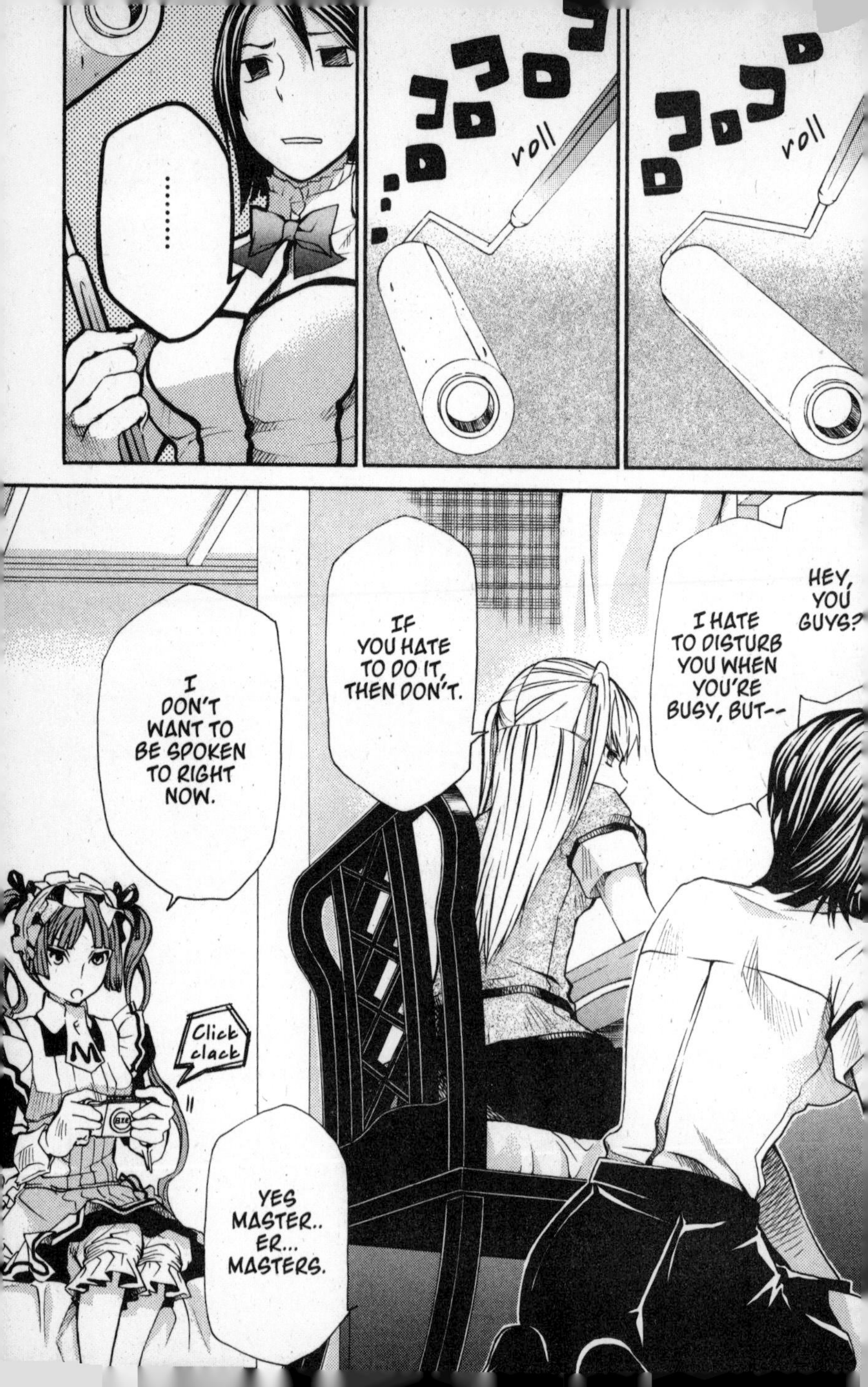
roll
roll
......
HEY, YOU GUYS?
I HATE TO DISTURB YOU WHEN YOU'RE BUSY, BUT--
IF YOU HATE TO DO IT, THEN DON'T.
I DON'T WANT TO BE SPOKEN TO RIGHT NOW.
Click clack
YES MASTER.. ER... MASTERS.

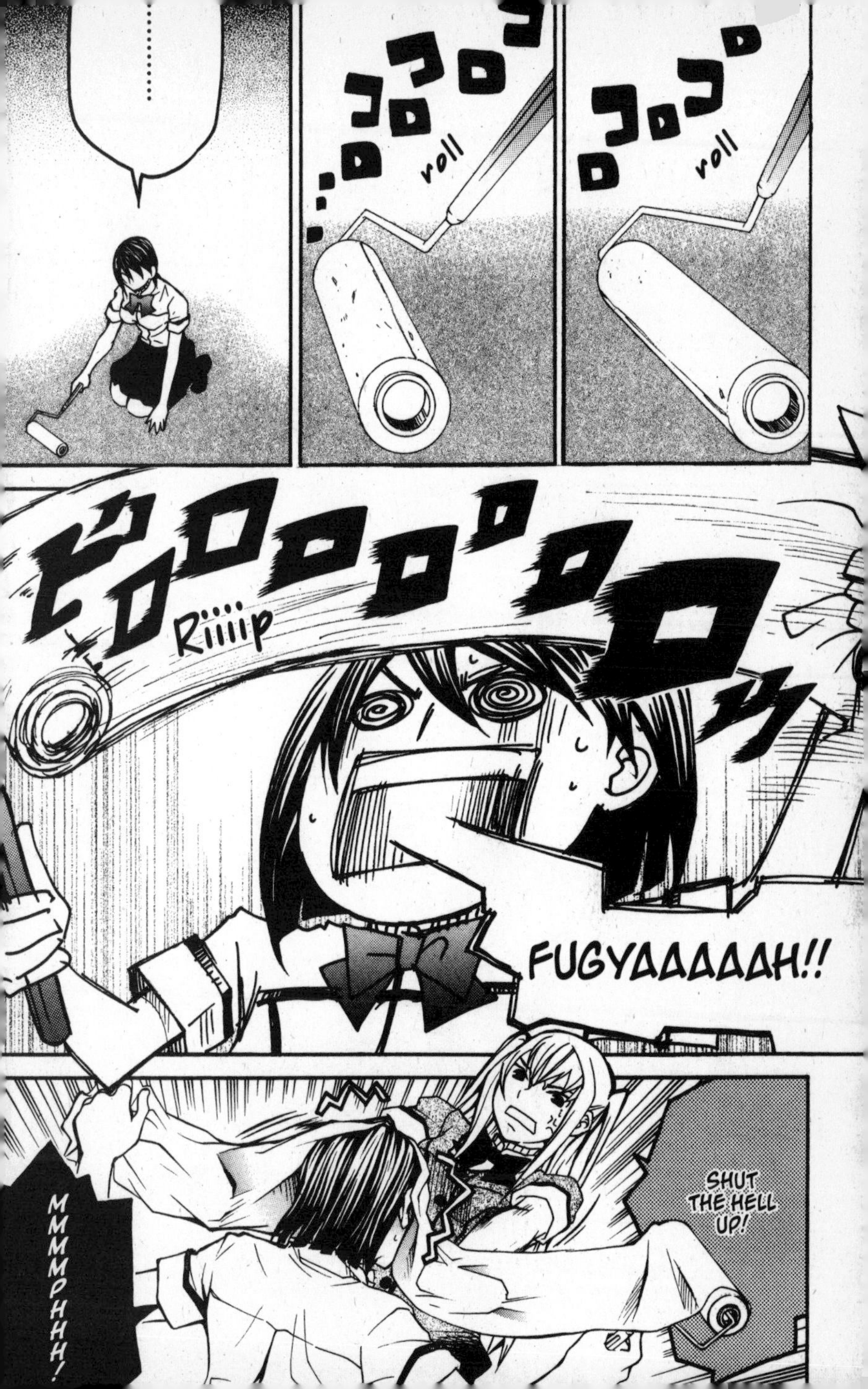

roll
roll
......
Riiiip
FUGYAAAAAH!!
SHUT THE HELL UP!
MMMMPHHH!

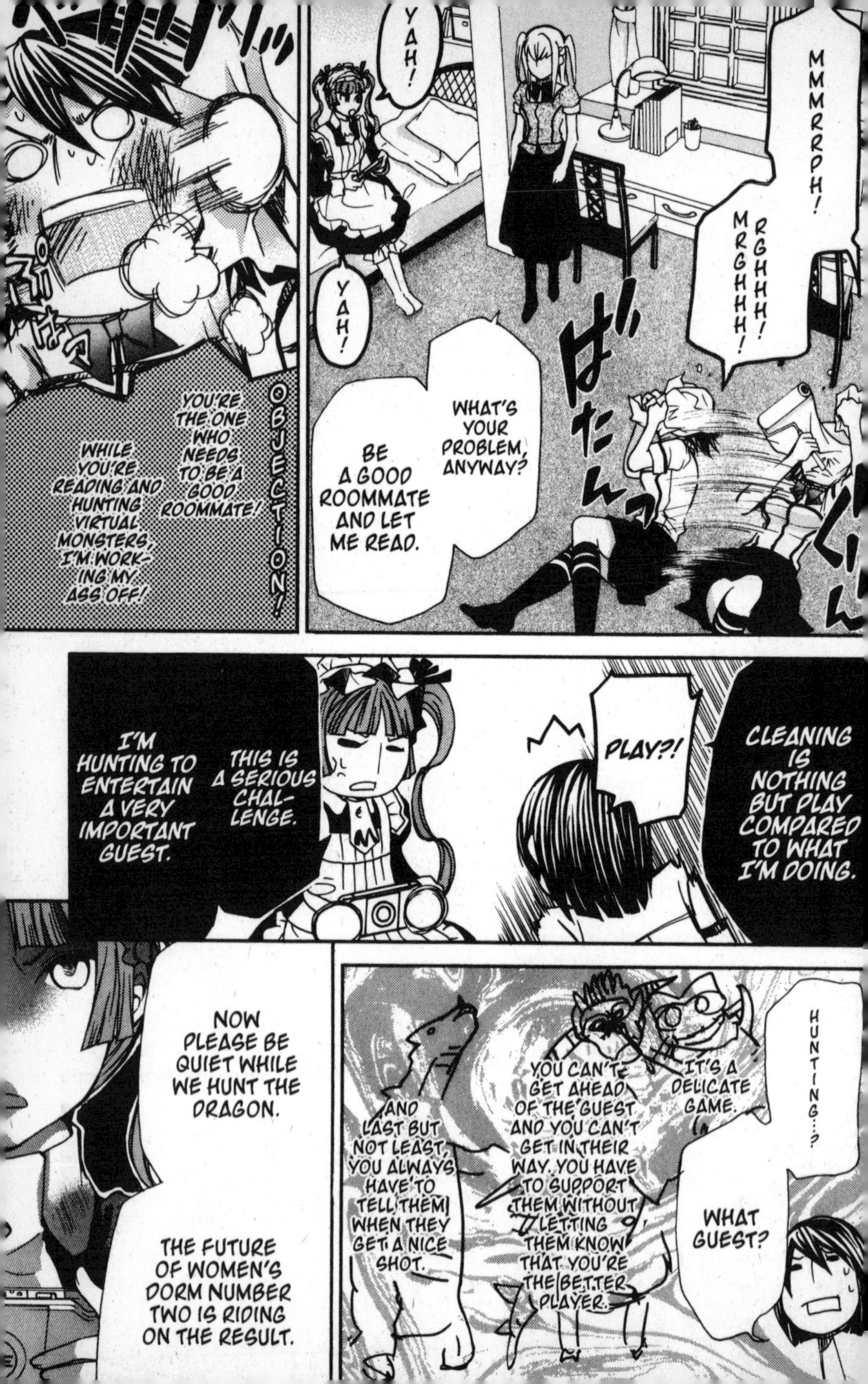
MMMRRPH!
RGHHH! MRGHHH!
YAH!
YAH!
WHAT'S YOUR PROBLEM, ANYWAY?
BE A GOOD ROOMMATE AND LET ME READ.
OBJECTION!
YOU'RE THE ONE WHO NEEDS TO BE A GOOD ROOMMATE!
WHILE YOU'RE READING AND HUNTING VIRTUAL MONSTERS, I'M WORKING MY ASS OFF!
CLEANING IS NOTHING BUT PLAY COMPARED TO WHAT I'M DOING.
PLAY?!
THIS IS A SERIOUS CHALLENGE.
I'M HUNTING TO ENTERTAIN A VERY IMPORTANT GUEST.
HUNTING...?
WHAT GUEST?
IT'S A DELICATE GAME.
YOU CAN'T GET AHEAD OF THE GUEST AND YOU CAN'T GET IN THEIR WAY. YOU HAVE TO SUPPORT THEM WITHOUT LETTING THEM KNOW THAT YOU'RE THE BETTER PLAYER.
AND LAST BUT NOT LEAST, YOU ALWAYS HAVE TO TELL THEM WHEN THEY GET A NICE SHOT.
NOW PLEASE BE QUIET WHILE WE HUNT THE DRAGON.
THE FUTURE OF WOMEN'S DORM NUMBER TWO IS RIDING ON THE RESULT.

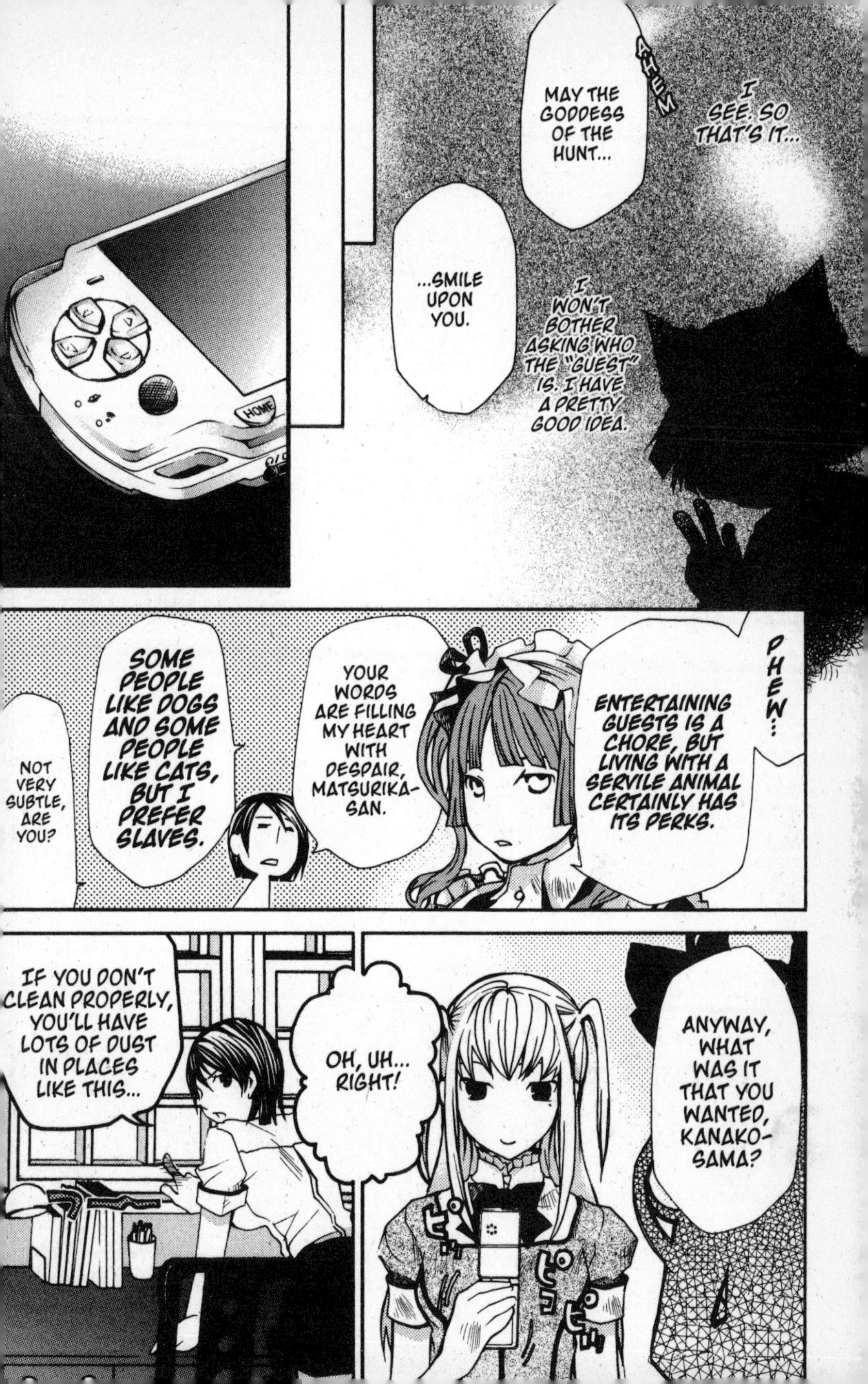
I SEE. SO THAT'S IT...
AHEM
MAY THE GODDESS OF THE HUNT...
...SMILE UPON YOU.
I WON'T BOTHER ASKING WHO THE "GUEST" IS. I HAVE A PRETTY GOOD IDEA.
PHEW...
ENTERTAINING GUESTS IS A CHORE, BUT LIVING WITH A SERVILE ANIMAL CERTAINLY HAS ITS PERKS.
YOUR WORDS ARE FILLING MY HEART WITH DESPAIR, MATSURIKA-SAN.
SOME PEOPLE LIKE DOGS AND SOME PEOPLE LIKE CATS, BUT I PREFER SLAVES.
NOT VERY SUBTLE, ARE YOU?
ANYWAY, WHAT WAS IT THAT YOU WANTED, KANAKO-SAMA?
OH, UH... RIGHT!
IF YOU DON'T CLEAN PROPERLY, YOU'LL HAVE LOTS OF DUST IN PLACES LIKE THIS...

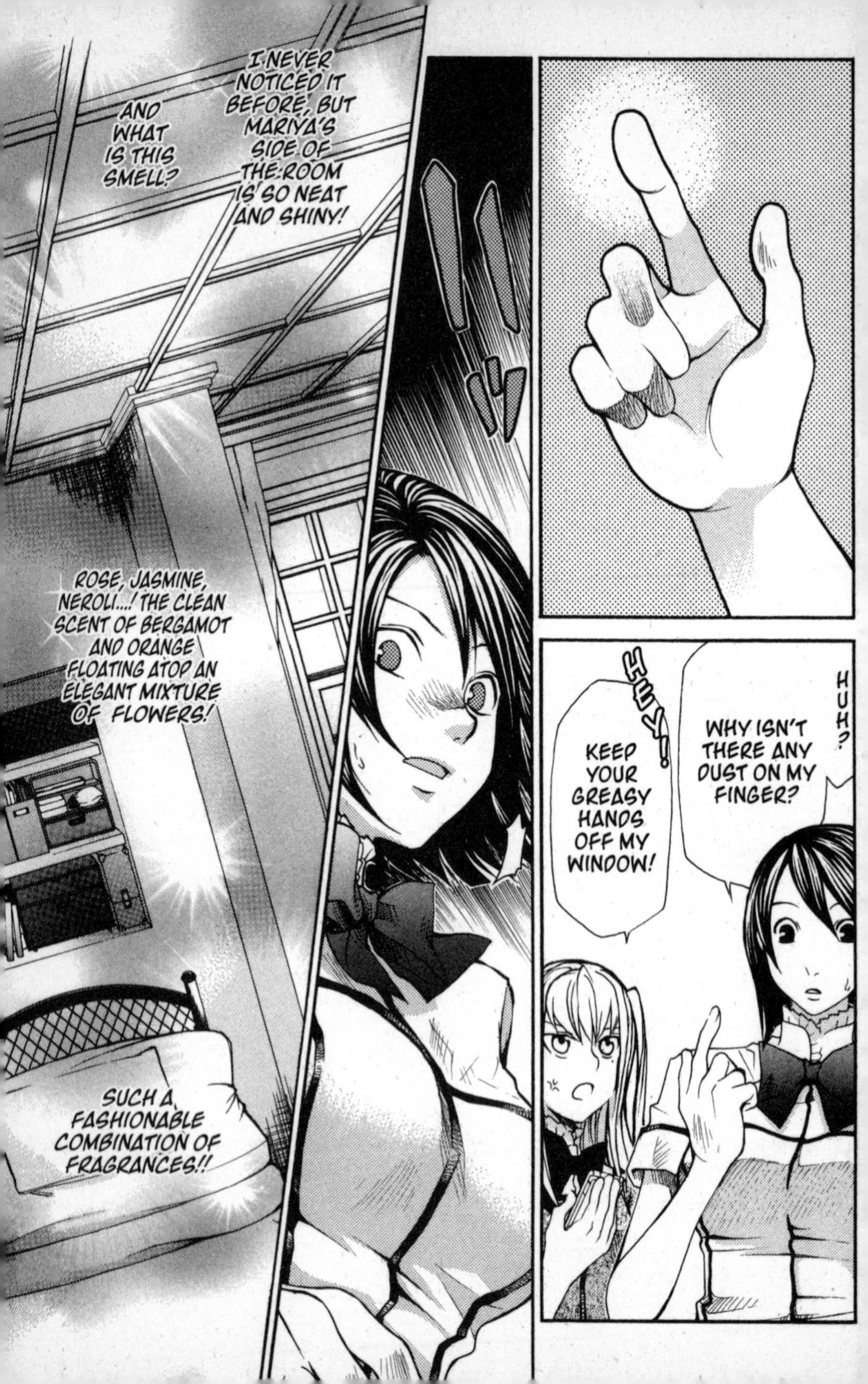
HUH?
WHY ISN'T THERE ANY DUST ON MY FINGER?
HEY!
KEEP YOUR GREASY HANDS OFF MY WINDOW!
I NEVER NOTICED IT BEFORE, BUT MARIYA'S SIDE OF THE ROOM IS SO NEAT AND SHINY!
AND WHAT IS THIS SMELL?
ROSE, JASMINE, NEROLI...! THE CLEAN SCENT OF BERGAMOT AND ORANGE FLOATING ATOP AN ELEGANT MIXTURE OF FLOWERS!
SUCH A FASHIONABLE COMBINATION OF FRAGRANCES!!

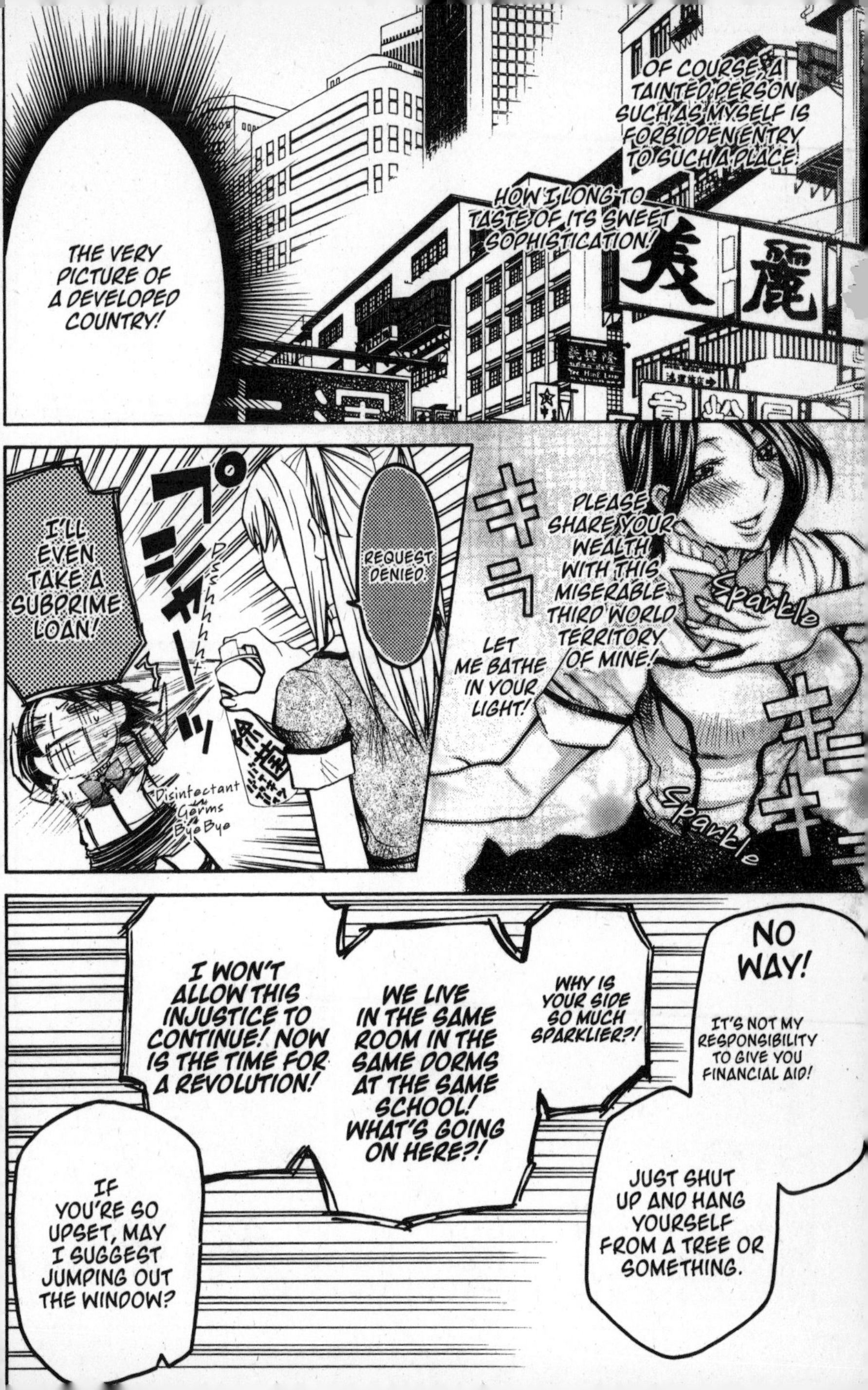
OF COURSE A TAINTED PERSON SUCH AS MYSELF IS FORBIDDEN ENTRY TO SUCH A PLACE.
HOW I LONG TO TASTE OF ITS SWEET SOPHISTICATION!
美麗
THE VERY PICTURE OF A DEVELOPED COUNTRY!
キラ
PLEASE SHARE YOUR WEALTH WITH THIS MISERABLE THIRD WORLD TERRITORY OF MINE!
LET ME BATHE IN YOUR LIGHT!
Sparkle
キラキラ
Sparkle
REQUEST DENIED.
I'LL EVEN TAKE A SUBPRIME LOAN!
プシャーッ
Pshhhhhht
Disinfectant
Germs Bye Bye
NO WAY!
IT'S NOT MY RESPONSIBILITY TO GIVE YOU FINANCIAL AID!
WHY IS YOUR SIDE SO MUCH SPARKLIER?!
WE LIVE IN THE SAME ROOM IN THE SAME DORMS AT THE SAME SCHOOL! WHAT'S GOING ON HERE?!
I WON'T ALLOW THIS INJUSTICE TO CONTINUE! NOW IS THE TIME FOR A REVOLUTION!
JUST SHUT UP AND HANG YOURSELF FROM A TREE OR SOMETHING.
IF YOU'RE SO UPSET, MAY I SUGGEST JUMPING OUT THE WINDOW?

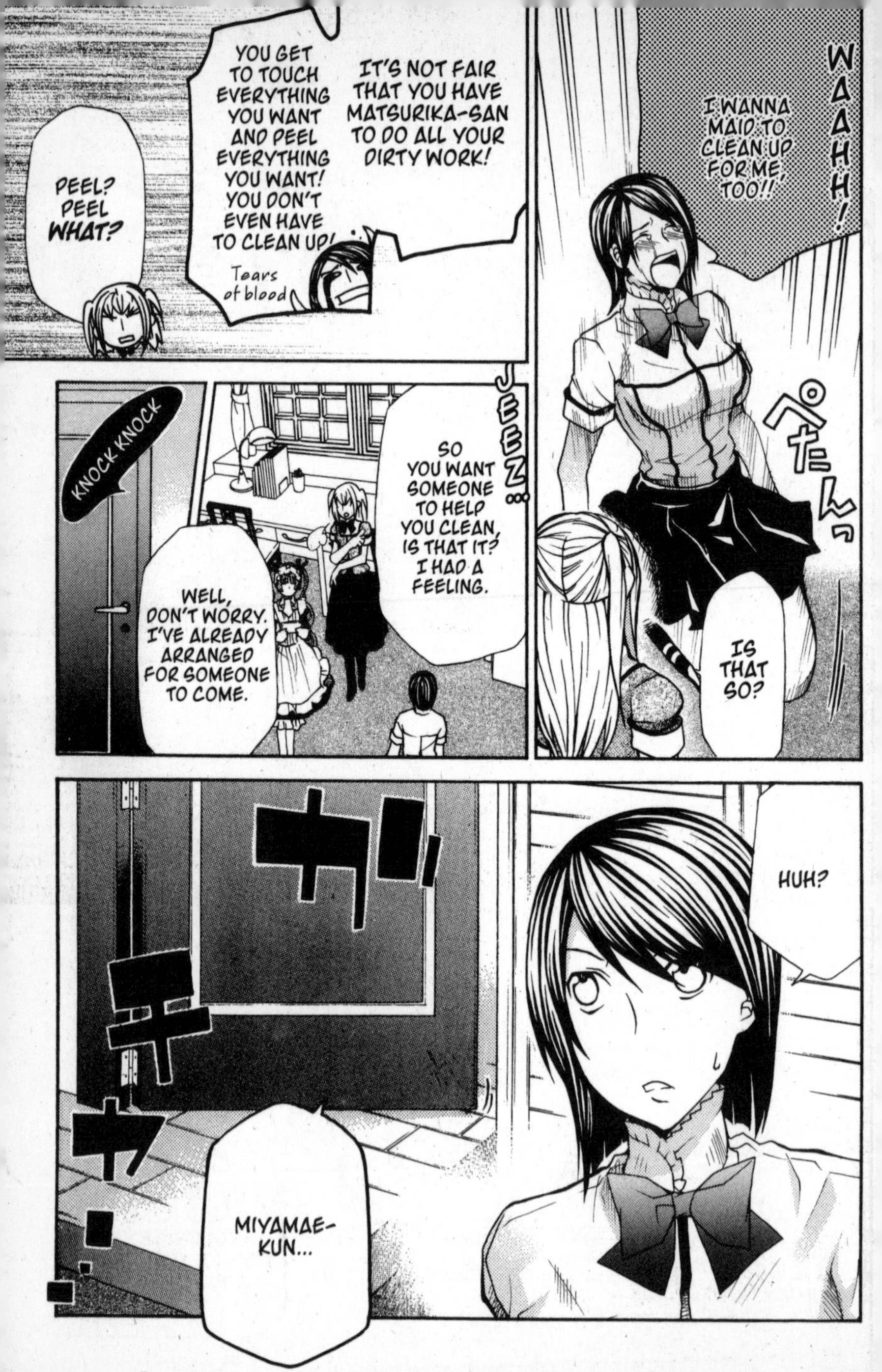
WAAHH!
I WANNA MAID TO CLEAN UP FOR ME, TOO!!
ぺたん
IS THAT SO?
IT'S NOT FAIR THAT YOU HAVE MATSURIKA-SAN TO DO ALL YOUR DIRTY WORK!
YOU GET TO TOUCH EVERYTHING YOU WANT AND PEEL EVERYTHING YOU WANT! YOU DON'T EVEN HAVE TO CLEAN UP!
Tears of blood
PEEL? PEEL WHAT?
JEEZ...
SO YOU WANT SOMEONE TO HELP YOU CLEAN, IS THAT IT? I HAD A FEELING.
WELL, DON'T WORRY. I'VE ALREADY ARRANGED FOR SOMEONE TO COME.
KNOCK KNOCK
HUH?
ガチャッ
MIYAMAE-KUN...

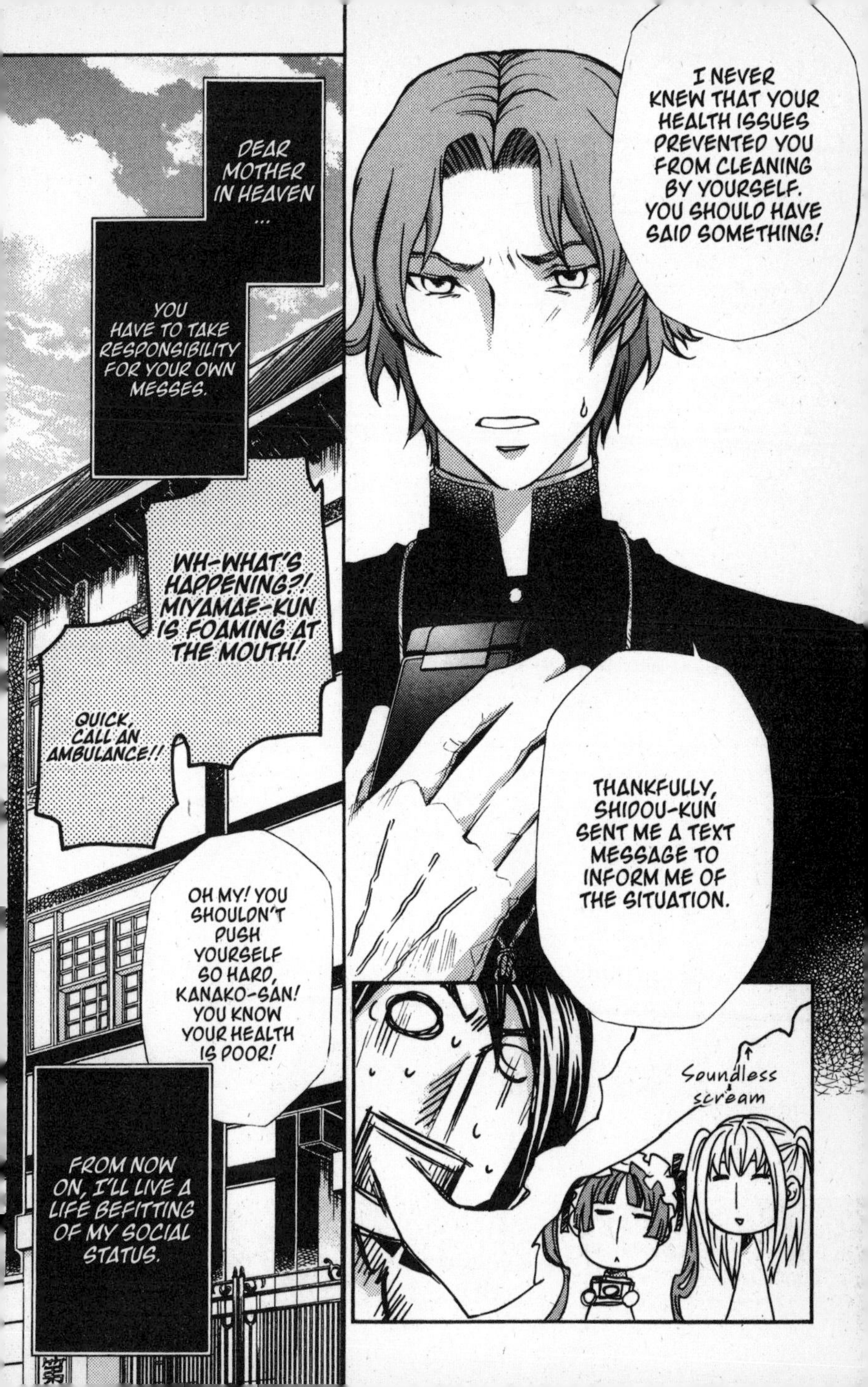
I NEVER KNEW THAT YOUR HEALTH ISSUES PREVENTED YOU FROM CLEANING BY YOURSELF. YOU SHOULD HAVE SAID SOMETHING!
THANKFULLY, SHIDOU-KUN SENT ME A TEXT MESSAGE TO INFORM ME OF THE SITUATION.
Soundless scream
DEAR MOTHER IN HEAVEN ...
YOU HAVE TO TAKE RESPONSIBILITY FOR YOUR OWN MESSES.
WH-WHAT'S HAPPENING?! MIYAMAE-KUN IS FOAMING AT THE MOUTH!
QUICK, CALL AN AMBULANCE!!
OH MY! YOU SHOULDN'T PUSH YOURSELF SO HARD, KANAKO-SAN! YOU KNOW YOUR HEALTH IS POOR!
FROM NOW ON, I'LL LIVE A LIFE BEFITTING OF MY SOCIAL STATUS.

MARIAHOLIC

Maria✝Holic

Maria✝Holic

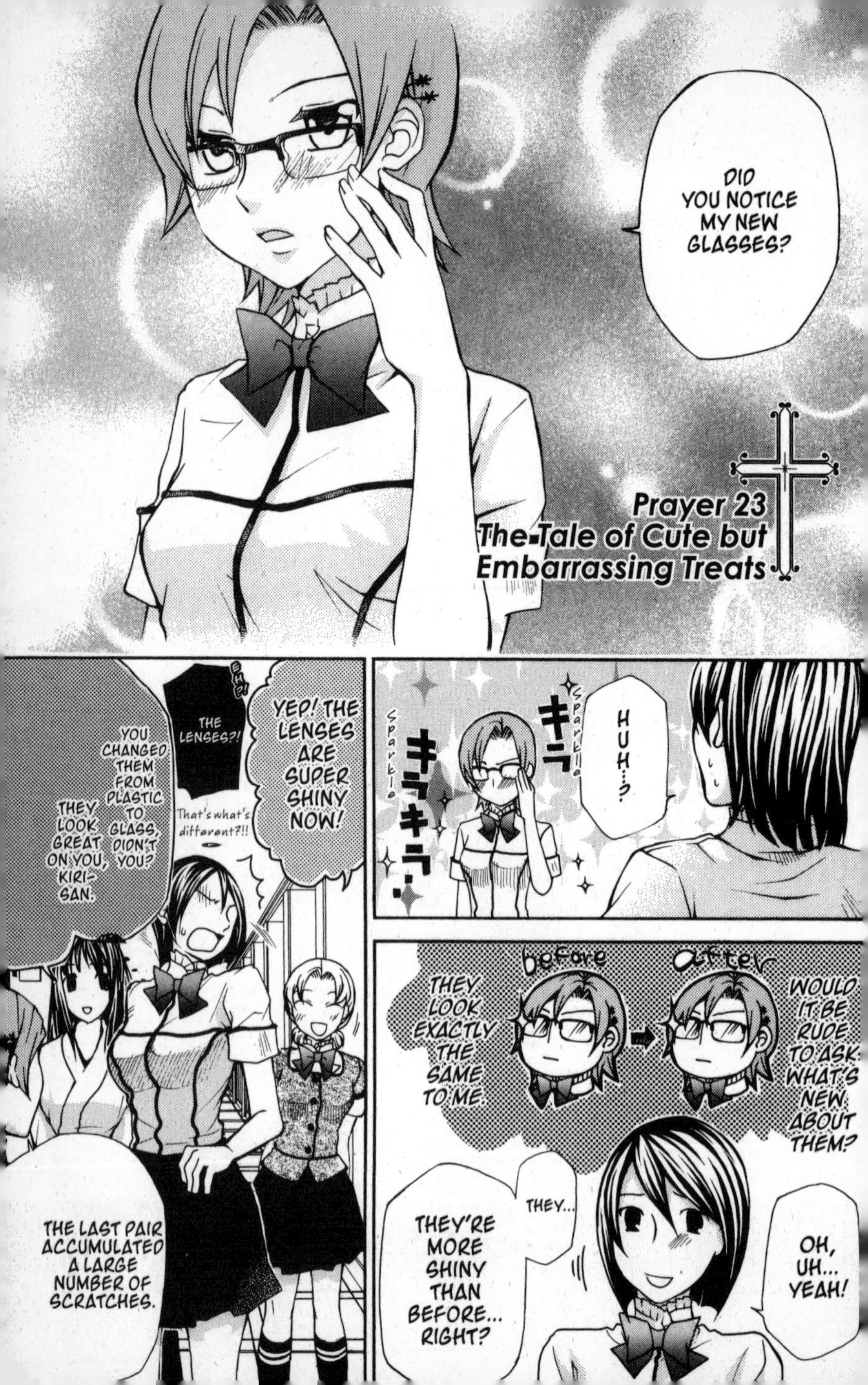
DID YOU NOTICE MY NEW GLASSES?
Prayer 23
The Tale of Cute but Embarrassing Treats
HUH...?
Sparkle
キラ
キラキラ
Sparkle
WOULD IT BE RUDE TO ASK WHAT'S NEW ABOUT THEM?
after
before
THEY LOOK EXACTLY THE SAME TO ME.
OH, UH... YEAH!
THEY...
THEY'RE MORE SHINY THAN BEFORE... RIGHT?
YEP! THE LENSES ARE SUPER SHINY NOW!
EH?!
THE LENSES?!
That's what's different?!!
YOU CHANGED THEM FROM PLASTIC TO GLASS, DIDN'T YOU?
THEY LOOK GREAT ON YOU, KIRI-SAN.
THE LAST PAIR ACCUMULATED A LARGE NUMBER OF SCRATCHES.

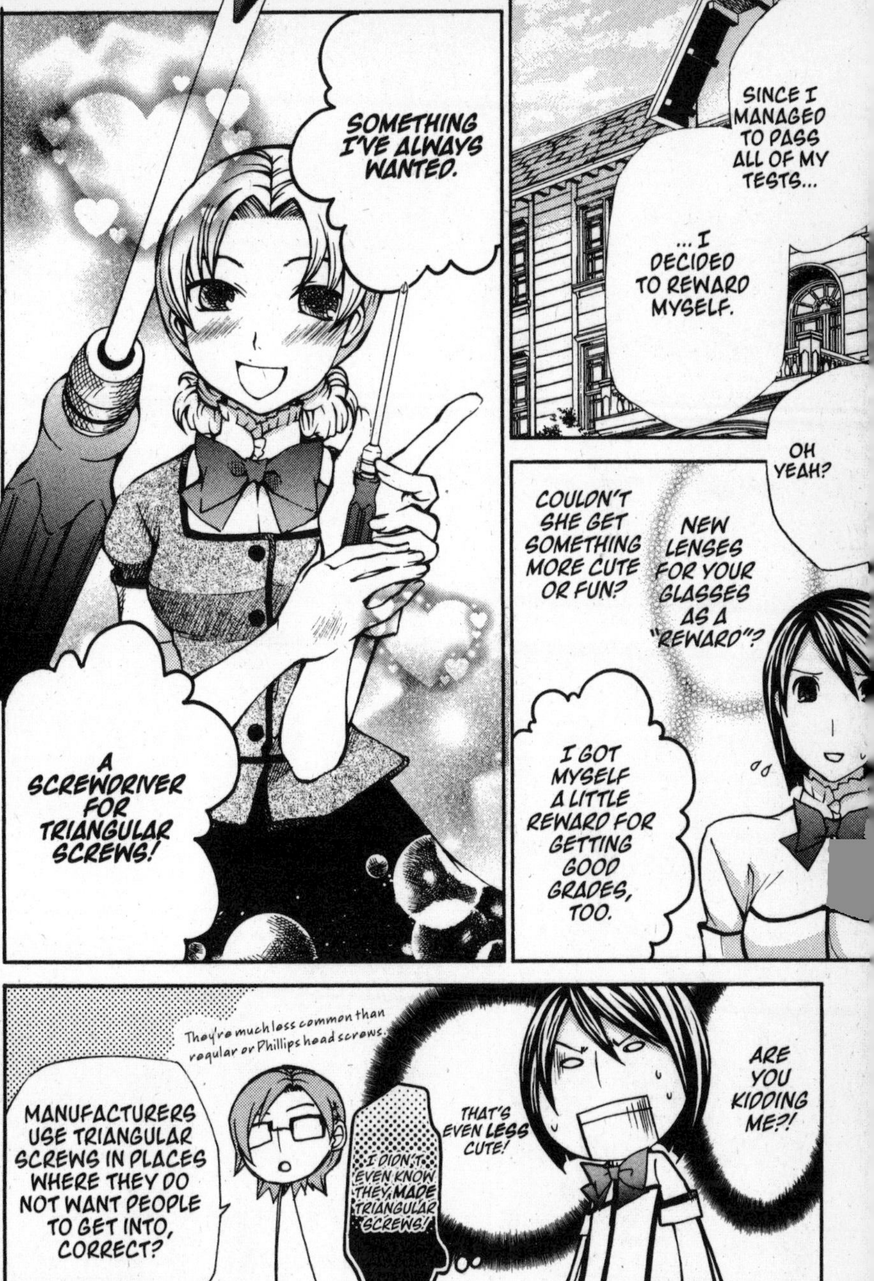
SINCE I MANAGED TO PASS ALL OF MY TESTS...
... I DECIDED TO REWARD MYSELF.
OH YEAH?
I GOT MYSELF A LITTLE REWARD FOR GETTING GOOD GRADES, TOO.
NEW LENSES FOR YOUR GLASSES AS A "REWARD"?
COULON'T SHE GET SOMETHING MORE CUTE OR FUN?
SOMETHING I'VE ALWAYS WANTED.
A SCREWDRIVER FOR TRIANGULAR SCREWS!
ARE YOU KIDDING ME?!
THAT'S EVEN LESS CUTE!
I DIDN'T EVEN KNOW THEY MADE TRIANGULAR SCREWS!
They're much less common than regular or Phillips head screws.
MANUFACTURERS USE TRIANGULAR SCREWS IN PLACES WHERE THEY DO NOT WANT PEOPLE TO GET INTO, CORRECT?

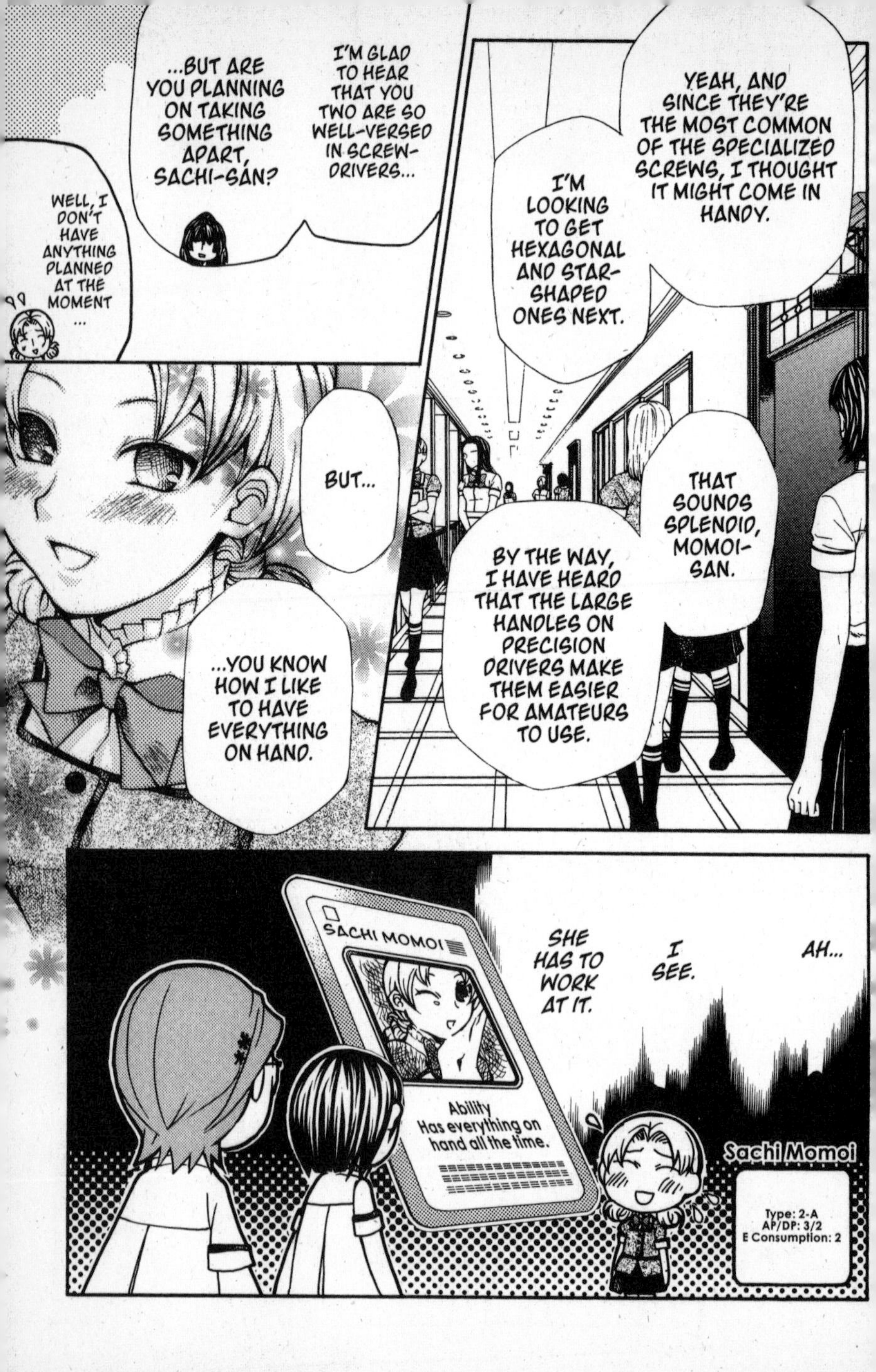
YEAH, AND SINCE THEY'RE THE MOST COMMON OF THE SPECIALIZED SCREWS, I THOUGHT IT MIGHT COME IN HANDY.
I'M LOOKING TO GET HEXAGONAL AND STAR-SHAPED ONES NEXT.
THAT SOUNDS SPLENDID, MOMOI-SAN.
BY THE WAY, I HAVE HEARD THAT THE LARGE HANDLES ON PRECISION DRIVERS MAKE THEM EASIER FOR AMATEURS TO USE.
I'M GLAD TO HEAR THAT YOU TWO ARE SO WELL-VERSED IN SCREW-DRIVERS...
...BUT ARE YOU PLANNING ON TAKING SOMETHING APART, SACHI-SAN?
WELL, I DON'T HAVE ANYTHING PLANNED AT THE MOMENT ...
BUT...
...YOU KNOW HOW I LIKE TO HAVE EVERYTHING ON HAND.
AH...
I SEE.
SHE HAS TO WORK AT IT.
SACHI MOMOI
Ability
Has everything on hand all the time.
Sachi Momoi
Type: 2-A
AP/DP: 3/2
E Consumption: 2

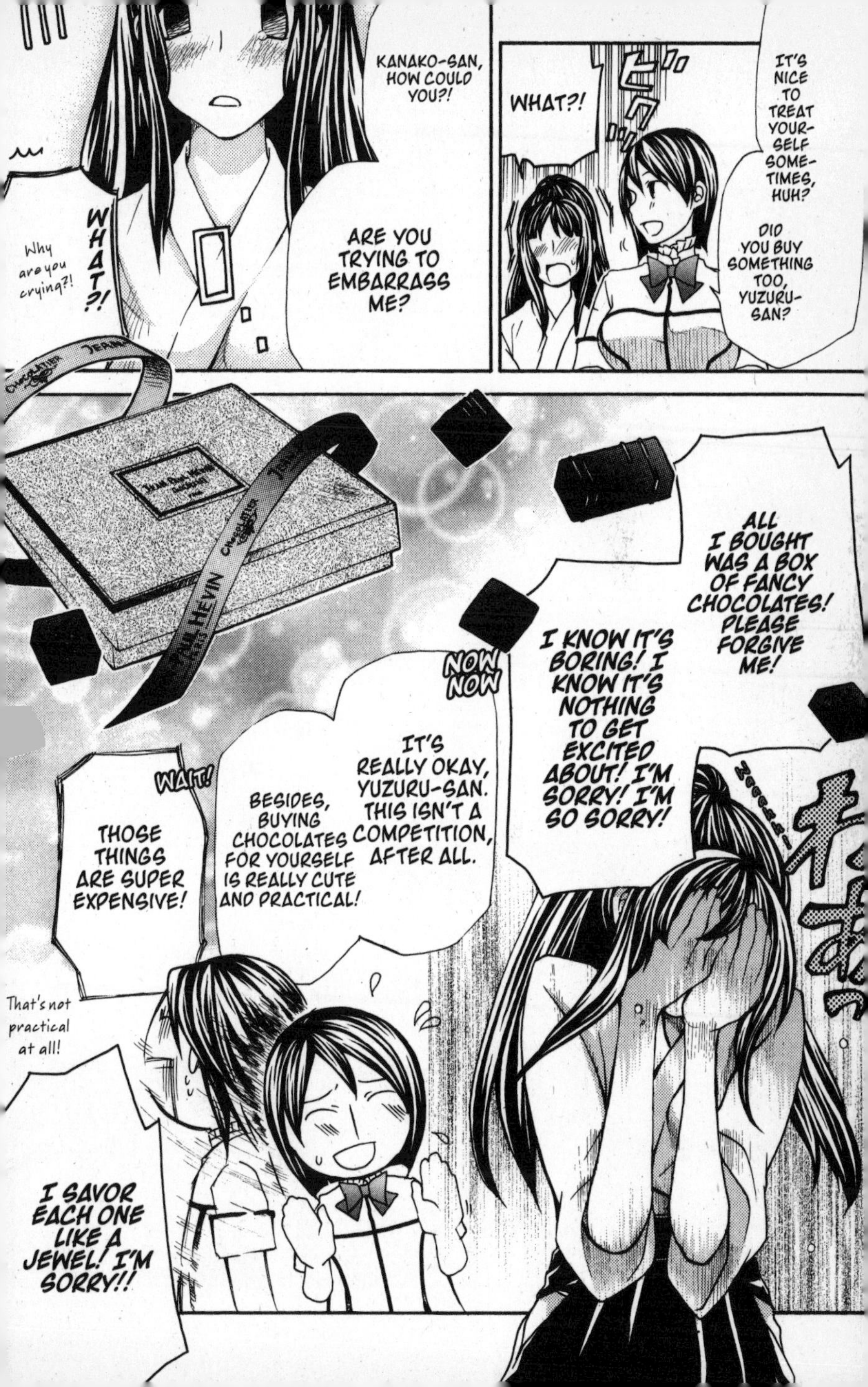
IT'S NICE TO TREAT YOURSELF SOMETIMES, HUH?
DID YOU BUY SOMETHING TOO, YUZURU-SAN?
WHAT?!
KANAKO-SAN, HOW COULD YOU?!
ARE YOU TRYING TO EMBARRASS ME?
WHAT?!
Why are you crying?!
ALL I BOUGHT WAS A BOX OF FANCY CHOCOLATES! PLEASE FORGIVE ME!
I KNOW IT'S BORING! I KNOW IT'S NOTHING TO GET EXCITED ABOUT! I'M SORRY! I'M SO SORRY!
NOW NOW
IT'S REALLY OKAY, YUZURU-SAN. THIS ISN'T A COMPETITION, AFTER ALL.
BESIDES, BUYING CHOCOLATES FOR YOURSELF IS REALLY CUTE AND PRACTICAL!
WAIT!
THOSE THINGS ARE SUPER EXPENSIVE!
That's not practical at all!
I SAVOR EACH ONE LIKE A JEWEL! I'M SORRY!!

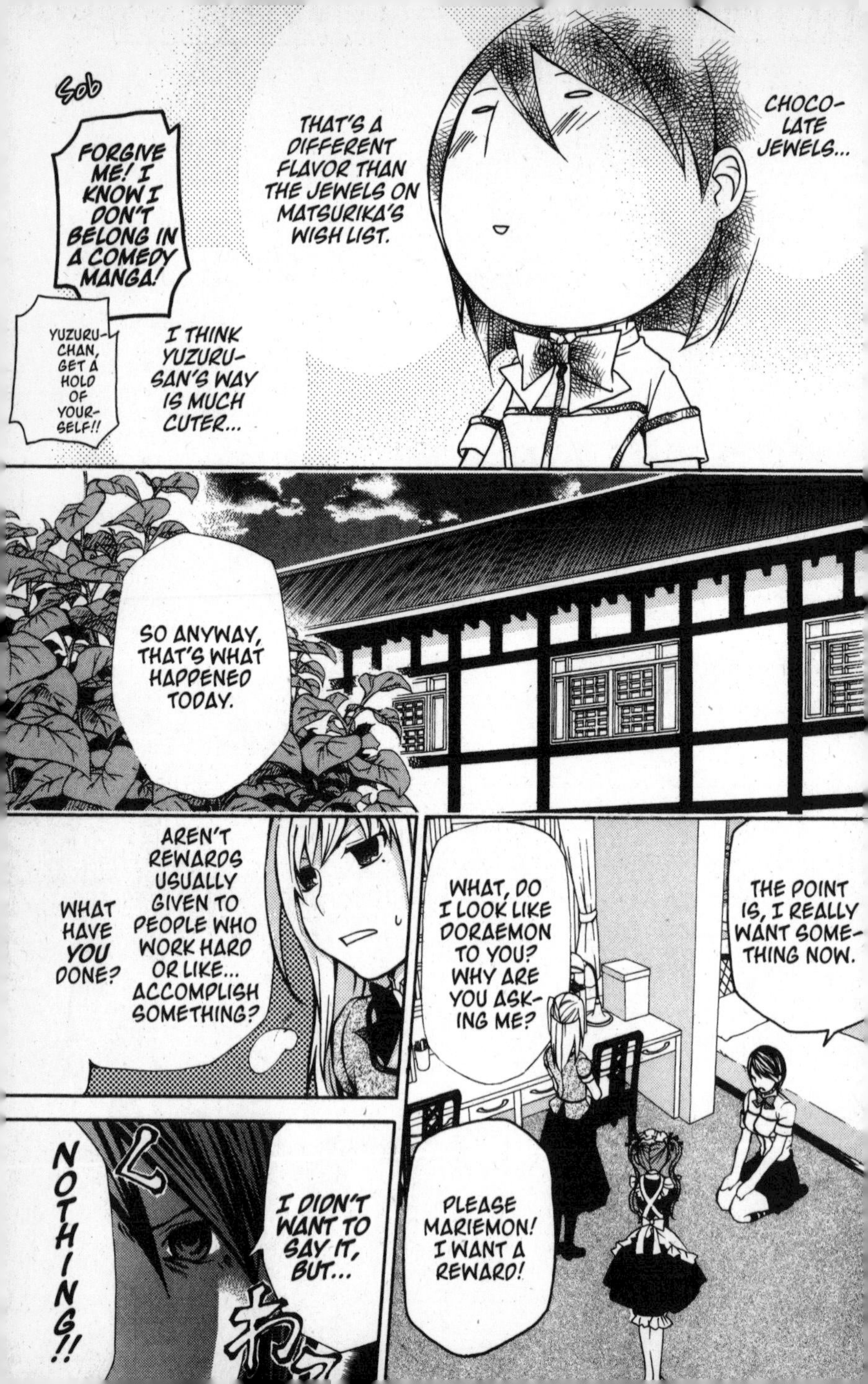
CHOCOLATE JEWELS...
THAT'S A DIFFERENT FLAVOR THAN THE JEWELS ON MATSURIKA'S WISH LIST.
FORGIVE ME! I KNOW I DON'T BELONG IN A COMEDY MANGA!
Sob
I THINK YUZURU-SAN'S WAY IS MUCH CUTER...
YUZURU-CHAN, GET A HOLD OF YOURSELF!!
SO ANYWAY, THAT'S WHAT HAPPENED TODAY.
THE POINT IS, I REALLY WANT SOMETHING NOW.
WHAT, DO I LOOK LIKE DORAEMON TO YOU? WHY ARE YOU ASKING ME?
PLEASE MARIEMON! I WANT A REWARD!
AREN'T REWARDS USUALLY GIVEN TO PEOPLE WHO WORK HARD OR LIKE... ACCOMPLISH SOMETHING?
WHAT HAVE YOU DONE?
I DIDN'T WANT TO SAY IT, BUT...
NOTHING!!

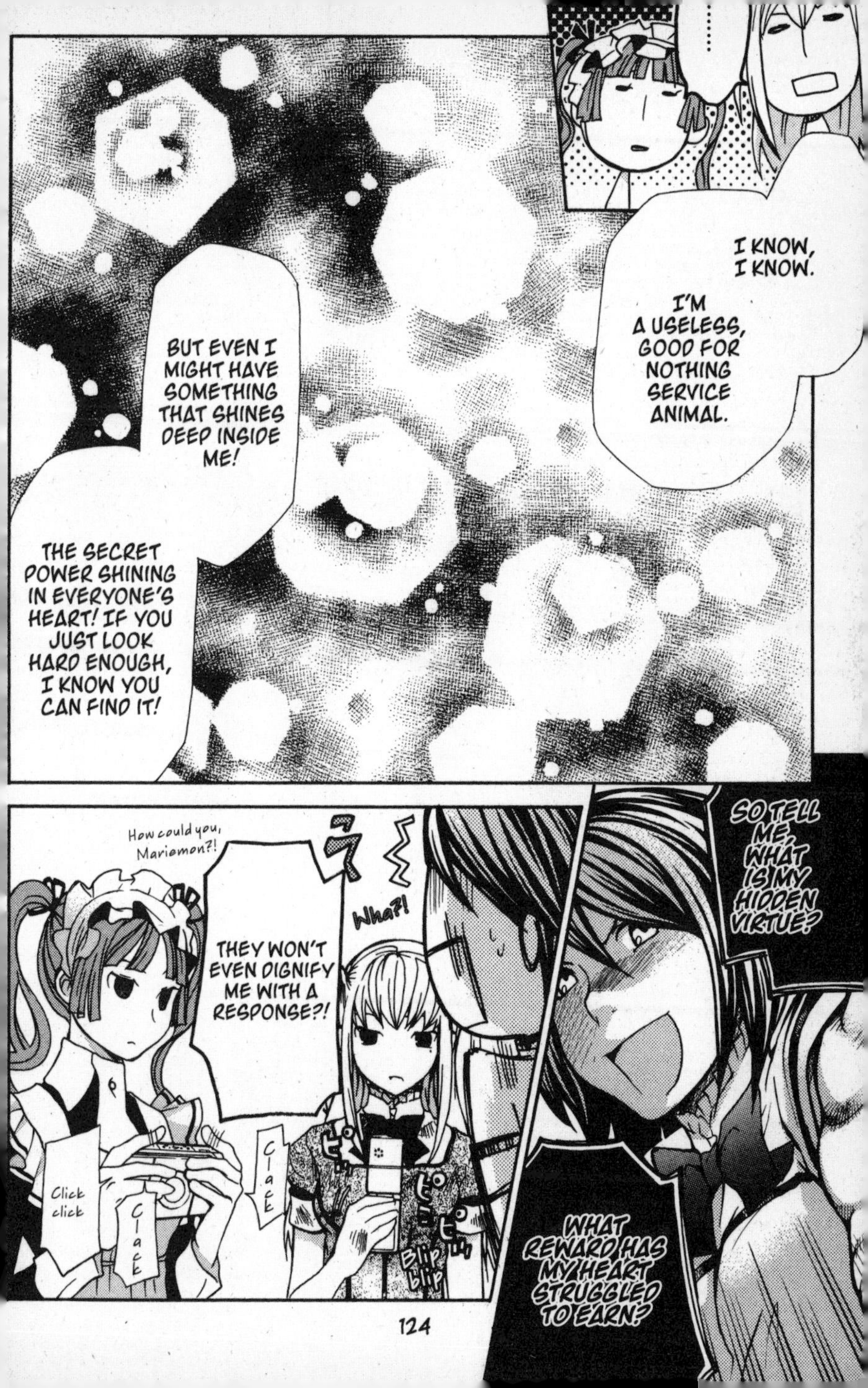
I KNOW, I KNOW.
I'M A USELESS, GOOD FOR NOTHING SERVICE ANIMAL.
BUT EVEN I MIGHT HAVE SOMETHING THAT SHINES DEEP INSIDE ME!
THE SECRET POWER SHINING IN EVERYONE'S HEART! IF YOU JUST LOOK HARD ENOUGH, I KNOW YOU CAN FIND IT!
SO TELL ME, WHAT IS MY HIDDEN VIRTUE?
WHAT REWARD HAS MY HEART STRUGGLED TO EARN?
Wha?!
THEY WON'T EVEN DIGNIFY ME WITH A RESPONSE?!
How could you, Mariemon?!
Clack
Blip blip
Click click
Clack

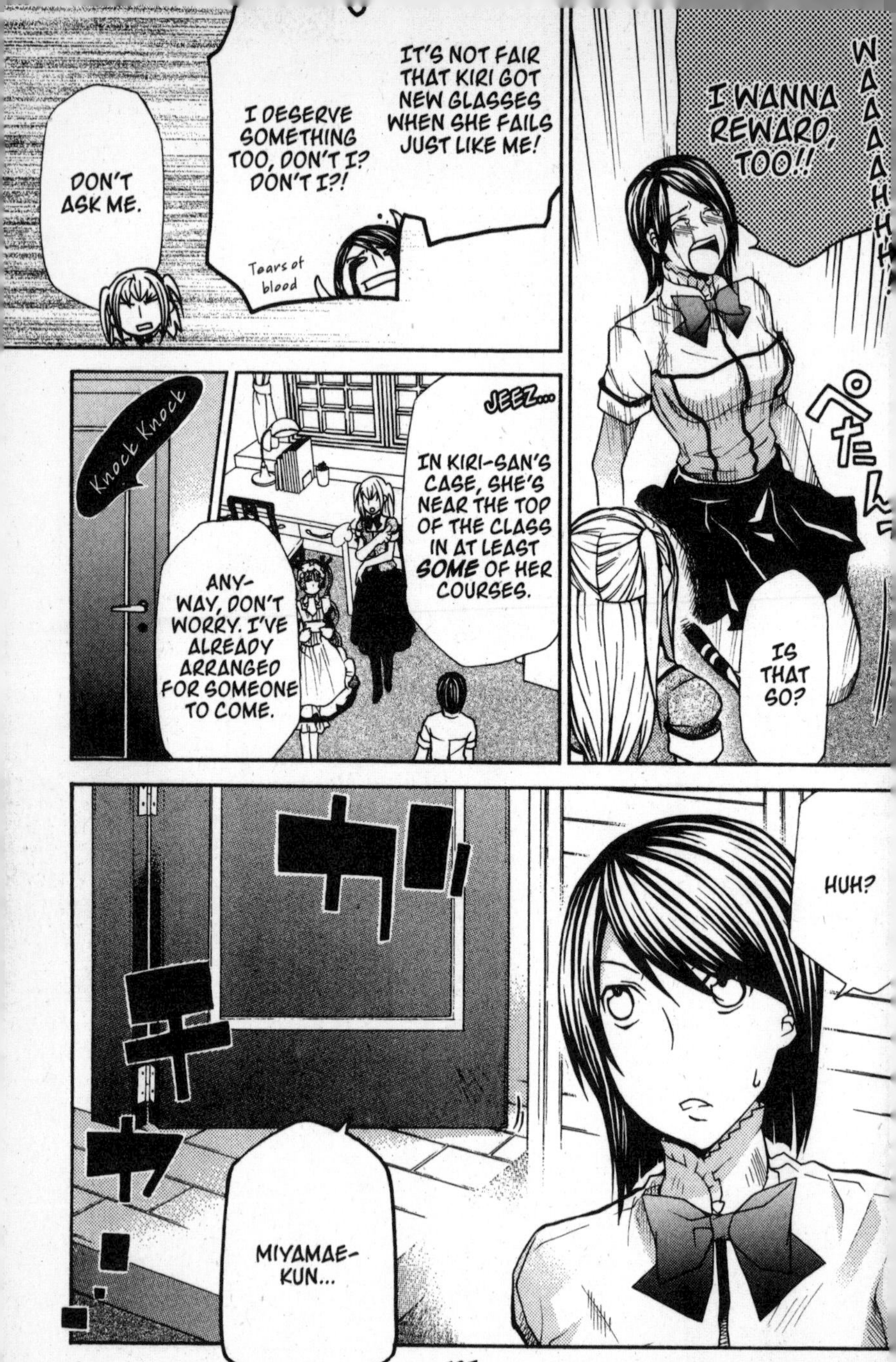
WAAAAAHHH!
I WANNA REWARD, TOO!!
ぺたーん
IS THAT SO?
IT'S NOT FAIR THAT KIRI GOT NEW GLASSES WHEN SHE FAILS JUST LIKE ME!
I DESERVE SOMETHING TOO, DON'T I? DON'T I?!
Tears of blood
DON'T ASK ME.
JEEZ...
IN KIRI-SAN'S CASE, SHE'S NEAR THE TOP OF THE CLASS IN AT LEAST SOME OF HER COURSES.
ANY-WAY, DON'T WORRY. I'VE ALREADY ARRANGED FOR SOMEONE TO COME.
Knock Knock
HUH?
ガチャ
MIYAMAE-KUN...

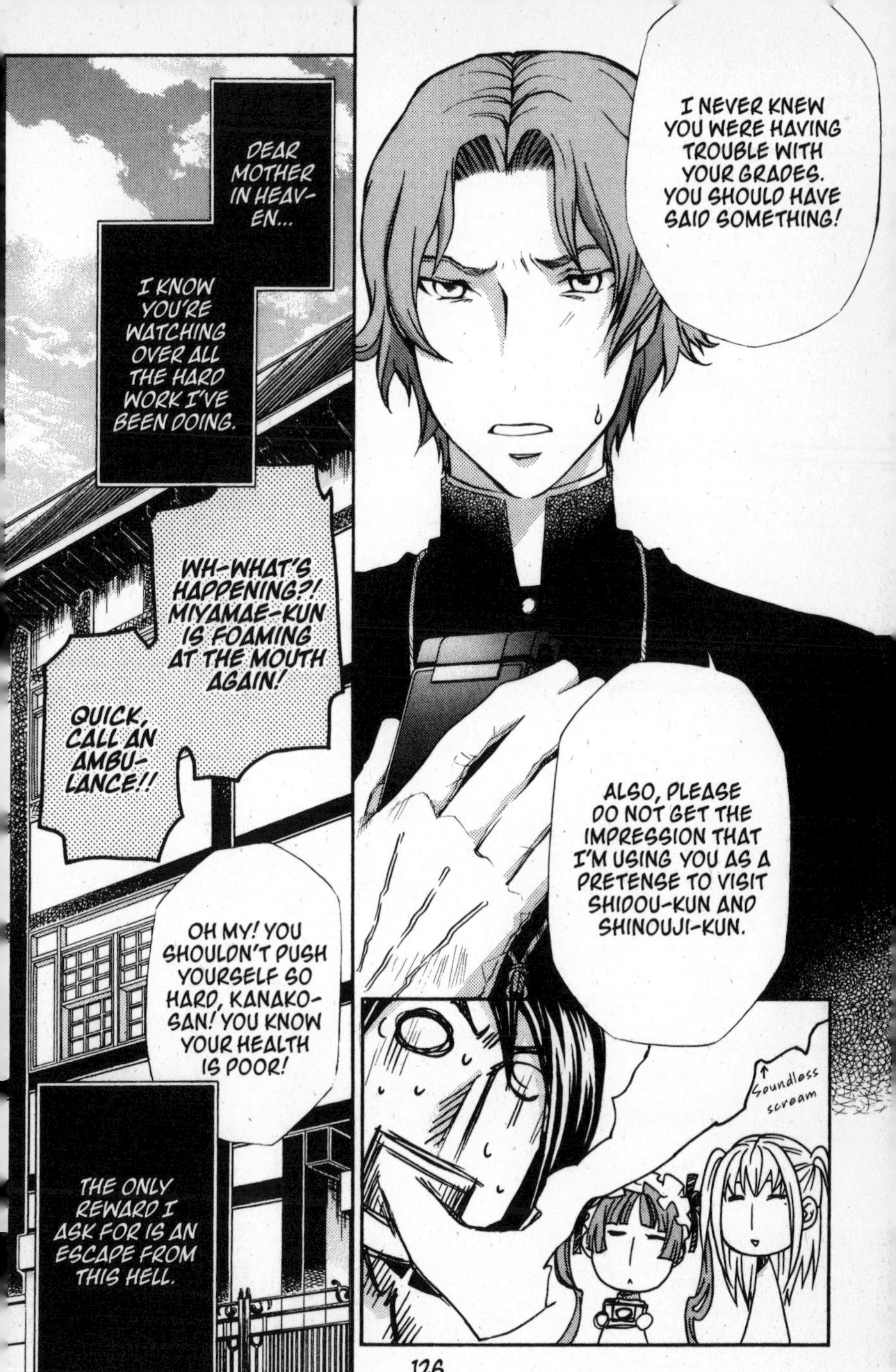
I NEVER KNEW YOU WERE HAVING TROUBLE WITH YOUR GRADES. YOU SHOULD HAVE SAID SOMETHING!
ALSO, PLEASE DO NOT GET THE IMPRESSION THAT I'M USING YOU AS A PRETENSE TO VISIT SHIDOU-KUN AND SHINOUJI-KUN.
↑ Soundless scream
DEAR MOTHER IN HEAV-EN...
I KNOW YOU'RE WATCHING OVER ALL THE HARD WORK I'VE BEEN DOING.
WH-WHAT'S HAPPENING?! MIYAMAE-KUN IS FOAMING AT THE MOUTH AGAIN!
QUICK, CALL AN AMBU-LANCE!!
OH MY! YOU SHOULDN'T PUSH YOURSELF SO HARD, KANAKO-SAN! YOU KNOW YOUR HEALTH IS POOR!
THE ONLY REWARD I ASK FOR IS AN ESCAPE FROM THIS HELL.

M A R I A H O L I C

Maria Holic

M A R I A H O L I C

Maria Holic

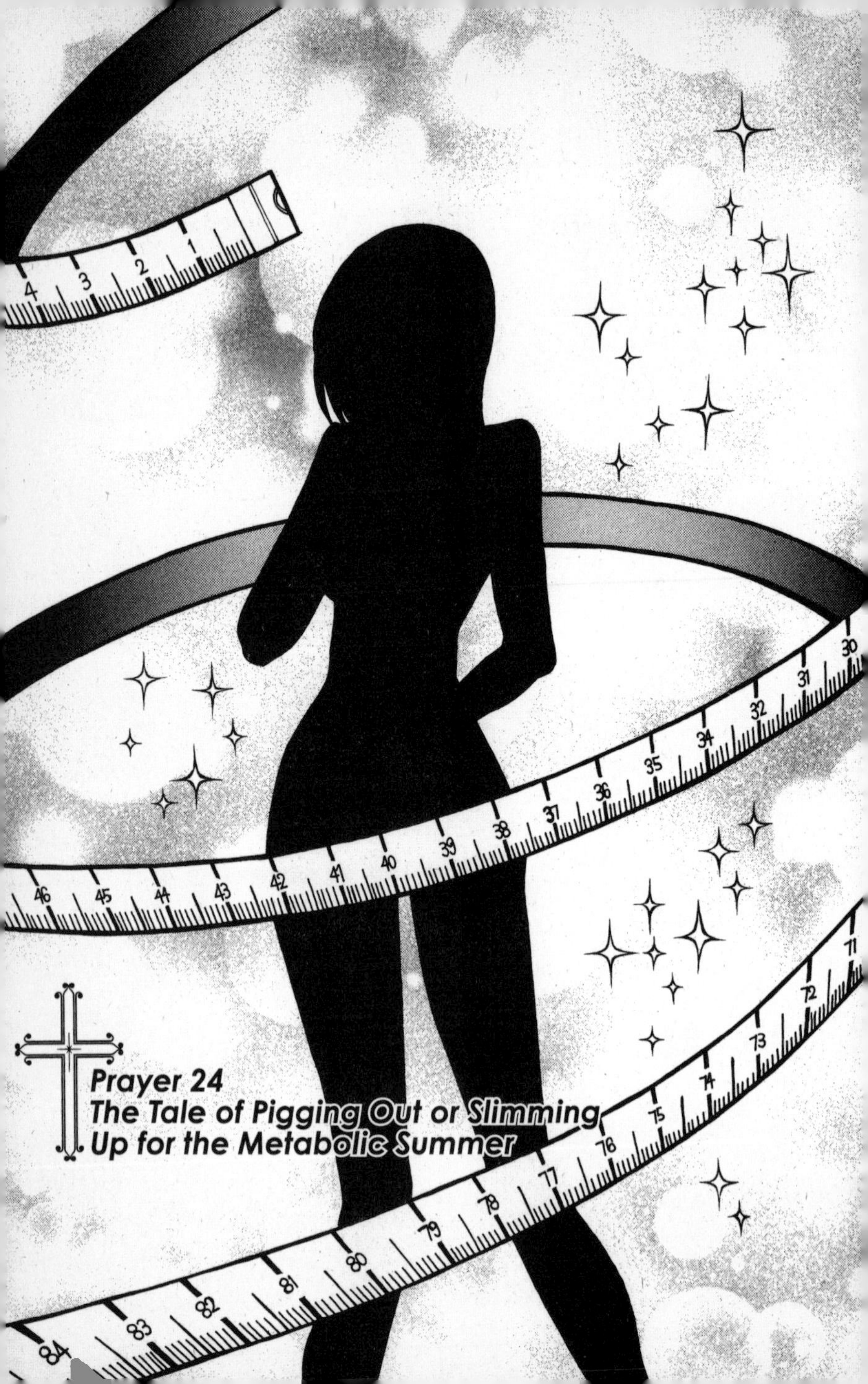
Prayer 24
The Tale of Pigging Out or Slimming Up for the Metabolic Summer

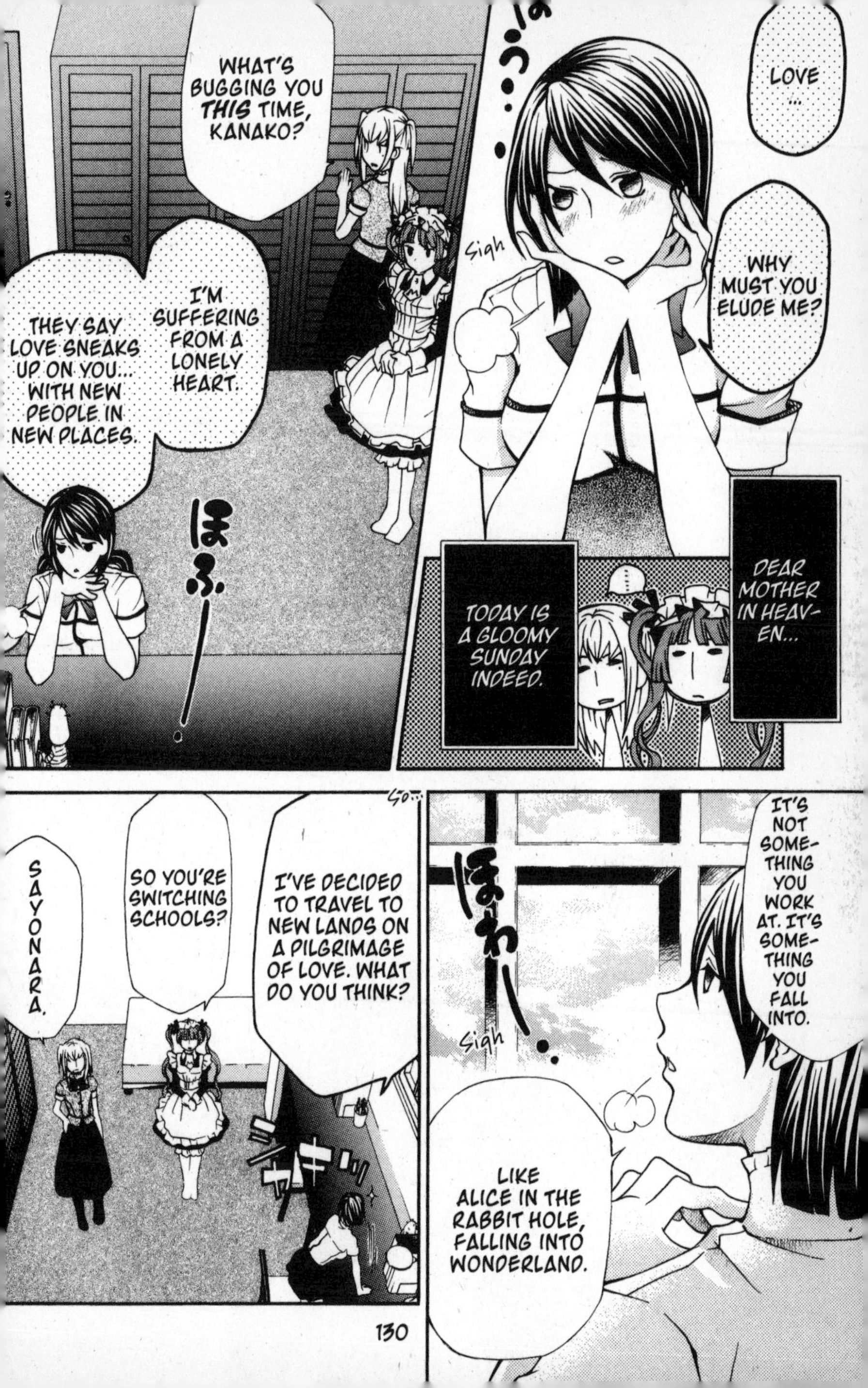
LOVE ...
Sigh
WHY MUST YOU ELUDE ME?
DEAR MOTHER IN HEAV- EN...
TODAY IS A GLOOMY SUNDAY INDEED.
WHAT'S BUGGING YOU THIS TIME, KANAKO?
I'M SUFFERING FROM A LONELY HEART.
THEY SAY LOVE SNEAKS UP ON YOU... WITH NEW PEOPLE IN NEW PLACES.
ほふー
IT'S NOT SOME- THING YOU WORK AT. IT'S SOME- THING YOU FALL INTO.
Sigh
LIKE ALICE IN THE RABBIT HOLE, FALLING INTO WONDERLAND.
So...
I'VE DECIDED TO TRAVEL TO NEW LANDS ON A PILGRIMAGE OF LOVE. WHAT DO YOU THINK?
SO YOU'RE SWITCHING SCHOOLS?
SAYONARA.

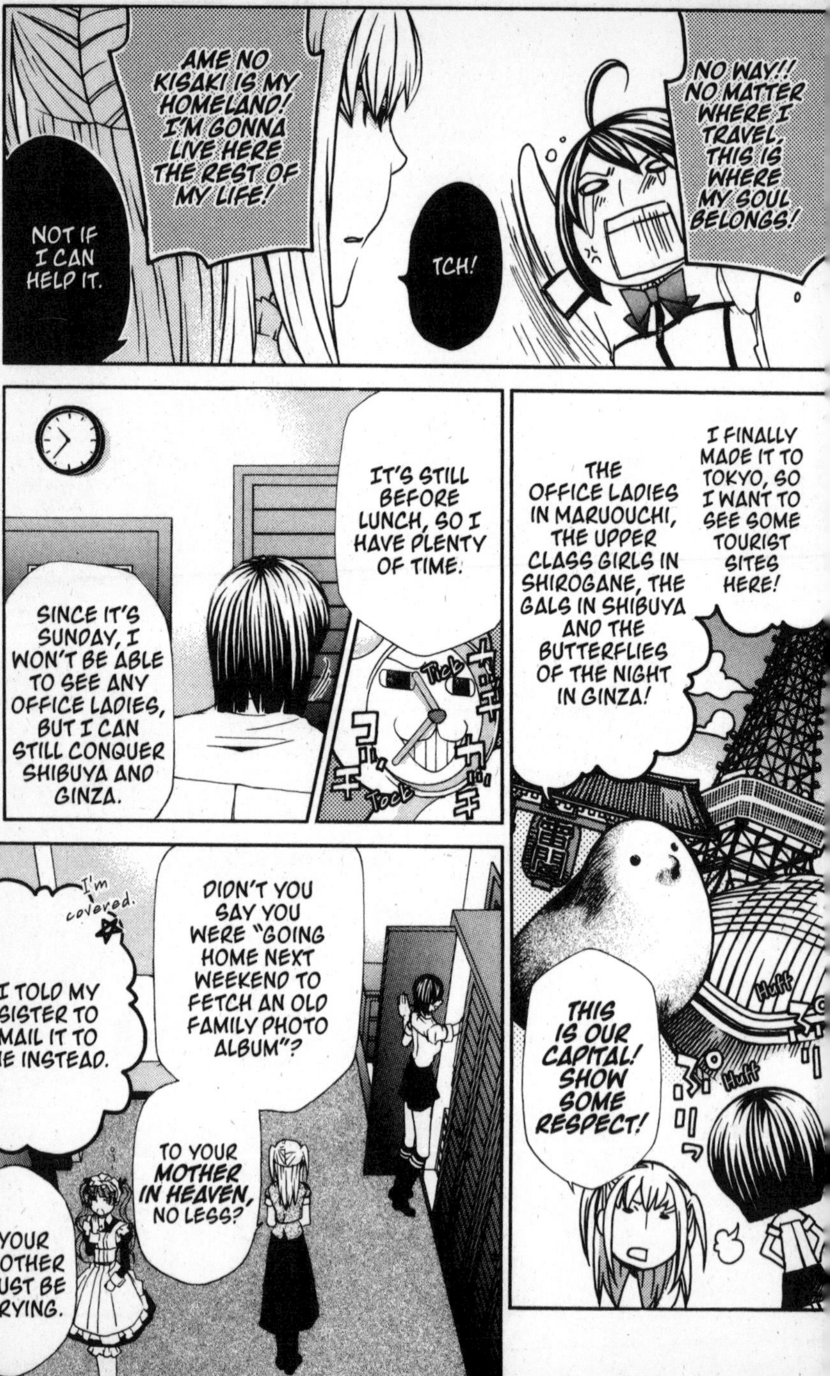
NO WAY!! NO MATTER WHERE I TRAVEL, THIS IS WHERE MY SOUL BELONGS!
AME NO KISAKI IS MY HOMELAND! I'M GONNA LIVE HERE THE REST OF MY LIFE!
TCH!
NOT IF I CAN HELP IT.
I FINALLY MADE IT TO TOKYO, SO I WANT TO SEE SOME TOURIST SITES HERE!
THE OFFICE LADIES IN MARUOUCHI, THE UPPER CLASS GIRLS IN SHIROGANE, THE GALS IN SHIBUYA AND THE BUTTERFLIES OF THE NIGHT IN GINZA!
Huff
Huff
THIS IS OUR CAPITAL! SHOW SOME RESPECT!
IT'S STILL BEFORE LUNCH, SO I HAVE PLENTY OF TIME.
Tick
Tock
SINCE IT'S SUNDAY, I WON'T BE ABLE TO SEE ANY OFFICE LADIES, BUT I CAN STILL CONQUER SHIBUYA AND GINZA.
DIDN'T YOU SAY YOU WERE "GOING HOME NEXT WEEKEND TO FETCH AN OLD FAMILY PHOTO ALBUM"?
I'm covered.
I TOLD MY SISTER TO MAIL IT TO ME INSTEAD.
TO YOUR MOTHER IN HEAVEN, NO LESS?
YOUR MOTHER MUST BE CRYING.

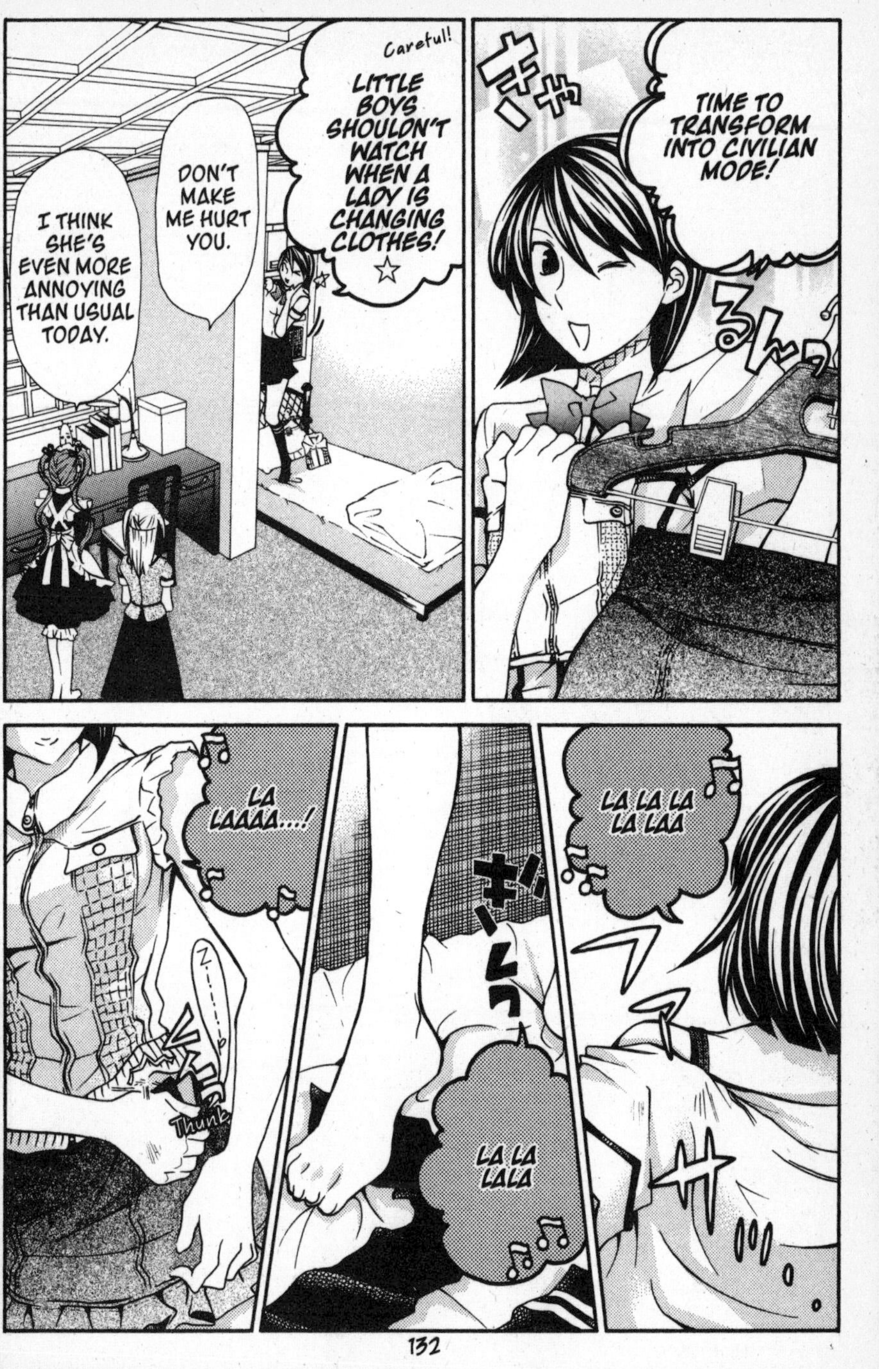
TIME TO TRANSFORM INTO CIVILIAN MODE!
Careful!
LITTLE BOYS SHOULDN'T WATCH WHEN A LADY IS CHANGING CLOTHES! ☆
DON'T MAKE ME HURT YOU.
I THINK SHE'S EVEN MORE ANNOYING THAN USUAL TODAY.
LA LA LA LA LAA
LA LA LALA
LA LAAAA...!
Thunk

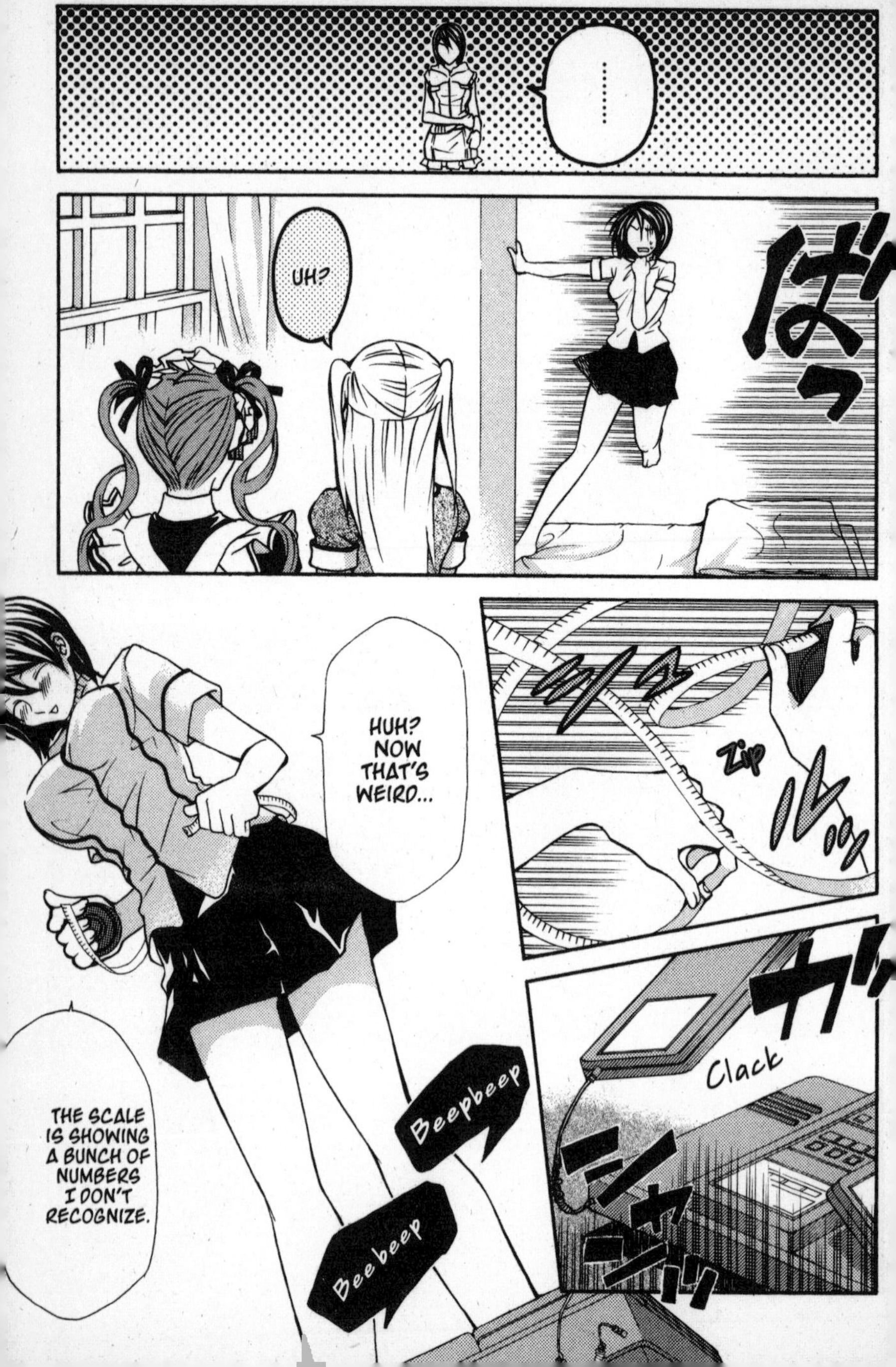
……
ぱっ
UH?
Zip
Clack
HUH? NOW THAT'S WEIRD...
Beepbeep
Beebeep
THE SCALE IS SHOWING A BUNCH OF NUMBERS I DON'T RECOGNIZE.

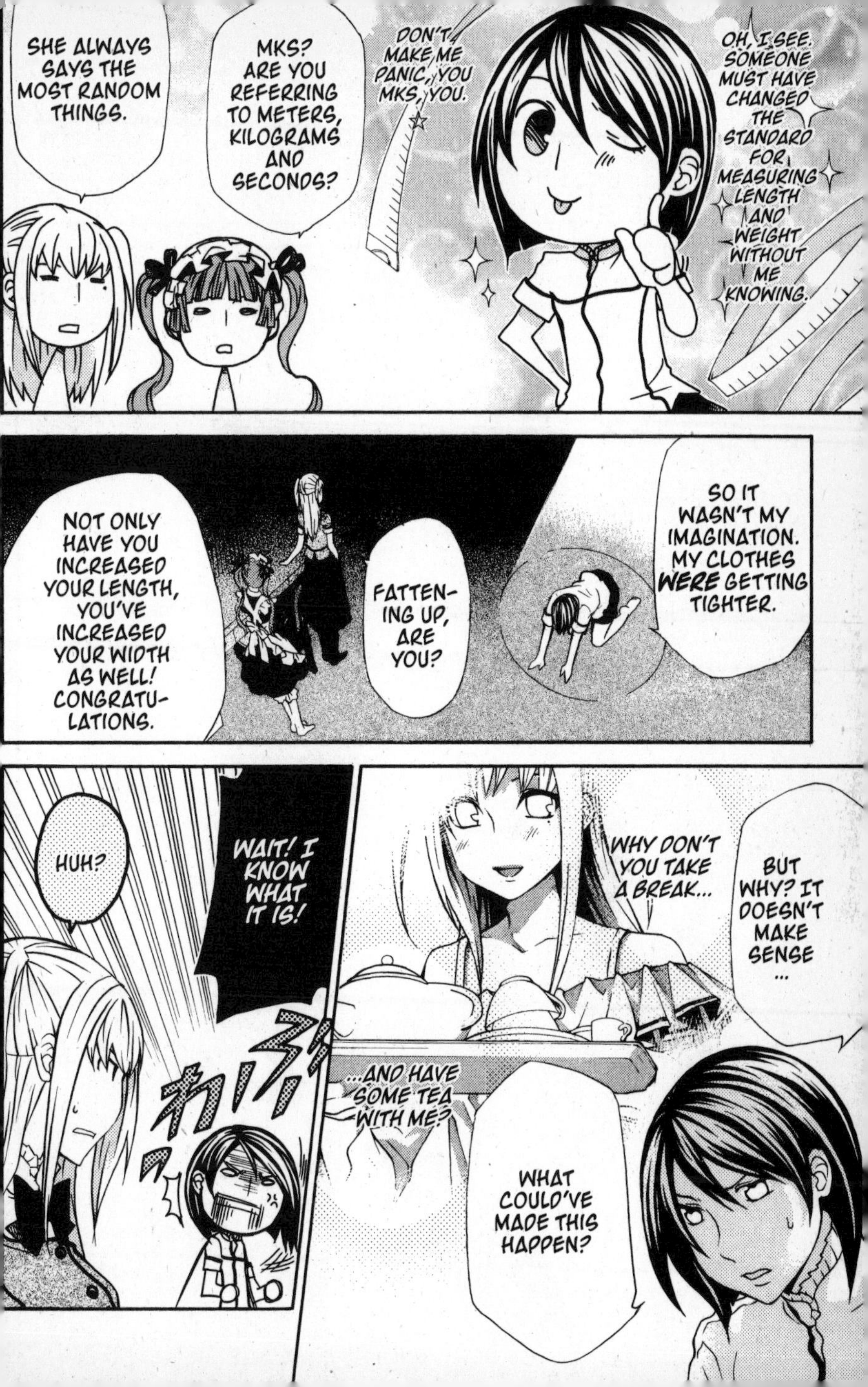
OH, I SEE. SOMEONE MUST HAVE CHANGED THE STANDARD FOR MEASURING LENGTH AND WEIGHT WITHOUT ME KNOWING.
DON'T MAKE ME PANIC, YOU MKS, YOU.
MKS? ARE YOU REFERRING TO METERS, KILOGRAMS AND SECONDS?
SHE ALWAYS SAYS THE MOST RANDOM THINGS.
SO IT WASN'T MY IMAGINATION. MY CLOTHES WERE GETTING TIGHTER.
FATTENING UP, ARE YOU?
NOT ONLY HAVE YOU INCREASED YOUR LENGTH, YOU'VE INCREASED YOUR WIDTH AS WELL! CONGRATULATIONS.
BUT WHY? IT DOESN'T MAKE SENSE...
WHAT COULD'VE MADE THIS HAPPEN?
WHY DON'T YOU TAKE A BREAK...
...AND HAVE SOME TEA WITH ME?
WAIT! I KNOW WHAT IT IS!
HUH?

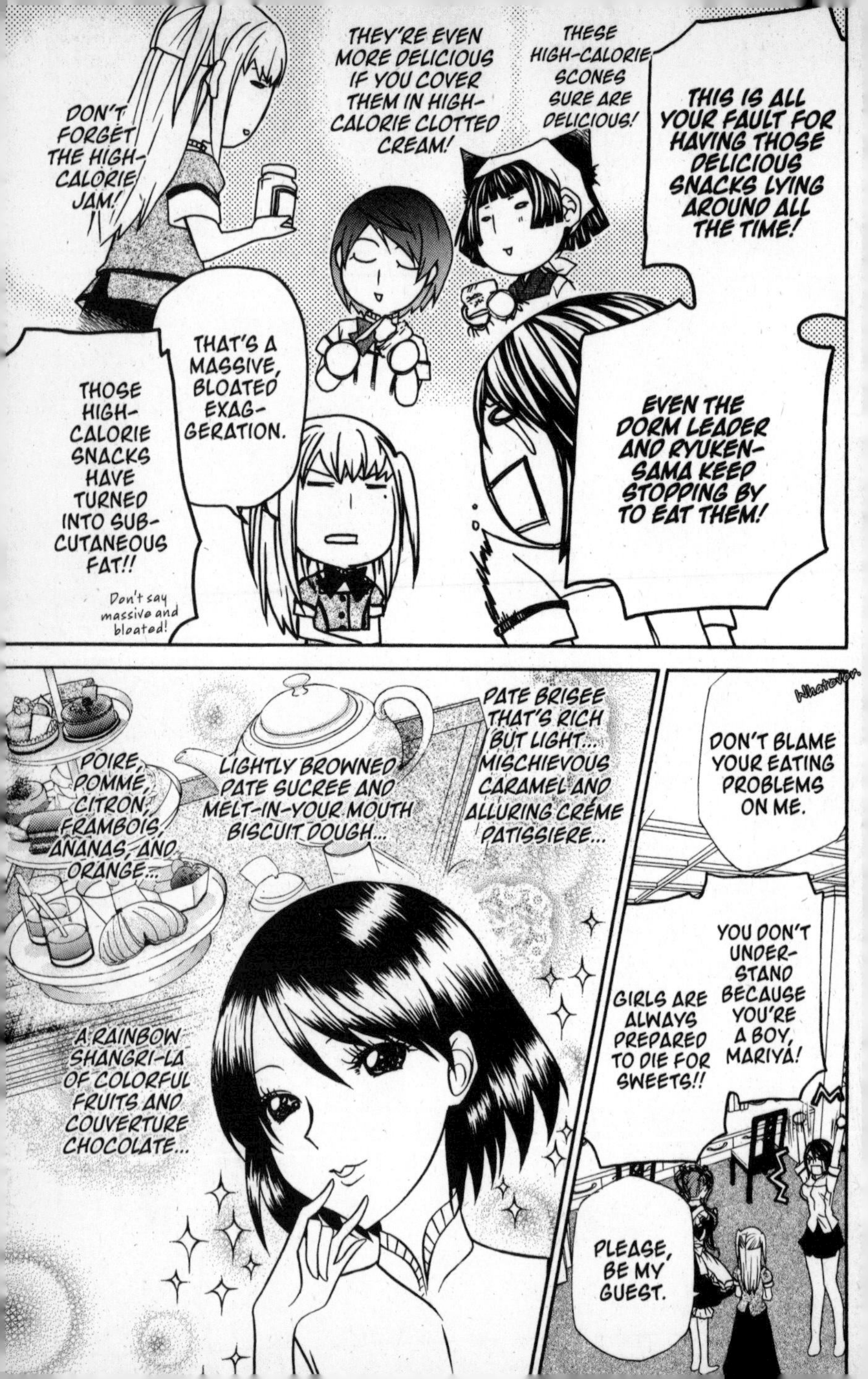
THIS IS ALL YOUR FAULT FOR HAVING THOSE DELICIOUS SNACKS LYING AROUND ALL THE TIME!
THESE HIGH-CALORIE SCONES SURE ARE DELICIOUS!
THEY'RE EVEN MORE DELICIOUS IF YOU COVER THEM IN HIGH-CALORIE CLOTTED CREAM!
DON'T FORGET THE HIGH-CALORIE JAM!
EVEN THE DORM LEADER AND RYUKEN-SAMA KEEP STOPPING BY TO EAT THEM!
THAT'S A MASSIVE, BLOATED EXAG-GERATION.
THOSE HIGH-CALORIE SNACKS HAVE TURNED INTO SUB-CUTANEOUS FAT!!
Don't say massive and bloated!
Whatever.
DON'T BLAME YOUR EATING PROBLEMS ON ME.
YOU DON'T UNDER-STAND BECAUSE YOU'RE A BOY, MARIYA!
GIRLS ARE ALWAYS PREPARED TO DIE FOR SWEETS!!
PLEASE, BE MY GUEST.
PATE BRISEE THAT'S RICH BUT LIGHT... MISCHIEVOUS CARAMEL AND ALLURING CRÉME PATISSIERE...
LIGHTLY BROWNED PATE SUCREE AND MELT-IN-YOUR MOUTH BISCUIT DOUGH...
POIRE, POMME, CITRON, FRAMBOIS, ANANAS, AND ORANGE...
A RAINBOW SHANGRI-LA OF COLORFUL FRUITS AND COUVERTURE CHOCOLATE...

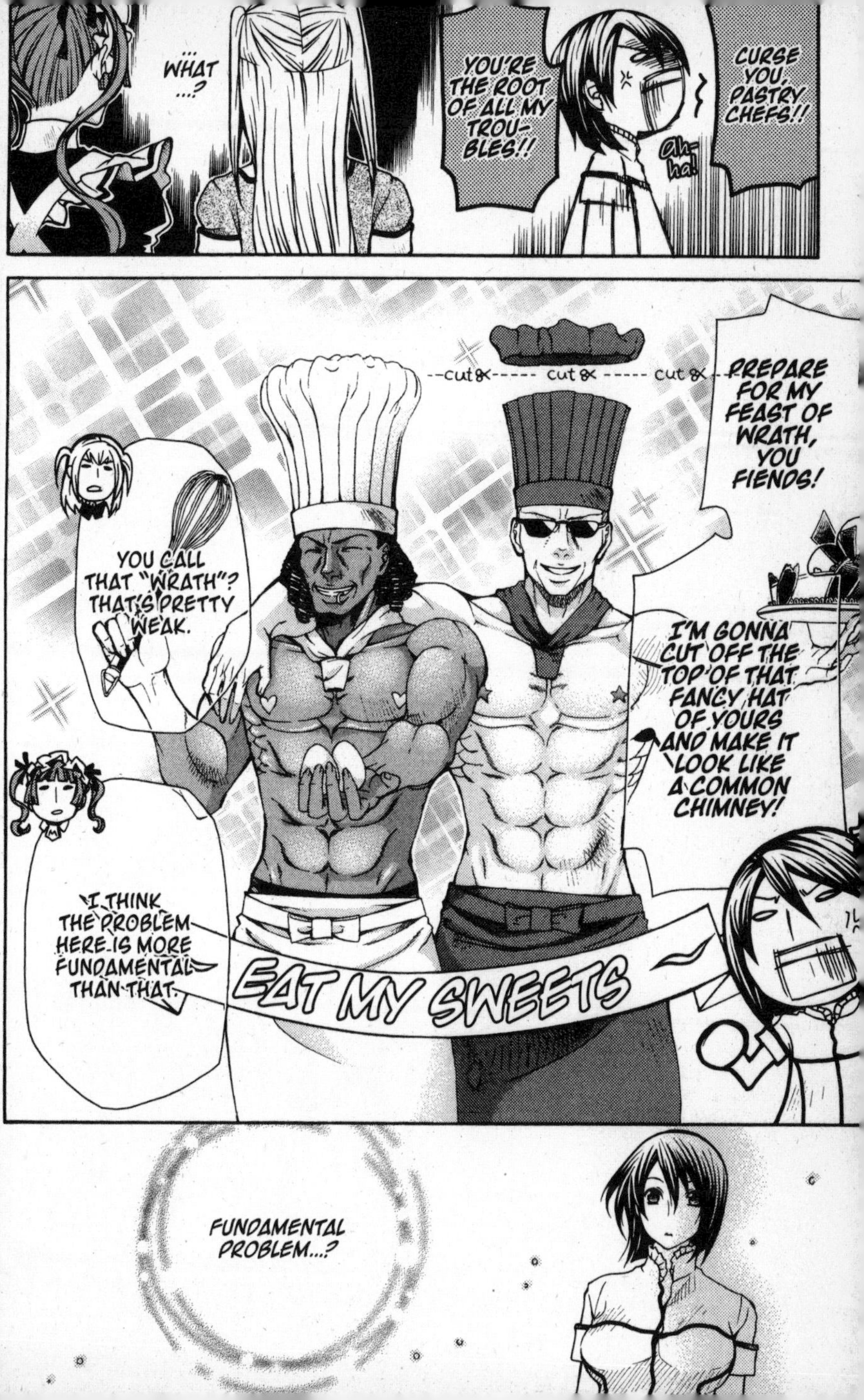
CURSE YOU, PASTRY CHEFS!!
Ah-ha!
YOU'RE THE ROOT OF ALL MY TROUBLES!!
... WHAT ...?
PREPARE FOR MY FEAST OF WRATH, YOU FIENDS!
cut cut cut
I'M GONNA CUT OFF THE TOP OF THAT FANCY HAT OF YOURS AND MAKE IT LOOK LIKE A COMMON CHIMNEY!
YOU CALL THAT "WRATH"? THAT'S PRETTY WEAK.
EAT MY SWEETS
I THINK THE PROBLEM HERE IS MORE FUNDAMENTAL THAN THAT.
FUNDAMENTAL PROBLEM...?

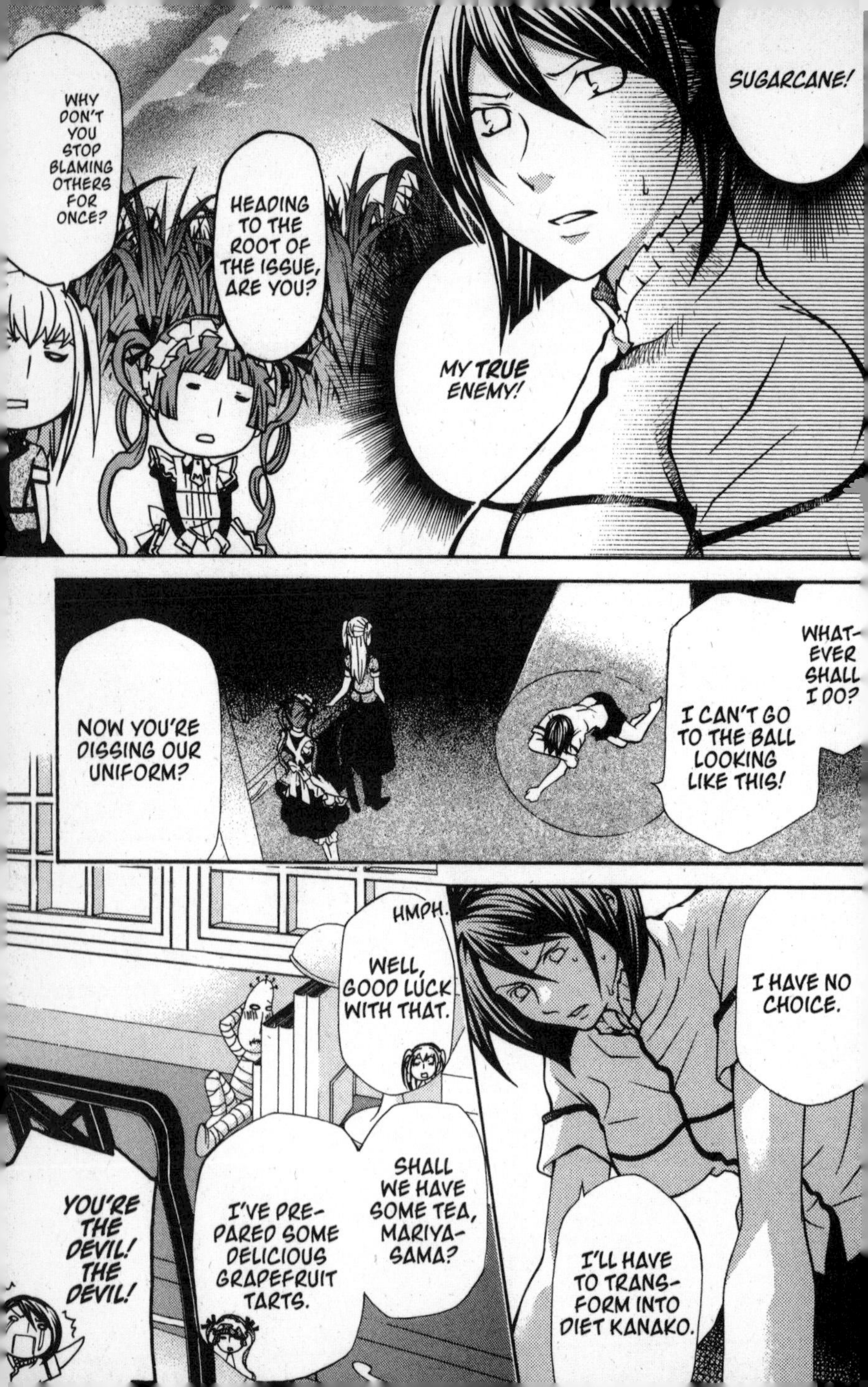
SUGARCANE!
MY TRUE ENEMY!
HEADING TO THE ROOT OF THE ISSUE, ARE YOU?
WHY DON'T YOU STOP BLAMING OTHERS FOR ONCE?
WHAT-EVER SHALL I DO?
I CAN'T GO TO THE BALL LOOKING LIKE THIS!
NOW YOU'RE DISSING OUR UNIFORM?
I HAVE NO CHOICE.
I'LL HAVE TO TRANS-FORM INTO DIET KANAKO.
HMPH.
WELL, GOOD LUCK WITH THAT.
SHALL WE HAVE SOME TEA, MARIYA-SAMA?
I'VE PRE-PARED SOME DELICIOUS GRAPEFRUIT TARTS.
YOU'RE THE DEVIL! THE DEVIL!

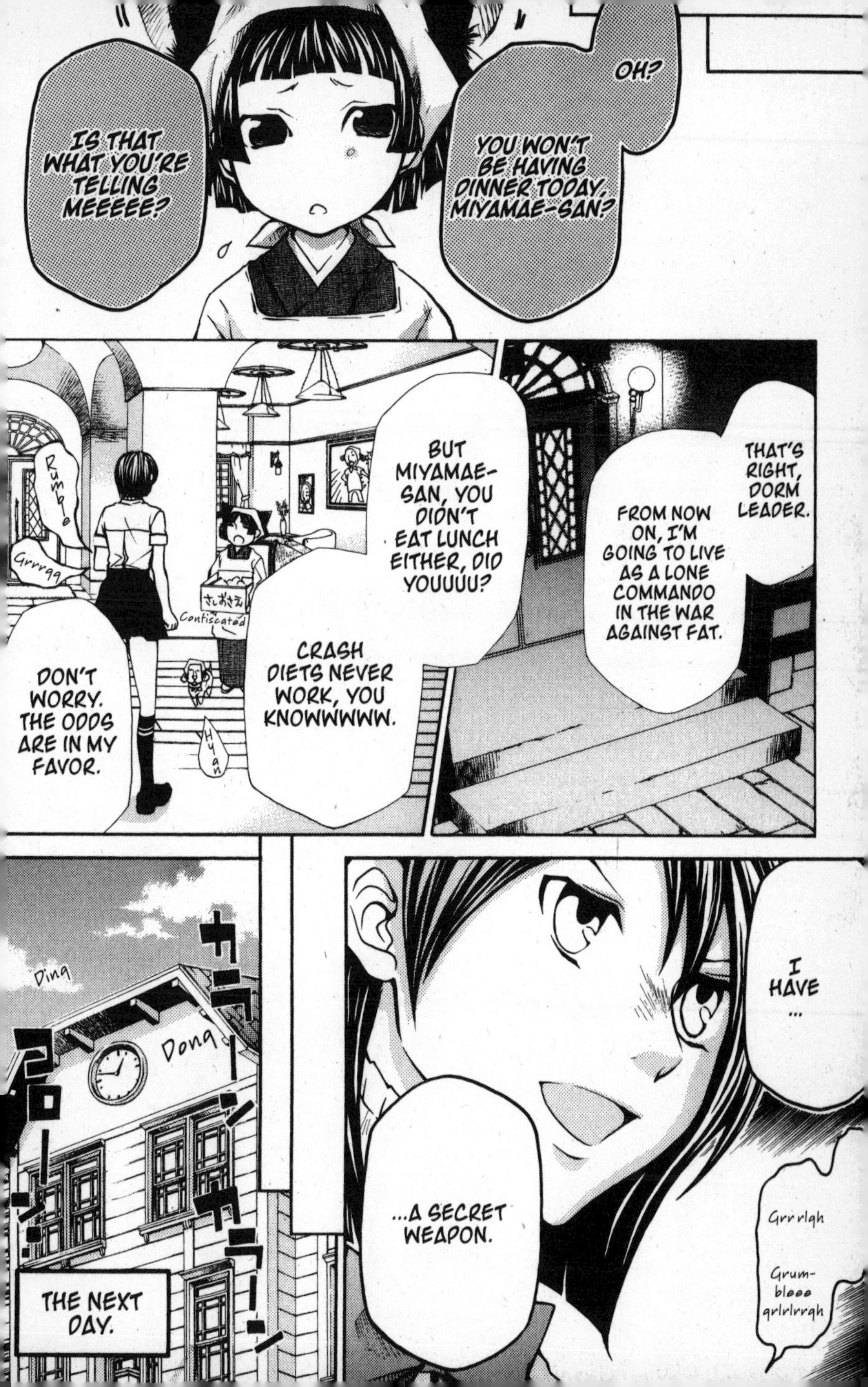
OH?
YOU WON'T BE HAVING DINNER TODAY, MIYAMAE-SAN?
IS THAT WHAT YOU'RE TELLING MEEEEEE?
THAT'S RIGHT, DORM LEADER.
FROM NOW ON, I'M GOING TO LIVE AS A LONE COMMANDO IN THE WAR AGAINST FAT.
BUT MIYAMAE-SAN, YOU DIDN'T EAT LUNCH EITHER, DID YOUUUU?
CRASH DIETS NEVER WORK, YOU KNOWWWWW.
Rumble
Grrrgg
さしおさえ
Confiscated
Hyan
DON'T WORRY. THE ODDS ARE IN MY FAVOR.
I HAVE ...
...A SECRET WEAPON.
Grrrlgh
Grum-bleee grlrlrrgh
Ding
Dong
THE NEXT DAY.

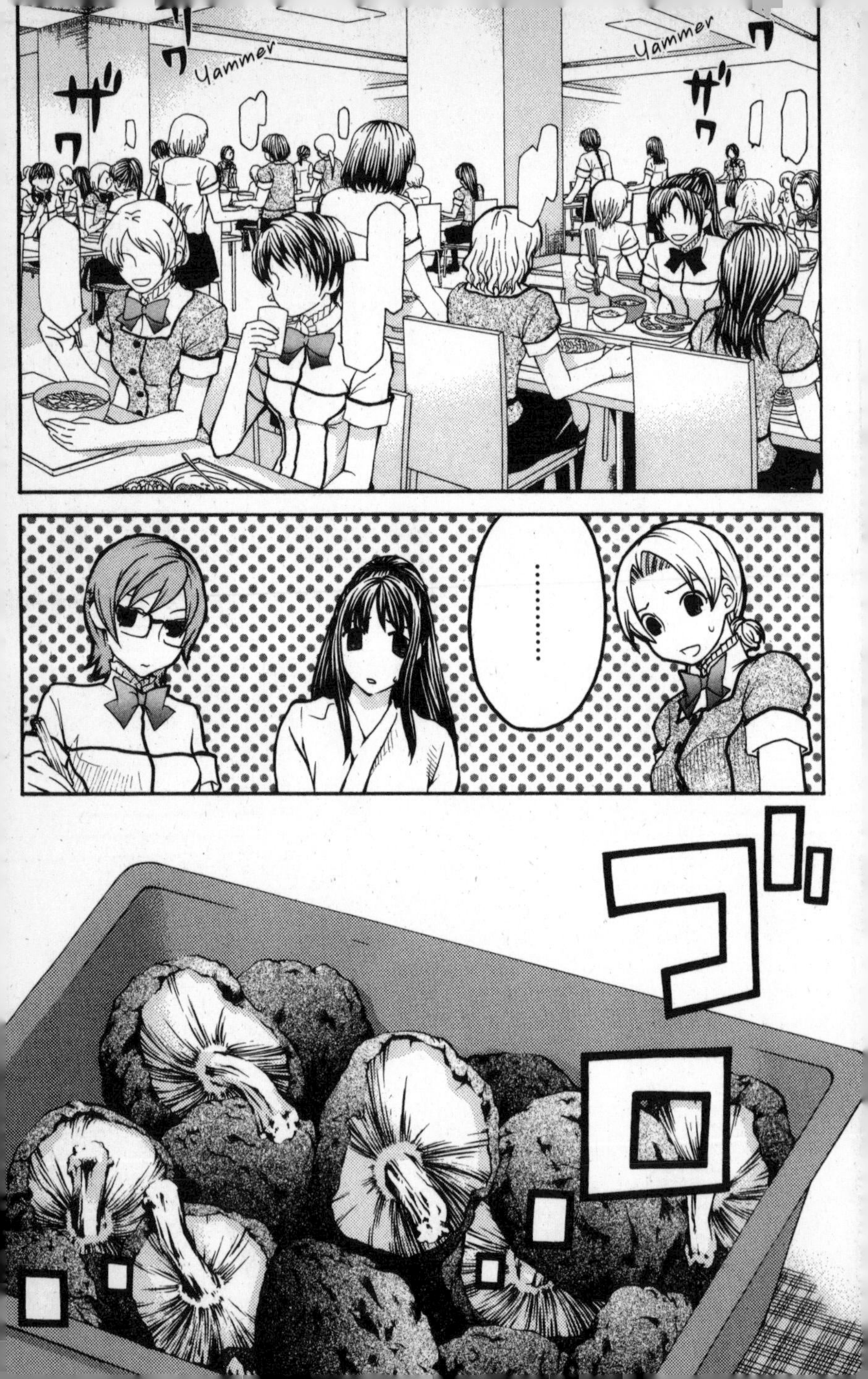
Yammer
ザワ
Yammer
ザワ
……

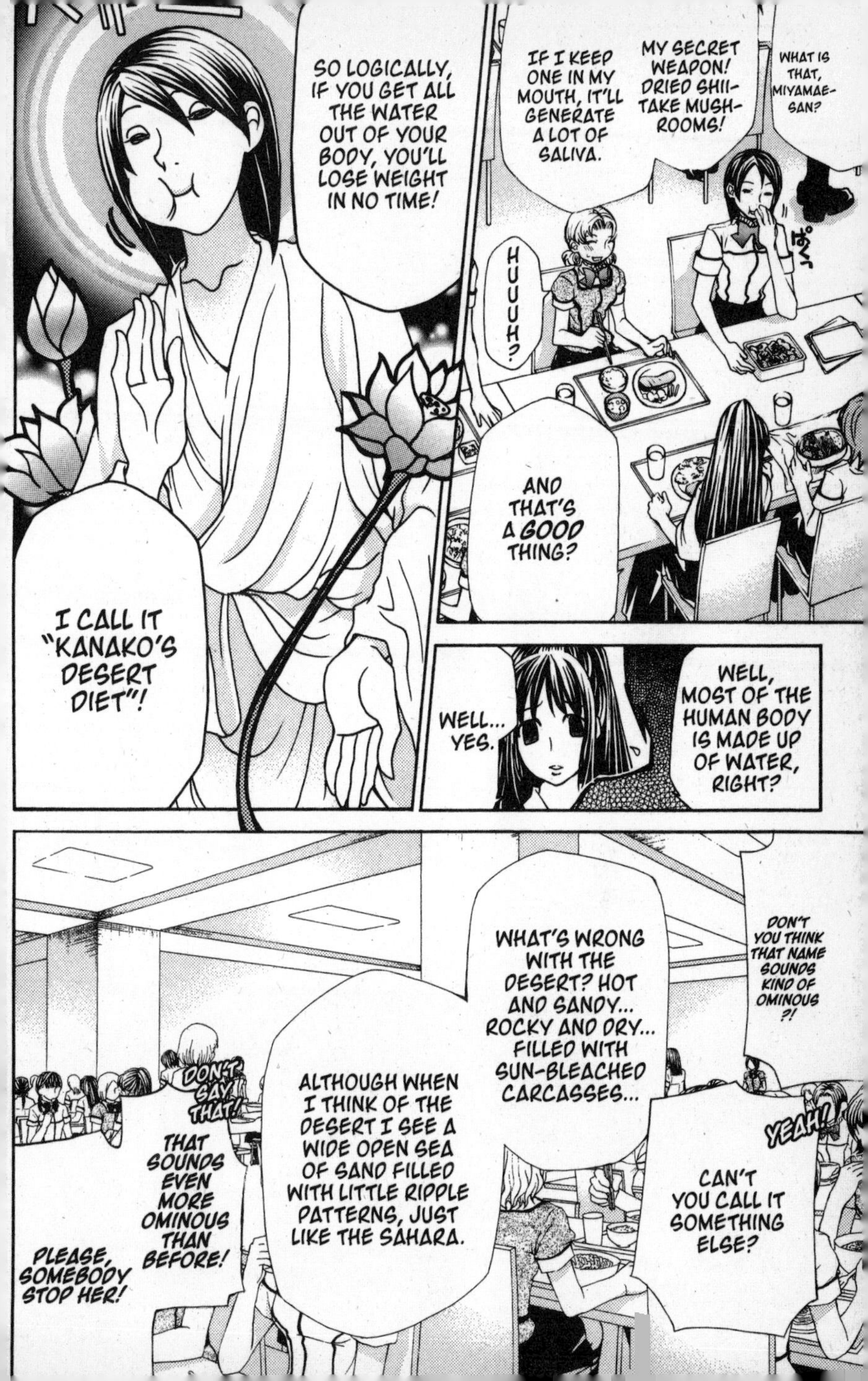
WHAT IS THAT, MIYAMAE-SAN?
MY SECRET WEAPON! DRIED SHII-TAKE MUSH-ROOMS!
IF I KEEP ONE IN MY MOUTH, IT'LL GENERATE A LOT OF SALIVA.
HUUUUH?
AND THAT'S A GOOD THING?
WELL, MOST OF THE HUMAN BODY IS MADE UP OF WATER, RIGHT?
WELL... YES.
SO LOGICALLY, IF YOU GET ALL THE WATER OUT OF YOUR BODY, YOU'LL LOSE WEIGHT IN NO TIME!
I CALL IT "KANAKO'S DESERT DIET"!
DON'T YOU THINK THAT NAME SOUNDS KIND OF OMINOUS ?!
WHAT'S WRONG WITH THE DESERT? HOT AND SANDY... ROCKY AND DRY... FILLED WITH SUN-BLEACHED CARCASSES...
YEAH!
CAN'T YOU CALL IT SOMETHING ELSE?
ALTHOUGH WHEN I THINK OF THE DESERT I SEE A WIDE OPEN SEA OF SAND FILLED WITH LITTLE RIPPLE PATTERNS, JUST LIKE THE SAHARA.
DON'T SAY THAT!
THAT SOUNDS EVEN MORE OMINOUS THAN BEFORE!
PLEASE, SOMEBODY STOP HER!

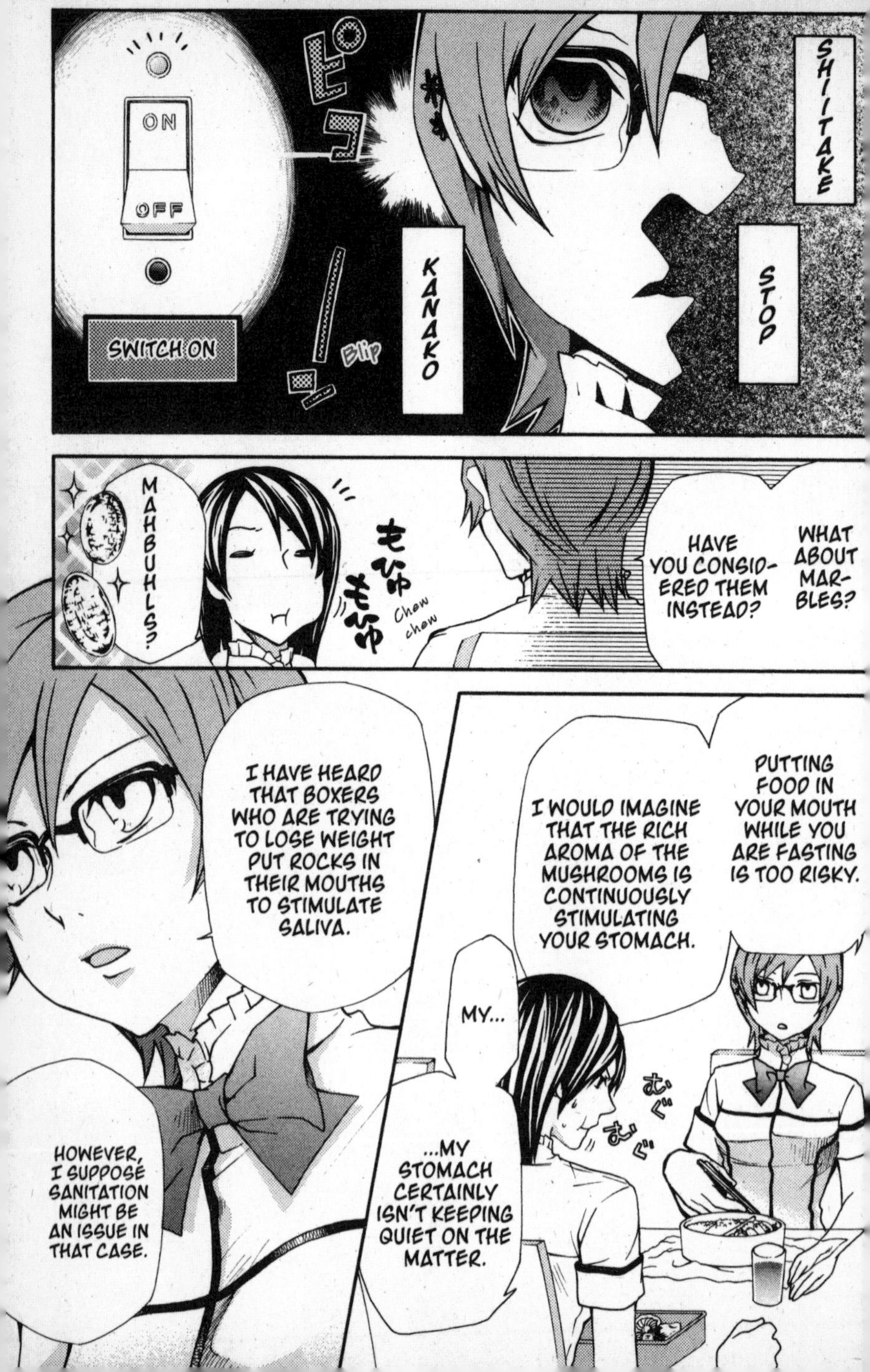
SHIITAKE
STOP
KANAKO
ピコ
Blip
ON
OFF
SWITCH ON
WHAT ABOUT MARBLES?
HAVE YOU CONSIDERED THEM INSTEAD?
もひゅもひゅ
Chew chew
MAHBUHLS?
PUTTING FOOD IN YOUR MOUTH WHILE YOU ARE FASTING IS TOO RISKY.
I WOULD IMAGINE THAT THE RICH AROMA OF THE MUSHROOMS IS CONTINUOUSLY STIMULATING YOUR STOMACH.
むぐむぐ
MY...
...MY STOMACH CERTAINLY ISN'T KEEPING QUIET ON THE MATTER.
I HAVE HEARD THAT BOXERS WHO ARE TRYING TO LOSE WEIGHT PUT ROCKS IN THEIR MOUTHS TO STIMULATE SALIVA.
HOWEVER, I SUPPOSE SANITATION MIGHT BE AN ISSUE IN THAT CASE.

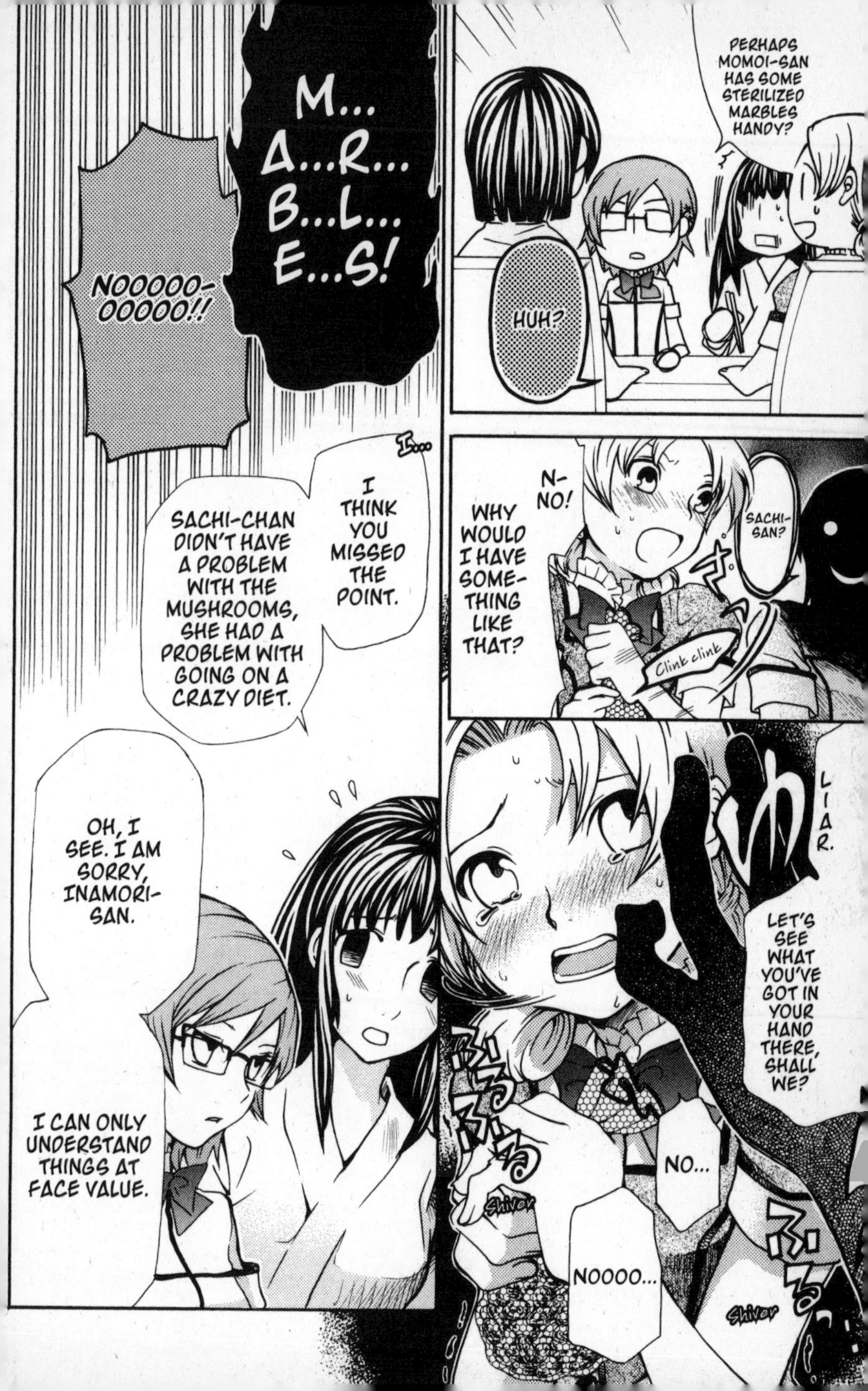
PERHAPS MOMOI-SAN HAS SOME STERILIZED MARBLES HANDY?
HUH?
M... A...R... B...L... E...S!
NOOOOO-OOOOO!!
N-NO!
WHY WOULD I HAVE SOMETHING LIKE THAT?
SACHI-SAN?
Clink clink
LIAR.
LET'S SEE WHAT YOU'VE GOT IN YOUR HAND THERE, SHALL WE?
NO...
NOOOO...
Shiver
Shiver
I...
I THINK YOU MISSED THE POINT.
SACHI-CHAN DIDN'T HAVE A PROBLEM WITH THE MUSHROOMS, SHE HAD A PROBLEM WITH GOING ON A CRAZY DIET.
OH, I SEE. I AM SORRY, INAMORI-SAN.
I CAN ONLY UNDERSTAND THINGS AT FACE VALUE.

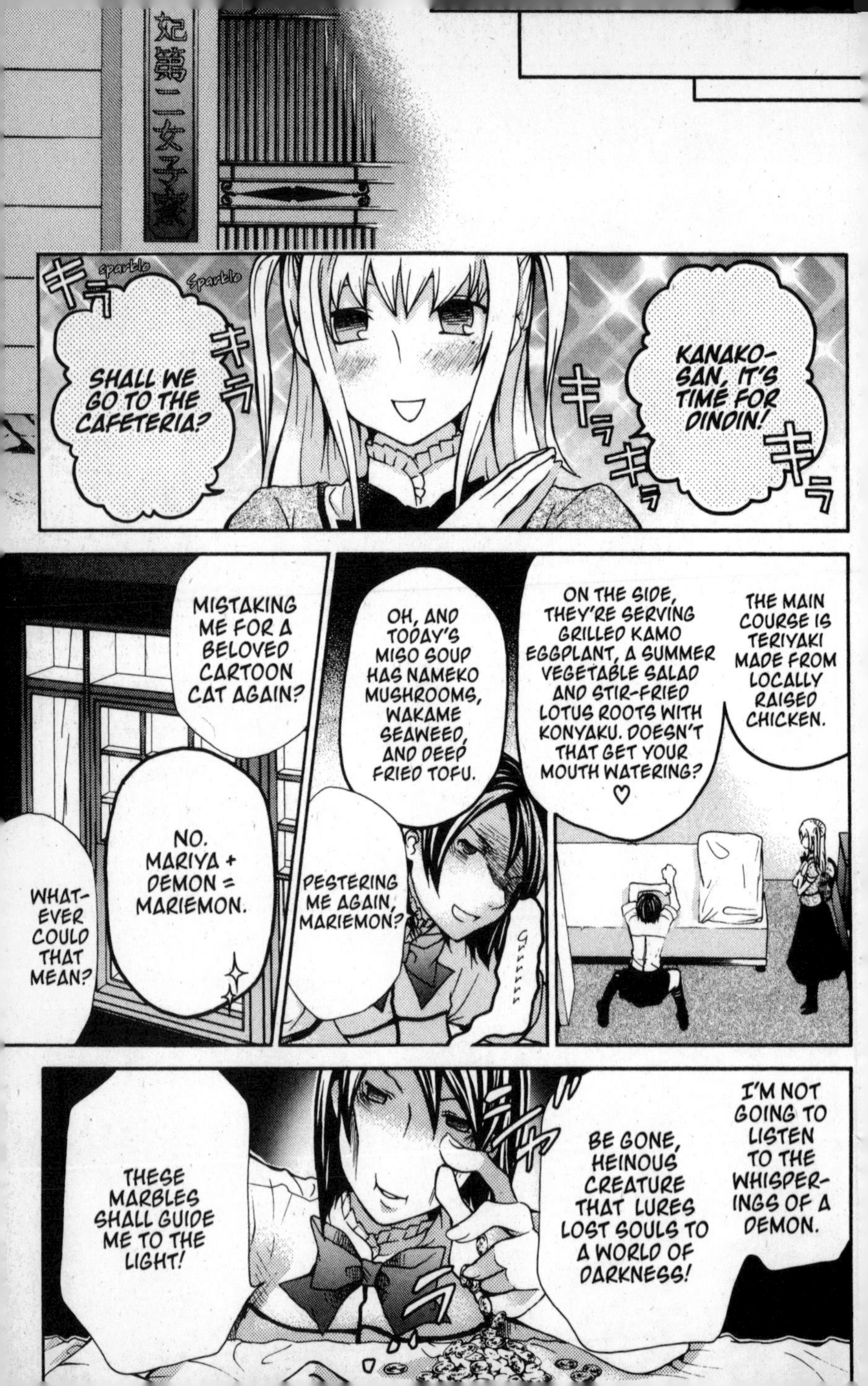

KANAKO-SAN, IT'S TIME FOR DINDIN!
SHALL WE GO TO THE CAFETERIA?
sparkle
sparkle
THE MAIN COURSE IS TERIYAKI MADE FROM LOCALLY RAISED CHICKEN.
ON THE SIDE, THEY'RE SERVING GRILLED KAMO EGGPLANT, A SUMMER VEGETABLE SALAD AND STIR-FRIED LOTUS ROOTS WITH KONYAKU. DOESN'T THAT GET YOUR MOUTH WATERING? ♡
OH, AND TODAY'S MISO SOUP HAS NAMEKO MUSHROOMS, WAKAME SEAWEED, AND DEEP FRIED TOFU.
PESTERING ME AGAIN, MARIEMON?
MISTAKING ME FOR A BELOVED CARTOON CAT AGAIN?
NO. MARIYA + DEMON = MARIEMON.
WHATEVER COULD THAT MEAN?
I'M NOT GOING TO LISTEN TO THE WHISPERINGS OF A DEMON.
BE GONE, HEINOUS CREATURE THAT LURES LOST SOULS TO A WORLD OF DARKNESS!
THESE MARBLES SHALL GUIDE ME TO THE LIGHT!

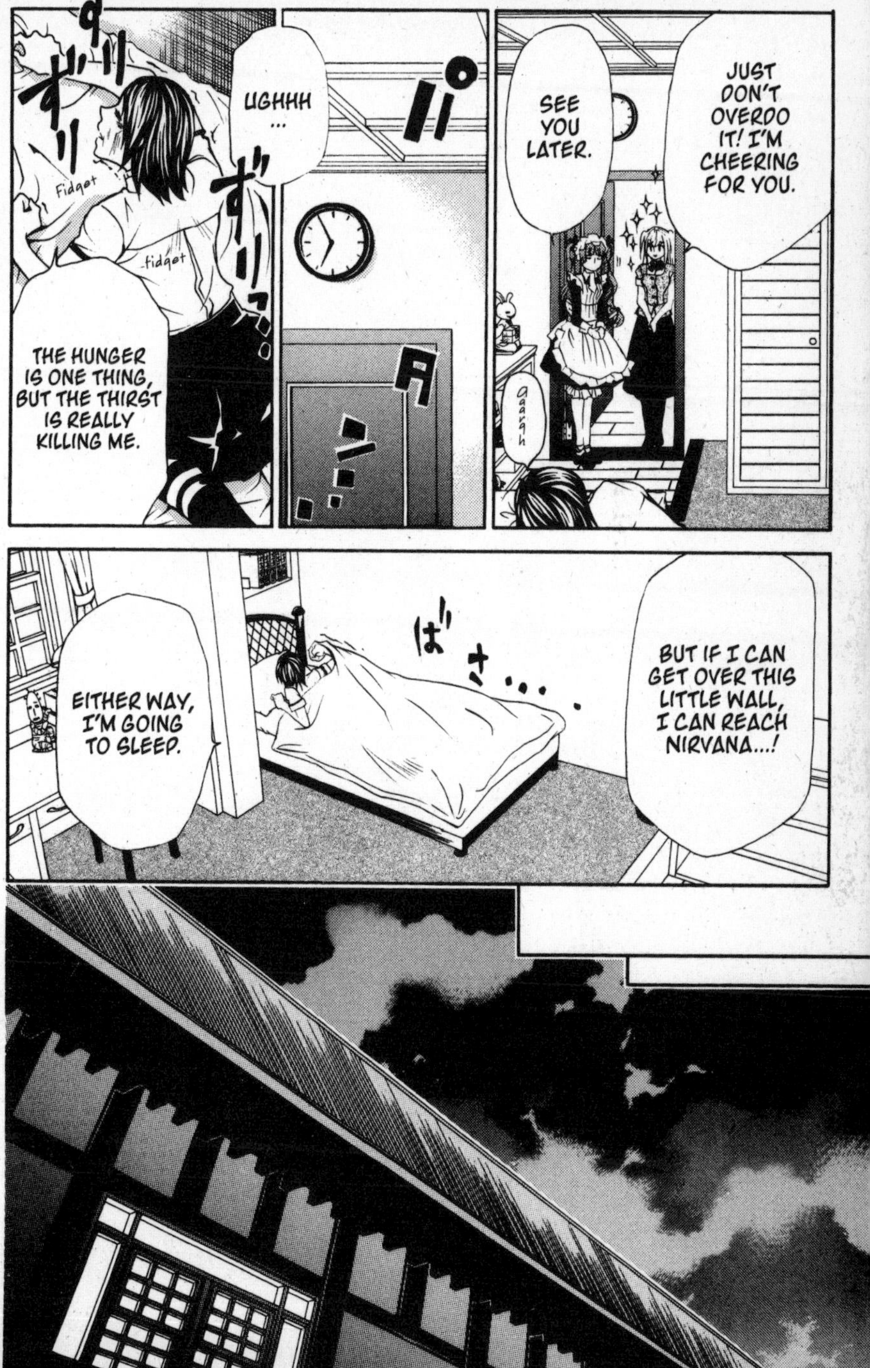
JUST DON'T OVERDO IT! I'M CHEERING FOR YOU.
SEE YOU LATER.
Aaargh
パ
UGHHH ...
ずり ずり
Fidget
fidget
THE HUNGER IS ONE THING, BUT THE THIRST IS REALLY KILLING ME.
BUT IF I CAN GET OVER THIS LITTLE WALL, I CAN REACH NIRVANA...!
ばさ...
EITHER WAY, I'M GOING TO SLEEP.

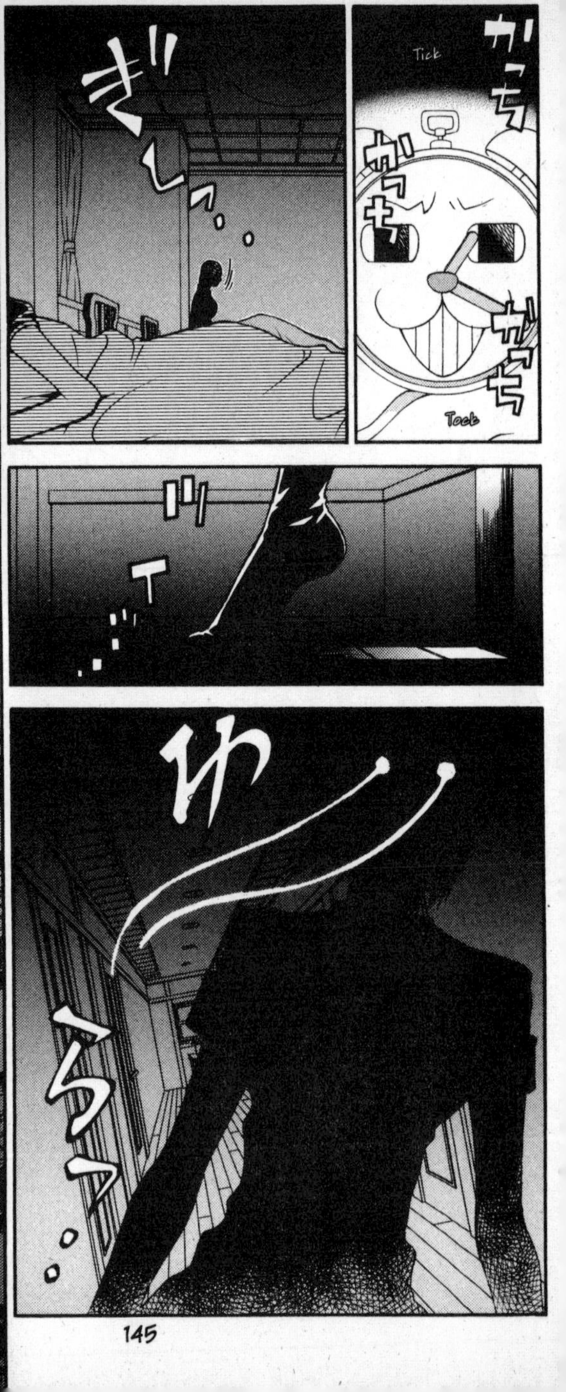
Tick
Tock
ぎしっ

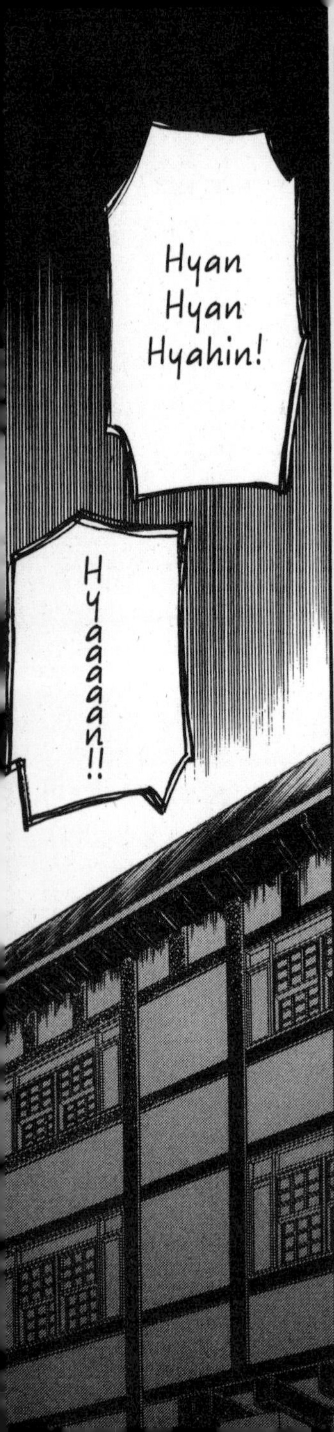
Hyan Hyan Hyahin!
Hyaaaaan!!

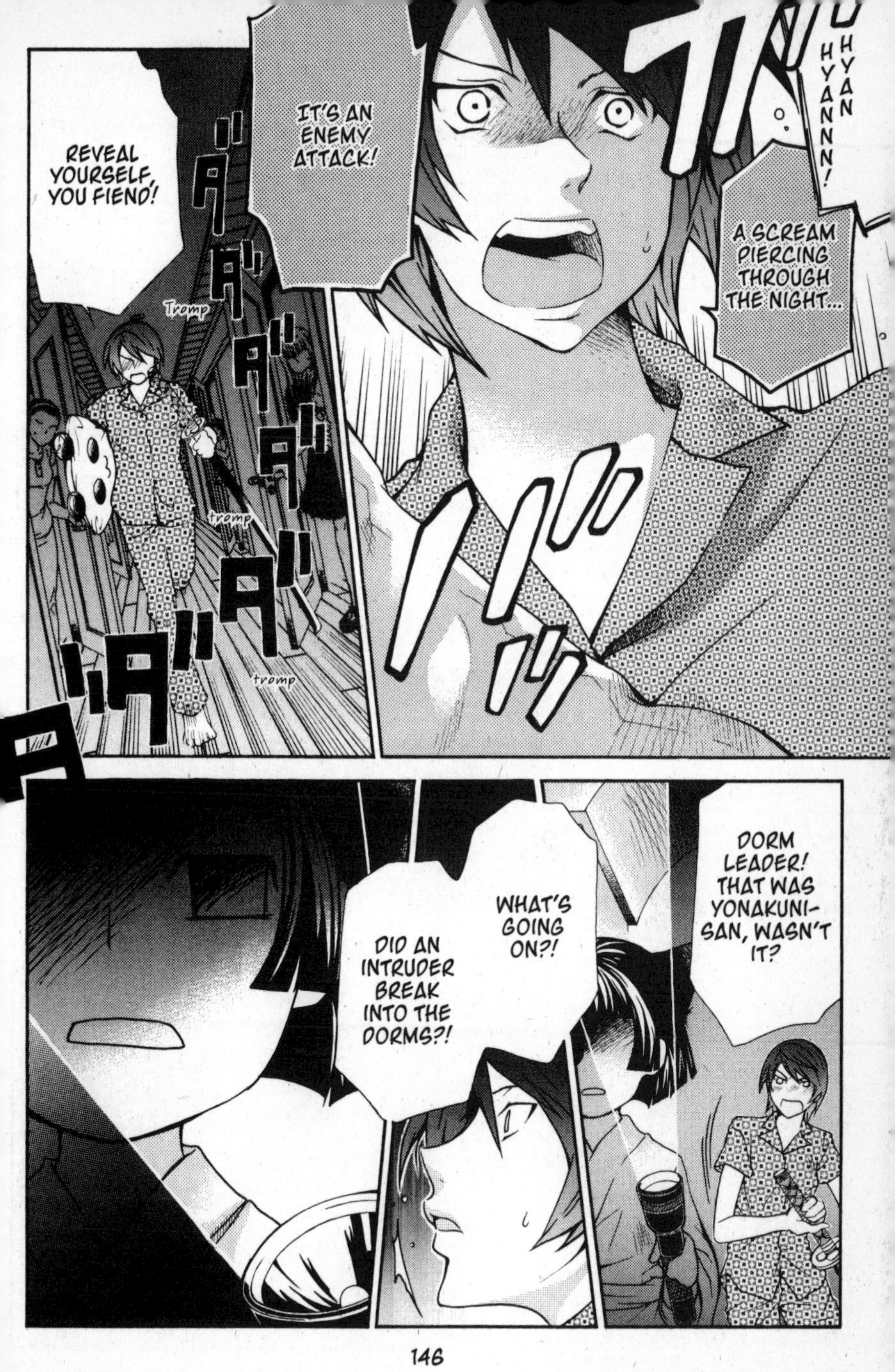
HYAN HYANNNN!
A SCREAM PIERCING THROUGH THE NIGHT...
IT'S AN ENEMY ATTACK!
REVEAL YOURSELF, YOU FIEND!
Tromp
tromp
tromp
DORM LEADER! THAT WAS YONAKUNI-SAN, WASN'T IT?
WHAT'S GOING ON?!
DID AN INTRUDER BREAK INTO THE DORMS?!

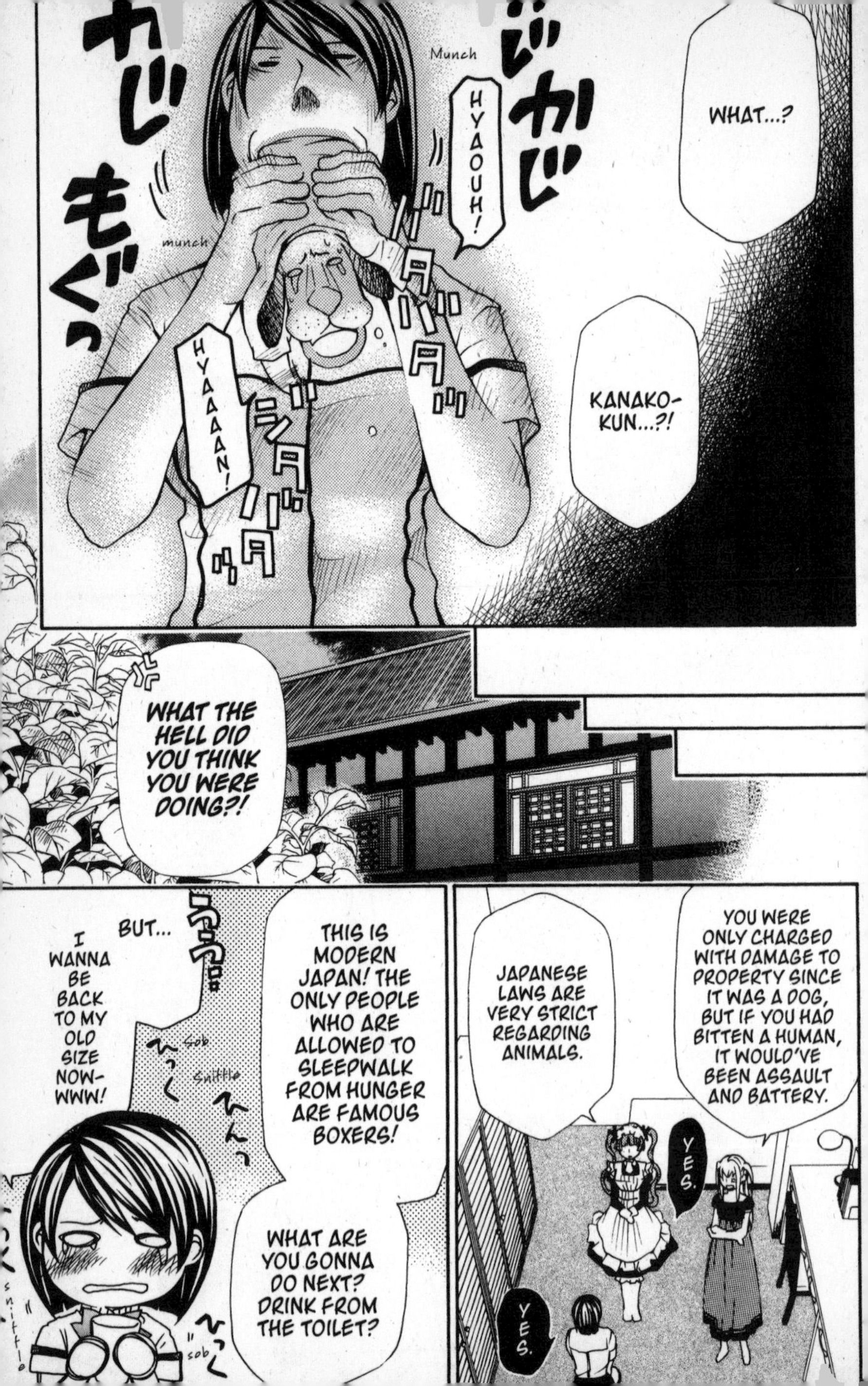
WHAT...?
KANAKO-KUN...?!
Munch
HYAOUH!
munch
HYAAAAN!
WHAT THE HELL DID YOU THINK YOU WERE DOING?!
YOU WERE ONLY CHARGED WITH DAMAGE TO PROPERTY SINCE IT WAS A DOG, BUT IF YOU HAD BITTEN A HUMAN, IT WOULD'VE BEEN ASSAULT AND BATTERY.
YES.
JAPANESE LAWS ARE VERY STRICT REGARDING ANIMALS.
YES.
THIS IS MODERN JAPAN! THE ONLY PEOPLE WHO ARE ALLOWED TO SLEEPWALK FROM HUNGER ARE FAMOUS BOXERS!
WHAT ARE YOU GONNA DO NEXT? DRINK FROM THE TOILET?
BUT...
I WANNA BE BACK TO MY OLD SIZE NOW-WWW!
Sob
Sniffle
sniffle
sob

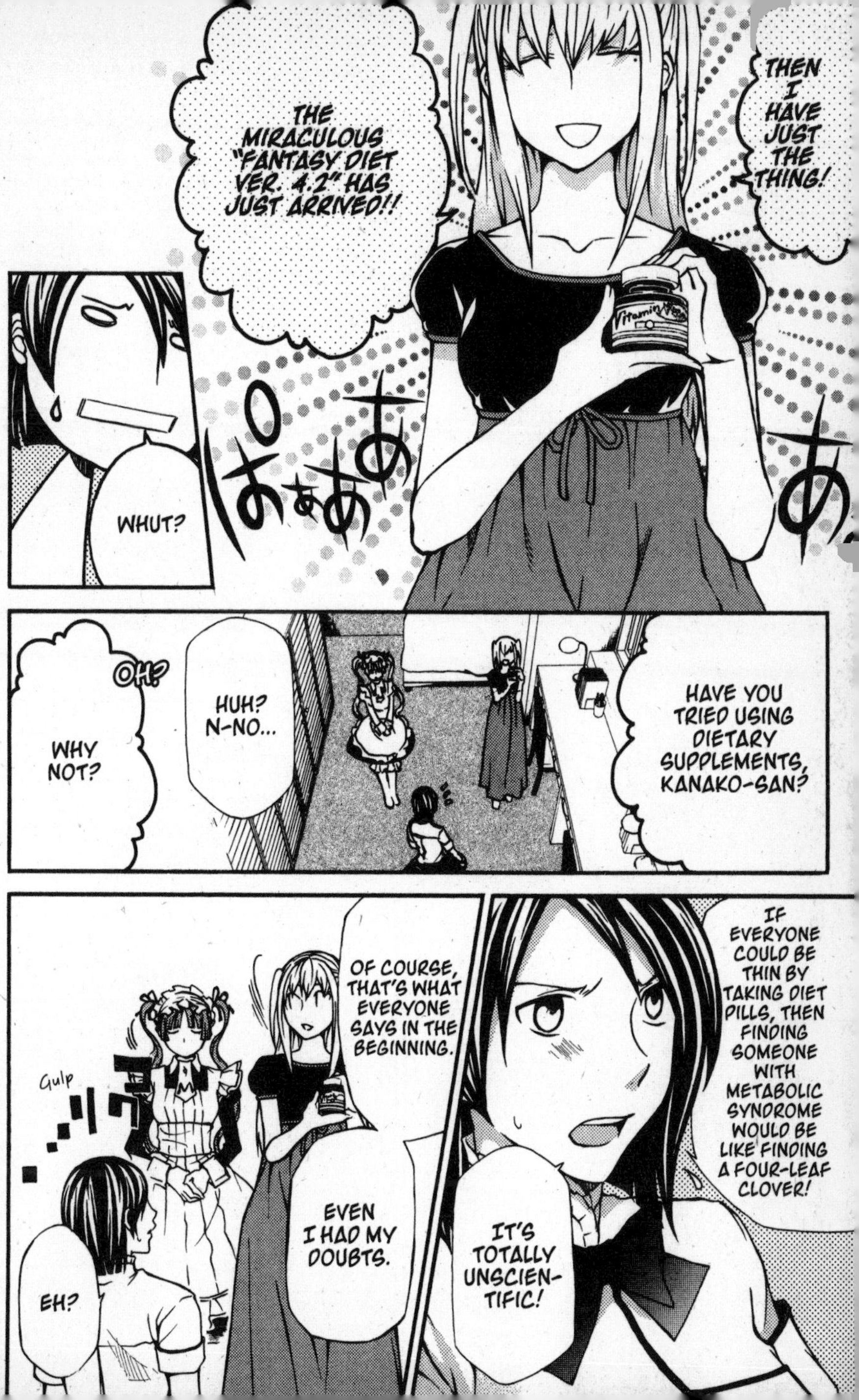
THEN I HAVE JUST THE THING!
THE MIRACULOUS "FANTASY DIET VER. 4.2" HAS JUST ARRIVED!!
WHUT?
HAVE YOU TRIED USING DIETARY SUPPLEMENTS, KANAKO-SAN?
HUH? N-NO...
OH?
WHY NOT?
IF EVERYONE COULD BE THIN BY TAKING DIET PILLS, THEN FINDING SOMEONE WITH METABOLIC SYNDROME WOULD BE LIKE FINDING A FOUR-LEAF CLOVER!
IT'S TOTALLY UNSCIENTIFIC!
OF COURSE, THAT'S WHAT EVERYONE SAYS IN THE BEGINNING.
EVEN I HAD MY DOUBTS.
Gulp
EH?

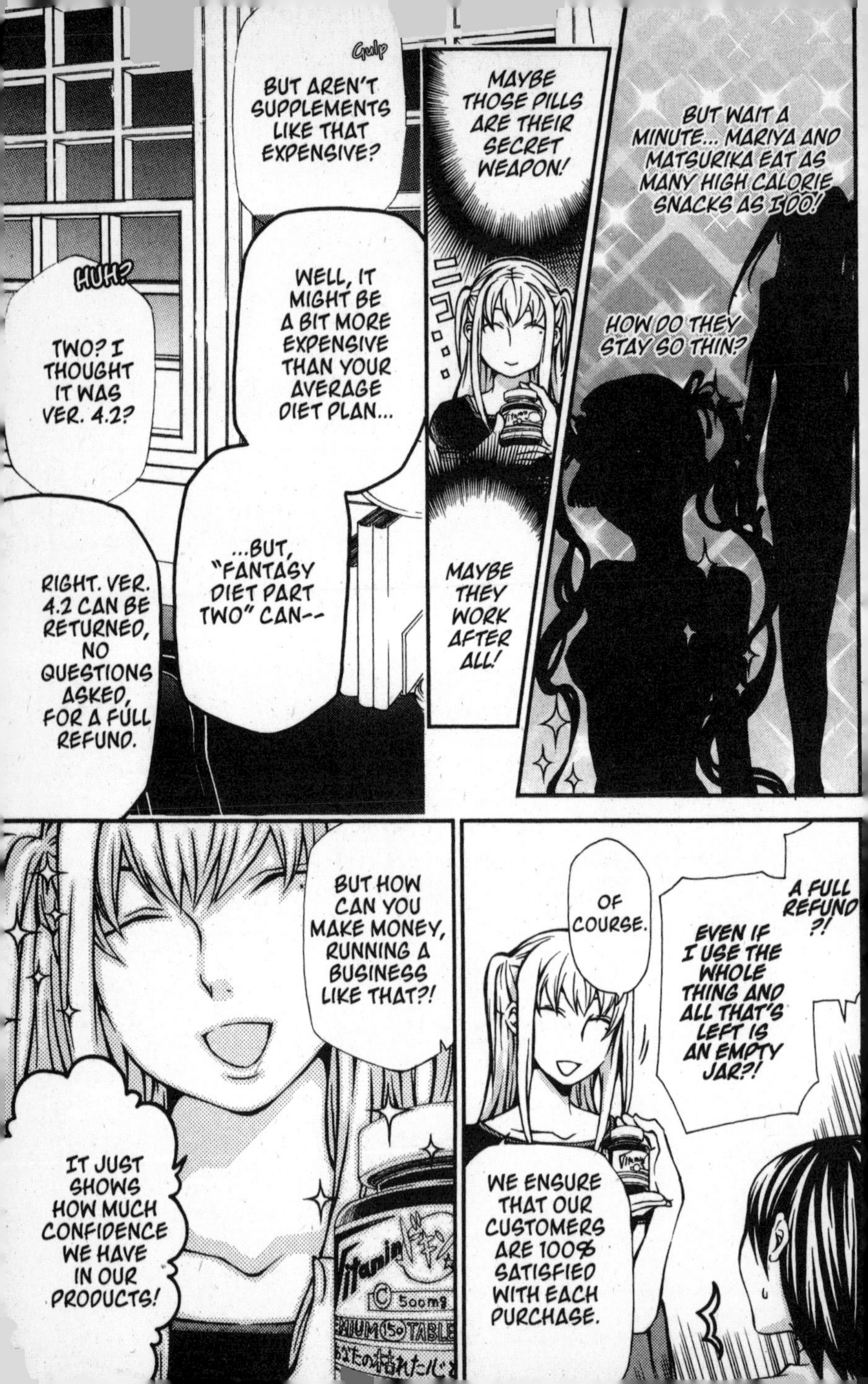
BUT WAIT A MINUTE... MARIYA AND MATSURIKA EAT AS MANY HIGH CALORIE SNACKS AS I DO!
HOW DO THEY STAY SO THIN?
MAYBE THOSE PILLS ARE THEIR SECRET WEAPON!
MAYBE THEY WORK AFTER ALL!
Gulp
BUT AREN'T SUPPLEMENTS LIKE THAT EXPENSIVE?
WELL, IT MIGHT BE A BIT MORE EXPENSIVE THAN YOUR AVERAGE DIET PLAN...
...BUT, "FANTASY DIET PART TWO" CAN--
HUH?
TWO? I THOUGHT IT WAS VER. 4.2?
RIGHT. VER. 4.2 CAN BE RETURNED, NO QUESTIONS ASKED, FOR A FULL REFUND.
A FULL REFUND?!
EVEN IF I USE THE WHOLE THING AND ALL THAT'S LEFT IS AN EMPTY JAR?!
OF COURSE.
WE ENSURE THAT OUR CUSTOMERS ARE 100% SATISFIED WITH EACH PURCHASE.
BUT HOW CAN YOU MAKE MONEY, RUNNING A BUSINESS LIKE THAT?!
IT JUST SHOWS HOW MUCH CONFIDENCE WE HAVE IN OUR PRODUCTS!

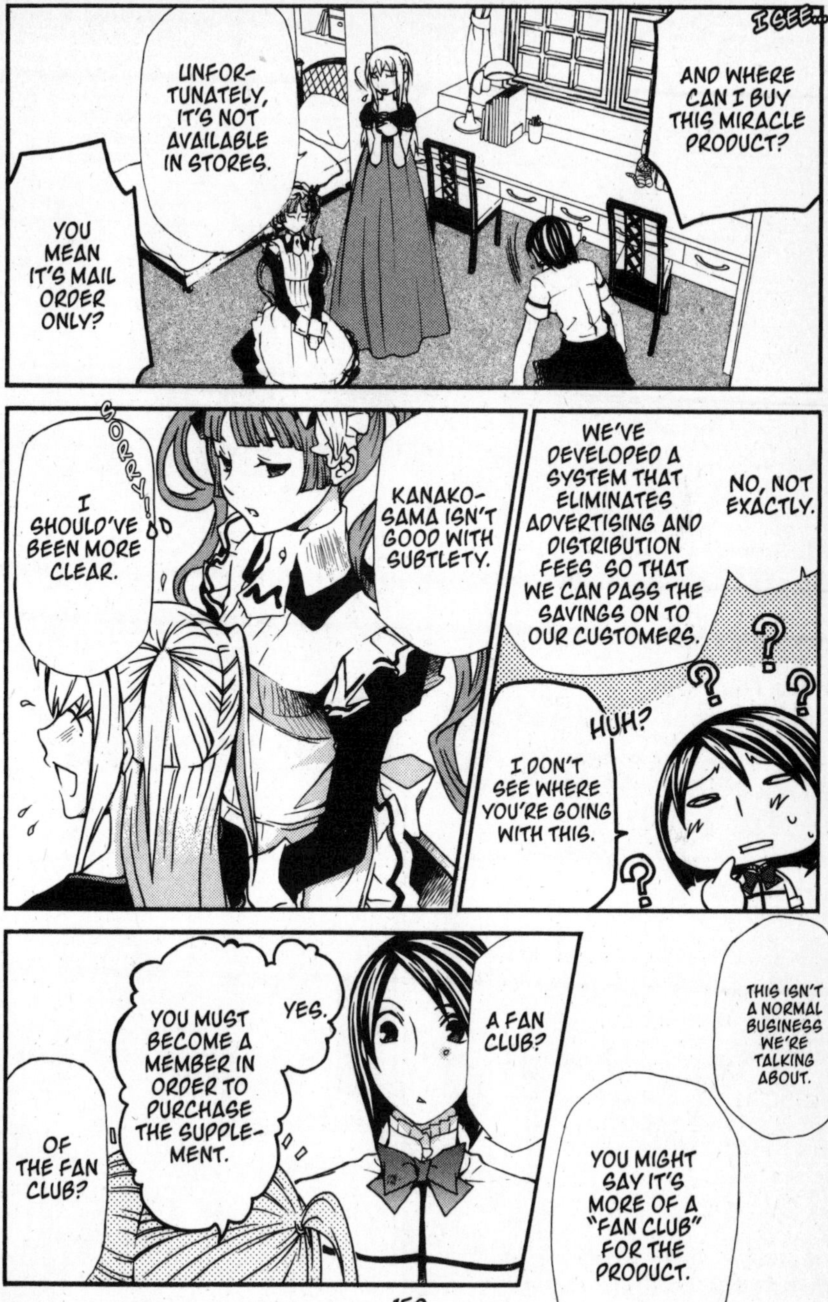
I SEE...
AND WHERE CAN I BUY THIS MIRACLE PRODUCT?
UNFORTUNATELY, IT'S NOT AVAILABLE IN STORES.
YOU MEAN IT'S MAIL ORDER ONLY?
NO, NOT EXACTLY.
WE'VE DEVELOPED A SYSTEM THAT ELIMINATES ADVERTISING AND DISTRIBUTION FEES SO THAT WE CAN PASS THE SAVINGS ON TO OUR CUSTOMERS.
HUH?
I DON'T SEE WHERE YOU'RE GOING WITH THIS.
KANAKO-SAMA ISN'T GOOD WITH SUBTLETY.
SORRY!
I SHOULD'VE BEEN MORE CLEAR.
THIS ISN'T A NORMAL BUSINESS WE'RE TALKING ABOUT.
YOU MIGHT SAY IT'S MORE OF A "FAN CLUB" FOR THE PRODUCT.
A FAN CLUB?
YES.
YOU MUST BECOME A MEMBER IN ORDER TO PURCHASE THE SUPPLEMENT.
OF THE FAN CLUB?

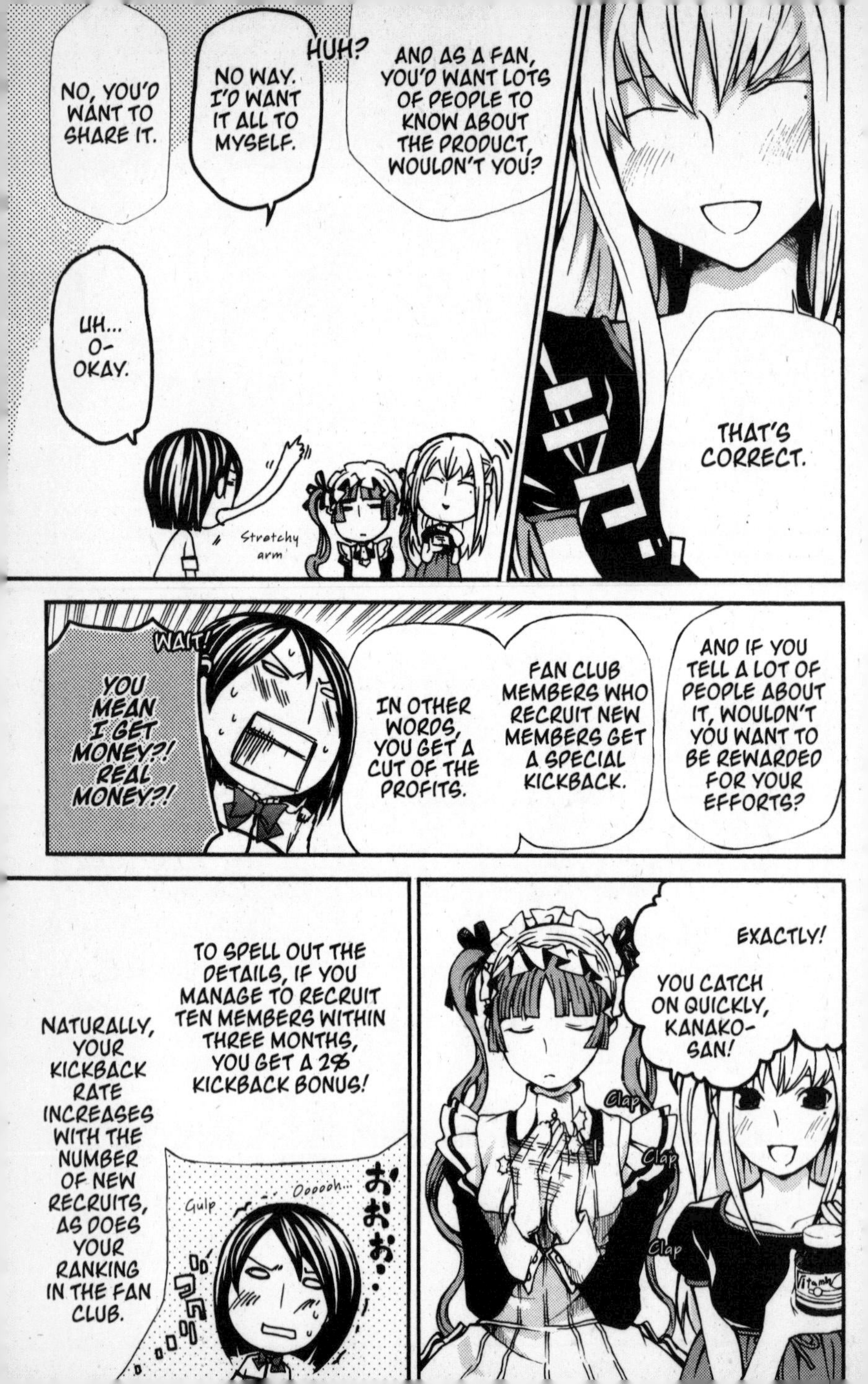
THAT'S CORRECT.
AND AS A FAN, YOU'D WANT LOTS OF PEOPLE TO KNOW ABOUT THE PRODUCT, WOULDN'T YOU?
HUH?
NO WAY. I'D WANT IT ALL TO MYSELF.
NO, YOU'D WANT TO SHARE IT.
UH... O-OKAY.
Stretchy arm
AND IF YOU TELL A LOT OF PEOPLE ABOUT IT, WOULDN'T YOU WANT TO BE REWARDED FOR YOUR EFFORTS?
FAN CLUB MEMBERS WHO RECRUIT NEW MEMBERS GET A SPECIAL KICKBACK.
IN OTHER WORDS, YOU GET A CUT OF THE PROFITS.
WAIT!
YOU MEAN I GET MONEY?! REAL MONEY?!
EXACTLY!
YOU CATCH ON QUICKLY, KANAKO-SAN!
Clap
Clap
Clap
TO SPELL OUT THE DETAILS, IF YOU MANAGE TO RECRUIT TEN MEMBERS WITHIN THREE MONTHS, YOU GET A 2% KICKBACK BONUS!
NATURALLY, YOUR KICKBACK RATE INCREASES WITH THE NUMBER OF NEW RECRUITS, AS DOES YOUR RANKING IN THE FAN CLUB.
おおお…
Oooooh...
Gulp

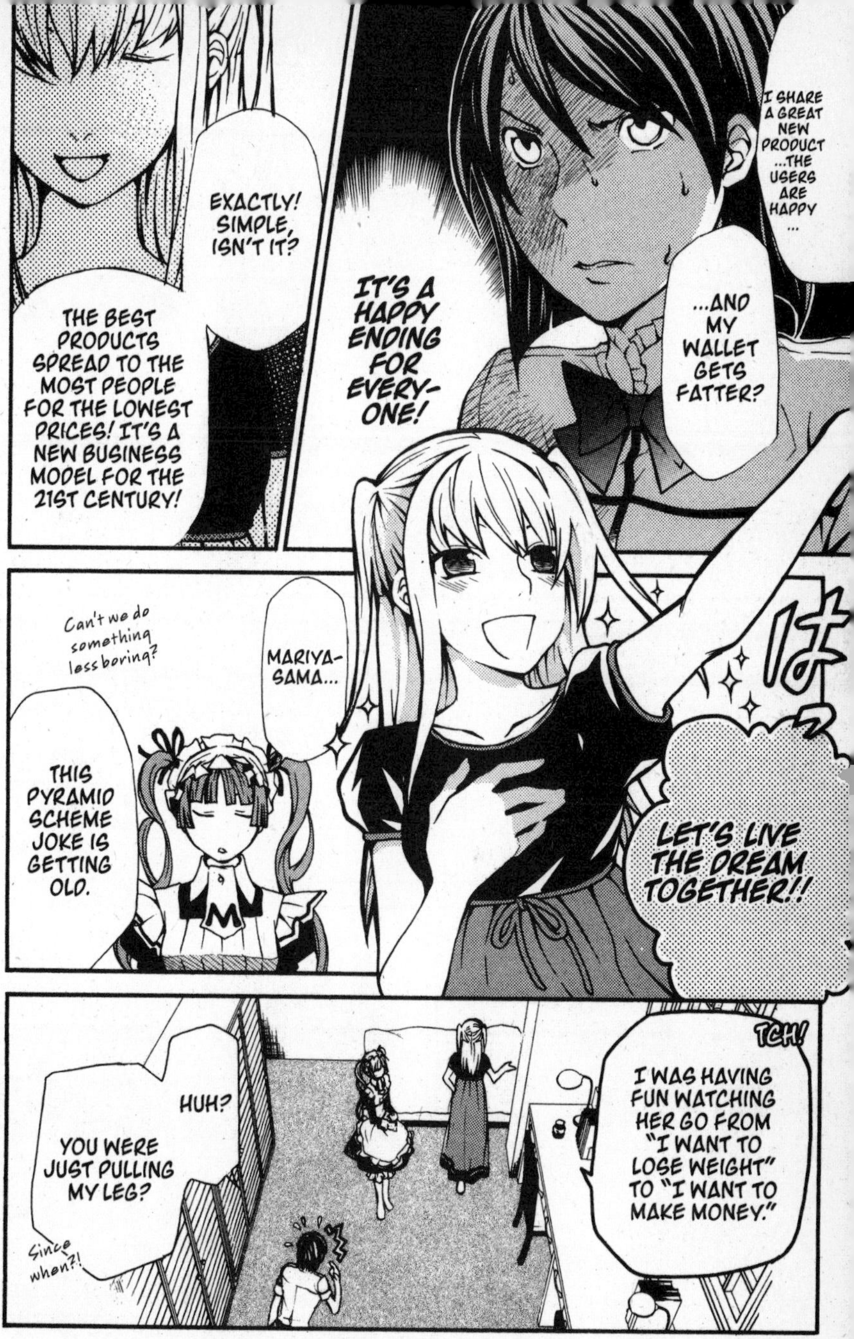
I SHARE A GREAT NEW PRODUCT ...THE USERS ARE HAPPY ...
...AND MY WALLET GETS FATTER?
IT'S A HAPPY ENDING FOR EVERY-ONE!
EXACTLY! SIMPLE, ISN'T IT?
THE BEST PRODUCTS SPREAD TO THE MOST PEOPLE FOR THE LOWEST PRICES! IT'S A NEW BUSINESS MODEL FOR THE 21ST CENTURY!
はっ
LET'S LIVE THE DREAM TOGETHER!!
MARIYA-SAMA...
THIS PYRAMID SCHEME JOKE IS GETTING OLD.
Can't we do something less boring?
TCH!
I WAS HAVING FUN WATCHING HER GO FROM "I WANT TO LOSE WEIGHT" TO "I WANT TO MAKE MONEY."
HUH?
YOU WERE JUST PULLING MY LEG?
Since when?!

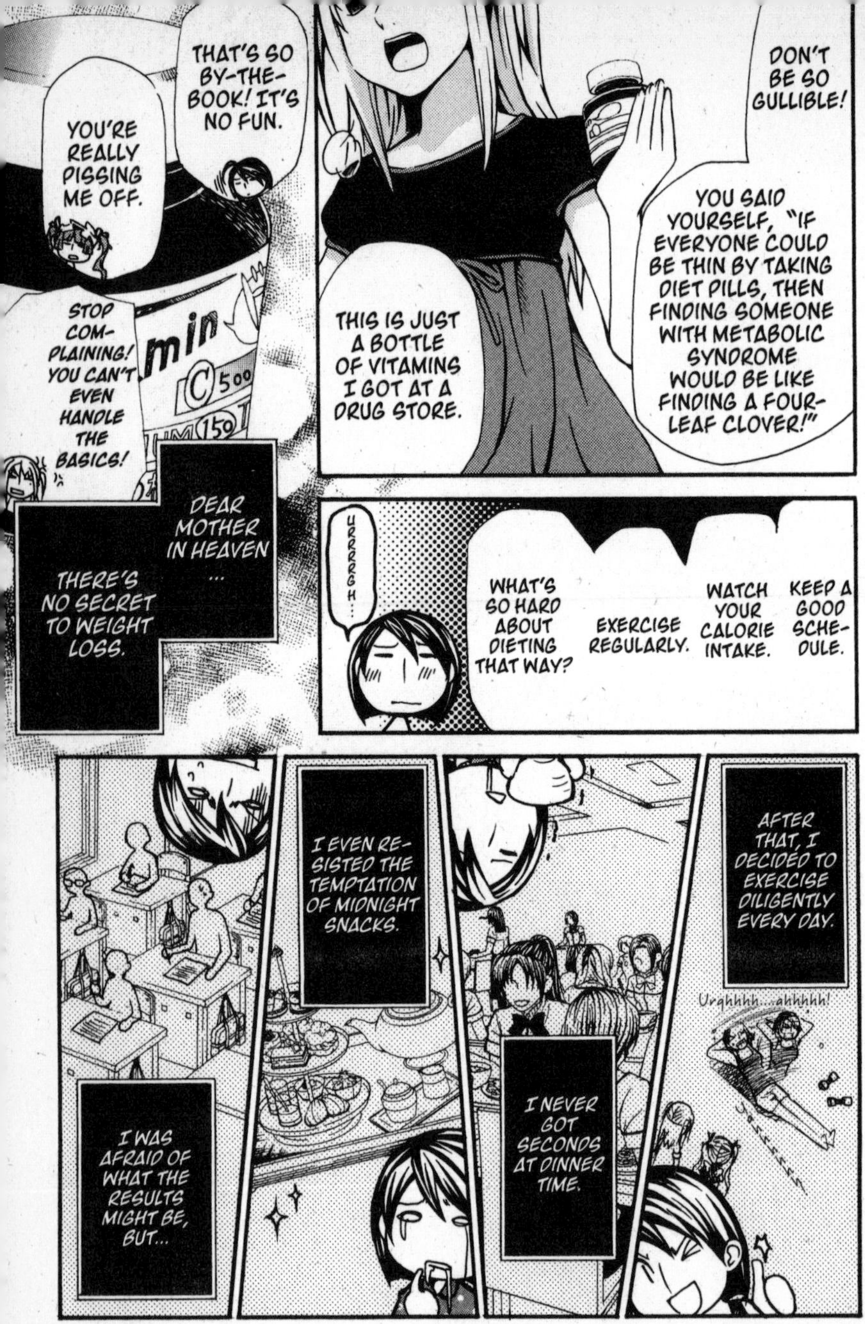
DON'T BE SO GULLIBLE!
YOU SAID YOURSELF, "IF EVERYONE COULD BE THIN BY TAKING DIET PILLS, THEN FINDING SOMEONE WITH METABOLIC SYNDROME WOULD BE LIKE FINDING A FOUR-LEAF CLOVER!"
THIS IS JUST A BOTTLE OF VITAMINS I GOT AT A DRUG STORE.
THAT'S SO BY-THE-BOOK! IT'S NO FUN.
YOU'RE REALLY PISSING ME OFF.
STOP COM-PLAINING! YOU CAN'T EVEN HANDLE THE BASICS!
KEEP A GOOD SCHE-DULE.
WATCH YOUR CALORIE INTAKE.
EXERCISE REGULARLY.
WHAT'S SO HARD ABOUT DIETING THAT WAY?
URRRRGH...
DEAR MOTHER IN HEAVEN...
THERE'S NO SECRET TO WEIGHT LOSS.
AFTER THAT, I DECIDED TO EXERCISE DILIGENTLY EVERY DAY.
Urghhhh...ahhhhh!
I NEVER GOT SECONDS AT DINNER TIME.
I EVEN RE-SISTED THE TEMPTATION OF MIDNIGHT SNACKS.
I WAS AFRAID OF WHAT THE RESULTS MIGHT BE, BUT...

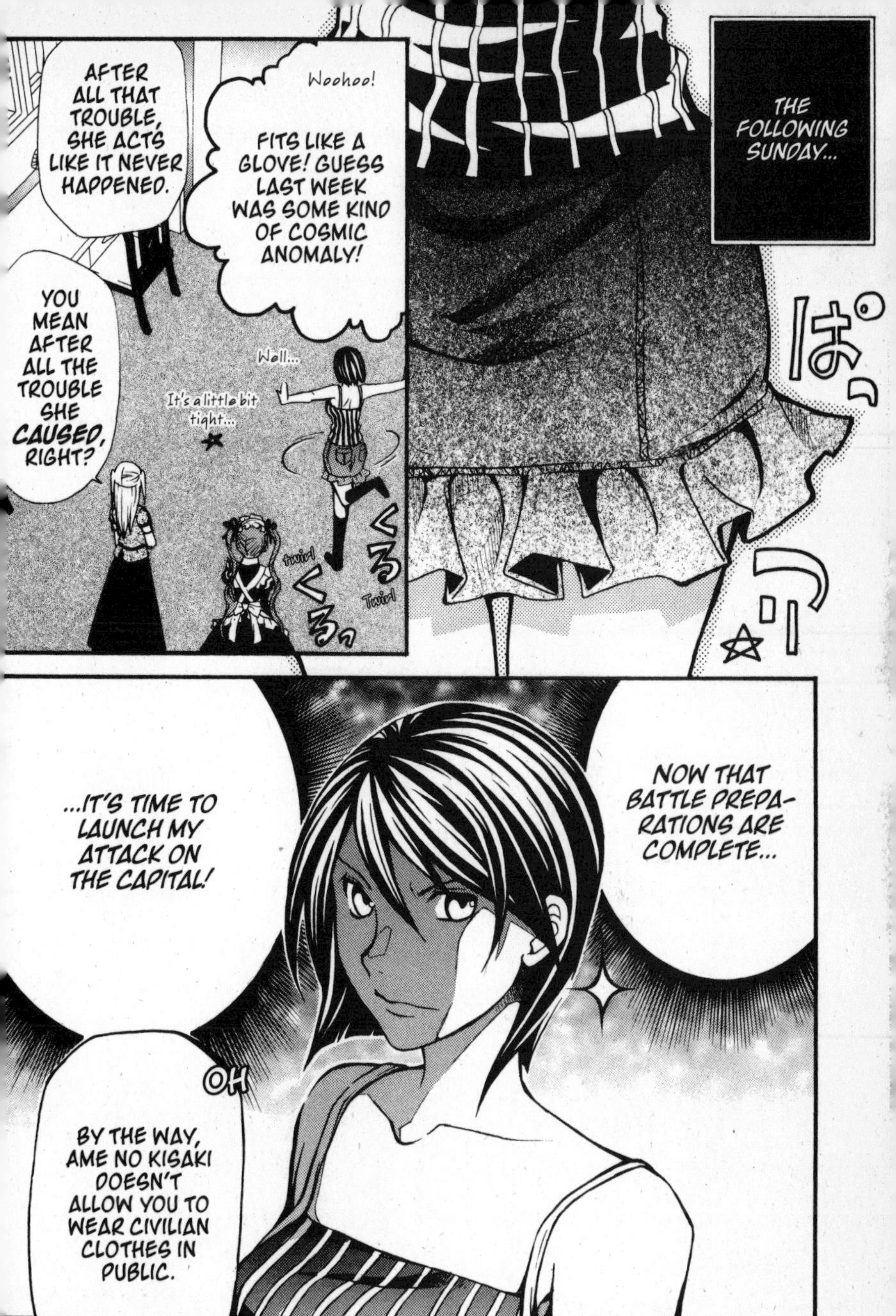
THE FOLLOWING SUNDAY...
ぱっ
Woohoo!
FITS LIKE A GLOVE! GUESS LAST WEEK WAS SOME KIND OF COSMIC ANOMALY!
AFTER ALL THAT TROUBLE, SHE ACTS LIKE IT NEVER HAPPENED.
Well...
It's a little bit tight...
YOU MEAN AFTER ALL THE TROUBLE SHE **CAUSED**, RIGHT?
くる
Twirl
くるっ
twirl
NOW THAT BATTLE PREPARATIONS ARE COMPLETE...
...IT'S TIME TO LAUNCH MY ATTACK ON THE CAPITAL!
OH
BY THE WAY, AME NO KISAKI DOESN'T ALLOW YOU TO WEAR CIVILIAN CLOTHES IN PUBLIC.

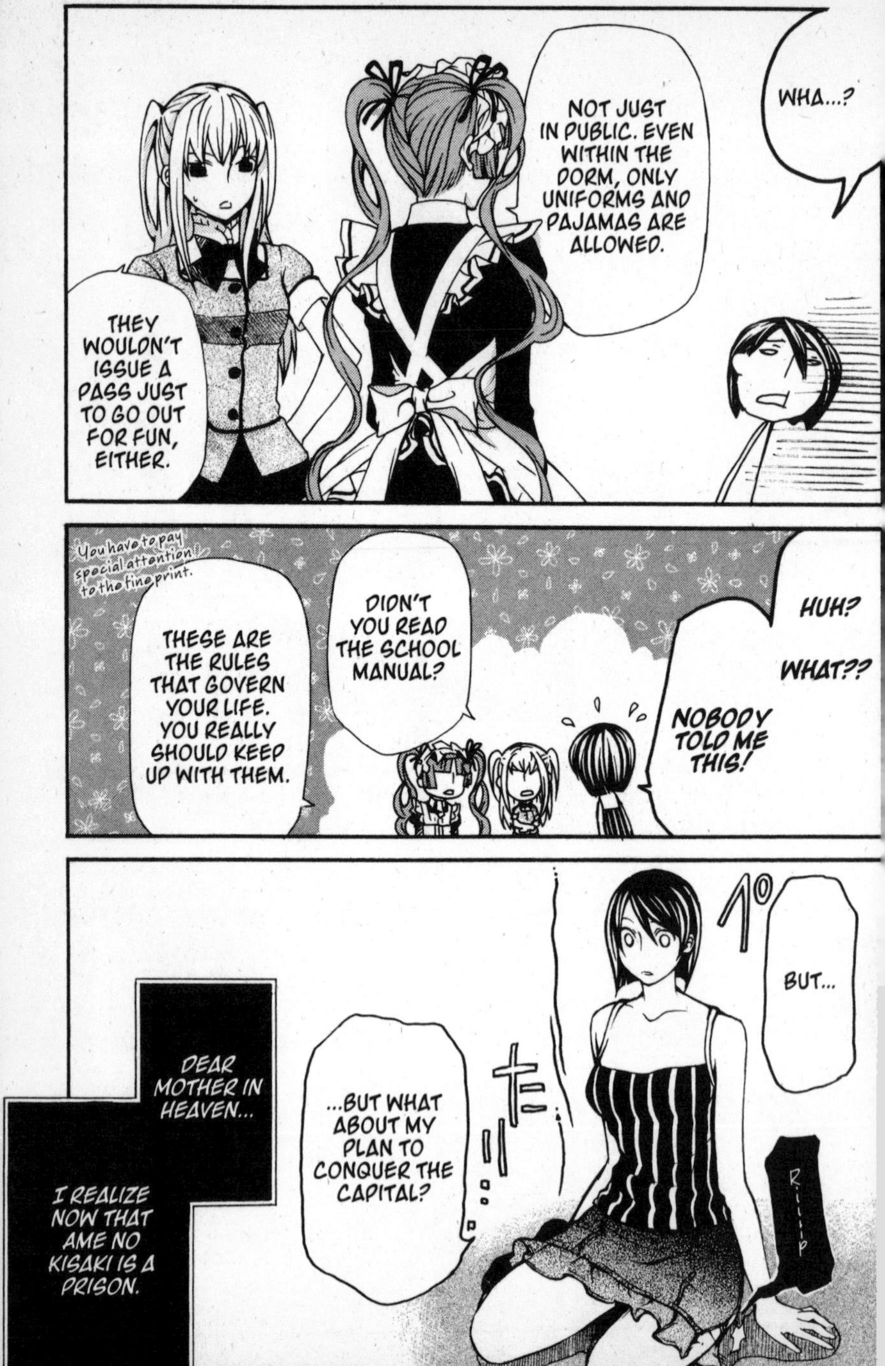
WHA...?
NOT JUST IN PUBLIC. EVEN WITHIN THE DORM, ONLY UNIFORMS AND PAJAMAS ARE ALLOWED.
THEY WOULDN'T ISSUE A PASS JUST TO GO OUT FOR FUN, EITHER.
HUH?
WHAT??
NOBODY TOLD ME THIS!
DIDN'T YOU READ THE SCHOOL MANUAL?
THESE ARE THE RULES THAT GOVERN YOUR LIFE. YOU REALLY SHOULD KEEP UP WITH THEM.
You have to pay special attention to the fine print.
BUT...
...BUT WHAT ABOUT MY PLAN TO CONQUER THE CAPITAL?
DEAR MOTHER IN HEAVEN...
I REALIZE NOW THAT AME NO KISAKI IS A PRISON.

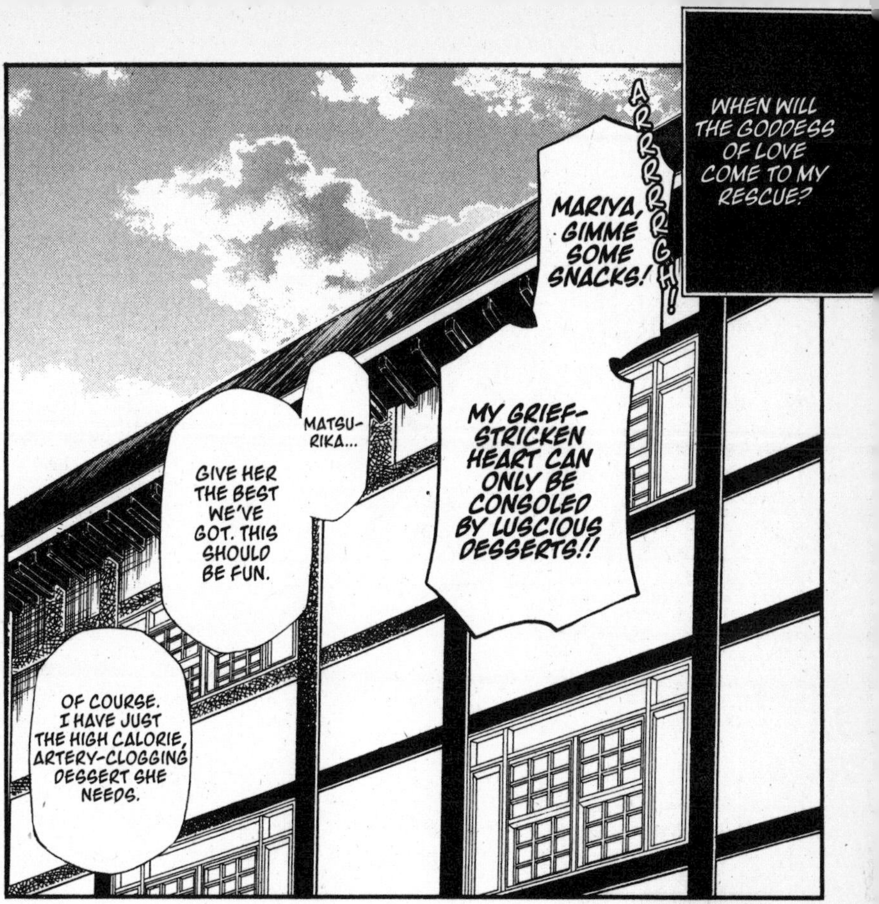
WHEN WILL THE GODDESS OF LOVE COME TO MY RESCUE?
ARRRRRRGH!
MARIYA, GIMME SOME SNACKS!
MY GRIEF-STRICKEN HEART CAN ONLY BE CONSOLED BY LUSCIOUS DESSERTS!!
MATSU-RIKA...
GIVE HER THE BEST WE'VE GOT. THIS SHOULD BE FUN.
OF COURSE. I HAVE JUST THE HIGH CALORIE, ARTERY-CLOGGING DESSERT SHE NEEDS.

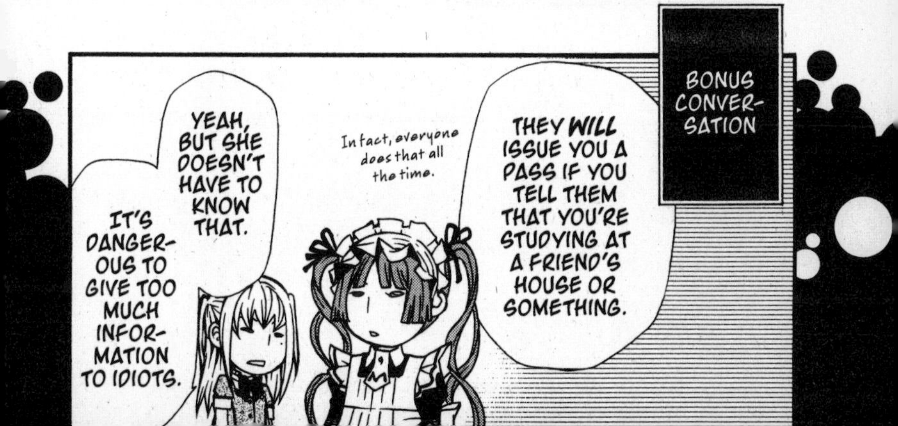
BONUS CONVER-SATION
THEY WILL ISSUE YOU A PASS IF YOU TELL THEM THAT YOU'RE STUDYING AT A FRIEND'S HOUSE OR SOMETHING.
In fact, everyone does that all the time.
YEAH, BUT SHE DOESN'T HAVE TO KNOW THAT.
IT'S DANGER-OUS TO GIVE TOO MUCH INFOR-MATION TO IDIOTS.

M A R I A H O L I C

Maria Holic

Maria✝Holic

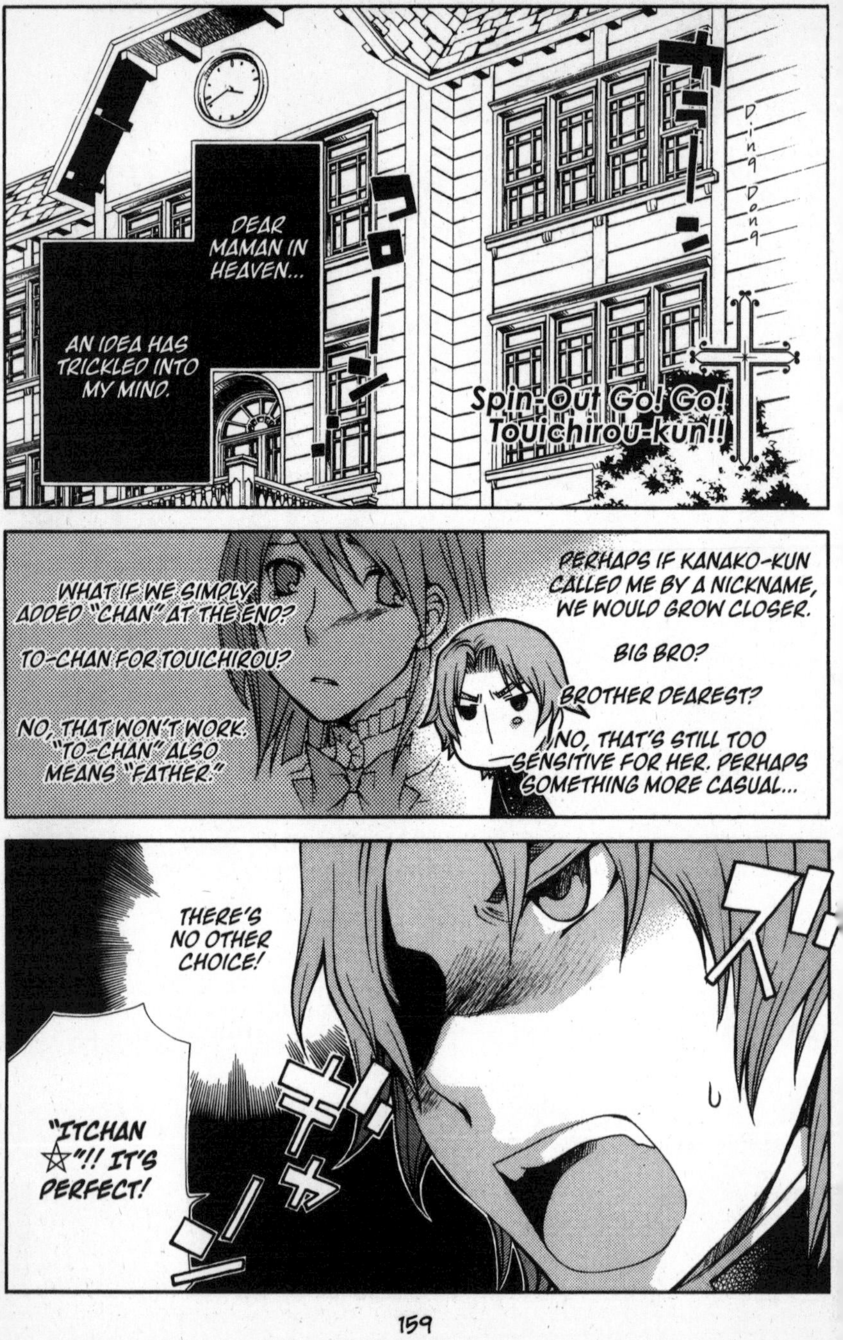
Ding Dong
Spin-Out Go! Go! Touichirou-kun!!
DEAR MAMAN IN HEAVEN...
AN IDEA HAS TRICKLED INTO MY MIND.
PERHAPS IF KANAKO-KUN CALLED ME BY A NICKNAME, WE WOULD GROW CLOSER.
BIG BRO?
BROTHER DEAREST?
NO, THAT'S STILL TOO SENSITIVE FOR HER. PERHAPS SOMETHING MORE CASUAL...
WHAT IF WE SIMPLY ADDED "CHAN" AT THE END?
TO-CHAN FOR TOUICHIROU?
NO, THAT WON'T WORK. "TO-CHAN" ALSO MEANS "FATHER."
THERE'S NO OTHER CHOICE!
"ITCHAN ☆"!! IT'S PERFECT!

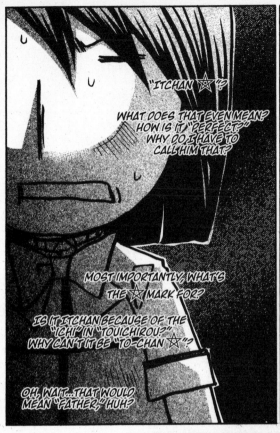

"ITCHAN ☆"?

WHAT DOES THAT EVEN MEAN? HOW IS IT "PERFECT?" WHY DO I HAVE TO CALL HIM THAT?

MOST IMPORTANTLY, WHAT'S THE ☆ MARK FOR?

IS IT ITCHAN BECAUSE OF THE "ICHI" IN "TOUICHIROU?" WHY CAN'T IT BE "TO-CHAN ☆"?

OH, WAIT...THAT WOULD MEAN "FATHER," HUH?

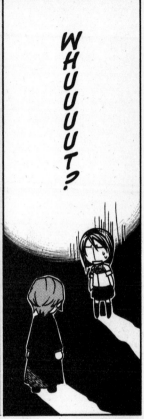

WHUUUT?

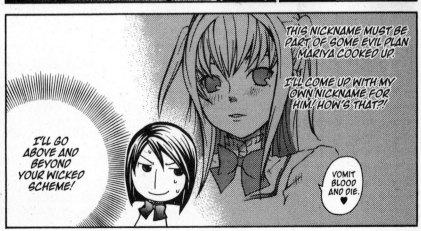

THIS NICKNAME MUST BE PART OF SOME EVIL PLAN MARIYA COOKED UP.

I'LL COME UP WITH MY OWN NICKNAME FOR HIM! HOW'S THAT?!

I'LL GO ABOVE AND BEYOND YOUR WICKED SCHEME!

VOMIT BLOOD AND DIE. ♥

160

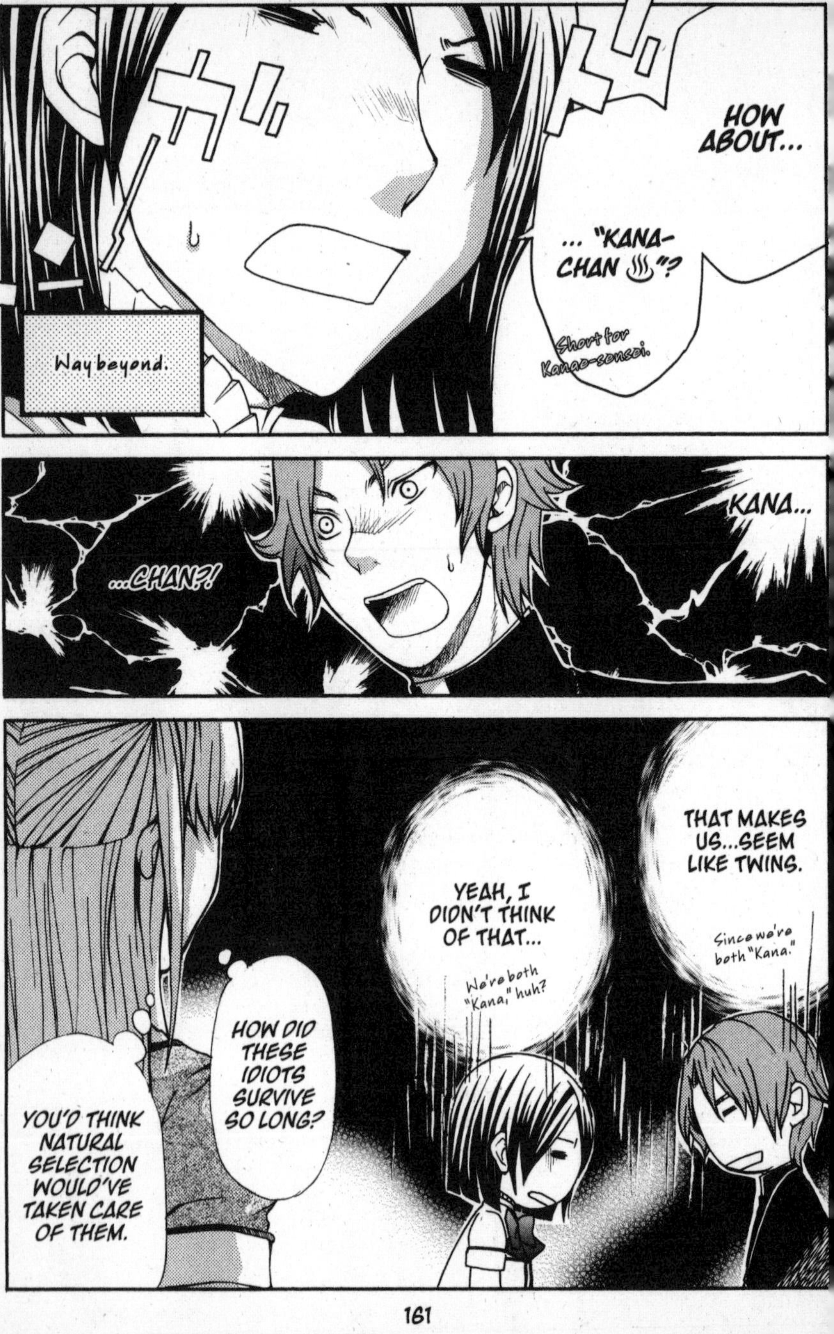
HOW ABOUT...
... "KANA-CHAN ♨"?
Short for Kanae-sensei.
Way beyond.
KANA...
...CHAN?!
THAT MAKES US...SEEM LIKE TWINS.
Since we're both "Kana."
YEAH, I DIDN'T THINK OF THAT...
We're both "Kana," huh?
HOW DID THESE IDIOTS SURVIVE SO LONG?
YOU'D THINK NATURAL SELECTION WOULD'VE TAKEN CARE OF THEM.

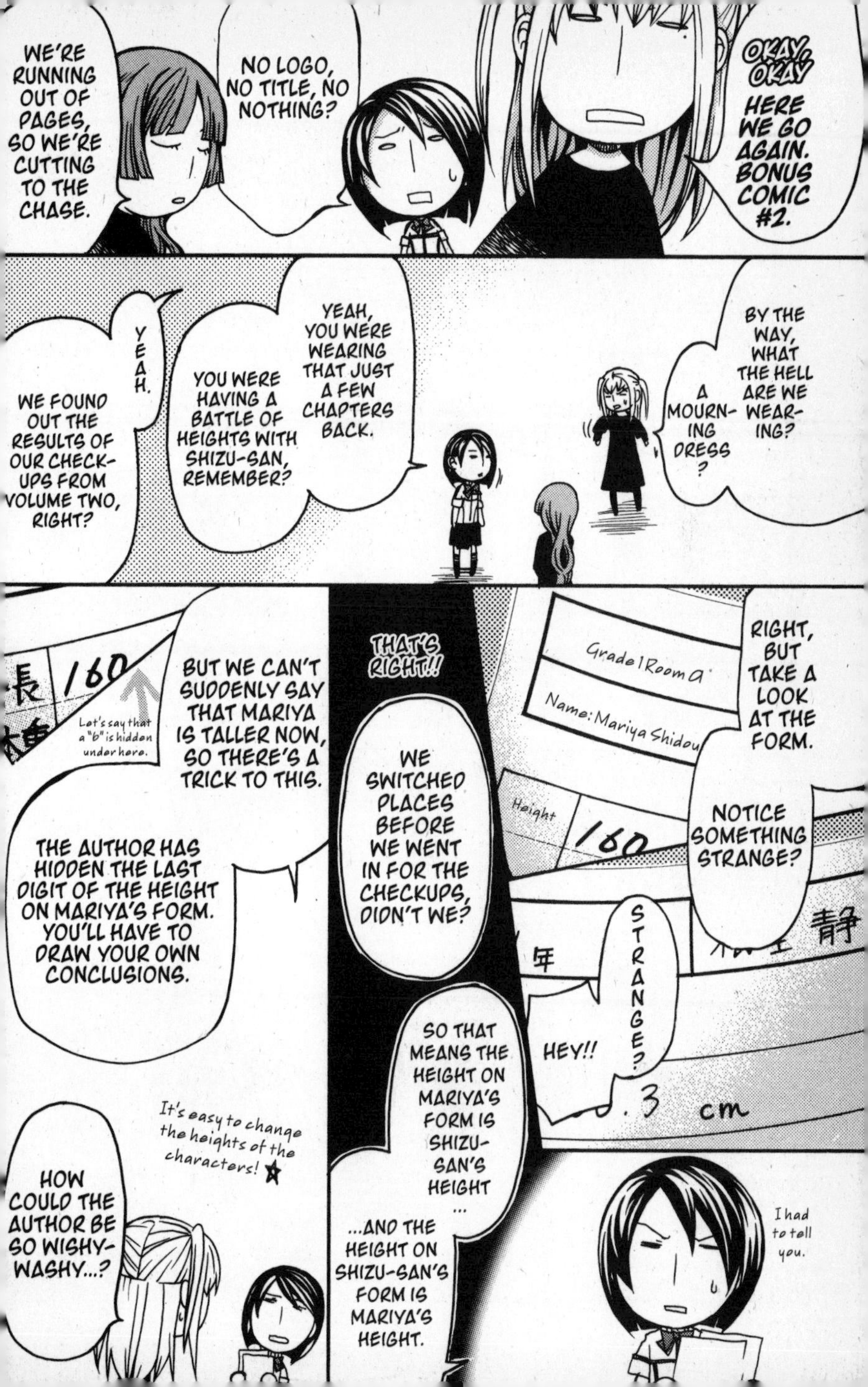
OKAY, OKAY
HERE WE GO AGAIN. BONUS COMIC #2.
NO LOGO, NO TITLE, NO NOTHING?
WE'RE RUNNING OUT OF PAGES, SO WE'RE CUTTING TO THE CHASE.
BY THE WAY, WHAT THE HELL ARE WE WEARING?
A MOURNING DRESS?
YEAH, YOU WERE WEARING THAT JUST A FEW CHAPTERS BACK.
YOU WERE HAVING A BATTLE OF HEIGHTS WITH SHIZU-SAN, REMEMBER?
YEAH.
WE FOUND OUT THE RESULTS OF OUR CHECK-UPS FROM VOLUME TWO, RIGHT?
RIGHT, BUT TAKE A LOOK AT THE FORM.
Grade 1 Room A
Name: Mariya Shidou
Height
160
NOTICE SOMETHING STRANGE?
STRANGE?
HEY!!
3 cm
年
静
I had to tell you.
THAT'S RIGHT!!
WE SWITCHED PLACES BEFORE WE WENT IN FOR THE CHECKUPS, DIDN'T WE?
SO THAT MEANS THE HEIGHT ON MARIYA'S FORM IS SHIZU-SAN'S HEIGHT...
...AND THE HEIGHT ON SHIZU-SAN'S FORM IS MARIYA'S HEIGHT.
長 160
Let's say that a "6" is hidden under here.
BUT WE CAN'T SUDDENLY SAY THAT MARIYA IS TALLER NOW, SO THERE'S A TRICK TO THIS.
THE AUTHOR HAS HIDDEN THE LAST DIGIT OF THE HEIGHT ON MARIYA'S FORM. YOU'LL HAVE TO DRAW YOUR OWN CONCLUSIONS.
It's easy to change the heights of the characters! ☆
HOW COULD THE AUTHOR BE SO WISHY-WASHY...?

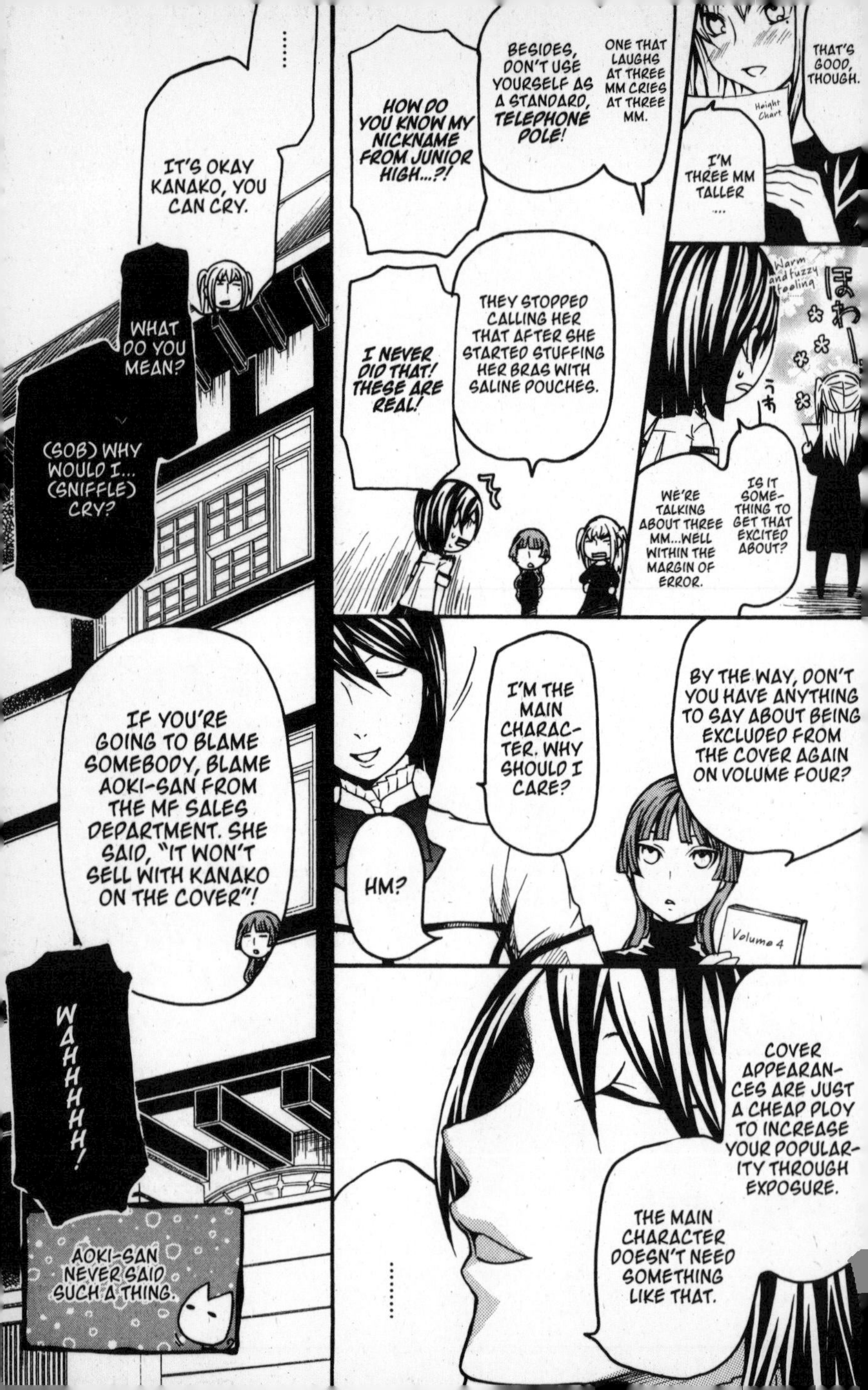

THAT'S GOOD, THOUGH.
Height Chart
I'M THREE MM TALLER ....
ONE THAT LAUGHS AT THREE MM CRIES AT THREE MM.
BESIDES, DON'T USE YOURSELF AS A STANDARD, TELEPHONE POLE!
HOW DO YOU KNOW MY NICKNAME FROM JUNIOR HIGH...?!
ほわー
Warm and fuzzy feeling
IS IT SOMETHING TO GET THAT EXCITED ABOUT?
WE'RE TALKING ABOUT THREE MM...WELL WITHIN THE MARGIN OF ERROR.
THEY STOPPED CALLING HER THAT AFTER SHE STARTED STUFFING HER BRAS WITH SALINE POUCHES.
I NEVER DID THAT! THESE ARE REAL!
BY THE WAY, DON'T YOU HAVE ANYTHING TO SAY ABOUT BEING EXCLUDED FROM THE COVER AGAIN ON VOLUME FOUR?
I'M THE MAIN CHARACTER. WHY SHOULD I CARE?
Volume 4
HM?
COVER APPEARANCES ARE JUST A CHEAP PLOY TO INCREASE YOUR POPULARITY THROUGH EXPOSURE.
THE MAIN CHARACTER DOESN'T NEED SOMETHING LIKE THAT.
.....
.....
IT'S OKAY KANAKO, YOU CAN CRY.
WHAT DO YOU MEAN?
(SOB) WHY WOULD I... (SNIFFLE) CRY?
IF YOU'RE GOING TO BLAME SOMEBODY, BLAME AOKI-SAN FROM THE MF SALES DEPARTMENT. SHE SAID, "IT WON'T SELL WITH KANAKO ON THE COVER"!
WAHHHHHH!
AOKI-SAN NEVER SAID SUCH A THING.

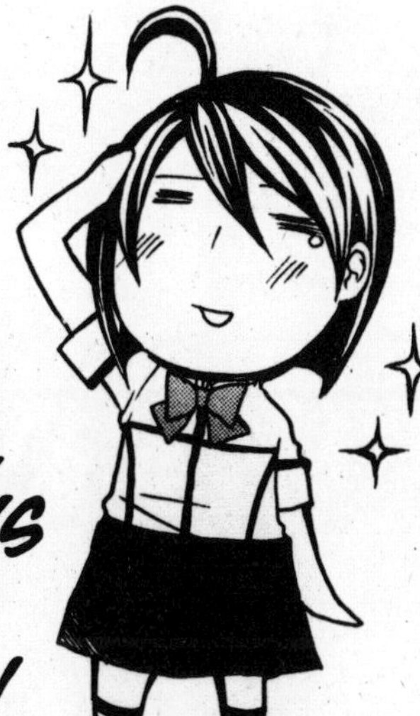
IT'S TIME TO THINK OUTSIDE THE BOX, KANAKO. THINK INSIDE OUT. ALTHOUGH THIS IS HIDDEN UNDER THE BOOK COVER, THIS IS STILL THE FRONT COVER.
THAT MEANS, KANAKO'S ON STAGE!!

"MAGICAL KANAKO" PARTS
HER HAIR DIFFERENTLY FROM
KANAKO-SAN ☆

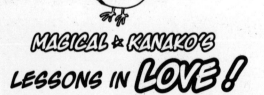

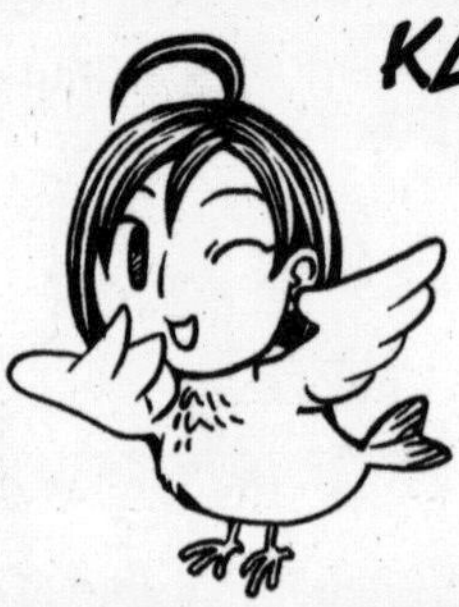

MAGICAL ☆ KANAKO'S
LESSONS IN *LOVE* !

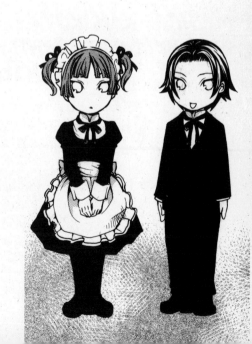

There's more maidenly mischief
to be had in the next volume of...

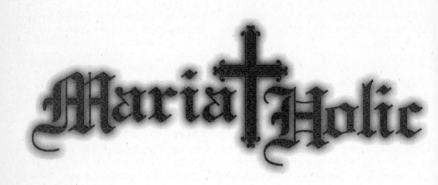

When Kanako ends up on trial for attempting
to eat Yonakuni the dog, she forgets all
about studying for the final exams. As a
result, she ends up the first person in Ame no
Kisaki's history to have failed all her classes.
An emergency committee is formed, and
Ryocho is appointed its head. She tells
Kanako to leave for a week of self-study
in the hope that she'll come back more
mature and responsible, but how will her
friends survive the week without her?

TOKYOPOP Insider
Stu Levy, May 2010

Hi everyone! Most of you don't know me but please allow me to introduce myself. While my parents named me Stuart Joel Levy, I really just go by "Stu". Ever since I was a child, people would tease me about being a food, calling me "Beef Stu" and the like. Even in Japanese, I get variations (although I'm 「スチュウ」 "Su-chu" whereas "stew" the food is actually 「シチュー」 "Shi-chu").

Now that we've gotten that sorted out, let me explain why I'm writing this. At TOKYOPOP, we decided to start a new column in our manga called "TOKYOPOP Insider" where some of our staff can write something casually – whatever's on their mind. I guess it's sort of a paper-based blog. I thought I'd be the first one to give it a go and see what you guys thought.

It may be hard to believe but it's been 13 years since I founded TOKYOPOP. Wow, time flies! Along with me, you manga readers have matured as well. We've seen some of our favorite series end, others begin, lots of content go online, and books evolve. Many more people know and love Japanese culture than when I first started – and I'm proud that I was a part of making that happen.

So, let me say ありがとう！("arigatou" - "thank you") to all of you for being interested in manga, Japan, and otaku culture overall. It's been a whirlwind of a ride over the past 13 years, but I've enjoyed every thrilling moment of it – working day and night for a passion that we all share.

This summer we're doing something I've wanted to do for years but never had the guts. I'm going on the road with Dice (from TOKYOPOP) and a very talented group of fans (the "Otaku Six") and we're going to search the nation for "America's Greatest Otaku" as well as give away lots of TOKYOPOP swag. Who knows what will happen – it's a crazy endeavor since we'll all be living on a humongous bus for 3 months – but my goal is to meet as many of you in person as I can (www.Americasgreatestotaku.com).

The details will be online but please come out and say hi if we're in your neighborhood – I'd love to meet you!

今後とも宜しくお願いします！("Kongo tomo Yoroshiku onegai-shimasu!" which roughly translates as "Looking forward to it!")

Cheers!
--Stu

A 🐾 TOKYOPOP® Manga
E-mail: info@TOKYOPOP.com
Come visit us online at www.TOKYOPOP.com

Editor's Notes
Cindy Suzuki

Hi All,

Thanks for purchasing this book! We hope you enjoyed it.

My colleague and I actually just got back from Japan. We had a series of meetings with our Japanese partners and licensors. These trips occur once or twice a year, and it's a crazy busy time.

It's always interesting to meet with the Japanese staff. I must mention their reaction to the TOKYOPOP Tour was priceless. Some sat in disbelief during our presentation while others laughed and shook their heads with that YOU ARE CRAZY look on their face. I also had some time to chat with the Japanese editors. It was a great learning experience.

We were also able to make it to Tokyo Anime Fair. While the show floor on business day was pretty quiet, I went back on Sunday, and it was packed with fans. Here are some pictures from the trip, but for a full summary, go to www.tokyopop.com/CindyPop/tp_article/3025583.html ☺

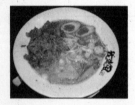 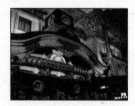 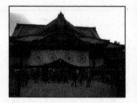

So back to the books! Be sure to check out the bookstores for new volumes of Happy Café, Maid Sama, Sgt. Frog, Samurai Harem, Suppli, NG Life, Maria Holic and last but not least, the first volume of .hack// Link. And if you haven't checked out Neko Ramen, Ratman or Alice in the Country of Hearts already, be sure to do so!

See you again next month!

Cindy Suzuki, Editor

For exclusive updates, be sure to find us here:

www.TOKYOPOP.com
www.Facebook.com/TOKYOPOP
www.Twitter.com/TOKYOPOP

A 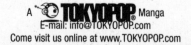 Manga
E-mail: info@TOKYOPOP.com
Come visit us online at www.TOKYOPOP.com

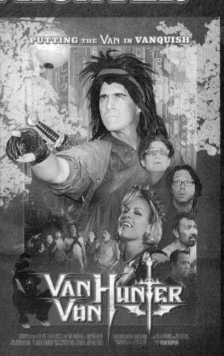

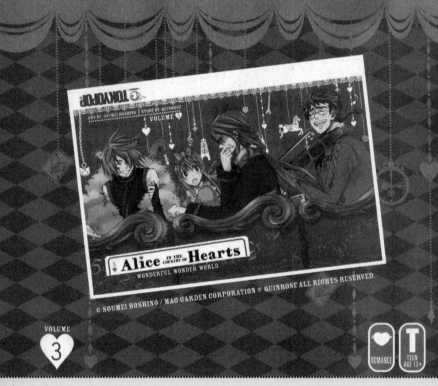

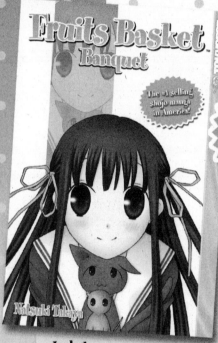
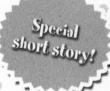

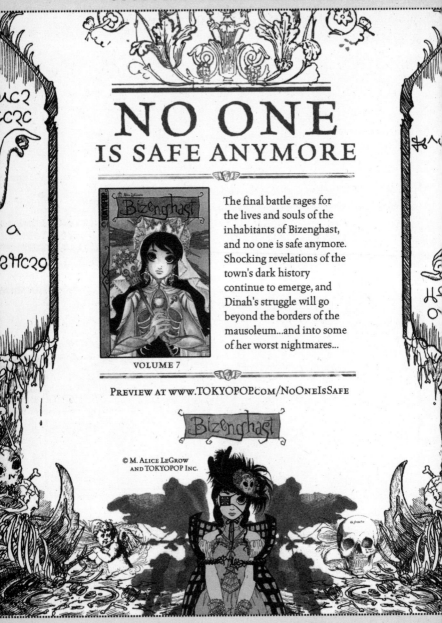

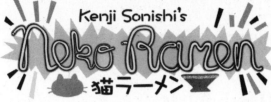
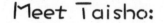
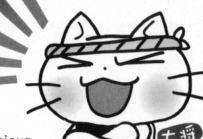
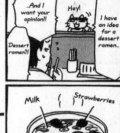
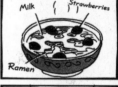
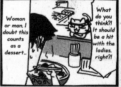
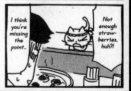

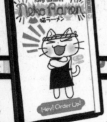

THE SMALLEST HERO!?

RATMAN

ラットマン

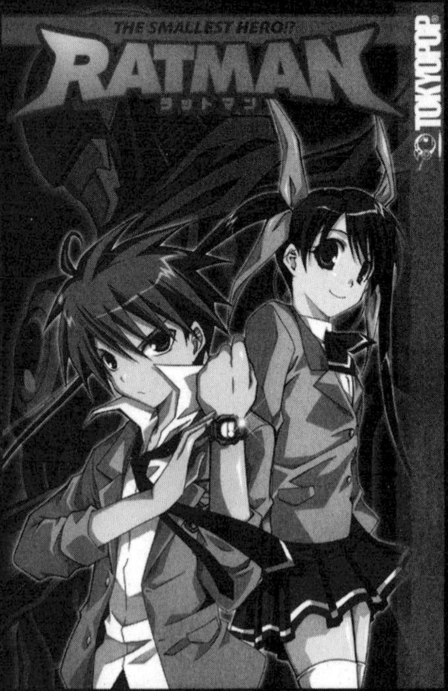
THE SMALLEST HERO!?
RATMAN
ラットマン
TOKYOPOP

Shuto Katsuragi is a superhero otaku. Only problem is, he's a shrimp always getting teased for his height...especially when he tries to emulate his favorite superhero! To make matters worse, Shuto suddenly gets abducted by his classmate and tricked into participating in some rather sketchy and super-villainous experiments! Why is it always one step forward and a hundred steps back for this little guy?

ACTION

OT
OLDER TEEN
AGE 16+

WWW.TOKYOPOP.COM/SHOP

STOP!

This is the back of the book.
You wouldn't want to spoil a great ending!

This book is printed "manga-style," in the authentic Japanese right-to-left format. Since none of the artwork has been flipped or altered, readers get to experience the story just as the creator intended. You've been asking for it, so TOKYOPOP® delivered: authentic, hot-off-the-press, and far more fun!

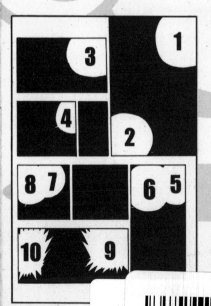

DIRECTIONS

If this is your first time reading manga-style, here's a quick guide to help you understand how it works.

It's easy... just start in the top right panel and follow the numbers. Have fun, and look for more 100% authentic manga from TOKYOPOP®!